A HISTORY *of the* THE SEAFORTH

A History of the Fourth Battalion The Seaforth Highlanders

With some Account of the Military Annals of Ross the Fencibles the Volunteers and of the Home Defence & Reserve Battalions 1914-1919

Compiled by
Lieut-Colonel M M Haldane
Illustrations by
Captain Finlay Mackinnon

London
H F & G Witherby

M. M. H.

Printed and bound by Antony Rowe Ltd, Eastbourne

To
the Brave Womanhood
which by example of Loyalty and Love
upheld the Hope and Honour
of those who served in
the Great War
this Record of the Faithful
is dedicated
with ever-grateful
Pride

(*Frontispiece*)

FOREWORD

On 6th January 1915 I took over the command of the Dehra Dun Brigade in the Meerut Division of the Indian Army Corps. The Brigade consisted of:

1st Battalion Seaforth Highlanders.
4th Battalion Seaforth Highlanders.
2nd Battalion 2nd Gurkha Rifles.
1st Battalion 9th Gurkha Rifles.
6th Jats.

The 4th Battalion The Seaforth Highlanders had only just joined the Brigade, and it was my first experience of a Territorial Battalion on service. I went down to see this battalion directly I took over command of the Brigade, and spoke to each officer individually and then collectively. I was much struck with the magnificent physique of all ranks. I very soon learned that, although the 4th Seaforths were new to fighting on service, they were a battalion that I could trust to fight under all circumstances. From 6th January to the end of November 1915, when the Battalion left the Dehra Dun Brigade, nothing could have been better than the fighting and work it did for me under the most trying circumstances.

This volume of the history of the Battalion is a fine record, and one to be proud of, and no Commander could wish for a finer Unit on service than the 4th Battalion The Seaforth Highlanders.

Claud W. Jacob, F.M.

28th June 1927.

PREFACE

To write the history of a regiment is a purely impersonal matter. It is drawn entirely from documents and is a simple record of the outstanding events in regimental history. During the Great War, when the number of battalions in a regiment varied from those of one to those of three or more divisions, the history could be little more than a brief summary of the share of each battalion in the deeds of the formation to which it belonged. The human touch is very hard to work into such books.

The history of a battalion is another matter. It is in the nature of a biography, for the battalion is a living thing. It may be touchy on this point, vain upon that. Its members have many memories of the war which—often just because they are trivial—are of the greatest value in bringing the soul of the battalion vividly to the reader.

This was not overlooked by Lieutenant-Colonel Cuthbert, who arranged a most interesting tour through the County for me, and I shall always be grateful for the kindness and hospitality that I had from the people of Ross. All were most anxious to help, and gave me many "tales of the trenches" that have been invaluable in compiling the history of the 4th Seaforths. Nor was it otherwise with the Dingwall, Glasgow and London gatherings which it has been my privilege to attend.

I wish to record my gratitude for all the help and support of the Committee under whose auspices this work appears; to one of the best friends the Battalion ever had—namely, to Mr D. M. Watt of *The Ross-shire Journal*—both for most helpful criticism and for placing at my disposal the matter contained in his files and in unpublished letters in his possession; to those members of the Battalion and their relatives who have lent letters and diaries or have verbally supplied reminiscences of their experiences in France, among which I would specially mention the remarkably interesting series of letters by the late Lieutenant P. H. Ballantyne; to Colonel D. Mason-MacFarlane, Lieutenant-Colonel J. S. Unthank and Lieutenant J. Davidson, whose contributions to the compilation of Part I. have been of the utmost help.

My heartiest thanks are due to The Lady Seaforth for kindly giving permission to reproduce the picture *Cuidich'n Righ*, and to Dr Matheson for the loan of the print for reproduction; to Captain Finlay Mackinnon for his colour plates and chapter headings; to Mr Frank Tennant for kind permission to publish Plate 6; and to Miss Kennedy (Tain) for the heading to Chapter II.

Brigadier-General J. E. Edmonds—whose advice has enabled me to escape many pitfalls—Major A. F. Becke—whose help in the compilation of the maps has been of inestimable service—and other members of the staff of the Historical Section of the Committee of Imperial Defence have gone out of their way to put matter at my disposal that could not otherwise have been accessible; Mr F. G. Hudleston, the War Office Librarian (whose recent death has been such a blow to his many friends), and his successor, Mr W. Y. Baldry, supplied most of the material relating to the Fencibles and Volunteers; while Sir Reginald Brade and Captain C. E. Etches provided me, at considerable trouble to themselves, with the means of checking certain important statements made herein. To all these I would express my gratitude.

Many thanks are likewise due to Mr D. F. Macdonald (Inverness) for having the draft MS. typed in his office, whereby the labours of both Committee and Compiler have been materially assisted; to the Rev. Dr MacLean Watt for writing the dedication; and to Messrs Hills & Saunders of Oxford for permission to reproduce the three photographs taken at Bedford.

I alone am responsible for the writing of Part I.; for Part II., I am indebted to Lieutenant-Colonel D. Matheson and Major W. Wilkie; while the account of the training of the Reserve Battalion in Part III. has been written entirely by Colonel D. Mason-MacFarlane and the officers he quotes.

Finally, I wish to record my thanks to those many personal friends who have so generously given their time to criticize the draft MS., to read the proofs and to compile the indices, especially to Mr Alexander Inkson McConnochie, F.Z.S.

To one and all of those named, as well as to the many whom space has forbidden to name, I give my most grateful thanks. Any pleasure that the book may give to its readers is due much more to them than to me.

M. M. H.

LONDON, *16th December* 1927.

CUIDICH'N RIGH

ALEXANDER III KING OF SCOTLAND RESCUED FROM THE FURY OF A STAG

BY THE INTREPIDITY OF COLIN FITZGERALD, THE ANCESTOR OF THE PRESENT MACKENZIE FAMILY.

BEDFORD GRAMMAR SCHOOL

BILLETS NEAR LOCON

BRIDGE AT VIELLE CHAPELLE

CRUCIFIX AT NEUVE CHAPELLE

WORKING PARTY AT NIGHT

RELIEFS OF THE 4TH SEAFORTHS IN NEUVE CHAPELLE

LOOS

VIMY

SUNSET IN ARTOIS

ARRAS

LOOKING TOWARDS KEMMEL

FONTAINE NOTRE DAME

THE GERMAN OFFENSIVE, 1918.

THE
4TH BATTALION
SEAFORTH HIGHLANDERS
B.E.F..

BATTLES AND ACTIONS IN WHICH THEY TOOK PART DURING THE WAR OF 1914~1918.

1914
Defence of Givenchy

1915
Neuve Chapelle
Aubers Ridge
(Attack at Rue du Bois)
Festubert

Loos
(Action of Pietre)

1916
The Somme
Bazentin Ridge
(Attacks on High Wood)
The Ancre
(Capture of Beaumont Hamel)

1917
Vimy Ridge
Second Battle of the Scarpe
Third Battle of the Scarpe
(Capture of Roeux)

Ypres
Pilckem Ridge
Poelcappelle
Cambrai
Tank Attack
German Counter-Attacks

1918
The Somme
Battle of Bapaume
The Lys
Estaires
Hazebrouck
Defence of Hinges Ridge
Béthune
The Marne
Tardenois
Fighting for the Ardre Valley
Second Battles of Arras
The Scarpe
The Drocourt-Quéant Line
The Selle
Valenciennes.

BAPAUME

Summary
of
Casualties sustained & Honours won
by
Officers & other Ranks.

Total who served with the Battalions overseas 1914-1918.

4056.

Officers - - - - - 273.
Other Ranks - - 3783.

Casualties.

Officers

Killed.	Died of Wounds.	Died.	Missing.	Total.
44.	11.	1.	4.	60.

Other Ranks.

Killed.	Died of Wounds.	Died.	Missing.	Total.
718.	235.	56.	101.	1110.

Honours.

Officers

C.M.G.	C.B.E.	O.B.E.	D.S.O.	Bar.	M.C.	Bar.	D.C.M.	M.M.	L.S.M	Despatches	R.H.S.M.	C. de G.
4.	1.	4.	13.	1.	32.	6.	2.	3.	1.	27.	1.	2.

Other Ranks.

V.C.	M.C.	D.C.M.	Bar.	M.M.	Bar.	M.S.M.	Dispatches.	C. de G.	Med St. G.
1.	1.	25.	3.	101.	6.	7.	11.	2.	1

CONTENTS

Note on the Arrangement of Text and Maps

When the word Battalion, standing alone, begins with a capital "B" it always refers to the 4th Battalion The Seaforth Highlanders. When it begins with a lower case "b" it refers to some other unit or units.

Similarly Division and Brigade, without other particularization, and beginning with a capital, refer to the formation to which the Battalion at that time belonged.

The Synopses are in no sense intended to be a history of the Great War, but merely to enable the reader to follow the purpose of the doings in which the Battalion had a part.

Unless otherwise stated, positions of units are given from right to left of the British line.

No index of subjects as such has been attempted. They are almost always connected with the name of some person or place and should be looked up under the appropriate name.

Map 1 is the strategical map, on which have been shown most of the names mentioned in the synopses as well as those outside the borders of Maps 2, 3 and 4. The area of these is shown on Map 1.

Maps 2, 3 and 4 contain practically every place-name mentioned in the book within their borders. They are arranged to overlap, so as to facilitate passage from one to another.

The remainder are taken mostly from sketch maps made in the field, and their accuracy is not always absolute, but they give detail too minute for record on the smaller-scale maps.

The names of places mentioned in Chapter XIV. have in many cases been omitted, as being of little importance as compared with those in the war chapters.

ILLUSTRATIONS

COLOUR PLATES

BLACK AND WHITE PLATES

CHAPTER HEAD-PIECES

MAPS

PART I

TAIN : ST DUTHUS TOWER

CHAPTER I

THE MILITARY HISTORY OF THE COUNTY OF ROSS AND CROMARTY, THE FENCIBLES AND THE VOLUNTEERS

Ross and Cromarty are now one county, as they were up till the beginning of the eighteenth century, when Sir George MacKenzie of Castle Leod, later Lord Tarbat, succeeded in erecting into an earldom the scattered estates that he had inherited or acquired, under the style of the Earldom of Cromarty. The county of Ross has had a great share in the history of Scotland, and indeed its fate for long was surely indicative of the fortunes of that country, to which at times it hardly seemed to belong.

Ross was one of the ancient divisions of Alban, the land north of the Forth, and formed part of the territory of the Northern Picts, whose capital is said to have been at Inverness, where St Columba baptized the then king, Brude MacMælchon by name. It is not, however, until the arrival of Ketill Flatneb and his followers in Caithness that the history, properly so called, of Ross begins to emerge from the mists of vague tradition. These newcomers were Norsemen who had fled from Norway to escape the exactions of Harold Harfagr; they founded in the Northern Isles and Caithness a line of rulers that long disputed with the Scottish kings of the race of Alpin the lordship of the northern portion of their kingdom. Sigurd the Stout, Jarl of Orkney, carried his conquests down to the Oykell, the *Ekkialsbakki* of the Sagas, if not further; but it was apparently Jarl Thorfinn, Sigurd's son by a daughter of King Malcolm II., who carried out the conquest of the Machair of Ross. This Jarl, who seems to have been one of the ablest warriors in an age that produced a great number, defeated his grandfather at a place called Torfness, identified by some with Knockfarrel, near Dingwall, after which he ravaged the kingdom of Scotland as far south as Fife. The considerable number of Norse names along the Cromarty Firth shows that the Norsemen must have settled in large numbers in the Machair. The county town proclaims by its name, Dingwall (*Thingvallr*), that it was the meeting-place of a Norse parliament and the centre of government of the invaders, and the district abounds in place-names similarly recalling the Norse settlement. After the death of Jarl Thorfinn, Ross seems to have passed, without any struggle, under the dominion of Malcolm Canmore, by his marriage with Thorfinn's widow, Ingibiorg. As happened with their kinsmen in the Western Isles, the Norsemen rapidly abandoned their own speech for the Gaelic, though one has only to look at the present people of Easter Ross to see what a large Norse element yet remains in its population.

Ross having become a favourite place of refuge for the Macwilliams, who claimed the throne as descendants of Duncan, son of Malcolm Canmore, Alexander II. created it into an earldom for Farquhar Macintaggart (son of the priest), who had aided in the suppression of one of their rebellions. The earldom at this time comprised not only the present county, but also the glens of the Affric, Cannich and Farrar. After the death of Haco and the purchase of the Western Isles the Lewis and Skye were added to the dominions of the Earl, who married the daughter of the Earl of Buchan, niece of the King. It was at this time that Kenneth, eponymous of the Mackenzies, made his appearance in Kintail, where he held the Castle of Ellandonan. He was not on good terms with his overlord—a fact that had momentous consequences for the history of Ross.

Walter, the son of the third earl, was killed at Bannockburn along with the Chief of the Clan Munro; but his grandson was guilty of something nearly approaching high treason. By the marriage of his daughter with Walter Lesley the earldom passed with her to the Lesley family, the male line being represented for long by the old family of Balnagown. Walter's daughter married the then Lord of the Isles, while his widow was forced to marry Alexander Stewart, the notorious "Wolf of Badenoch," who, fortunately for the county, does not seem to have paid it many visits. Walter's son succeeded "the Wolf," and left but one daughter, Euphemia, who, though described as a "crouch-backit" creature, was a prize of the first magnitude for the ambitious. The Regent Albany arranged that she should go into a convent, and that the earldom should then be resigned by her for reconveyance to the Earl of Buchan, thus cutting out the claims of Donald of the Isles in right of his wife. Donald therefore invaded Ross in July 1411. He was repulsed in his advance on Dingwall by Mackay of Farr and the Munros, but continued his march into Aberdeenshire.

At the battle of "the Red Harlaw" Donald was decisively defeated, yet he held the greater part of Ross under his power for about a year more, when he was forced to abandon all claims to the earldom and to give hostages for his good conduct.

John, Earl of Buchan, with Douglas and Swinton, won the battle of Beaugé, and their Scottish troops were the origin of the famous Garde Ecossaise and the Gens-d'armes Ecossais. He became the ninth Earl of Ross, and was killed at Verneuil in 1423.

James I. introduced a novel procedure into the history of these turbulent lands by convening a Parliament at Inverness, to which all the prominent chiefs of the North were invited. Practically all were apprehended, and many were interned in the Castle of Dingwall. Murdoch, fifth Chief of the Mackenzies, seems to have been favourably received, while the Chief of the Mathesons, at that time perhaps, next to the Macdonalds, the most powerful of the clans of Ross, escaped with a caution. Alexander of the Isles was held for some time, but eventually released, though his mother was interned in Inchcolm. This resulted in an invasion of Ross, the wasting of the Crown lands and the burning of Inverness by the Lord of the Isles, whose forces were, however, dispersed by the King in Lochaber in the following year. The assassination of James in the year 1437 led to the restoration to Alexander of his inherited rights, whereby he became the tenth Earl of Ross. He was involved in the great Douglas conspiracy, but died before his complicity could recoil on his head, leaving three sons—John, who succeeded as a minor; Celestine, who succeeded to the lands of Lochalsh in right of his mother, heiress of the last of the Macintaggarts of Applecross, descendants of the first earl; and Hugh, Lord of Sleat.

Like his father, John became involved in the Douglas conspiracy, which continued through at least three generations, and actually took the field, seizing the castles of Inverness, Urquhart and Ruthven in Badenoch. The King being unable to take effective measures against the rebel confirmed him in the possession of Castle Urquhart on payment of a rent! There followed the murder of Douglas by the King's own hand and the defeat of his successor at Arkinholme. The vanquished barons fled to John, who sent a fleet of one hundred galleys to take reprisals, which, however, amounted only to some abortive raids on the islands in the Firth of Clyde. The Douglases then went to England, leaving their ally to the King's mercy, which, after some delay, was shown to him. John was present with a division of well-armed Highlanders at the siege of Roxburgh, where James II. was killed.

During James III.'s minority, John entered into an alliance with the English, and actually sent a force as far as Inverness; but, like so many Highland armies, it melted away. John was once more pardoned; but, on his resuming his traitorous correspondence with England, an army under the command of Crawford and Athole was sent against him. Again followed submission, with surrender by the Earl to the Crown of his earldom of Ross and his possessions in Glenmoriston and Cantyre. Thus did Ross become a county palatine. Its administration was entrusted to the Earl of Sutherland, Alexander, Chief of the Mackenzies, and John, fifteenth Baron of Foulis.

Meanwhile began the long struggle between the Mackenzies and the Macdonalds. The former family had gained much, both in lands and power, from the transfer of the earldom to the Crown—a matter greatly resented by John's illegitimate son, Angus Og. The bitterness was increased when Kenneth Mackenzie, Younger of Kintail, was on a visit to Angus. In consequence of an insult fixed on him by one of the Macdonald vassals Kenneth repudiated his wife, the sister of Angus. There was recourse to arms. Government forces under the Earl of Atholl were defeated at Lag-a-bhraid, but Angus was eventually assassinated by an Irish harper.

The feud was continued by Angus's successor, Alexander of Lochalsh. In 1491 Alexander led both branches of the Clan Donald, together with the Camerons and the Clan Chattan, on an inroad designed apparently to punish the Mackenzies. Inverness was taken and much of the Sheriffdom was laid waste. Meanwhile Alexander himself appears to have started off with a force to hunt for Kenneth, taking the road to Kinellan. On his way he burnt the church of Contin, wherein a number of old men, women and children had sought sanctuary. Alexander met the Mackenzies at a place not yet satisfactorily identified, and was utterly defeated owing to the tactical dispositions of Red Hector, brother of Kenneth Mackenzie and founder of the Gairloch family. The Macdonalds were cut off almost to a man. The Government again intervened. John was declared to have forfeited his title and estates, although it is very uncertain how far he was privy to the doings of his kinsmen. In January 1494 he waited on the King and formally surrendered his honours. He died in Dundee in a common lodging-house five years later.

Thus ended the line of the Lords of the Isles, the descendants of the great Somerlid, called by the Gael Somhairle, and by the English Samuel! They had drawn the men of Ross into many a bloody fight during their two hundred and fifty years of rule, usually in rebellion against the Scottish Crown, or in attacks on its loyal supporters. The power in the county was now to pass to another family.

Red Hector (*Eachain Ruadh*) was the virtual chief of the Clan Coinnich while tutor during the minority of his nephew. He commanded the Clan contingent at Flodden; failed in an assault on the Castle of Dingwall (an entirely lawless act), seized, and was confirmed in the possession of, the Red Castle, and soundly routed the Munros at Bealach'n Cor.

With the Reformation the county of Ross begins to share in a less erratic manner in the history of Scotland. It had its part in the troubles concerning Episcopacy, but, on the whole, because of its longer and stronger attachment to the Episcopate, seems to have suffered less in these quarrels than the counties in the South. It was, however, considerably troubled with personal quarrels, usually ending in a resort to violence, whereby sundry of the King's lieges were from time to time killed or wounded. It would seem that the county had its full share of "fighting parsons," and these not by any means confined to the Episcopalians and Catholics, as some have maintained.

At the end of the sixteenth century the Lewis became a storm centre, the Macleods using it as a base for piratical raids carried out in a good old fashion that was felt even then to be somewhat of an anachronism. A company of Fifeshire lairds accordingly was formed to make a "plantation" of the island, such as their sovereign, James VI., afterwards carried out in Ulster. The Islesmen, however, contrived to capture their camp, and they departed after making humiliating terms. Three separate attempts did these "Adventurers" make to establish their claim to the island, but between the open hostility of the Macleods and the tortuous intrigues of Kenneth Mackenzie of Kintail they failed utterly. The Macleods, however, had incurred the hostility of the Government; their lands were, therefore, forfeited and conferred on Kintail.

In the confused and crooked policies of the middle of the seventeenth century the Ross-shire chiefs seem to have been almost as bewildered as the modern student of that extraordinary time. They consequently took little part in the civil wars, although the Clans of Munro and Ross bore a share in the final defeat of the "Great Marquis." In the wars on the Continent, however, we find several distinguished officers from the county, foremost among them being the celebrated author of the *Expedition*, Major-General Munro, originally an officer in Mackay's Highlanders, and the constant friend of Sir John Hepburn, commander of the famous Green Brigade in the army of Gustavus. He makes frequent mention in his book of "my cousin, Obisdell," who also served in Mackay's Highlanders, and who later on became Sir Robert Munro, Chief of the Clan. About thirty-four officers from this family alone held commissions in the Swedish army.

The end of the seventeenth century saw the continuance of the steady rise of the Rosses, Munros and Mackenzies to power in the county, and the diminution of that of the Macdonalds, Macleods and Mathesons.

Photo by Hills & Saunders.

THE OFFICERS, 4TH SEAFORTHS,
BEDFORD: NOVEMBER, 1914.

Seaforth was out with his clan in the '15, but only the Cromarty branch of the clan went out in the '45, a small company of about eighty men being the sole representatives of the county in the army of Prince Charles.

In 1778 Lord Macleod, the heir to the Cromarty title, raised the 74th Regiment in Ross. This later became the 71st, now the 1st Battalion Highland Light Infantry. In the same year Lord Seaforth raised the 78th, afterwards renumbered the 72nd, later the Duke of Albany's, and now the 1st Battalion Seaforth Highlanders. In 1793 the third of the Ross-shire regiments, again the 78th, was formed, chiefly through the Seaforth influence. This was known as the Ross-shire Buffs, now the 2nd Battalion Seaforth Highlanders. It is a very noteworthy circumstance that no less than three of the twelve Highland regiments raised during fifteen years should have been recruited in the county.

The wars of the French Revolution imposed a great strain on Great Britain. Her regular army was inadequate for its tasks, even after new regiments had been raised; for, as usual, we were unprepared for war. To relieve the army of the duties of home defence new corps were called into being.

First came the Fencibles—troops raised, officered and equipped like regular troops, but enlisted on a limited engagement or for the duration of the war, and liable to be sent out of their own county only if they volunteered to go. A great number of these regiments were formed in the Highlands. The first were those of Argyll and of Sutherland, permission for their embodiment being given by the Government with much hesitation, for fear that they might display Jacobite tendencies. The Sutherland Regiment was embodied at Fort George on 1st March 1793, its strength being 1084 with drummers and pipers. One company was raised in Ross-shire by Captain R. B. Æneas Macleod of Cadboll.

The Duke of Gordon's Northern Fencible Regiment enlisted twenty-three men in Ross whose average height was only 5 feet 4 inches.

On 20th November 1794 the Ross-shire Highland Fencible Regiment was raised. It wore the Highland garb, with yellow facings. It was commanded by Major-Commandant Colin Mackenzie of Mountgerald, and had two companies, noted for "exemplary character and physical capacity. No man was punished; nor died during its service." It was reduced in 1799.

The Ross and Cromarty Rangers was raised on 6th June 1799. It was commanded by Colonel Lewis Mackenzie, Younger of Scatwell, the Lieutenant-Colonel being George Mackenzie and the Major, John Mackenzie. It consisted of eight companies. The name was changed in 1801 to the Ross and Cromarty Fencibles. It volunteered for service in any part of Europe.

In 1801 it was quartered in Aberdeen. On the evening of the King's birthday there was a crowd in the main street, where stood the guard-house. According to custom the crowd was in a boisterous mood, and a number of young men began throwing squibs, crackers, and dead cats about. The guard stood to arms outside the guard-house, but were driven in again by the crowd, which broke the windows and tried to force the door. Word of this reached the barracks, and a number of men seized their arms and ran down to rescue their comrades. They formed up on seeing the mob, and were joined by some of their officers. The mob became more turbulent. Someone gave the order to fire, and two of the townsmen were killed and several wounded. No magistrate was present, nor was the order given by an officer. The affair made a great sensation, and two officers, two sergeants and some privates were tried by the Court of Justiciary and acquitted. The affray was unfortunate; it originated in no ill will, for the troops had so far been on the best of terms with the townsfolk.

On 9th June 1799 Colonel John Macleod of Colbeck raised the Princess Charlotte of Wales or Macleod Fencibles, the last Fencible regiment raised in the Highlands. It is probable that it was raised largely in Ross, though actually embodied at Elgin. It served in Ireland, where it was very popular with the people, who said of the Highland soldiers that they were "like children of the family" on which they were billeted, and "like lambs in the house." This regiment was reduced in 1802.

In the closing years of the eighteenth century ten Militia regiments were raised in Scotland. Of these the 2nd (or Ross-shire) North British Militia was raised on 23rd April 1798. It was commanded by Colonel Francis, Lord Seaforth. The Lieutenant-Colonel was James, Earl of Caithness; the Major, William Wilson, and the Adjutant, Donald Fraser. There were six companies.

Volunteer companies were formed in Easter Ross as under:

Tain Company: Captain George Murray, 28th December 1794.
Tarbutt (*sic*) Company: Captain Donald M'Leod, 31st March 1795.
Nigg Company: Captain John Cockburn Ross, 3rd April 1795.
Fortrose Company: Captain David Urquhart, 23rd May 1795.
Dingwall Companies: Captain Kenneth M'Kenzie, Captain George Munro, 23rd May 1795.

By October 1798 they had been formed into a battalion under the style of the East Ross Volunteers: Lieutenant-Colonel-Commandant, Donald M'Leod; Lieutenant-Colonel, Alexander Baillie; and Major, David Urquhart, who was succeeded in command of the Fortrose Company by George Lockhart. The Adjutant was Hugh Roy.

In Wester Ross there were three companies:

Ulapool (*sic*) Company: Major-Commandant Robert Melvile, 12th September 1794.
Kintail Company: Captain Colin Macdonnell, 16th August 1797.
Lochalsh Company: Captain John Matheson, 16th August 1797.

Cromarty had a separate corps, apparently of three companies, raised on the 3rd of May 1797, and commanded by Major-Commandant Walter Ross.

At the Peace of Amiens the British Government hastily disbanded every regiment it possibly could, and only the Militia were left, with the pompous title of the Ross, Caithness, Sutherland and Cromarty Militia! The Colonel was Lord Seaforth, with a new commission dated 6th November 1802, and its Lieutenant-Colonel the Earl of Caithness, commission dated 18th December in the same year. Headquarters were at Dingwall. It ultimately became the 3rd Battalion The Seaforth Highlanders.

The renewed outbreak of war revived the Volunteers. On 27th August 1803 there existed six companies, styled, it would seem, the Ross Regiment; but as no field officers are shown on the list they may have been independent companies.

By October the following additional battalions had made their appearance:

Ross (1st, or Eastern Ross): Lieutenant-Colonel-Commandant Donald M'Leod. Headquarters, Tain. Eight companies.

Ross (2nd, or Western Ross): Lieutenant-Colonel-Commandant Sir George Stewart M'Kenzie, Bart. Headquarters, Dingwall. Three companies.

Ross (3rd, or Black Isle): Lieutenant-Colonel-Commandant Sir Hector Mackenzie, Bart. Three companies.

Ross (4th, or Lewis Island or Sternway (*sic*)): No officers named.

Ross (5th, or West Island District): Captain Hugh Innes. One company.

Cromarty Volunteers: Lieutenant-Colonel-Commandant Walter Ross. Three companies.

The number of companies is not given in the 1804 Army List, but is easily deduced from the numbers and ranks of the officers.

By 1807 the Ross companies and the 5th of the above battalions had disappeared. The 4th had dropped its numeral and was now called the Stornoway; it had apparently two companies, commanded by Captains John Mackenzie and James Robertson, with commissions dated 27th August 1803.

In 1808 the Volunteers became "Local Militia." In the Militia Lists for that year we find the Ross-shire Western Regiment: Headquarters, Dingwall; Lieutenant-Colonel-Commandant, Duncan Munro, commission dated 24th September 1808; and the Ross-shire Eastern Regiment: Headquarters, Tam [an evident misprint for Tain]; Lieutenant-Colonel-Commandant, Donald M'Leod, commission dated 10th April 1809. In the former a considerable number of the old Volunteer officers continued to serve, but comparatively very few in the Eastern Regiment. Both regiments were reduced at the close of the Napoleonic Wars.

A very noticeable thing in the old Fencible, Militia and Volunteer Lists is the difficulty the simplest Highland names presented to the London printer, of which several examples have been given. Patronymics in "Mac" are practically all spelt with the "M'," a form comparatively rare in the North to-day.

Save for the doings of the Regular regiments, the 71st, 72nd and 78th, with which we are not here concerned, the military history of Ross is confined to that of individuals who adopted the military profession, until the year 1859. In that year Cadboll, Robert Bruce Æneas Macleod, called a meeting in the

Commercial Bank at Invergordon. Among those present were Messrs John Ross, Andrew Munro (banker), Henry Oakes, Andrew Malcolm, George McGregor, James Mackillichan, George Mackenzie, Donald McKillechan and Norman Walker. Cadboll explained that the object of the meeting was to raise a company of Volunteers for the defence of Britain against the French, whose policy at that time was one of military aggression, which it was feared might be directed against this country. He gave particulars as to the number of men required to form a company, the time to be taken up by training, and the approximate cost of the uniform. It was decided that the necessary numbers could not be raised and equipped without extending the area to be included, and that it would be essential to get the co-operation of the Tain district. A meeting accordingly was called at Tain on 27th May 1859, which was very enthusiastic, forty of those present volunteering to join the corps. Recruits came in rapidly, and on 1st August the Invergordon section met at Invergordon Mains, when Sergeant Munro, Northfield, gave an address. The first drill was held on 8th August, both the Tain and Invergordon sections parading at their respective headquarters on that day.

The Invergordon Times of 20th February 1860 contained the following advertisement:

FIRST COMPANY, ROSS RIFLE VOLUNTEERS

Subscription List

The following gentlemen are effective members, fully armed and equipped, or have supplied a rifle, sword, accoutrements and uniform to one or more substitutes:

	Yearly Subscription			*Donation*		
Robert Bruce Æneas Macleod of Cadboll	£10	0	0	£29	15	0
W. H. Murray of Geanies . .	3	3	0	23	2	0
David Monro of Allan . . .	5	5	0	13	5	0
George Ross, Esq., of Pitcalnie .		..		8	5	0
Kenneth Murray, Tain . . .	2	10	0	8	5	0

It is noteworthy that the five sergeants of the company, besides subscribing £8, 5s., which was evidently the cost of uniform and rifle, put down their names for a yearly subscription of £1 each.

The uniform of this corps, which afterwards became the 1st Company of the Ross-shire Rifle Volunteers, was a grey tunic, trousers and cap. There were no facings, but there was a band of black braid round the cap. The waist-belt was brown. It was armed with the short Enfield rifle. The official date of its formation is given as 15th February 1860. The officers, whose commissions bear the same date, were Captain R. B. Æ. Macleod, Lieutenant David Monro, and Ensign Kenneth Murray.

Other companies—or corps, as they were commonly called—were formed in quick succession.

On 16th February 1860 the 2nd Company was formed at Dingwall. The uniform was the same as that of the 1st Company, but with black leggings and a black plume in the cap. The officers were Captain Keith Stewart Mackenzie, Lieutenant Alexander Hay and Ensign Edward Hay M. Matheson.

On the same day a meeting was held in the Town Hall, Cromarty, for the purpose of raising a Cromarty Company; Provost Ross was elected Captain; Mr Mackay, factor, Lieutenant, and Mr George Macdonald, Customs Officer, 2nd Lieutenant. By 3rd March this company was seventy strong, but it can have had but a brief existence, since it does not appear in the Army Lists of 1864.

On the 17th of the same month the 3rd Company was formed at Avoch, after a meeting at the Royal Hotel, Fortrose, whereat Sir James Mackenzie, Bart., gave a donation of £125 and undertook to equip any of his tenants or their sons, paying a rent of from £10 to £100, who might join. The uniform was a grey tweed jacket, knickerbockers and cap—the material of which was made at Mr Alexander George Mackenzie's mill at Avoch—brown leggings and waist-belt. The officers were Captain Sir James Mackenzie, Lieutenant Alexander George Mackenzie, Ensign Roderick Mackenzie of Flowerburn, and Hon. Assistant Surgeon Alexander R. Mackenzie.

On 22nd February the 4th Company was formed at Knockbain (spelt Knockbairn in the Army Lists). The uniform was a light grey tunic with red facings, light grey trousers with black braid, light grey cap with stag's head badge, black leggings, and black patent leather waist- and shoulder-belts. The officers, whose commissions bore date the 12th April 1860, were Captain

James Wardlaw (who appears already to have held the rank of Major in the Regular Army), Lieutenant James Fowler Mackenzie and Ensign James Cameron.

The 5th Company was formed at Alness on 20th May. The uniform was grey. The officers were Captain Andrew Munro, Lieutenant David Forsyth and Ensign Alexander Maclean.

On the following day the 6th Company also was formed at Alness. Sir James Grierson is of opinion that it was originally a section of the 5th Company—an opinion which is borne out by the fact that it had no captain till 2nd April 1864, when the Lieutenant, Frederick Walton, became its Captain. The first Ensign was Roderick Mackenzie. It would appear that there was, in fact, some feeling on the part of certain of the inhabitants that there should be a "Celtic" company, and this is probably the explanation of the appearance in Alness of two companies.

In 1864 all these companies, except the 3rd, adopted a common uniform, consisting of a scarlet tunic with blue facings, white cord on the collar and cuffs, and black braid down the front, which was not buttoned but hooked. The trousers were blue with red piping, shakos blue with a red band, stag's head badge and horsehair plume. The waist- and pouch-belts were of white patent leather. The 3rd Company adopted scarlet doublets with blue facings, Mackenzie tartan kilts and plain glengarries.

Keith Stewart Mackenzie of Seaforth was the moving spirit in the Volunteer movement in Ross, and it was he who brought about the formation of these companies into the Administrative Battalion of Ross-shire Rifle Volunteers. On 25th May 1865 he became its first Lieutenant-Colonel. There were two Majors, R. B. Æ. Macleod and James Wardlaw. The Adjutant, who was appointed on 12th November 1863, was Edward Francis Cash, late of the School of Musketry, Hythe; the Surgeon was A. R. Mackenzie; and the Hon. Chaplain the Rev. John Gibson, M.A.

Closely connected with the Battalion was a rifle club, the Ross-shire Service Rifle Association. It was always remarkable for fine marksmanship and had no less than fourteen separate rifle ranges. In 1865 Captain Horatio Ross, of the 6th Company, won the Wimbledon Cup. Both he and his father were noted shots, the latter having won the first Queen's Prize when serving with the 7th North York, and the former the first Association Cup when serving with the 6th Kincardine.

In 1865 the 5th Company was transferred from Alness to Ullapool. The officers were all new, Captain Duncan H. C. R. Davidson of Tulloch and Lieutenant Alexander MacDonald being commissioned on 24th May 1865, and Ensign Walter G. Mundell on 1st September.

On 12th May 1866 a 7th Company was formed at Evanton. It wore, at first, grey tunics, 42nd tartan trews and plain glengarries; but towards the end of the year changed to scarlet doublets with blue facings, Mackenzie tartan kilts, heather-mixture hose with green tops, plain grey goat-skin sporrans, plain glengarries with stag's head badge, and white patent leather belts. The officers were Captain Charles Munro, Lieutenant David Forsyth (presumably he who had been in the 5th Company), and Ensign James Forbes.

On 11th August 1866 the 8th Company was formed at Moy. Its uniform was the same as that of the 7th, except that it had white facings. The Captain was Hector Munro, the Lieutenant Alexander Blake, and the Ensign George M'Lennan.

The last Company, the 9th, was formed at Gairloch on 23rd February 1867. Its uniform was the same as that of the 7th Company. The officers were Captain Sir Kenneth S. Mackenzie, Bart., of Gairloch, Lieutenant Alexander Burgess and Ensign Murdo MacRae.

In 1876 a further step in the consolidation of the Battalion was taken in the adoption of an identical uniform. This was a scarlet doublet with blue collar and cuffs, black Austrian knots on the sleeves and blue pipings; trews of Mackenzie tartan; diced glengarries with stag's head badge, and white belts.

In 1880 the Battalion became the 1st Ross-shire (Ross Highland) Rifle Volunteers, with headquarters at Dingwall. The headquarters of the Avoch Company were transferred to Fortrose and those of the Knockbain to Munlochy. Letters also were substituted for numbers, the 1st Company becoming A, the 2nd B, and so on to the 9th, which became I.

The Ross-shire Volunteers were not represented at the Royal Review in Holyrood Park in 1860, but Major Duncan Davidson, with 27 officers and 556 other ranks, attended the "coming of age" review on the same ground in August 1881. The weather was very bad. The troops got soaked through and had to travel for many hours in their wet uniforms; there was in consequence much sickness and some deaths.

In 1887 the Battalion became the 1st (Ross Highland) Volunteer Battalion, The Seaforth Highlanders. The headquarters of G Company were transferred from Evanton to Dingwall, and those of H from Moy to Fairburn. In the following year authority was given to wear the uniform of the Seaforth Highlanders, substituting the glengarry for the feather bonnet, and subject to the universal rules as to distinctions, such as the wearing of silver instead of gold lace, pouch belts instead of sashes, and so forth.

In 1888 the Battalion was assigned to the "Highland Brigade," which was allocated to the defences of London.

In 1897 it was represented in the Diamond Jubilee Procession.

Lieutenants W. M. Macphail and James Oliphant Black (Gairloch), with about 110 other ranks, served in the South African War, some with the Volunteer Company of the regiment and some in other units.

In 1902, when the Brodrick Scheme came into force, the 1st and 3rd Volunteer Battalions, the 1st Sutherland Rifle Volunteer Corps and the 1st Volunteer Battalion Cameron Highlanders were brigaded together as the Seaforth and Cameron Infantry Brigade.

In September 1905 Colonel A. R. B. Warrand, with 22 officers and 329 other ranks, took part in the Royal Review in Holyrood Park before King Edward VII.

The following figures may be of interest, as showing the strength of the Battalion at various times:

	1862	1881	1907
Establishment	..	910	1044
Efficient officers	..	896	34
Efficient other ranks	..		835
Non-efficient officers	..	8	1
Non-efficient other ranks	..		37
Total strength	330	904	907

The commanding officers, with dates of appointment, were:

Lieutenant-Colonel K. W. Stewart Mackenzie of Seaforth, V.D., 26th May 1865.

Lieutenant-Colonel D. H. C. R. Davidson of Tulloch, 17th August 1881.

Lieutenant-Colonel (Hon. Colonel) A. J. C. Warrand, V.D., 29th March 1889.
Lieutenant-Colonel (Hon. Colonel) A. R. B. Warrand, 1st July 1897.

In 1903 Bt.-Colonel J. A. F. H. Stewart Mackenzie of Seaforth (subsequently Lord Seaforth) was appointed Honorary Colonel of the Battalion.

The adjutants were:

Captain E. F. Cash, 12th November 1863.
Captain A. R. B. Warrand, Seaforth Highlanders, 7th July 1890.
Captain A. Stirling, Seaforth Highlanders, 1st November 1895.
Captain T. Fetherstonhaugh, Seaforth Highlanders, 2nd February 1901.
Bt.-Major K. W. Arbuthnot, Seaforth Highlanders, 10th August 1907.

Colonel A. R. B. Warrand continued to command the Battalion after it became a unit of the Territorial Force, relinquishing on 15th June 1909.

Before proceeding with the history of the Territorial Battalion a few notes on the Volunteers may not come amiss.

They had always a splendid record for marksmanship—not, perhaps, surprising in a battalion that had in its ranks many deerstalkers, gamekeepers and gillies, but none the less creditable to those who had no such chances of becoming good shots in civil life.

They were noted also for their fine physique. About 1867 none of the Gairloch Company was under 5 feet 10 inches in height, and most of them were over 6 feet. One of them was so tall that, on battalion parades, he was taken from his company and put on the right of the line in A Company, to act as fugleman—a thing that he bitterly resented, for he was proud of belonging to I Company.

The old Volunteers were very keen, but they took their duties in a light-hearted way. They were essentially *amateurs* and were proud of it. In consequence of this they were not taken very seriously by the majority of the Regular soldiers of their time, though there were a few even then who dreamed of converting them into a second-line army that should be really effective.

This light-hearted manner of soldiering sometimes led to

rather dangerous situations, as when two contending forces on a field day got so close as to cause a good many casualties from wads and stones thrown up by the blast of the rifles. It was very rarely that the Battalion could be collected for a battalion parade, owing to the great distances to be covered and the lack of rapid means of transport. The commanding officer's main duty was an occasional inspection of each company, when a few evolutions were carried out to test the efficiency of the officers and N.C.O.'s, followed by an inspection of the company-books. At one of these inspections the colour-sergeant had braced himself for the ordeal with whisky before he came on parade. He was called out to put the company through some movements and got them hopelessly "clubbed." Undaunted he turned to his captain and said: "We'll just try it another way." But the remedy was as bad as the disease!

Another of these worthies rejoiced greatly when extended order was introduced. Like many of them he was an elderly man and found field days dry work. The new method gave him welcome opportunities to get behind a rock and slake his thirst.

A great many of the West Coast men had very little English, and could not understand the orders they got on parade. On one occasion, when the instructor was explaining to the squad the meaning of the word "Attention," one of the newly enrolled recruits turned to his neighbour and said in Gaelic: "Isn't it good of him to be talking of a pension already?"

Yet these old Volunteers deserve every honour from their country, for without them the Territorial Force could not have come into existence, and that force undoubtedly saved the situation in the winter of 1914, when the original Expeditionary Force and the Regular troops from India and elsewhere had been worn down in the struggle against overwhelming odds to mere shadows of what they had once been.

In the Army List of October 1908 the Battalion first figures as the 4th Battalion The Seaforth Highlanders. Under Lord Haldane's scheme the old Volunteers were converted into the Territorial Force. It was, in some ways, a very similar conversion to that which transformed the volunteers of the Napoleonic Wars into Local Militia, for it very definitely affected their previous amateur status. They were no longer to be a congeries of units, but definite parts of an army, organized in all respects, and trained, so far as their civilian occupations would allow, in the same manner as the Regular army. How this new force enabled the phantom remains of the old army to hold at bay the largest and, so far as material preparedness goes, the most efficient engine of war ever produced in peace time, will be sketched in the pages of this book. That it was able to bring real help to that army was due, not so much to its training, which was of need but partial, but to the fact that it had begun to regard itself as a real second line, and that it brought to the front the same "will to victory" as inspired the Regulars—a will that expressed itself, not in heroics of any sort, but in the entire absence of any idea that anything but ultimate victory was possible.

On 16th June 1909 Lieutenant-Colonel H. M. Fraser, V.D., succeeded Lieutenant-Colonel Warrand in command of the Battalion, and on 11th October of the same year Lieutenant D. H. Davidson, Seaforth Highlanders, succeeded Major Arbuthnot as Adjutant, with the temporary rank of Captain.

The difference between the Volunteers and the Territorial army is brought out by the stress now laid by the military authorities on expending more extra ammunition on bad shots than on good, and on special training for N.C.O.'s.

On 24th February 1910 the companies were reorganized as follows:

A, Tain, with sections at Fearn, Edderton and Portmahomack.
B, Dingwall.
C, Munlochy, with sections at Fortrose, Muir of Ord, Avoch and Rosemarkie.
D, Gairloch, with sections at Poolewe, Opinan, Kinlochewe and Torridon.
E, Ullapool, with sections at Braemore and Coigach.
F, Invergordon, with sections at Kildary.
G, Alness, with sections at Evanton.
H, Maryburgh, with sections at Fairburn, Garve and Strathpeffer.

The Battalion furnished a Guard of Honour in front of the Burgh Buildings at Dingwall on 12th May 1910, on the occasion of the proclamation by the Sheriff of the accession of King George V.

On 18th June the Battalion went into camp with the Seaforth and Cameron Infantry Brigade at Aviemore. A and F Companies, acting as a double company under Captain and

Hon. Major W. Robertson of Monteagle, were fourth in the competition for Colonel The Mackintosh of Mackintosh's Cup, and the Battalion was first in the machine gun competitions, making the highest total in both. The camp broke up on 2nd July.

Lieutenant C. G. Hogg, one sergeant, two corporals and twenty-two other ranks went to London for duty at the Coronation of King George V. in June 1911.

The Brigade Camp in 1911 was at Tain, lasting from 17th June till 1st July. There was a parade in camp to celebrate the Coronation, at which Lieutenant Ian Forsyth and 2nd Lieutenant J. H. Budge carried the Battalion colours. The troops marched through Tain, past Major-General Woolcombe, C.B., commanding the Highland Division, who took the salute at the Town Cross. The parade formed up in front of the new Drill Hall, where it received the General Officer Commanding with a general salute. Major-General Woolcombe then opened the Drill Hall, and a Coronation service in the Academy Park followed. B Company had in the meanwhile sent a party, consisting of one officer, two pipers and twenty-two other ranks, for the Coronation ceremonies at Dingwall.

In this year Private K. MacLennan, C Company, took first place in putting the shot, and second in throwing the hammer, at the Territorial Force Athletic Sports at Stamford Bridge, London.

In 1912 the Brigade Camp was held from 15th to 29th June at Burghead, where the County Association Challenge Trophy was won by H Company.

The Imperial Service Section at this time was composed as follows:

Company	*Officers*	*Other Ranks*
A	..	45
B	3	18
C	..	4
D	..	9
E	1	3
F	..	..
G	..	11
H	..	..
Field officers	1	..
Total	5	90

Lieutenant-Colonel Fraser retired, after thirty-six years' service in the Battalion, a few months before the normal expiration of his period of command, in order to allow of Major D. Mason MacFarlane, T.D., taking over command sufficiently long before the Battalion went into camp to learn something of his new unit. Major Mason MacFarlane, who had been second-in-command of the 4th Battalion, Berkshire Regiment, assumed command on 26th February 1913.

Camp that year was at Dornoch, and lasted from 14th to 28th June.

On 10th October Lieutenant Sir John Fowler, Bart., Seaforth Highlanders, succeeded Captain Davidson as Adjutant, with the temporary rank of Captain.

By a vigorous recruiting campaign begun in November 1913 the strength of the Battalion was increased by 120 of all ranks, till in June 1914 its total strength was 707.

Camp in 1914 was held at Kingussie from 13th to 27th June. It was highly successful, and the efficiency of the Battalion showed a marked improvement. Little did anyone think that within six weeks of breaking camp the Battalion would be on active service, and that ere a year had passed many of those who had attended camp would have died for their country.

Photo by Hills & Saunders.

THE SERGEANTS, 4TH SEAFORTHS,
BEDFORD: NOVEMBER, 1914.

MAP

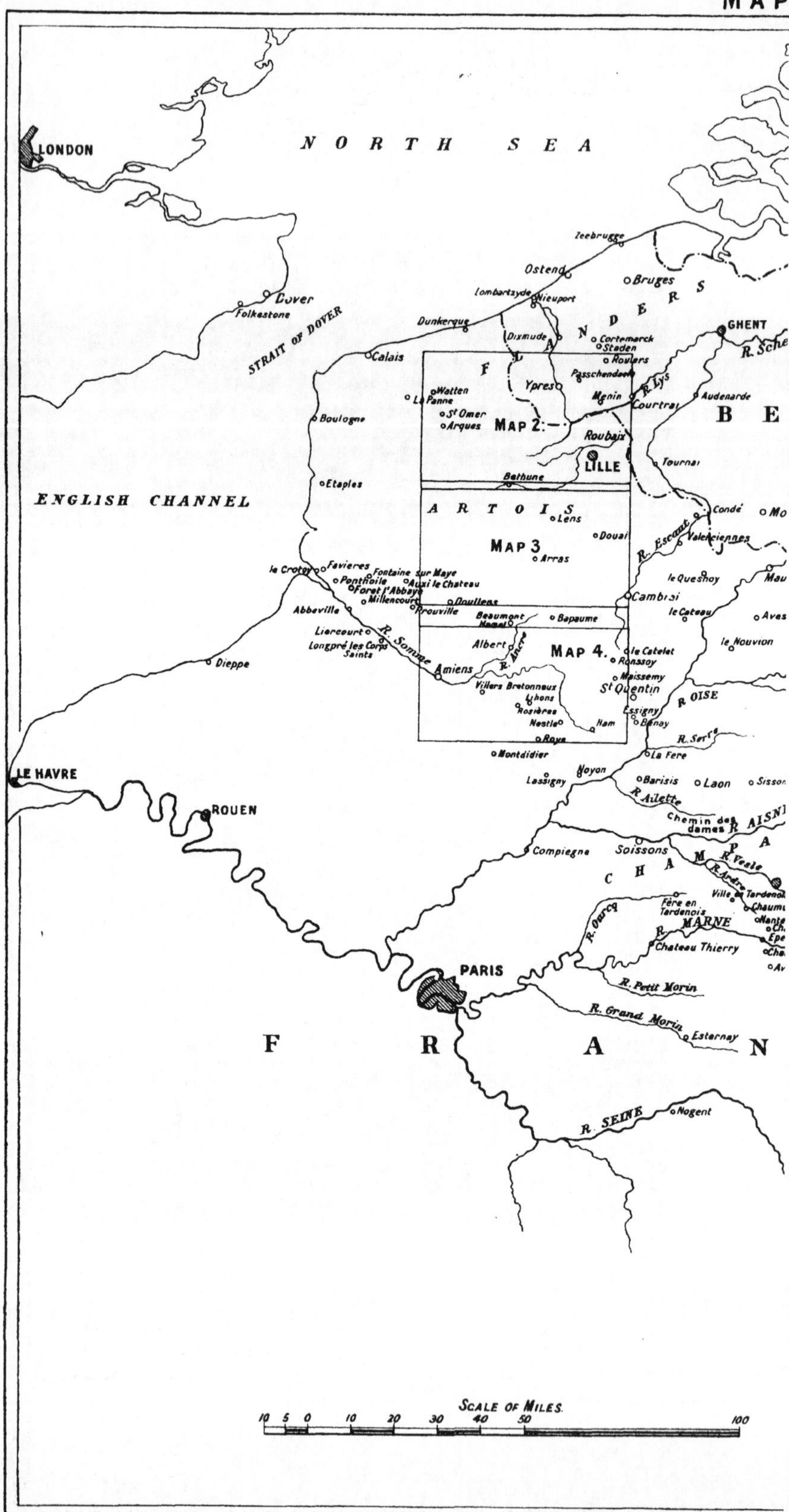

FROM HAVRE

1.

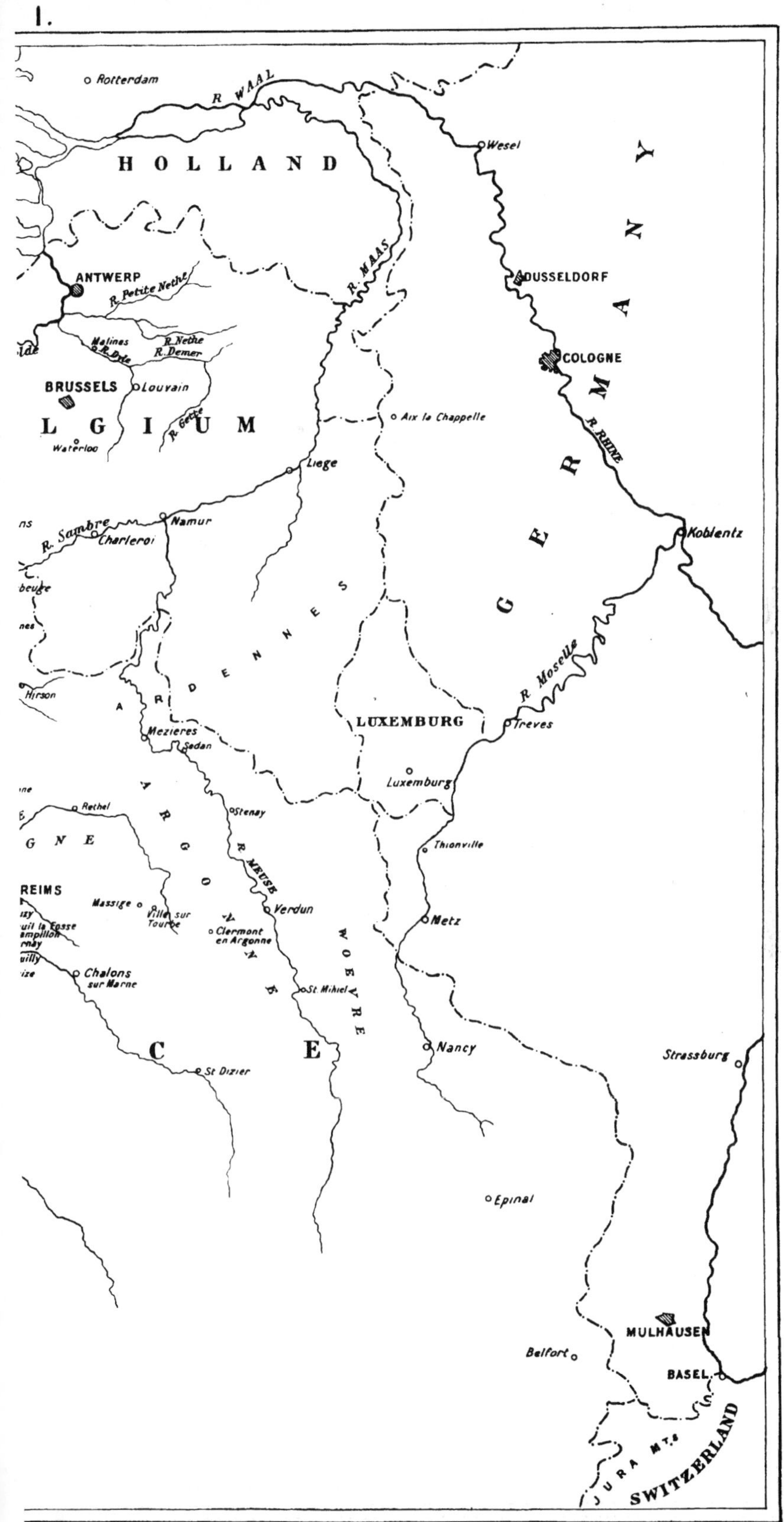

Rotterdam
R. WAAL
HOLLAND
Wesel
GERMANY
ANTWERP
R. Petite Nethe
R. MAAS
DUSSELDORF
Malines
R. Nethe
R. Dyle
R. Demer
BRUSSELS
Louvain
COLOGNE
R. Gette
Waterloo
Aix la Chappelle
R. RHINE
Liege
Namur
R. Sambre
Charleroi
Koblentz
ARDENNES
Hirson
R. Moselle
LUXEMBURG
Treves
Mezieres
Sedan
Luxemburg
Rethel
Stenay
ARGONNE
Thionville
R. MEUSE
REIMS
Massige
Ville sur Tourbe
Verdun
Clermont en Argonne
Metz
WOEVRE
Chalons sur Marne
St. Mihiel
Nancy
Strassburg
St Dizier
Epinal
MULHAUSEN
Belfort
BASEL
JURA MTS
SWITZERLAND

TO COLOGNE

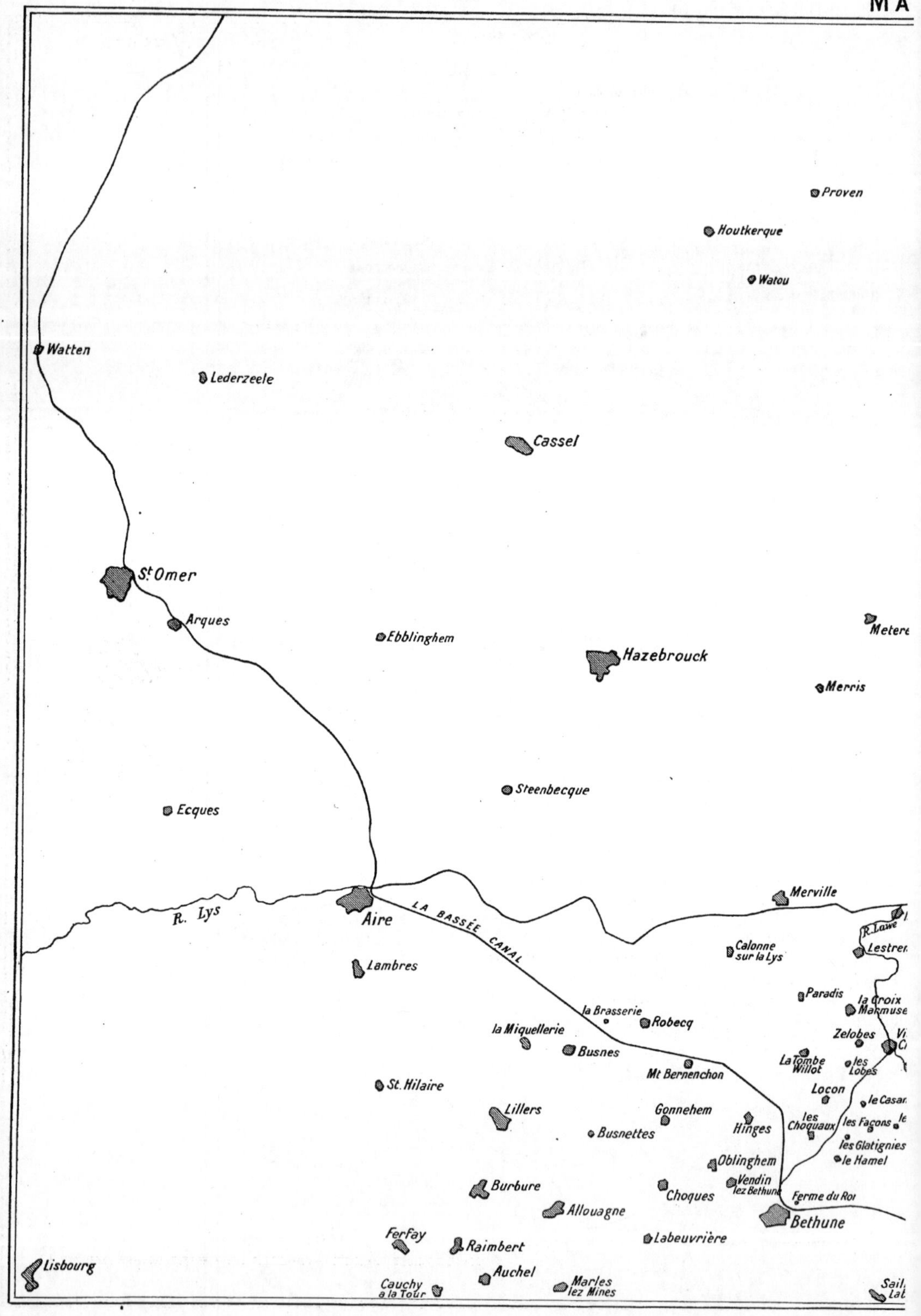
MA
Proven
Houtkerque
Watou
Watten
Lederzeele
Cassel
St Omer
Arques
Ebblinghem
Hazebrouck
Metere
Merris
Steenbecque
Ecques
R. Lys
Aire
LA BASSÉE CANAL
Merville
R. Lawe
Lestrem
Calonne sur la Lys
Lambres
Paradis
la Croix Marmuse
la Brasserie
Robecq
la Miquellerie
Busnes
Zelobes
Mt Bernenchon
La Tombe Willot
les Lobes
St. Hilaire
Locon
Lillers
Gonnehem
Hinges
les Choquaux
les Façons
les Glatignies
le Hamel
Busnettes
Oblinghem
Vendin lez Bethune
Burbure
Choques
Ferme du Roi
Allouagne
Bethune
Ferfay
Raimbert
Labeuvrière
Lisbourg
Auchel
Cauchy a la Tour
Marles lez Mines
FLAN

P 2.

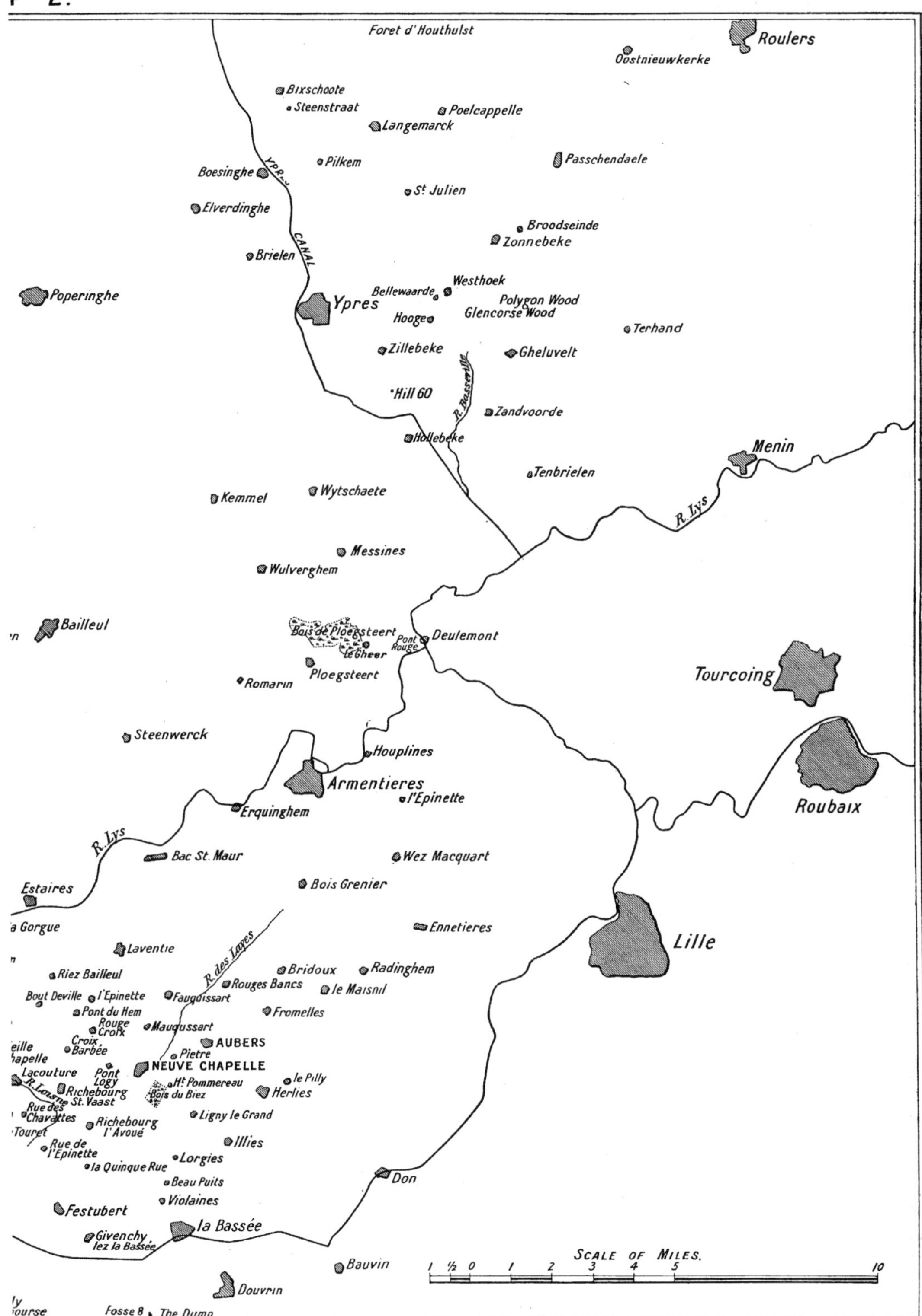

Foret d'Houthulst
Roulers
Oostnieuwkerke
Bixschoote
Steenstraat
Poelcappelle
Langemarck
Pilkem
Passchendaele
Boesinghe
YPRES CANAL
St Julien
Elverdinghe
Broodseinde
Zonnebeke
Brielen
Poperinghe
Ypres
Bellewaarde
Westhoek
Polygon Wood
Glencorse Wood
Hooge
Terhand
Zillebeke
Gheluvelt
R. Bassevillo
Hill 60
Zandvoorde
Hollebeke
Menin
Tenbrielen
Kemmel
Wytschaete
R. Lys
Messines
Wulverghem
Bailleul
Bois de Ploegsteert
Pont Rouge
Deulemont
Le Gheer
Ploegsteert
Tourcoing
Romarin
Steenwerck
Houplines
Armentieres
Roubaix
l'Epinette
Erquinghem
R. Lys
Bac St. Maur
Wez Macquart
Estaires
Bois Grenier
a Gorgue
Ennetieres
Lille
Laventie
R. des Layes
Riez Bailleul
Bridoux
Radinghem
Rouges Bancs
le Maisnil
Bout Deville
l'Epinette
Fauquissart
Pont du Hem
Fromelles
Rouge Croix
Mauquissart
Croix Barbée
AUBERS
Pietre
NEUVE CHAPELLE
Lacouture
Pont Logy
Ht Pommereau
le Pilly
Richebourg St. Vaast
Bois du Biez
Herlies
R. Lawe
Rue des Chavattes
Ligny le Grand
Richebourg l'Avoué
Touret
Illies
Rue de l'Epinette
Lorgies
la Quinque Rue
Don
Beau Puits
Violaines
Festubert
la Bassée
Givenchy lez la Bassée
Bauvin
SCALE OF MILES.
1 ½ 0 1 2 3 4 5 10
Douvrin
Fosse 8
The Dump

DERS

MA

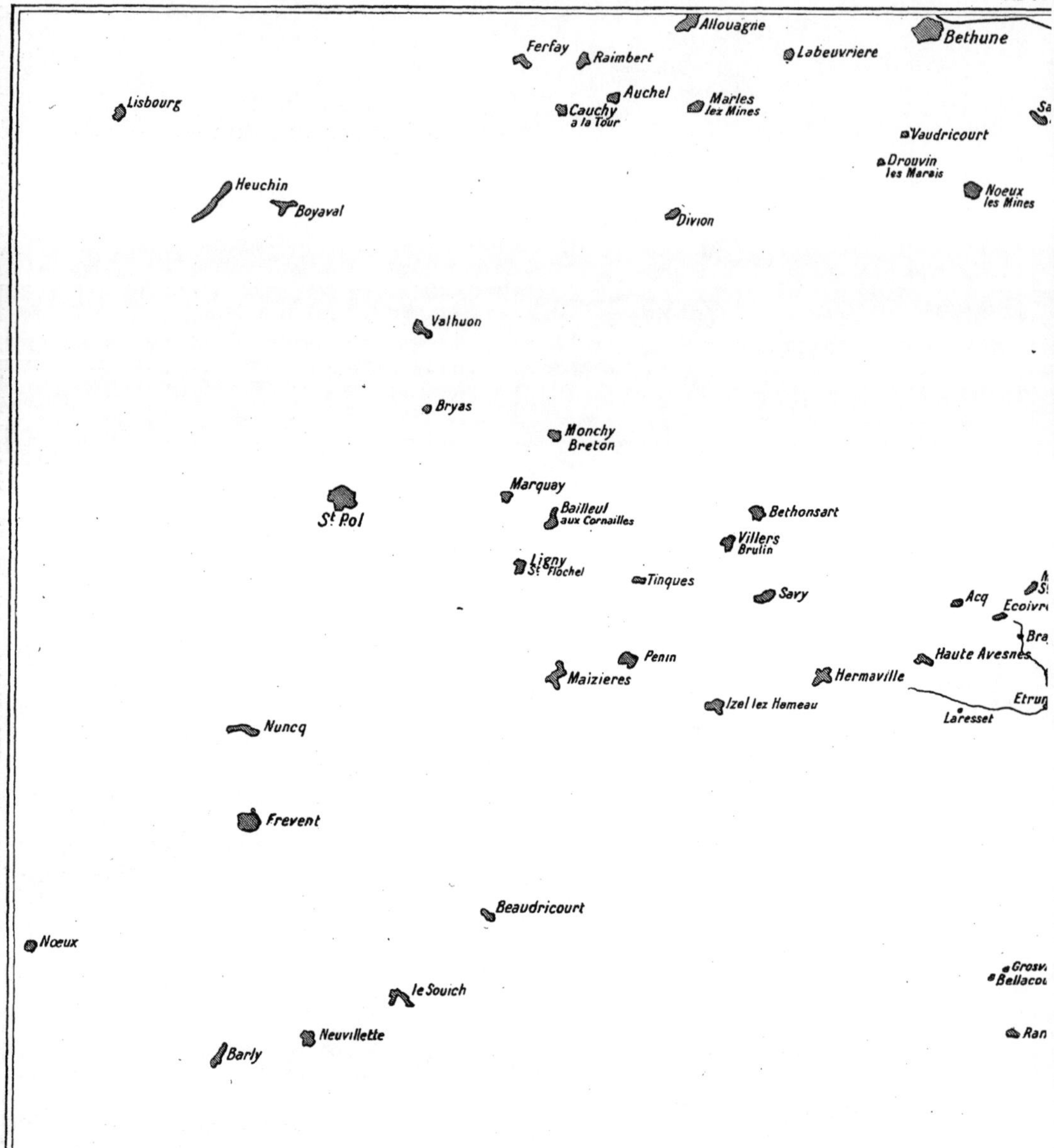

Allouagne
Bethune
Ferfay
Raimbert
Labeuvriere
Lisbourg
Auchel
Marles lez Mines
Cauchy a la Tour
Sa
Vaudricourt
Drouvin les Marais
Heuchin
Noeux les Mines
Boyaval
Divion
Valhuon
Bryas
Monchy Breton
Marquay
St Pol
Bailleul aux Cornailles
Bethonsart
Villers Brulin
Ligny St Flochel
Tinques
Savy
Acq
Ecoivr
Bra
Penin
Haute Avesnes
Maizieres
Hermaville
Izel lez Hameau
Etrun
Laresset
Nuncq
Frevent
Beaudricourt
Noeux
Grosv
Bellacou
le Souich
Neuvillette
Barly
Ran
Doullens
Pas
Souastre
Hébuterne
Sarton
Sailly au Bois
Candas
Courcelles au Bois
Serre
Berneuil
Bus les Artois
Colincamps
Louvencourt
Auchonvillers
BEAUMONT HAMEL

ART

AP 3.

P 3.

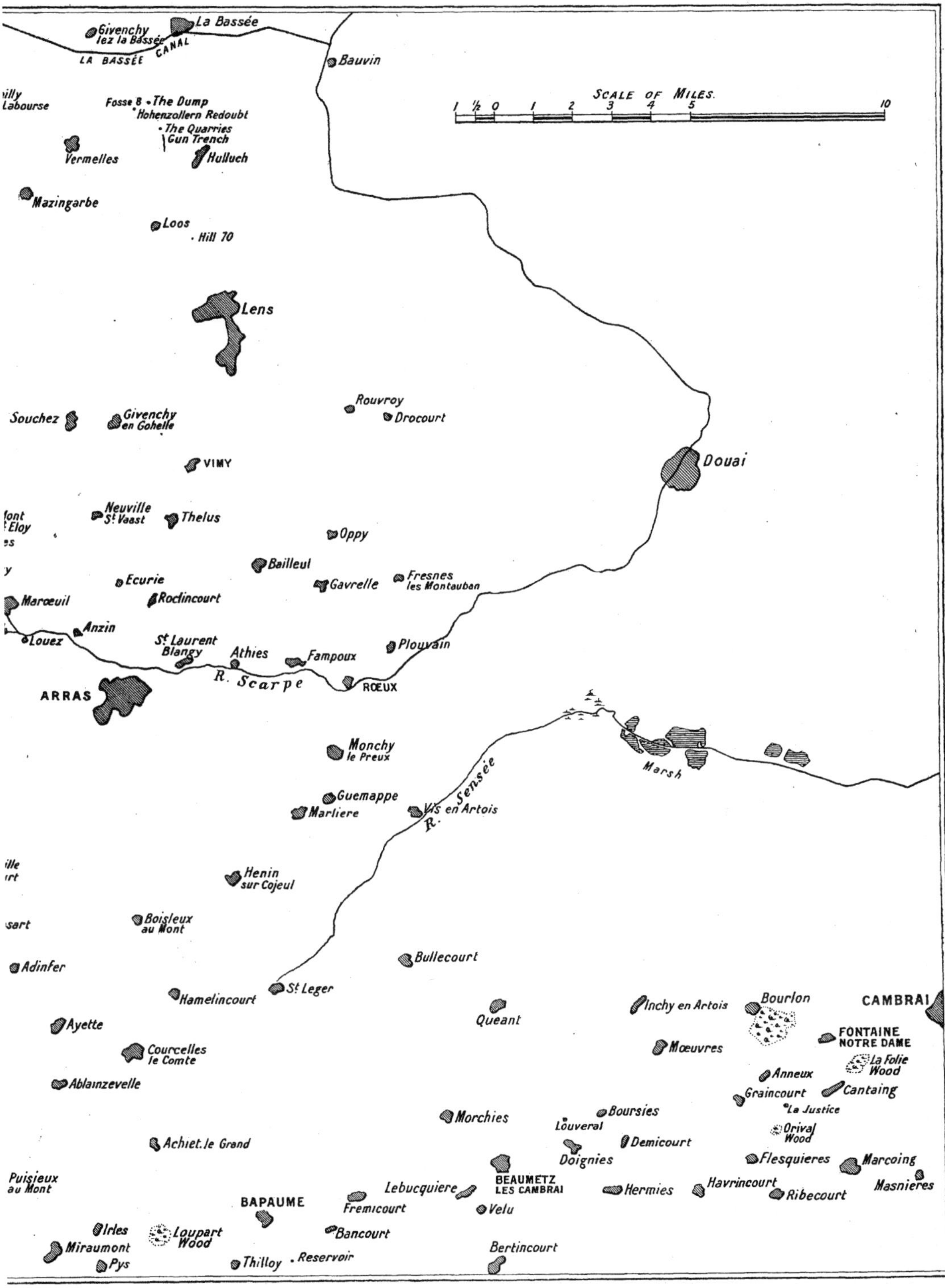

La Bassée
Givenchy lez la Bassée
LA BASSÉE CANAL
Bauvin
illy Labourse
Fosse 8 · The Dump
Hohenzollern Redoubt
· The Quarries
Gun Trench
SCALE OF MILES.
1 ½ 0 1 2 3 4 5 10
Vermelles
Hulluch
Mazingarbe
Loos
· Hill 70
Lens
Rouvroy
Drocourt
Souchez
Givenchy en Gohelle
VIMY
Douai
Neuville St. Vaast
Thelus
Mont St. Eloy
Oppy
Bailleul
Ecurie
Gavrelle
Fresnes les Montauban
Marœuil
Roclincourt
Anzin
Louez
St. Laurent Blangy
Athies
Fampoux
Plouvain
R. Scarpe
ARRAS
RŒUX
Monchy le Preux
Marsh
R. Sensée
Guemappe
Marliere
Vis en Artois
Henin sur Cojeul
Boisleux au Mont
sart
Adinfer
Bullecourt
St. Leger
Hamelincourt
Queant
Inchy en Artois
Bourlon
CAMBRAI
Ayette
FONTAINE NOTRE DAME
Courcelles le Comte
Mœuvres
La Folie Wood
Anneux
Ablainzevelle
Graincourt
Cantaing
· La Justice
Morchies
Boursies
Louveral
Orival Wood
Achiet le Grand
Demicourt
Doignies
Flesquieres
Marcoing
Puisieux au Mont
Lebucquiere
BEAUMETZ LES CAMBRAI
Hermies
Havrincourt
Masnieres
Ribecourt
BAPAUME
Fremicourt
Velu
Irles
Loupart Wood
Bancourt
Miraumont
Bertincourt
Pys
Thilloy
· Reservoir

OIS

W

MA

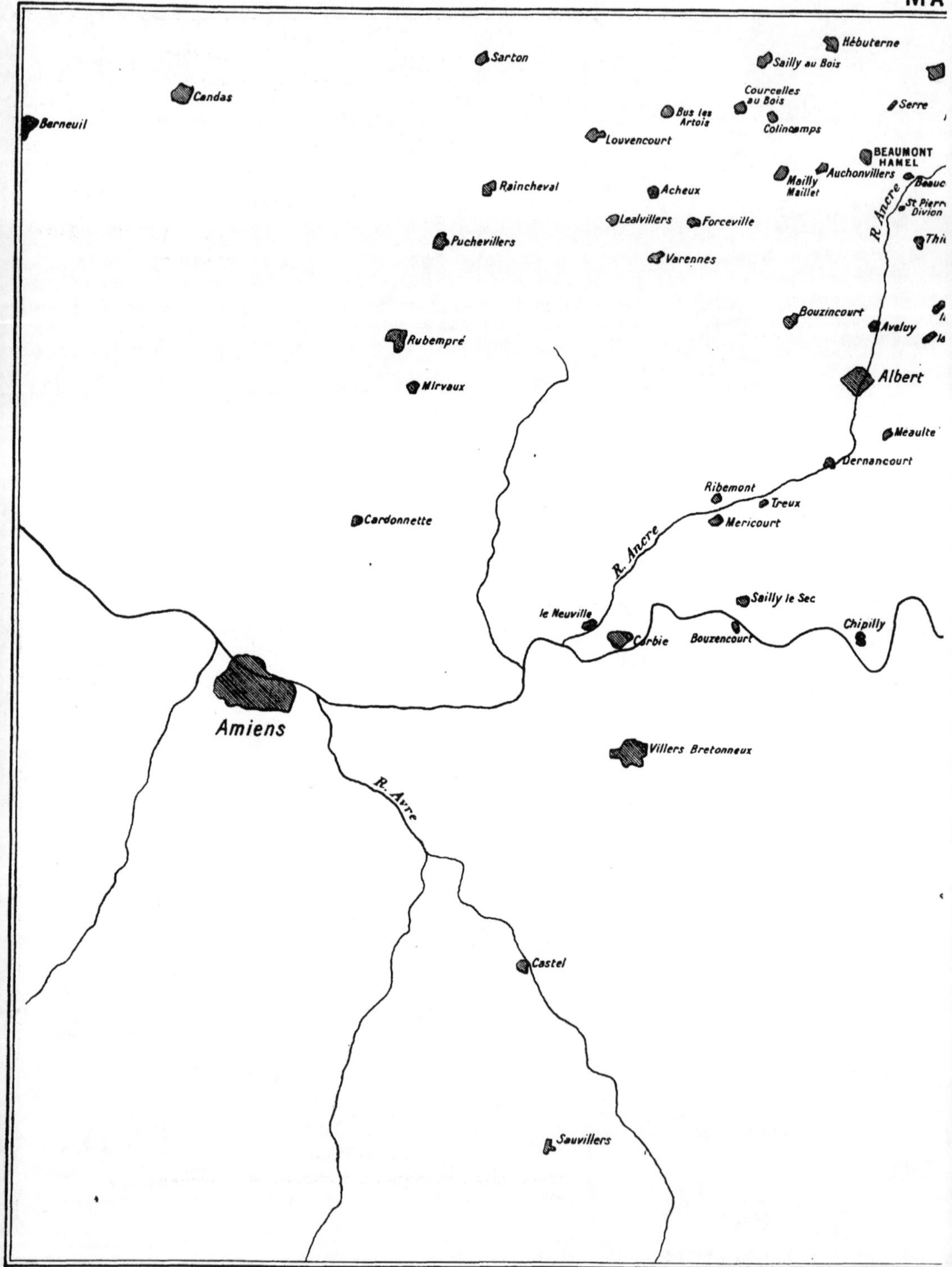

Hébuterne
Sarton
Sailly au Bois
Candas
Courcelles au Bois
Serre
Bus les Artois
Berneuil
Colincamps
Louvencourt
BEAUMONT HAMEL
Auchonvillers
Mailly Maillet
Raincheval
Acheux
R. Ancre
St Pierre Divion
Lealvillers
Forceville
Puchevillers
Varennes
Bouzincourt
Aveluy
Rubempré
Albert
Mirvaux
Meaulte
Dernancourt
Ribemont
Treux
Cardonnette
Mericourt
R. Ancre
Sailly le Sec
le Neuville
Chipilly
Corbie
Bouzencourt
Amiens
Villers Bretonneux
R. Avre
Castel
Sauvillers

PICA

P 4.

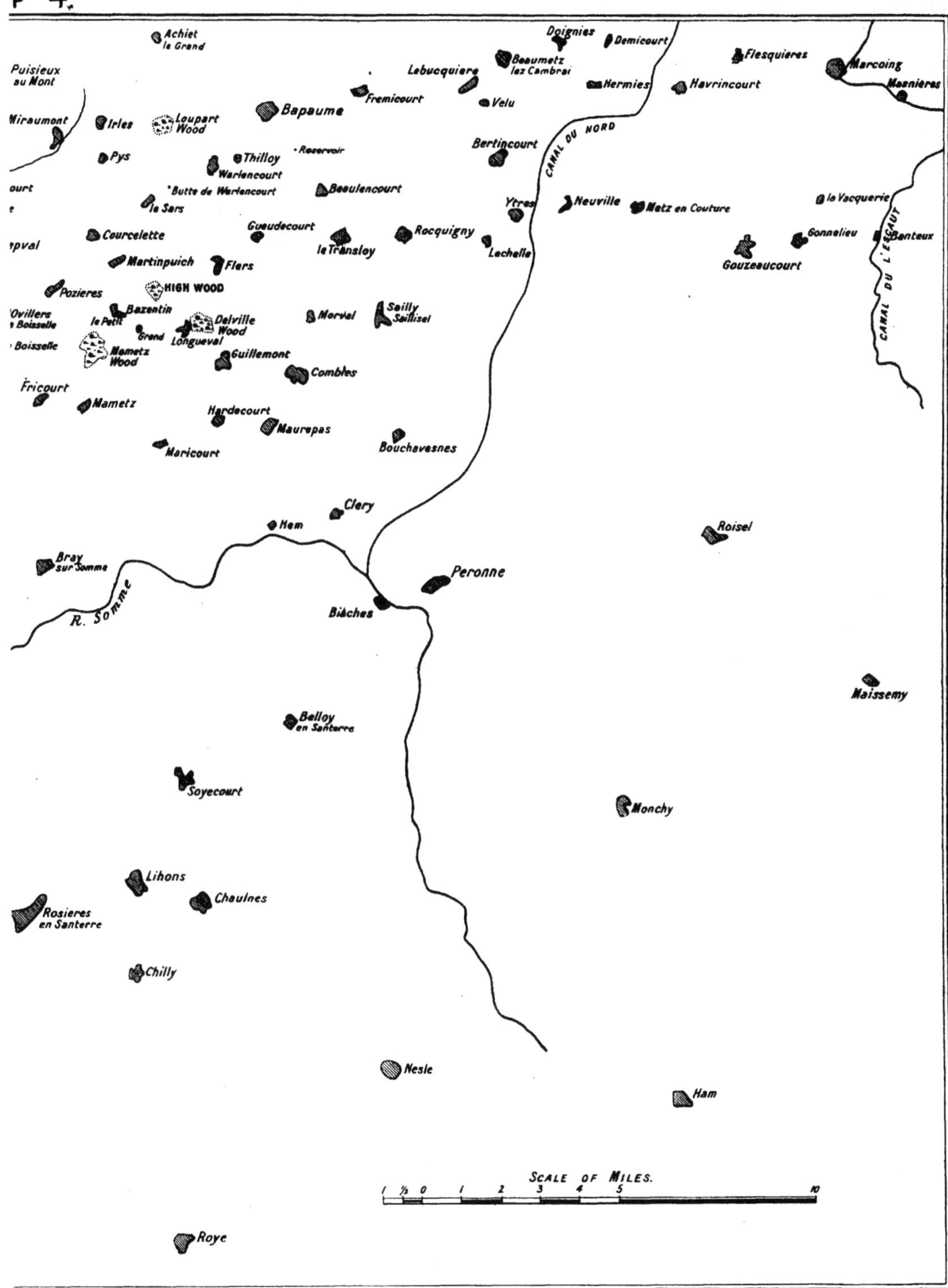

Achiet le Grand
Doignies
Demicourt
Puisieux au Mont
Beaumetz lez Cambrai
Flesquieres
Marcoing
Lebucquiere
Hermies
Havrincourt
Masnieres
Fremicourt
Velu
Miraumont
Irles
Loupart Wood
Bapaume
CANAL DU NORD
Bertincourt
Reservoir
Pys
Thilloy
Warlencourt
ourt
Butte de Warlencourt
Beaulencourt
le Sars
Ytres
Neuville
Metz en Couture
le Vacquerie
Gueudecourt
Courcelette
le Transloy
Rocquigny
Gonnelieu
Banteux
pval
Lechelle
Gouzeaucourt
Martinpuich
Flers
CANAL DU L'ESCAUT
HIGH WOOD
Pozieres
Bazentin
Sailly Saillisel
Ovillers Boisselle
le Petit
Delville Wood
Morval
Boisselle
Grand
Longueval
Mametz Wood
Guillemont
Combles
Fricourt
Mametz
Hardecourt
Maurepas
Maricourt
Bouchavesnes
Clery
Hem
Roisel
Bray sur Somme
Peronne
R. Somme
Biaches
Maissemy
Belloy en Santerre
Soyecourt
Monchy
Lihons
Chaulnes
Rosieres en Santerre
Chilly
Nesle
Ham
SCALE OF MILES.
1 ½ 0 1 2 3 4 5 10
Roye

RDIE

SYNOPSIS OF EVENTS FROM THE SARAJEVO MURDERS TO THE DEFENCE OF GIVENCHY

(*28th June* 1914 *to* 18*th December* 1914)

THE murder of the Archduke Francis Ferdinand, heir-presumptive to the thrones of Austria and Hungary, on 28th June 1914, gave to Germany and the Dual Monarchy the long-sought pretext for reducing Serbia to a condition of vassalage and thereby preparing for a further thrust to the East. The humiliating Austrian ultimatum to Serbia was presented on 23rd July, and although Serbia, under Russian advice, accepted nearly all its terms, her request to refer two articles to The Hague Tribunal was treated as a refusal and the Austrian Minister left Belgrade. Serbia mobilized at once, and Austria ordered a partial mobilization.

Despite the earnest efforts of Sir Edward Grey and M. Sazonov, the British and Russian Ministers for Foreign Affairs, the situation became more threatening. The British Fleet, which was about to disperse after manœuvres, left for the North Sea on the 29th, on which day Russia ordered a partial mobilization, the Austrians bombarded Belgrade, and Belgium, in virtue of her treaty obligations, placed her army on a war footing.

Germany, which had been for long secretly recalling reservists and officers—while using every artifice to secure the neutrality of Great Britain—mobilized on the 1st of August, and France at once followed suit.

The next day German troops violated the neutrality of Luxembourg and German patrols crossed the French border. In the evening Germany demanded a passage through Belgian territory. King Albert refused, and on the 3rd appealed for support to King George. That day German troops crossed the Belgian border.

On 4th August 1914 Britain mobilized, and the Germans entered Russian territory.

Von Emmich, the commander of the besiegers, did not complete the capture of the fortress of Liége till the 16th. General Leman's stubborn defence had thereby gained the Allies at least four days.

On the 18th the Belgian army was forced to fall back from the line of the River Gette and retired on Antwerp. The Germans attacked Namur, and on the 23rd the garrison withdrew into France.

The French began a movement designed to seize the initiative and pierce the German centre, but both their right and left wings were forced back; for Germany had decided to make her great effort in the West. To this end she had concentrated seven armies, each more than 200,000 strong. While two were to hold the French to their ground along the eastern border, the other five, pivoting on Thionville, were to make a gigantic wheel through Belgium, overwhelm the French left, and crush the French army against Switzerland.

It appears that, but for the withdrawal of the Belgians into Antwerp, the German reserve corps that were detailed to invest it would have pushed on to seize the Channel ports. Once more the Belgian army proved of inestimable value to the Allies.

The British concentration about Le Cateau and Avesnes was virtually complete on 20th August. The British Expeditionary Force was commanded by General Sir John French, G.C.B., G.C.V.O., K.C.M.G., and comprised a cavalry division of four brigades under Major-General E. H. H. Allenby, C.B.; the 5th Cavalry Brigade; the I Corps (1st and 2nd Divisions), under Lieutenant-General Sir Douglas Haig, K.C.B., K.C.I.E., K.C.V.O., A.D.C.-General; the II Corps (3rd and 5th Divisions), under Lieutenant-General Sir James Grierson, K.C.B., C.V.O., C.M.G., A.D.C.-General, with Army and Line of Communication troops. A III Corps, under Major-General W. P. Pulteney, C.B., D.S.O., was formed on 31st August. It at first comprised only the 4th Division, but was later joined by the 19th Brigade, and still later by the 6th Division.

Sir James Grierson died in the train on the way to the front on 17th August. He was one of the most distinguished officers in the British army, and probably the one who best understood the German psychology. He was succeeded by Lieutenant-General Sir Horace Smith-Dorrien, G.C.B., D.S.O.

Aeroplane reconnaissance reported the advance of a huge German column through Louvain on the 20th; next day the British Expeditionary Force moved up to support the French left wing. On 23rd August it was occupying a line bent at an angle round Mons, the I Corps from Peissant to Hermignies, and the II Corps from thence to Condé. The 19th Infantry Brigade, formed from the Line of Communication troops, was with the II Corps.

The Germans attacked in dense masses. They were so severely dealt with by the British musketry that they believed it to be the fire of many batteries of machine guns! The 3rd Division had to withstand the attack of three and a half German Divisions and the 5th that of two and a half, which were successfully checked until the retreat of the Fifth French Army compelled the British Expeditionary Force to conform. During the retirement the 4th Division came up on the left of the II Corps.

Owing to our line of march being crossed by Sordet's French Cavalry Corps, the retirement of the II Army was so delayed as to become a running fight. The weather was very hot, the reservists found the French *pavés* terribly trying to the feet, and crowds of refugees congested the roads.

On 26th August the II Corps found itself to the west of Le Cateau, too closely in contact with the Germans to effect a retreat. Men and horses were tired out and hungry. Sir Horace Smith-Dorrien, therefore, stood to fight on the anniversary of Crécy.

The Germans steadily enveloped the British right, which by noon jutted into the line of its assailants in a blunt curve; they also had compelled a slight withdrawal of the left flank of the 4th Division on the left.

About 3 P.M. the retirement began, and by nightfall the II Corps and 4th Division had successfully extricated themselves from an almost hopelessly impossible position, with a loss of less than 8000 men and 38 guns. Bodies of troops that had been accidentally left behind both disturbed and perturbed the Germans all that night, and most of them cut their way through. It was a "soldiers' battle," and the men showed themselves worthy descendants of the men of Albuera and Inkermann. There seems little doubt but that this battle greatly upset the German ideas as to what was either fitting or decent in an enemy who, by all the rules of the game, was routed!

The I Corps meanwhile retreated with little molestation, and the whole British Expeditionary Force fell back rapidly across the Oise, the Aisne and the Marne, in touch on the right with the Fifth, and on the left with the Sixth, French Army.

The operations entailed a change of base from the Channel ports to St Nazaire, which delayed the arrival of the 6th Division by some days.

Now it became clear that the German plan was beyond the power of the German army. Instead of continuing south-westward, so as to envelop Paris, the German left was forced to swing south-eastward —a move which enabled Joffre, in his turn, to strike at his opponent's flank. On 5th September the two lines resembled the letter **N** as seen in a mirror, but whereas the French outer flank rested on Switzerland, and that group of armies was effectively resisting the Germans, the outer flank of the Germans was in the air and being bent back by the French inner flank.

Fatigue, coupled with the necessity for masking Antwerp, investing Maubeuge, and guarding their long and very vulnerable line of communications, had brought the German armies to a halt, with their heads in danger of being caught between the pincers prepared by Joffre.

They, therefore, hastily fell back to the Aisne, where, on 15th September, the arrival of fresh troops enabled them to stop the Allies. Trench warfare had begun.

The French continued their attempts to outflank the enemy, and now began what is known as "the race to the sea." Northward and westward, but mainly northward, went the French and German armies. On 3rd October the British began to hand over their line to French units, preparatory to a move to Flanders; and on the 19th the I Corps, the last to leave, completed its detrainment near Hazebrouck.

Meanwhile the Germans began their attacks on Antwerp on 28th September. On 4th October the Royal Marine Brigade of the Naval Division began to arrive, followed on the 5th by the other two brigades. On the 6th the Germans had crossed the River Nethe and the Belgian army began to withdraw towards Ghent. On the 7th there was desperate rearguard fighting, which continued for the next two days, during which the 7th Division and the 3rd Cavalry Division were landing at Ostend and Zeebrugge. On the 9th Antwerp fell.

Lille was occupied by the Germans on 12th October, but Maud'huy succeeded in holding Arras and Albert. On the 18th the British II Corps were in Aubers and Illies, and the III Corps, by now complete, was holding the line Bois Grenier-Le Gheir.

All this time the Belgians were falling back, covered by the 7th Division and the 3rd Cavalry Division. On the 14th these latter were in touch with the 1st Division and were covering Ypres, while the Belgians were taking up the line of the Yser from Dixmude to Nieuport. In between were French Territorial troops. The line was complete from the Jura Mountains to the North Sea.

The Allies pushed forward in the effort to seize Lille and Menin, but were forestalled by the enemy at both places. On 19th October the high-water mark of the Allied offensive was reached, the situation of the line from the left of the Sixth French Army on La Bassée Canal being:

II Corps: Givenchy—Herlies—Aubers.
Conneau's French Cavalry Corps: Fromelles—Le Maisnil.
III Corps: Radinghem—Ennetières—Epinette—Pont Rouge.
Cavalry Corps: Opposite Deulemont—Tenbrielen.
IV Corps: Zandvoorde—Terhand—Passchendaele—Oostnieukirke.
Bidon's French "Group": Roulers — Staden — Cortemarke — Boesinghe.
Belgian Army: Boesinghe—Nieuport.

Hitherto the British had had comparatively little dealings with their French comrades-in-arms. From now on they saw a great deal of one another, fighting side by side, and sending each other help when needed. Hence sprang up a feeling of mutual respect and confidence that was steadily to increase. Of those chiefly responsible for this good feeling the ever-helpful Generals Conneau and Du Bois deserve special mention.

On the 18th the Germans began the attack on the Belgians known as the Battle of the Yser. During this they were shelled with great moral effect by units of the Royal Navy. It will be seen that their hopes of success were foiled at the critical moment.

There was as yet no "unity of command," and the armies of the nations fought side by side, sometimes as if belonging to the same army, owing to the excellent relations between General Foch, General Joffre's lieutenant in the North, and his allies.

Foch's plan at this time contemplated an advance towards Roulers, so as to separate the German III Reserve Corps, now engaged against the Belgians, from the main armies; to be followed by a wheel outwards, so as to force the III Reserve Corps against the sea and roll up the right of the main forces.

The attempt to put this plan into action resulted in an encounter battle, and by 21st October the British line had been pushed back about Neuve Chapelle and Ypres, with the I Corps on the extreme left. The whole much resembled a mark of interrogation, Ypres being in the centre of the loop. Seven and one-third British divisions and five Allied cavalry divisions, reduced by fighting, were holding a front of about 35 miles against eleven German divisions (eight of them fresh) and eight cavalry divisions. The German objective was to envelop the British from North-east and South, and so to achieve a great success.

The British trenches, mere disconnected lengths of shallow shelters, without communication trenches or wire, were described by the Germans as "a well-planned maze of trenches behind barbed wire!" This is a great tribute to the marksmanship and use of cover, as well as to the tenacity of the British troops; but it is impossible in a mere synopsis to give any idea of the difficulties under which they were fighting at this time.

The Allies still attempted to advance on the front around Ypres, but succeeded only in holding their own, though the II and III Corps had to withdraw slightly, and the former was driven out of Neuve Chapelle on 26th October. The opportune, if gradual, arrival of the Indian Corps was now beginning to relieve some of the strain on the II, III and Cavalry Corps.

The Allies persisted in their offensive plans until the 29th, on which the tide of battle definitely began to turn against them. The Belgians had just begun to make the inundation of the coastal levels that was finally to make their front secure, while the British began to shift their bases back to Havre and Rouen.

On the 29th the Germans drove the British back from the Gheluvelt cross-roads and on the 30th carried Zandvoorde and Hollebeke, forcing the line Messines-Gheluvelt. Whilst north of Langemarck the opponents were fairly evenly matched, the disparity in favour of the Germans increased as the line went southward, till south of the Menin Road their superiority in rifles and field guns rose to about six to one. Realizing the danger of the situation General Dubois immediately reinforced the British about Zillebeke.

Whether from a fear that the British were concealing large reserves with a view to a counter-offensive, or to a belief that the troops in the line were actually superior to their own—a fine tribute to our musketry—the Germans showed over-caution on 30th October.

On the 31st came the crisis. The main attack was delivered on Messines, most of which was taken by a force at least six times as strong as the twelve squadrons that defended it. It was between Messines and Wytschaete that the London Scottish, sent to relieve the cavalry, gained the distinction of being the first Territorial Force battalion to go into action, although Yeomanry units had already been engaged.

Meanwhile the Germans captured the ruins of Gheluvelt by sheer weight of numbers. Their losses must have been enormous. One of their regiments, the 143rd Infantry Regiment, covered itself with eternal disgrace by its brutality to the prisoners taken by it. The situation was very critical; the British line had been pierced and there were practically no reserves.

The situation was saved by the 2nd Worcestershire Regiment—11 officers and 450 other ranks. They recovered the village and stopped the gap in the line. After dark, nevertheless, the British troops were withdrawn to a new position in rear.

The 7th Division on the right also was driven back, but established its line again by a magnificent counter-attack, while on the left the British were able to hold their own.

Meanwhile the Indian Corps was relieving the II Corps, while the 4th Division still held its old front.

French counter-attacks on 1st November made but little progress, though they probably made the enemy over-cautious. He achieved little this day, though the British abandoned Messines, and Wytschaete was taken by a night attack, only to be recovered later by some British cavalry, supported by the 32nd French Division. The 2nd November was much like the 1st: Wytschaete was again lost, but a second break through on the Menin Road was stopped, though ground was yielded.

The effect of Hindenburg's defeat before Warsaw and the retreat of the Austrian and German armies was beginning to have an effect on the German Higher Command, which was hoping for some relief of the pressure in the East by a Turkish advance in the Caucasus; for Turkey had now openly joined the Central Powers.

There was comparatively little change in the situation until 11th November. The Germans gained some ground on the Messines side; but though to our troops their activity must have seemed fairly constant, they brought but little pressure to bear.

On the 11th they drove in a section of the British front on the Menin Road. A Prussian Guard Division and a Pomeranian and West Prussian Division, both fresh and at full strength, were the assailants. The latter have ever been a byword in Germany for dogged perseverance and efficiency: "A Pomeranian will march till he dies, a Brandenburger till he drops, a Saxon till he is tired, and a Rhinelander till he feels inclined to stop," runs the proverb. Yet it was the Guard that broke our line, only to be hunted out like straying sheep by battalions that had forgotten what rest meant, and varying in numbers from that of a company to that of a platoon! Only our first line trench was not recovered, for the Germans had dug themselves in, and night had fallen. The German losses had been enormously high; they attributed their failure to resistance of troops "in numerical superiority!"

Our men were by now utterly worn out; some fell asleep standing to fire while enemy troops were actually attacking. Mud jammed the rifles. Some units had practically disappeared; the 1st (Guards) Brigade could muster only 4 officers and 227 men, and the 1st Division numbered only about a tenth of its establishment. The worst losses had been suffered by the infantry and the Royal Engineers. These valuable technical troops had indeed many times been called on to fight as infantry, and well did they sustain their proud record. Our artillery, superior in skill, was much inferior numerically and in guns of large calibre. Outranged always, they were never for a moment out-fought. The British cavalry, fighting as infantry, were more than a match for the German battalions that attacked them. Gun ammunition was almost exhausted, and there were but the smallest reserves. Never had an army, called on for so supreme a test, been worse provided for by those responsible for sending it to fight. But for the magnificent efforts of all ranks for many years past, which had given it a training in musketry and the use of ground surpassing that of any other army, and, above all, but for the immortal heroism of the British Regular soldier, Germany must inevitably have won the war. This is no slur on our gallant and skilfully led Allies. For the rest of the first eighteen months the brunt of the fighting fell on them. Still it remains true that in the first battles of Ypres the old army was almost destroyed; yet its grim skeleton kept open the gate to Menin and therewith the road for the advance to final victory.

For a time there was fighting, hard enough for the war-worn troops; but by 22nd November the French had taken over the salient, and the British Expeditionary Force stood in line from La Bassée Canal to a point opposite Wytschaete:

Indian Corps: Givenchy to near Neuve Chapelle.
IV Corps: To Bridoux.
III Corps: To Wulverghem.
II Corps with a Cavalry Division: To opposite Wytschaete.
I Corps and Cavalry Corps (less one division): In reserve behind Bailleul.

The British army was a mere ghost of what it had been. Notwithstanding this, in the Higher Command, in staff work, in infantry and artillery fire, in the courage and determination of all ranks, in everything that makes for success in war—but numbers—it had obtained a moral ascendancy over the Germans that it never lost. Could we have put fourteen Territorial divisions in line in October we might well have rolled the Germans up against the Ardennes. As it was, they and the new armies had to find for themselves that the British *had* obtained that moral ascendancy, as, indeed, they quickly did at Neuve Chapelle and Loos.

Those who would read the full and glorious story of this early part of the war should read the official *History of the War, Military*

Operations, France and Belgium, 1914. (By Brig.-Gen. C. E. Edmonds, C.B., C.M.G., R.E.(*p.s.c.*). Macmillan & Co. Ltd., London, 1925.)

The repulse of the German rush on Paris and the immortal stand of the seven divisions on the road to the Channel ports raised high hopes of the imminence of a victorious counter-thrust. Yet from the close of the first battles of Ypres to October 1915 events were bitterly disappointing, for now began the monotonous drag of trench warfare, when a gain of a thousand yards on a two-mile front was a signal victory, and men well-nigh lost the art of marching in their long vigils in sodden trenches.

Our attempt to emulate at the Dardanelles Grant's Mississippi campaign ended in a failure, relieved only by the skill with which the troops were withdrawn. The enemy drove back the Russians in Poland and Galicia and overran Serbia. Against this our gains were utterly insignificant.

New or revived means of destruction were ever making their appearance, and always was it the enemy that introduced them. Bombs, trench mortars, gas and liquid fire made the struggle like a nightmare wherein one grapples with a protean yet inexorable foe.

The old army was practically annihilated. But for the arrival of the Indian Army Corps and of the first units of the Territorial Force it seems now as if the annihilation must have been complete.

Ideas of the use of large-calibre guns and underground warrens had been regarded hitherto as fantastic. Now the reality surpassed the wildest dreams of peace-time students. Victory could be won only by breaking a front, for here were no flanks to be turned. Had Germany concentrated on the Western front, success must surely have been hers.

The first battles of Ypres ended on 22nd November and a redistribution of the British and French lines ensued. The British front ran for twenty-one miles from Givenchy to a point opposite Wytschaete, with French troops on either flank.

Now began in earnest the construction of that strange city of trenches, equipped with its baths, its tramways and its dwellings; the line that, ever plastic in the hands of sapper and gunner, ran from the Jura Mountains to the North Sea. Nothing like it has been seen since the legions left the Roman Wall. Men settled to a new and strange life, to goatskin jerkins and gum-boots, to hand-bombs, slings and catapults. The needs of the population of this vampire city increased far quicker than they could be supplied. Gun ammunition was terribly short for many months; of the complicated paraphernalia of trench warfare there was practically no certainty of supply, while units were rarely above four-fifths of their establishment.

BEDFORD: BUNYAN MONUMENT

CHAPTER II

MOBILIZATION AND TRAINING

TOWARDS the end of July 1914 it was evident that war was imminent, and all possible preparations for mobilization were made by the Battalion Headquarters.

At 6.30 P.M. on 4th August the order to mobilize was received. Drum-Major Hugh Fraser, 4th Battalion The Seaforth Highlanders, was at once sent to proclaim the news by sounding the "Assemble," followed by the "Fall In," at three places in the Burgh of Dingwall: first at the Mercat Cross, in front of the Municipal Buildings; then at the eastern end, in front of the National Hotel; and lastly, at the western end.

Few of those who saw what followed will forget it. At once the streets became crowded with people. Young men belonging to His Majesty's Forces were to be seen leaving shops and offices to answer the call. One man going his rounds with a horse and milk-cart left them to take care of themselves while he hurried away to report for duty. There was a striking absence of all outward excitement; everyone seemed to realize that Britain had entered on a conflict that must for ever leave its mark on her destiny, and that the men who were already making their way to Headquarters in kilt and khaki were among those responsible for the fate of their native land.

Meanwhile the Battalion staff were hard at work dispatching

telegrams to the outlying companies, while motor-cyclists were sent off to warn those beyond the reach of the telegraph. Not for over two hundred years had the fiery cross been sent throughout the county of Ross, and never had it awakened a more notable response.

The late Lady Fowler has left a vivid description of the arrival of the news at Loch Broom: "About half-past nine on the evening of 4th August (when we were gathered in the drawing-room at Inverbroom, with windows open and blinds up, watching the last glow fading in the western sky, and the shadows of night were beginning to fall around us), my daughter sprang to her feet, exclaiming that she had caught a glimpse in the garden of a man in motor-cyclist's dress. A few minutes later he was delivering to her the expected message from her brother, and quickly were the necessary papers filled in, acknowledging receipt of the order to 'Mobilize,' and entries in mobilization forms were rapidly completed in accordance with instructions previously given by my son.

"The motor-cyclist dispatch rider" (the late Councillor John MacKay) "at once continued his forty-seven miles' ride from Dingwall to Ullapool (not pausing to accept proffered hospitality), and our young relative, Daniel Bayley (later a gallant officer of the Royal Artillery), mounted his bicycle and vanished into the darkness, to deliver the necessary intimations of mobilization to the various lads of the Territorial Force resident on the estate of Braemore.

"Thus did the Fiery Cross come to Loch Broom." [1]

Owing to the necessity of protecting the naval base at Invergordon, with its huge oil stores, the Seaforth and Cameron Infantry Brigade was ordered to garrison the North and South Sutors, the two headlands that guard the entrance to Cromarty Firth. By the afternoon of 5th August over five hundred men of the 4th Seaforths were digging entrenchments at Nigg, where they had their first experience of billets. Meanwhile the Battalion Headquarters remained in Dingwall to collect stores, horses and equipment. On the 8th the companies returned from Nigg to complete mobilization, and were billeted in Dingwall. On Sunday, 9th August, they attended an impressive service in the Parish Church. That evening orders arrived for the 4th Seaforths to join the Brigade at Inverness on the following day. Just as the Battalion was parading to

[1] *Records of the Men of Loch Broom*, by Mrs Fraser of Leckmelm.

march to the station on the Monday morning a telephone message was received asking how many, by ranks and companies, would volunteer for service overseas. The Commanding Officer addressed the Battalion, and ordered any officer, non-commissioned officer or man who was unable to fight overseas to fall out on the flank. Although two officers, doubtless for excellent reasons, and three aged men fell out, the Commanding Officer had the satisfaction of telephoning to Brigadier-General D. A. MacFarlane, D.S.O., that the Battalion had volunteered as a complete unit.

Training continued at Inverness until 15th August, when the Seaforth and Cameron Brigade entrained for Bedford to join the Highland (later known as the 51st) Division. At least 25 per cent. of the men of the Battalion spoke Gaelic as their mother-tongue, and it has been claimed that it was the passage of the troop-trains bearing these big fellows, who spoke an unknown tongue and were understood to say they came from "Rossha," that gave rise to the assiduously spread rumour that Russian armies were being transported from Archangel to fight on the Western Front.

Intensive training began in grim earnest at Bedford, where Battalion Headquarters were at the Grammar School. Here the Battalion was brought up to its war establishment of 1020 of all ranks, partly by recruits from Ross-shire, but chiefly by a vigorous recruiting campaign in London. These recruits were mainly men of Scottish parentage or extraction for whom there were no vacancies in the London Scottish.

The help given to the 4th Seaforths by the London Scottish has always been held in grateful remembrance by the officers of the former. Especially does this apply to the Commanding Officer, Colonel James Greig, C.B., V.D., M.P., and the Adjutant, Captain R. Whyte, as well as to Mr Willie Smith and Recruiting-Sergeant W. Martin. To this day there is a very close comradeship between the two battalions, while the present Second-in-Command of the London Scottish is Major L. D. Henderson, M.C., for long one of the best-known officers of the 4th Seaforths.

One of these London Scots has left most vivid sketches of the life at Bedford, too long unfortunately to be quoted at length, but interesting as being the first impressions of a University graduate and Civil servant suddenly enlisted into the ranks of a purely Highland battalion.

He speaks with real appreciation of the Ross-shire men, whom he describes as " great fellows—quiet, jolly, simple and companionable—real country men, shepherds, fishermen and so on." They were " a happy, reckless crowd of chaps and very good tempered." He says: " It will take about ten years to get us all licked into proper fighting form; good enough for garrison duty, but nothing better. . . . But if the Highlanders aren't quite *au fait* as regards drill they can march and no mistake." Four miles an hour seems indeed to have been kept up on more than one route march. He notes that the old Regular permanent staff were rapidly taken away to train the New Army Units, but considers that on the whole the men were better handled by the officers and non-commissioned officers from their own country. The fatherly attitude of the officers towards their men seems particularly to have struck him. It is evident that in spite of the many changes in the last hundred and fifty years the old Highland spirit still lives in this relation between officers and their men.

The Battalion was still a very raw unit by the middle of September, and the accession of drafts from London must have done something to retard the progress of its training. Yet a month later one is struck with the difference in the outlook of those whose letters and diaries one had been privileged to read. No longer is it the individual trying to fit himself into a changed world, but the member of a body corporate recording—often quite unconsciously—the steady gain in efficiency of his unit. These records strikingly reveal from the inside what was so very noticeable to the observer from the outside, that the raw material from the universities, the business offices, the workshops and the countryside was being worked up into the type so familiar to all nowadays—the British soldier. Utterly diverse they came into that mill, to be turned out in the space of only a few weeks in that mould of cheerful detachment from all personal feelings in the performance of the work that has to be done, in that wonderful tolerance of men and circumstances that has ever been the most striking mark, and one of the most valuable qualities, of the British soldier. And yet, with all this wonderful uniformity of spirit, this Battalion, like every other unit in the army, had its own character and individuality, that marked it off from every other.

Owing to the generosity of friends in the county of Ross the 4th Seaforths became possessed of thirty-two sets of bayonet fighting equipment, and the only remaining Regular non-commissioned officer (besides the Regimental Sergeant-Major) spent the whole of each day training successive squads. It was very unfortunate that three machine guns of the latest pattern, that were being kept by Messrs Vickers for the Battalion, in the use of which the machine gun officer and his sergeant had been trained at Erith, were commandeered by the War Office for the New Armies before the Battalion went abroad. They had been made available by the initiative of the late Mr Duncan Davidson of Tulloch and the kindness of his shooting tenant, Mr Douglas Vickers. The training at this time was most strenuous, and, owing both to the rivalry between the different companies and to the high standard of intelligence and education of the men, the improvement not only in technical efficiency but in discipline became rapidly more and more marked. Lieutenant-Colonel Mason-MacFarlane was attaining to the fulfilment of his ideals; for everyone worked with such real interest that when, on 22nd October, the Division was inspected by His Majesty the King, the 4th Seaforths were reported as the best Battalion in their brigade, and as being equalled by only one other in the Division.

Like all other units at this time, the Battalion was hard put to it for clothing and equipment. The regimental tailors could not turn out kilts quickly enough to clothe the new drafts. One man who enlisted on 9th September did not get his kilt till the beginning of October, and had to wait even longer for his spats and glengarry. Spats and glengarries were indeed at a premium, for everyone wanted to be photographed in full service dress uniform. One reads of squads parading of their own accord at the quartermaster's stores on the mere rumour that a new consignment had arrived. Many of the men had to get their first training with damaged rifles. Indeed the unit when paraded at full strength must have been a curious-looking collection of men in every stage of clothing and equipment. In spite of these drawbacks, officers and other ranks were working in grim earnest, forging a weapon which was to sustain some of the fiercest fighting in history.

Bedford was not all hard work, however, for the whole Battalion managed to make themselves very popular, and the Bedford people spared themselves neither trouble nor expense to make the men comfortable. Some bought camp beds for those who were billeted in empty houses, while others gave them coal and wood to make fires with. The life was a great change for some of the men. One of them wrote that it was all holidays! Others record their increased physical fitness and improved health.

About this period a man on leave telegraphed for an extension, but got the reply "Extension not granted." As he nevertheless took the extension he was duly brought before the Commanding Officer, who asked him what he had to say. His reply was that he had an extension, and he put the telegraph form on the table. "But," said the Commanding Officer, "this says 'Extension *not* granted.'" The absentee looked at the form with an expression of well-feigned surprise. "My thumb must have been on the 'not' when I read it," said he. Another incipient warrior disappeared for several days. On his return he accounted for his absence by producing a photograph of himself with a new-born infant on each arm, explaining that he had been detailed for infantry training!

Rumours flew round the Battalion and as suddenly died away: now they were destined for Malta, now for Ipswich; South Africa, Egypt, Cromarty, Hong-Kong, Marseilles, each had its vogue. Finally one wag spread the rumour that they were going to garrison the South Pole till relieved by Shackleton! At last all doubts were resolved.

On the night of Sunday, 1st November 1914, Brigadier-General MacFarlane was discussing with the Battalion commanders the scheme for a divisional field day on the Monday. The telephone bell rang, and after a short conversation in monosyllables the General turned to Lieutenant-Colonel Mason-MacFarlane and said: "What is the first moment you can be ready for France?" "To-morrow, if we get our rifles, transport and clothes for the men," was the reply. "Get ready at once," said the Brigadier, "and everything you require will be given to you." The news spread like wildfire among the men, who could be heard cheering far into the small hours.

By Wednesday, 4th November, most of the requirements had been met. It was certainly a lack of foresight that new rifles were issued to the Battalion only the day before it embarked for France, and but for the outbreak of scarlet fever at Ecques each man might have gone into action knowing nothing of the peculiarities of his own weapon. The transport was overhauled and completed, but it was found that the new service dress jackets sent down from Pimlico were far too small, most of the men requiring a 38-, 40- or even a 42-inch size. The Royal Army Clothing Department was at once informed, and fresh jackets were found waiting at Southampton and fitted on the voyage.

On Thursday, 5th November 1914, the Battalion entrained in two special trains for Southampton. The half Battalions moved off at 11.40 and 12.25 respectively. One of the latest joined recruits records the event thus: "The great day arrives. All is excitement and hurry. We fell in at the Grammar School and received heartening words from the Brigadier. Benediction is pronounced, and with bands playing we marched to the station. It was a scene I will never forget—the cheering hundreds on the march, the waving of handkerchiefs, and the bidding of farewells."

The Battalion embarked at 8.30 P.M. on the *City of Dunkirk* for Havre, the entraining, detraining and embarkation being carried out with perfect discipline and precision. About midnight the steamer cast off, with all lights out, under an almost perfect moonlight sky, and escorted by a French destroyer. The Ross-shire men had set forth like those valiant Ross-shire men of old, Munro of Obisdell and his more famous cousin "Bully" Munro, to fight alongside the Ancient Allies—but this time not against "our auld enemies of England."

The convoy arrived at Havre about midday on the 6th, but the *City of Dunkirk* could not berth till 11 P.M. This involved the consumption of the emergency ration for men and beasts, because the Battalion had been rationed on the assumption that it would disembark immediately on arrival. A cipher radiogram from the Commanding Officer to the Officer in Charge of Reinforcements received no reply; it transpired later that there had been an omission of one letter in the code word handed by the Staff Officer at Southampton to the Commanding Officer, and the message could not be read. While no one in the 4th Seaforths was to blame for the error, it was a good lesson in the vital necessity of making sure that in dealing with cipher there is no possibility of mistake or misunderstanding.

The 4th Seaforth Highlanders landed in France about 8.30 A.M. on 7th November 1914. As they paraded on the quay an ambulance train drew up alongside. Among the wounded were some of the London Scottish, the first of the Territorial battalions to distinguish itself on active service. It was a dramatic introduction to the Theatre of War! Then to the tunes of *Dornoch Links* and *The Black Bear* (ever favourites of the 4th Seaforths) the Battalion swung along through the streets of Havre, past the cheering crowds, up the hill that dominates the historic town, to Bléville Rest Camp, four miles away.

The Battalion was not forgotten by this its first place of sojourn in France; for after the Armistice the Mayor of Havre sent a most cordial letter of thanks for its timely aid, and in reply the Battalion sent the three photographs taken just before it left Bedford—namely, those of the officers, the non-commissioned officers and the Battalion on parade, which appear in this book. These now hang in the Hôtel de Ville at Havre.

The Battalion reached Bléville at about 1 o'clock, but it was not till 8 o'clock that its transport arrived. The men were well-nigh worn out, for the excitement of the last four or five days and the lack of all sleeping accommodation on the *City of Dunkirk* had left them little time or chance for sleep. The ground on which the tents were pitched was, however, a sea of mud, quite unfit for them to lie on. Lieutenant-Colonel Mason-MacFarlane therefore ordered a large stack of straw to be pulled down; this, covered with the men's waterproof sheets, made a dry, if cold, bed.

Instructions had been received that the Battalion was to remain at Havre for three or four days; but at 8.30 P.M. a motor-cyclist arrived with orders to leave Havre the next morning for the front. Réveillé was therefore ordered for 5 A.M., so that the Battalion might march at 7, and maps of the Franco-Belgian frontier were issued.

About 11 o'clock the Commanding Officer was walking up and down outside his tent when one of the men came up and asked if he might speak to him. It was pitch dark, and the Commanding Officer had no idea who the man was. He therefore explained that he could hear any complaints only in the presence of the man's Company Commander, but the youngster insisted that he could only say what he wanted to say to the Commanding Officer privately. He then said: "I thought we were going to be here for four days; now I hear we're going into a fight to-morrow. I don't want to disgrace the Regiment, so just send me back to Ross-shire, as I'm sure to run away." The Commanding Officer told him that he was the bravest man in the Battalion and that when the time came he would find that out. Lieutenant-Colonel Mason-MacFarlane never knew who the man was. He has since said that the only sign of fear he ever saw among his men was the fear lest they might be thought afraid.

After an all too brief sleep the men were roused at 5 o'clock and soon after marched back through Havre to entrain for St-Omer. It was the first time the transport had been entrained on French railway wagons, and as these were limited in number and had to be loaded from ramps it was no easy matter for F Company, who acted as baggage guard, to get it properly stowed. But all was done in a much shorter space of time than the Railway Transport Officer had thought possible for a Territorial battalion. Indeed when the 4th Seaforths were ready to entrain in the normal time they found that they had generously been given an extra two hours to allow for their inexperience! Fortunately the Commandant of the French Infantry Barracks came to the rescue, and the men were marched into the barrack square, where they were given coffee. The Commandant was most complimentary on their military bearing, refusing at first to believe that they were a Territorial and not a Regular battalion.

The men did not appreciate the French trains. "In the evening a 'train '(?) does come, and we depart for the 'GREAT UNKNOWN,'" says one of the men in his diary. So abruptly, indeed, did the engine start and pull up that two men were stunned by rifles being jerked off the rack!

Havre was left at 1.19 P.M. on 8th November and St-Omer reached at 11.30 A.M. on the 9th. The crowded carriages, the creeping train and the scanty meals had made the men tired, and they were glad to detrain. "Weary but keen" is the phrase of one of our diarists. During the daylight, at each of the many halts, the French populace crowded round to get a souvenir, regimental buttons or badges being the favourites, until it was explained to the men that by giving these away they were disposing of His Majesty's property. An incident that well illustrates the French craze for souvenirs at that time and the efficient co-operation between the British military authorities and the French was the loss of his false teeth by one of the non-commissioned officers. He had had the ill luck to break the plate, and accidentally dropped them out of the window at one of the wayside stops. A French boy pounced on them and rushed off, crying: "Souvenir écosse!" The train was already on the move, and although the non-commissioned officer reported the matter to the stationmaster at the next stop he forgot to give the name of his unit. On 20th November a motor-cyclist arrived early at Battalion Headquarters. There was great excitement, everyone thought this must be the order to move into the line; amid tense silence the Commanding Officer read out the message: "Has any officer or man in the 4th Seaforth Highlanders lost some false teeth?" They apparently had travelled round most of the units of the First Army: their owner was glad enough to get them back.

From St-Omer the Battalion at once marched to Ecques, some six miles away.

Wearing what used to be known as the "Christmas Tree" —Sam Browne belt, sword, revolver, field-glasses, haversack, water-bottle, etc., with all their several cross straps—most of the officers felt well-nigh cut in two by the weight of their gear at the end of the march, and all took an early opportunity of providing themselves with the more comfortable web equipment. It was, indeed, as much the question of utility and comfort as of inconspicuousness that led to its general adoption by the officers of the army.

One of the first things some of the officers did on arrival at Ecques was to have their swords sharpened by the village blacksmith. Very shortly after all these weapons were packed off home. Here, too, the sound of the guns was heard for the first time.

At Ecques the 4th Seaforths were billeted in most insanitary quarters. To quote one of the men: "Our first billet. This is a little village of about 300 inhabitants and we wonder where our Battalion of 1050 men is likely to get billets. All corners of the place are commandeered, barns, pigstys, lofts, etc., and the Battalion receives its first dose of French billets. Our Company was billeted in a barn, a very airy barn too, and I am safe to say I never felt so cold in my life."

During the fortnight that the Battalion remained at Ecques it was training hard all day and every day. The recently issued rifles were the long mark with new barrels, and as no man knew anything about his weapon the first thing to be done was to put the whole Battalion through a course of musketry. Targets were improvised out of anything that could be picked up at Ecques by the Company Commanders. Besides musketry there were route marches, for the Commanding Officer set the greatest store on keeping his men fit, rightly holding that physical fitness is the basis of all efficiency.

Photo by Hills & Saunders.

4TH BATTALION, THE SEAFORTH HIGHLANDERS,
BEDFORD: NOVEMBER, 1914.

About this time buses and lorries began to be used for the transport of troops. They were, naturally, allotted to units that had far to go or were being hurried up into the line, neither of which conditions applied to the Battalion until much later. To the sight of these troops in motor-transport is, however, probably due the tradition—absolutely unfounded on fact—that Lieutenant-Colonel Mason-MacFarlane always sternly refused the proffer of buses to move the men, with the remark: "The laddies can walk." Hence the tale of how, when the Battalion was passing another that was being taken up in lorries, someone called out: "Who are you?" "West Riding. Who are you?" was the reply. "Seaforths walking," shouted the Battalion!

Entrenching and practice in various fighting formations completed the round of a training that knew nothing of trade union rules. The various diarists have little to record beyond such entries as the following: "Advanced in diamond formation over plough, etc., and through a wood a quarter of a mile in width at least, with dense undergrowth of thorns and brambles, very detrimental to the knees. The whole advance through the wood was excellent, the lines being beautifully preserved in the right half battalion."

"It was," writes Colonel Mason-MacFarlane, "a real pleasure to train the Battalion in the attack over ground two miles in depth and six hundred yards in breadth, and to feel that the men could go anywhere, instead of the experience we had training at home, where every hundred yards some portion of the ground was out of bounds. One saw at once that a week or ten days of this would do the Battalion untold good, and it did."

Snow, intense cold, heavy rain, long hours of training and wretched billets seemed only to raise the *moral* of the men, and it was a great source of pride to all the officers to see how they improved. Their pride was justified when the General Officer Commanding the Reinforcement Area told the Colonel that no Regular battalion could do better work than his men were doing.

Although twenty-five miles from the firing line the 4th Seaforths always had one company on outpost duty. This was, of course, mainly for instruction, but the men lived in hopes of catching some German motor-car or patrol that might have got through the front lines, for many were the tales of spies dressed as British officers walking or driving unchallenged into St-Omer.

At one time there was a belief that German spies were going about the country on motor-cycles, and it was announced—or at any rate it was believed that it was announced, which is not quite the same thing—that anyone who caught one of these spies would be given leave home. One of the men spent most of his spare time in trying to catch one of these "flying Dutchmen," although he had no clear idea as to how he would do it. He used to watch the dispatch riders rushing along the roads, and even penetrated as far as the motor-cycle depot to examine the machines. His reception was not over-friendly, and he never caught his leave home.

One of the chief things that struck the Royal Engineers and other officers who had to do with training the men in special duties was their extraordinary keenness to learn and the thoroughness with which they learned. Long after the war was over a distinguished Irish General expressed the hope that if ever he had troops under him again they might be Scots. A Scotsman present expressed surprise at his preference for foreigners, to which the General replied that he held that hope because of the high standard of Scottish education, which ensured that the youngest lance-corporal would intelligently try to carry out his Commander's intentions even after all his officers were killed.

It was at Ecques that scarlet fever broke out, which not only kept the Battalion for a long time out of the front line, but also formed grounds for the refusal to award to its members the bar to the 1914 Star, despite the Battalion's being shown in the Order of Battle of the first seven divisions for November 1914.

While at Ecques some of the men began to grow beards. This was soon forbidden, but one of them went to Captain Brodie and said that, since he had grown a beard, he had never had catarrh, from which he had suffered much. The doctor therefore got leave for him to keep his beard. His beard, however, once got him into trouble; for, being in Lillers on one occasion, he was arrested as a spy. This same man later on became a great sufferer from rheumatism, so he was made corporal and put in permanent charge of the bridge guard at La Gorgue. He had a goat from which he got his milk, and generally he managed to make himself very comfortable.

On 15th November Lord Roberts died at St-Omer. It was a worthy end to a long life spent in the service of his country in peace and war, for he died within sound of the guns, at the ripe age of eighty-four. But for the scarlet-fever epidemic the 4th Seaforths would have provided the pipers for the first stage of the funeral at St-Omer, an honour which thus fell to the Liverpool Scottish. The Battalion was, however, represented by the Commanding Officer and the Adjutant.

Some excellently carried-out night marches and a night attack through a wood showed that the men had been brought to a very high pitch of training. Trenches were at this time dug under the supervision of an officer of the Royal Engineers. Part of a general scheme of preparation for a further possible retirement, they were of the same type as those used by the Boers in the South African War, and were over a mile in length. The severity of the weather was, however, very trying to all, and the Commanding Officer was exceedingly dissatisfied with the billets allotted by the Mayor of Ecques, for it was almost impossible to dry the men's clothing in them. It was in vain that he represented that as the men were there to defend France, it was reasonable that the inhabitants should house them comfortably. The Mayor merely replied that as we were fighting in France to defend Britain as much as France we must take what the French chose to give us. This was characteristic of the inhabitants of Ecques, who were by no means friendly; some, in fact, openly declared that they would rather have the Boches!

Things, however, got so bad that after a fortnight the Commanding Officer insisted that the Battalion must be moved. As he was an Honours Doctor of Medicine of Edinburgh University he was able to speak with authority, and, on 22nd November, the Battalion moved to Arques, a much more satisfactory spot in every respect. The billets there consisted mainly of schoolrooms; they were often bitterly cold, but compensated for a lot of drawbacks by being dry. "Though we had no straw to lie on we felt quite warm and comfortable," says one of the diarists. Here, too, the officers, who up to this period had been wearing spats and shoes, began to discard them in favour of boots and puttees, a more suitable footwear for heavy plough and muddy trenches.

It was about this time that the Battalion was reorganized for field work into four companies instead of eight, in conformity with the formation in Regular battalions.

The grouping was as follows:

A and B formed No. 1 Company.
C and G formed No. 2 Company.
D and E formed No. 3 Company.
F and H formed No. 4 Company.

The days at Arques were spent very much as were those at Ecques. Four times did the orders for a move into the line arrive, and as surely did a fresh case of scarlet fever, so that the order had to be cancelled. More time was now spent on entrenching, the work being, as before, the preparation of a defensive position to be taken up by the Allies in case they were forced to retire. These were days of work in snow and rain, when fuel was scarce and men had to walk themselves dry. The brusque and cheery Major Brodie had big sick parades every day, but he was—and still is—a student of psychology, and had effective, if unorthodox, ways of dealing with the malingerer.

Battalion Headquarters at Arques were opposite those of the French 1st Cavalry Corps commanded by General Conneau, who was most kind, and did everything in his power to assist the Seaforths. The French gave a concert on the 25th November, some of the items being provided by the 4th Battalion. As will be seen from the programme, many of the performers were professionals of high standing in Paris. A few days later General Conneau invited the officers of the Battalion to a cake-and-wine banquet. He received them in a long *salon*, down the centre of which ran a table covered with cakes and sweets, and going round with a number of his staff who carried glasses, he filled one with champagne for each officer in turn before drinking his health. All that the officers could do to return this hospitality was to ask the General and his staff, as well as the Mayor of Arques (who, unlike his colleague of Ecques, was a great friend of the Battalion), to dinner on St Andrew's Night. The General himself was, unfortunately, unable to come, but his staff and the Mayor spent a very cheery evening. There was nothing to drink but whisky, which at first rather took their breath away, but when mixed with water they thoroughly enjoyed it.

International courtesies were not, however, the only relief to the hard work at Arques. First the blood of the old cattle-lifting clansmen began to stir, and if hens and eggs took for the most part the place of cattle, dexterity in their acquisition was

CONCERT du 25 NOVEMBRE 1914

Fantaisie Musicale Franco-Britannique

PREMIÈRE PARTIE

1. Piano. ALÉRINI, brigadier au 1er Chasseurs Indigènes.
2. DELAUNAY, cav. au 5e Dragons. **La Valse des Faubourgs.**
3. OLLIBET, cav. au 15e Dragons. **Le Zéphir.**
4. SIMAR, cav. au 1er Chasseurs Indig. **Marie.**
5. Mc KEE, 4e Seaforth. **The Rag Time Cow Boy Joe.**
6. GARBAL, Mal-des-Lis au 1er Chass. Indigènes. **Margot reste au village.**
7. HAREM, cav. au 14e Chasseurs. **Sa Muguette. Le Zambèze.**
8. **TROUPE MAROCAINE**
   Danses et Chants.
9. Piano. **Sélection.**
   M. le Capitaine **LE GORREC**, du 1er Chasseurs Indigènes.
10. **GEO BURY**, conducteur aux Auto-Mitrailleuses du 1er Corps de Cavalerie,
    des Concerts classiques de Paris.
    Accompagné par M. le Capitaine LE GORREC.

ENTR'ACTE 5 MINUTES

Piano tenu par G. W REAFORD.

DEUXIÈME PARTIE

11. DAVID WILSON, 4e Seaforth, Prestidigitateur.
12. PERSEVOT, cav. au 5e Dragons. **L'Evasion du Capitaine Lux.**
13. **T. TONES**, du 4e Seaforth, basse-soliste.
14. CHEVALIER, dit Rigadin, télégr. au 8e Génie, **Bien, Marie. Mais elle est revenue...**
15. **TOMM SHANLEY**, du 4e Seaforth, **Step Danse (The Old Banjo).**
16. GUÉRINGER, cav. au 1er Cuirass. **Je respecte ma concierge. Je fais du crochet.**
17. **GEO BURY.**
18. STRACKAN, MACKENZIE, MACKAY, MAGILLOWAY,
    du 4e Seaforth.
    Danses et Chants Ecossais.
19. **CHŒURS.**
    Beantiful Doll
    Alexander's Rag Time Band
    It's a Long Way To Piperary
20. **God Save The King**
    Marseillaise.

RETRAITE

Programme composé et mis en scène par le cavalier LABARTHE, du 8e Hussards, conducteur au Groupe d'Autos-Canons, ex-Secrétaire général de l'Alhambra et du Moulin Rouge de Paris.

Imp. LELEU & ALLAUT.

MAP 5.

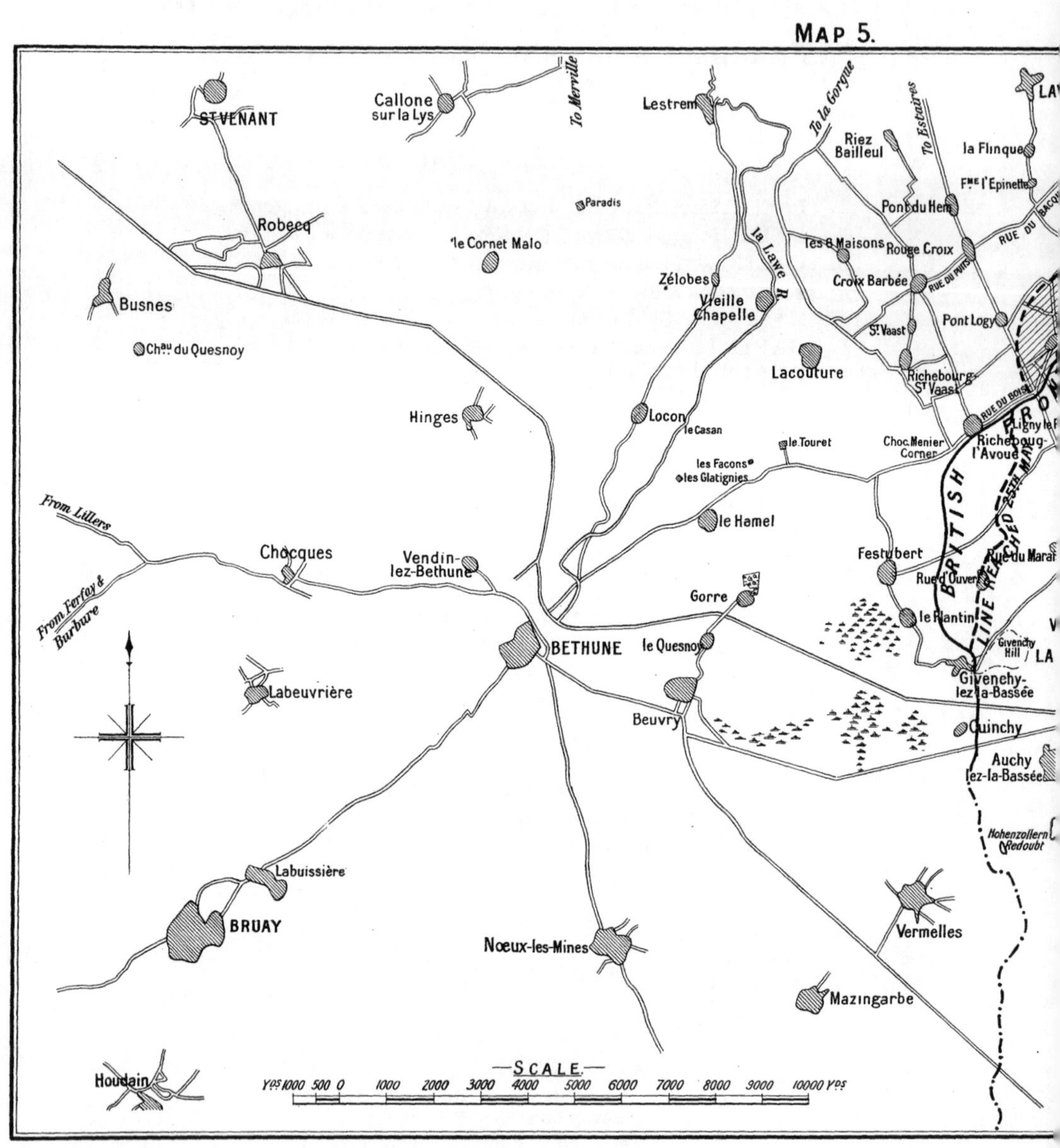

ST VENANT
Callone sur la Lys
To Merville
Lestrem
To la Gorgue
To Estaires
Riez Bailleul
la Flinque
Fme l'Epinette
Pont du Hem
Paradis
Robecq
le Cornet Malo
la Lawe R.
Les 8 Maisons
Rouge Croix
RUE DU BACQUEROT
Croix Barbée
RUE DU PUITS
Zélobes
Vieille Chapelle
Busnes
St. Vaast
Pont Logy
Chau. du Quesnoy
Lacouture
Richebourg-St. Vaast
Hinges
Locon
le Casan
RUE DU BOIS
le Touret
Choc. Menier Corner
Richebourg-l'Avoué
les Facons
les Glatignies
BRITISH
FRONT
LINE REACHED 25TH MAY
From Lillers
le Hamel
Chocques
Vendin-lez-Bethune
Festubert
Rue du Marais
Rue d'Ouvert
From Ferfay & Burbure
Gorre
le Plantin
BETHUNE
le Quesnoy
Givenchy Hill
Givenchy-lez-la-Bassée
Labeuvrière
Beuvry
Quinchy
Auchy lez-la-Bassée
Hohenzollern Redoubt
Labuissière
BRUAY
Noeux-les-Mines
Vermelles
Mazingarbe
Houdain
SCALE
Yds 1000 500 0 1000 2000 3000 4000 5000 6000 7000 8000 9000 10000 Yds

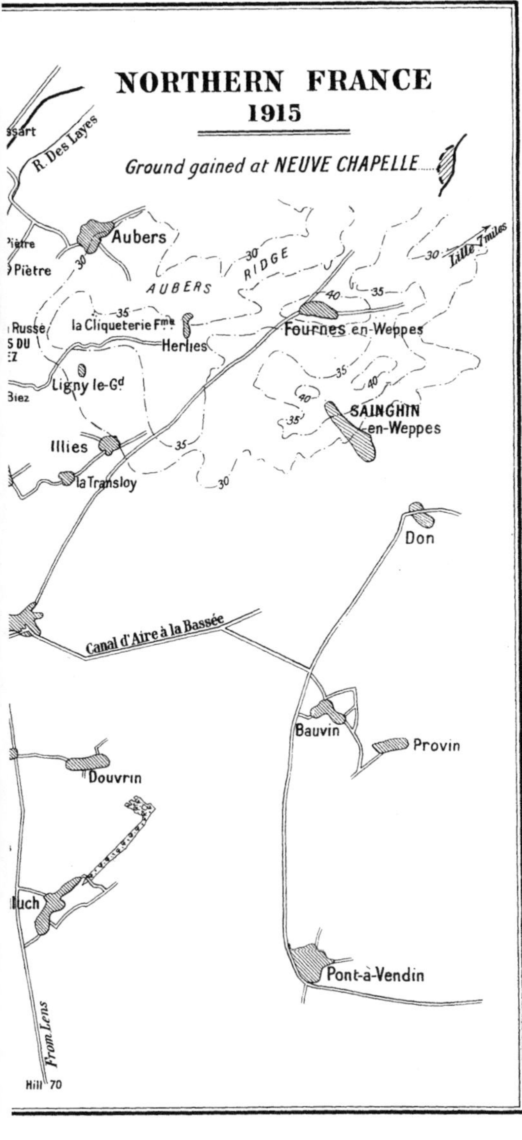

NORTHERN FRANCE
1915
Ground gained at NEUVE CHAPELLE
R. Des Layes
Aubers
Pietre
AUBERS
RIDGE
Lille 7 miles
Fournes en-Weppes
la Cliqueterie Fme
Herlies
Ligny le-Gd
Biez
SAINGHIN
en-Weppes
Illies
la Transloy
Don
Canal d'Aire à la Bassée
Bauvin
Provin
Douvrin
Pont-à-Vendin
From Lens
Hill 70

soon acquired. It is said that one of the men became so expert that he could, with one movement, take from its perch and kill a fowl without the bird making a sound. The taste for poultry seems to have been started one day at field-firing, when a number of hens wandered across the line of targets. A company proved their skill in marksmanship in a remarkably short time. While discipline demanded that they should get extra duty for their pains, the Commanding Officer records in his diary, with evident amusement: " I do not think *one* hen escaped! The men's dinners that night were more savoury than usual!" For long the favourite marching song was *Who Killed Cock Robin?* In a farm in another village the cow began to yield a very small supply of milk, and Madame could not understand why she should be going dry. One of " the boys " always had plenty of milk for his tea, and later on explained that he had always milked the cow at night. The peasants were, of course, compensated for such losses; but while every man in the Battalion was liable to be put under stoppages for the purpose, it by no means followed that all those who paid benefited by each raid. The poor old peasant women had a rather trying time. One, whom the men called " Maggie Bash," began to scream one morning. It turned out that the weight of some of the stalwart Ross-shire men who were billeted in her loft had made the floor to sag, and the old cow's back was nearly broken by the effort to support both floor and men!

The incident that is probably most vividly remembered by those who were in Arques was that of the rum boats. While No. 1 Company was loading up some boats on the canal one of the cases was accidentally dropped, and broke open, displaying a number of rum jars. After its return to billets the company was care-free and happy. No. 2 Company was detailed for this fatigue the next day, and, curiously enough, there was another accident, and No. 2 also spent a happy evening. When No. 3 Company was detailed for the duty on the third day there were those who expected the men of Wester Ross to prove more careful than their eastern neighbours. The few unprejudiced observers left say that the only noticeable difference was that, whereas Nos. 1 and 2 got happy after their return to billets, No. 3 was quite happy enough on its arrival.

Rum, in fact, and rum of the strength issued, was something new to nearly all the men. When they first arrived in France the people on whom they were billeted used to give them a mixture of coffee and rum; until they got used to it its effect, even in small quantities, was often quite surprising.

Nor was the training allowed entirely to eclipse higher things! On 27th November one diarist records: "An easy day for washing. Had a hot bath in St-Omer; first since Bedford"; and on 6th December: "Church parade conducted by the Colonel; first since Bedford."

On 1st December the Battalion was held up at a level-crossing while on a route march, when three motor-cars came up. The King was in the second with Lord Kitchener and Sir John French, and the Prince of Wales, now Colonel-in-Chief of the Seaforth Highlanders, was driving the third. The Battalion gave the Royal Salute. It was noticed that His Majesty looked much more cheerful than when he inspected the Battalion at Bedford six weeks before, while the Prince looked very happy.

About noon on 15th December the welcome order came to march next day to join the Dehra Dun Brigade in the Meerut Division of the Indian Corps. The Brigade then consisted of the 1st Battalion Seaforth Highlanders, 2/2nd Gurkhas, 1/9th Gurkhas and 6th Jat Light Infantry. At 9 o'clock the next morning accordingly the Battalion marched to Lambres, a small village about one and a half miles south of Aire, covering the twelve miles' march in the good time of three hours forty-five minutes. After a comfortable night the march was resumed at 9 A.M. *via* Lillers and Choques to Labeuvrière, which was reached at 2 P.M. A good many of the men were recent convalescents from scarlet fever, and, in addition to this, the boots issued were of such bad leather that they soon wore out on the abominable *pavés*. This meant that numbers of the men were marching in new boots, and it speaks volumes for their spirit that practically every one completed these twelve- and thirteen-mile marches on his own feet. On 18th December the Battalion again moved off at 9 A.M. through Locon, arriving at Vieille Chapelle, a distance of ten miles, at 1 P.M. Though rain fell earlier in the day the Battalion got in with dry jackets. This stage of the march was the most interesting that the Battalion had done as yet, for everything spoke of its approach to the front, especially the passing of British and French units that had been in the line. One batch of soldiers was the tattered remnant of a battalion of the Royal Irish Rifles, under the command of the Transport Officer, himself wounded and the last survivor of the officers of the battalion. This brought the war very close. To quote from one of the diaries: "We are now in the zone of war and the village shows the marks of war. Here is a church with the roof blown off, there a cottage razed to the ground, and away in the distance the cannons boom with a muffled roar. Thus the 4th Seaforths sleep their first night under the sound of guns."

Here the Battalion made its first acquaintance with Brigadier-General C. E. Johnson, commanding the Dehra Dun Brigade, under whom it was to serve, who came over that evening to have a chat with the officers of his new unit.

Before closing this chapter, it is of interest to record what Brigadier-General D. A. MacFarlane says of the Battalion: "As an old commander of the Seaforth and Cameron Infantry Brigade for more than three years preceding the Great War, and at the time of mobilization and early training at Bedford, my vivid recollection of the 4th Battalion Seaforth Highlanders is that of a battalion in which there was always an excellent tone and a high feeling of *esprit de corps*. With an enthusiastic and keen Commanding Officer, a Second-in-Command—afterwards to command—of unbounded energy and unfailing good humour, and an Adjutant belonging to the county who thoroughly understood and appreciated every man in the Battalion, it was no wonder, perhaps, that they were one of the very first Territorial battalions to be considered fit to take their place in the front line in France. On the afternoon of the first day of mobilization I was astonished to find the numbers that had already arrived from far and near, and this in a country which is wild and mountainous, with but few roads, and very little available rail communication. At Bedford, with the same zeal and energy they set to work to get themselves ready for war in the shortest possible time, and to my pride and regret they passed from under my command, a splendid lot of officers and men."

SYNOPSIS OF EVENTS FROM THE DEFENCE OF GIVENCHY TO THE BATTLE OF NEUVE CHAPELLE

(*14th December* 1914 *to 9th March* 1915)

TAKING advantage of the transfer of large German forces to the East, the Allies, on 14th December, began a general offensive in France. The British attack was weak, and by 18th December fighting ceased. The French gained some small success in Champagne. The Germans counter-attacked the right of the Indian Corps on 20th December, taking Givenchy and making a deep salient opposite Festubert. The 1st Corps reinforced and finally relieved the Indian Corps, retaking practically all the lost ground.

On Boxing Day, 1914, the Expeditionary Force was regrouped into two armies, as follows:

First Army, General Sir D. Haig.

I Corps: Lieutenant-General Sir C. C. Monro.
IV Corps: Lieutenant-General Sir H. Rawlinson.
Indian Corps: Lieutenant-General Sir J. Willcocks.

Second Army, General Sir H. L. Smith-Dorrien.

II Corps: Lieutenant-General Sir C. Ferguson.
III Corps: Lieutenant-General W. P. Pulteney.
27th Division: Major-General T. D'O. Snow.

Cavalry Corps: Lieutenant-General Sir E. H. H. Allenby.
Indian Cavalry Corps: Major-General M. F. Rimington.

In spite of the diversion of troops for the ill-starred Dardanelles Campaign the British Expeditionary Force was steadily growing in number both of units and effectives, as, for instance, by the arrival, before the end of February, of the Canadian and 46th (North Midland) Divisions; but it was impossible to replace the experience and training of men who had fallen. As the preoccupation of Germany in the East had weakened her position in the West, it was decided to co-operate with the French attack on the Vimy Ridge by one on the Aubers Ridge, with a view to cutting the German communications in the Noyon salient.

In the meantime the Russian reverses in Galicia and the advance of the Turks on the Caucasian front hastened the preparations for the Dardanelles offensive. This, by diverting the 29th (Regular) Division from France, prevented the relief of the French IX Corps in Flanders by British troops, on which General Joffre's plans depended. Intermittent affairs in January and February had, however, led to a gradual gain of moral ascendancy by the British. Sir John French, therefore, decided to attack independently.

MAP 18.

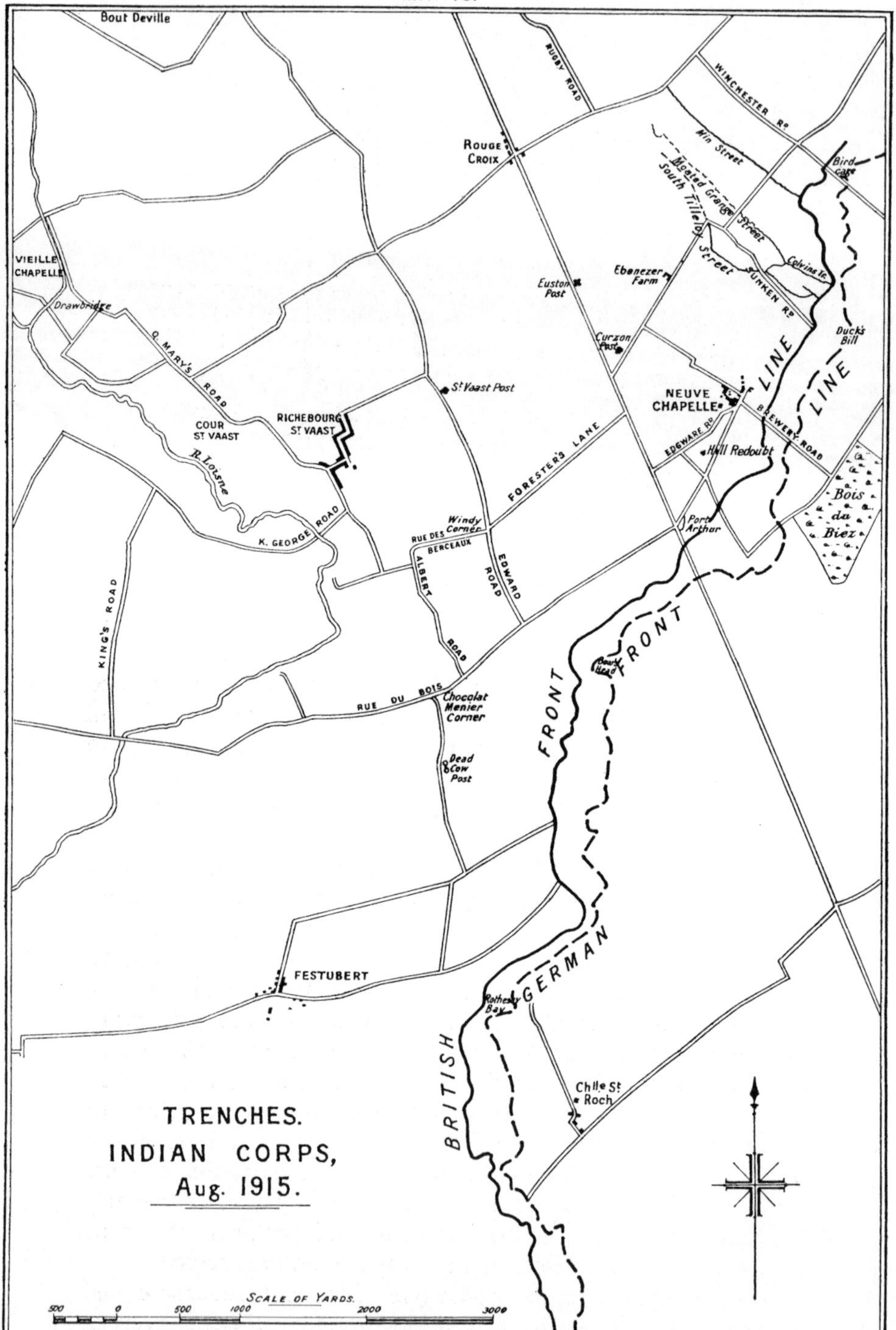

TRENCHES.
INDIAN CORPS,
Aug. 1915.

Bout Deville
Rugby Road
Winchester Rd
Min Street
Rouge Croix
Bird cage
Moated Grange Street
South Tilleloy Street
Colvins La.
Sunken Rd
Vieille Chapelle
Drawbridge
Q. Mary's Road
Euston Post
Ebenezer Farm
Curzon Post
Duck's Bill
St Vaast Post
Neuve Chapelle
Richebourg St Vaast
Cour St Vaast
R. Loisne
Forester's Lane
Edgware Rd
Hill Redoubt
Brewery Road
Bois du Biez
Port Arthur
Windy Corner
Rue des Berceaux
K. George Road
Albert Road
Edward Road
King's Road
Boar's Head
Rue du Bois
Chocolat Menier Corner
Dead Cow Post
Festubert
Rothesay Bay
Chlle St Roch
British Front Line
German Front Line

Scale of Yards.
500 0 500 1000 2000 3000

VIEILLE CHAPELLE

CHAPTER III

GIVENCHY

THE 4th Battalion The Seaforth Highlanders had now passed for good and all from a state of training to one of war. Up till this it had been a unit changing but little in numbers and personnel and forming day by day its own distinctive character as a living entity. From now on it was to face tests that were to prove the value of its training, both technical and moral. It was to go into action a unit of splendid youth, to emerge as a ragged remnant of worn-out men; it was to be built up again and again by drafts of new soldiers—eager volunteers, raw conscripts, patched-up survivors of former battles; it was to go through the same ordeal again and yet again; and still the stamp that had been set on it, the mould in which it had originally been cast, was to mark it with its own distinctive personality till the day of demobilization. The new drafts might hail from any part of the British Isles, they might have served in any of the hundreds of battalions in the Army List, yet the influence of Lieutenant-Colonel Mason-MacFarlane and the original officers, non-commissioned officers and men from Ross and Cromarty was impressed till the end on this splendid Battalion, which on 18th December completed its first stage of active service.

On the 19th Lieutenant-Colonel Mason-MacFarlane and his Adjutant, Sir John Fowler of Braemore, rode over to see Lieutenant-Colonel Ritchie, who was then commanding the 1st Battalion of the regiment. The ground all around the estaminet which formed his headquarters was honeycombed with shell-holes, some of which were large enough to have buried an elephant. Later on these would have been looked upon as quite small affairs, but at that time they created a great impression.

On the following morning, which was a Sunday, the Commanding Officer held a church parade. The Transport Officer had thoughtfully provided, as a pulpit, a wagon which, formerly a hearse, had been converted and issued to the Battalion at Bedford, but had always been looked at askance by the men, so the Commanding Officer decided to take the service on horseback. The proceedings were somewhat disturbed by the fact that our anti-aircraft guns were engaged in firing at some German aeroplanes circling overhead, and at the end of the service the men were dismissed at the double. About noon the Battalion was inspected by Lieutenant-General Sir James Willcocks, K.C.B., K.C.S.I., K.C.M.G., D.S.O., Commanding the Indian Corps. He praised the steadiness of the men and then explained that the Battalion was to go into the fire trenches in support of the 1st Battalion, one company at a time. When all the companies had had their baptism of fire the Battalion as a whole would take over a sector of trench. Hardly had Sir James finished when an orderly arrived with a message that the German attack was in full swing and that his presence was required at his headquarters. He says: "It amused me to think, after all my explanations and injunctions, that this corps was in fact to learn its lesson in the thick of the fighting without any preliminary practice at all. . . . The officers and men looked like fighters, and they did not belie their looks." [1]

At 1 P.M., therefore, about half-an-hour after the General had left, orders came to cancel the move of the first company and to move the Battalion as soon as possible into a line of reserve trenches on the Rue des Chavattes, between the Richebourg St-Vaast - Hulloch Road and the River Loisne. The right half Battalion occupied these trenches, while the left half was kept in reserve in billets at La Couture, about 1500 yards back. On the right were the 107th Pioneers, but the left was in the air. Everything pointed to the imminence of a big

[1] *With the Indians in France*, p. 153. By the late General Sir James Willcocks: London, Constable, 1920.

battle. All night there was heavy firing along the front; star shells lit up the surrounding country, and our own guns kept up a heavy fire over the 4th Seaforths' heads. On 21st December the left half Battalion relieved the right and in the evening the whole returned to billets at Vieille Chapelle. It was a most useful experience to a new unit thus to have been under heavy fire with practically no danger, for it gave the men a confidence that was invaluable later on.

One of our diarists records his experiences thus: "Hasty message summoned us from Vieille Chapelle to go out and occupy the reserve trenches. This was our first real experience and was anything but attractive. The night was bitterly cold and wet, and we had to post sentries on the trench. We had to do one hour on and four off—the four off we spent sleeping in an old loft, but could not take off our equipment or have a light for fear of shells. The battle was raging half-a-mile away and the star shells made the night into day. It was a long night for us, but we were relieved at 7 A.M. on Monday and we marched back to billets."

The next forenoon, 22nd December, when everyone was busy cleaning himself and his kit, another sudden order was received to return to the Rue des Chavattes. The Battalion moved off at 3 P.M. and spent the night in the trenches at Chocolat Menier Corner.

"Our first night passed actually in the trenches. We were summoned from Headquarters in the evening and posted in reserve trenches about half a mile behind the firing line. It was a very cold night and we had to sleep in the trench. It was a soft bed, but wet, and my pack was a hard pillow; but we managed to snatch a few hours' sleep and the morning came. It was 9.30 A.M. on Wednesday before we got relieved, and I came back with a good dose of cold."

Another diarist, however, says: "It was a bit cold at 4 A.M. The men were very contented, and some made quite comfortable huts of waterproof sheets, with straw underneath."

On 23rd December the 2/2nd Gurkhas were withdrawn from the line, being exhausted with the fighting of the last few days, and the 4th Seaforths were ordered to send half a battalion into the trenches in front of Richebourg l'Avoué in support of the 6th Jats. It was nearly dark when the Rue du Bois was reached, on the south side of which lay the trench line to be occupied. When the Battalion got there the battalion which it had been sent to relieve had retired, and the Staff Captain who was guiding it did not know exactly where the trenches were. Those nearest, however, were occupied by one company, while the other went into billets in shell-riddled barns. These trenches had been dug by a battalion of Gurkhas, and the big Highlanders stood head and shoulders above the parapet. The first thing to be done was to deepen and strengthen these trenches. They were held in reliefs of two hours by one company at a time. There was a good deal of rifle fire all night and hundreds of bullets were flying along the Rue du Bois, showing that the Germans were sniping the trench line from the open ground in front. One young officer proved this by putting his glengarry above the parapet on the point of a bayonet, which drew fire at once. It was more " unhealthy " in the Rue du Bois than in the trenches, and only slightly less so in the barns of the reserve. One officer lay down to read by the light of a candle, when a bullet very nearly extinguished both. The night was an anxious one, for the Battalion could not get in touch with any troops either in front or on its flanks. It was found out later that there was no battalion in front!

Sentries sometimes suffered from " nerves." One man who was posted on the Rue du Bois saw something move and fired at it. Again the thing moved and he fired again. Still no result. So he fired a third time, and was answered by the voice of a stray cow.

The companies, on being relieved by the Guards, retired at 2.45 P.M. on the 24th, after having been shelled for a short time without any casualties.

At 9 A.M. on Christmas Day, 1914, the 4th Seaforths marched ten miles to Robecq, due west from Vieille Chapelle, arriving at noon. The billets were good ones and the hard frost made the march a pleasant one. On the 26th the Battalion moved at 10 o'clock, reaching Ferfay, four miles south-west of Lillers, about 2 P.M. The billets were inferior and the men crowded, so it was not much wonder that there was a good deal of sickness during the next fortnight. The Rev. John Macleod, Free Church, Urray, joined on the march in time to take the service on the 27th. "He preached to us in Gaelic—the first Gaelic sermon we heard since we landed in France. I could not help but thinking of home and wondered how things were in the old country."

Another diarist evidently thought more of the secondary virtue, for he records: "Started a grand washing programme, clothes, men, etc."

"The one great excitement was the return of the 1st Battalion Seaforth Highlanders from the firing line to rest billets about a mile farther south than Ferfay. The battalion, we knew, had lost very heavily in officers and men. We heard they would march through Ferfay. The 4th Battalion lined the road as the 1st Battalion marched through the village and cheered with deafening cheers, as only Ross-shire lads know *how* to cheer. The 1st Battalion looked wonderfully fit, and though much depleted in numbers they were full of life and spirits. Major Stewart (who, fifteen months later, was killed while in command of the 4th Seaforths) was riding at the head of the Battalion. They were a *splendid* body of men in every respect. The General told us no battalion could have done better than the 1st Seaforth Highlanders, and one had just to see them march to know it must be true."

On the 30th fur jerkins were issued to the men.

Hogmanay was a cheery night. Each company had its concert in its billets. This is how No. 3 Company held its sing-song: "A big barn was found, and all the furniture consisted of a small box and one short bench. The box held the candles and the bench the officers. The boys had no seats, but we sat on the bare floor and admired the stars through the ceiling. Captain Mackenzie (E) took the chair, and later on the Colonel, Major Cuthbert and the Chaplain came in. Songs Gaelic and English were sung, and then when twelve o'clock came we cheered and wished each other a Happy New Year as if we were at home."

New Year's Day, 1915, was given up to "Highland Games" in conjunction with the 1st Battalion. "It was a grand day and everybody thoroughly enjoyed themselves." New Year's Day also marked the beginning of a period during which leave home was granted.

For the next twelve days the Battalion remained at Ferfay, undergoing special courses in entrenching and bombing. On 4th January, Lieutenant-General Sir James Willcocks inspected the Dehra Dun Brigade. He complimented the Battalion most highly on its discipline on parade and its general appearance. On the 6th, Brigadier-General C. W. Jacob, who had just taken over command of the Brigade, came to Headquarters and spoke to every officer in the Battalion. He was much impressed by the 4th Seaforths.

The next day Sir John French inspected the Indian Corps. "The day opened cold and misty and we thought the great man would not come. We fell in on the road and our poor bare knees turned blue with the cold. When Sir John did come we could hardly hear him, but by the smile on 'Cuthie's' face we knew he was very complimentary."

On 14th January 1915 the Battalion spent the morning entrenching and in the afternoon received orders to join the Sirhind Brigade (Brigadier-General W. G. Walker, V.C., C.B.) of the Lahore Division (Major-General H. D'U. Keary, C.B., D.S.O.). It left Ferfay at 4.30 P.M., arriving at Vendin-les-Bethune at 9 P.M., where it went into billets. An officer and eight junior non-commissioned officers went on ahead on cycles, and as the column reached Vendin the non-commissioned officer marched the half-company for which he was responsible to the billets allotted to them. This saved the men a lot; they had been digging hard all morning and had had a ten-mile march in the darkness. One of them wrote: "Our rest is up. We marched by night from Ferfay and felt quite done up when we came to Vendin-les-Bethune. I was ready to drop by the wayside, but I managed to stick it till we came to a place called Chocques, where we were expecting to get buses to take us right into the firing line. No buses for us. We had to march again, and when we got in we were dead-beat. I never bothered to take off my greatcoat nor my puttees, but I got into a barn among the straw and I slept as soundly as though I had a feather bed."

At 11 A.M., on 15th January, the march was resumed to Richebourg St-Vaast (seven miles), which was reached at 3.30 P.M. Captain Gilbert Fraser, with the two machine guns, was ordered to report himself at once to the 1st Battalion Highland Light Infantry, who were holding the front line. In the evening Major-General Keary visited the Battalion and made the acquaintance of the officers. Though much damaged the billets at Richebourg were good, as billets go. On the 16th the 4th Seaforths had a rest, the double Company Commanders being taken round the trenches held by the Highland Light Infantry, whom they were to relieve the following day. Major Cuthbert had a narrow escape when a shell burst outside Battalion Headquarters. A piece hit his boot, but he was, luckily, unhurt. On Sunday, the 17th, the Padre held service in the church in Richebourg St-Vaast, attended by the whole Battalion. The church had been badly shelled, and the men were carefully instructed how to get away at the double if the Germans began to shell again. Fortunately they did not, for there was only one little door.

As soon as it was dark three companies marched down the Rue du Bois to take over the trenches from the Highland Light Infantry. The fourth was held in reserve 600 yards in rear at the north end of the Rue des Berceaux. There was a very dangerous piece of road joining the Rue du Bois and the trench line at right angles. A German machine gun had been trained on this and opened fire as the Battalion was moving up in fours. The whole Battalion dropped into the side of the road, some into a ditch full of ice-cold water. Luckily the gun jammed or for some other reason ceased fire. Private Robertton, Alness, was shot through the thigh and Private Strickland through the arm. As soon as the firing ceased the Battalion crossed the danger spot at the double, and each company took over its section of trench from the Highland Light Infantry according to plan. When Major Cuthbert came up to one of the H.L.I. officers the latter said to him in a hurried manner: "Who are you?" "I'm Cuthbert. But what the devil is all the hurry about?" said the Major. "If you'd been here as long as I have," came the reply, "you'd know." Which saying, he vanished.

It was a severe test for the Battalion to take over in the dark trenches that they had never seen. They remained there for twelve hours, till relieved at dawn. What it felt like to the man in the ranks may be gathered from the following notes made at the time:

"*Sunday*, 17. D Company marched off to the Rue du Bois road and rested in a shelled house by the roadside. There were no doors or windows and the place was shivering. We could not light a match even, for the shells were falling near us, so we crouched behind the walls and tried to sleep. In the evening (7 P.M.) No. 1 Section of our company left for the trenches and our Section were to relieve them in the morning.

"*Monday*, 18. At 4.30 A.M. we left the house. There were ten of us and one corporal. We marched in file down the road till we came to a barricade across it, where we turned off. We were now going across the field in the open and the danger was that star shells would be thrown up and expose us. When one of these went up we had to lie quite flat on the ground, for the German snipers are keen to spot a moving object. It was a great experience. We sometimes lay in the mud for ten minutes and then got up covered with clay. We got into the trench and found it up to our knees with water and clay. We had to wade through this slush right up to where our loopholes were, and then we had to stand up all day there, cold and wet. We were blazing away at the German trenches 200 yards in front, but at 8 A.M. snow began to fall and continued all day. The snow got into the bolts of our rifles and spoilt them, until at last only one or two could fire a shot. My own rifle got quite choked, but I oiled it and got 100 rounds away, until at last it absolutely refused to open. The other boys were as badly off. We should have been relieved by Section 3 at 6 P.M., but it was 9 P.M. before we got out—wet, weary, but happy. We marched three miles back to Richebourg and had a wash and some hot tea, which we were badly in need of, as we had only three biscuits and one tin of meat each all day."

The Battalion had, indeed, been told to expect mud in the trenches, but, as another of them said: "Our expectations never rose above our ankles." When they did reach the trenches they flopped in up to the waists, carrying full equipment.

Another of the men records with gratitude that the H.L.I. told his section how to make themselves comfortable internally by showing them where fresh vegetables could be gathered: "I think we had a finer dinner that day than anyone else in the Battalion. We had a good bit of steak from the cooks, and cut it up into nice smallish bits and put it on an oven tray with some water, haricot beans, potatoes, leeks and cabbages, all of which vegetables we dug out from about the farm gardens and barns. The result was one of the best dinners we've had this side of the Channel, and, as things turned out, was a godsend to us, for we were relieved about three o'clock on Monday afternoon and were looking forward to a night's rest. Instead of which we were told we should have to move forward to the village just behind the firing line, to lie there for the night as a reserve, in case of attack." He goes on to describe the desolation of the village, the gaunt skeletons of houses standing out above the newly fallen snow, and the water dripping in through the riddled roof of the farm in which they lay for the night. He described how his bolt was jammed with mud, so that he had to sit and wait for the dawn; how he could hear the Germans singing in their trenches, and sometimes the sound of a gramophone. He blesses the kilt, "for our legs above the knees were dry at any rate," and comments on the smallness of the losses in the Battalion.

There were, indeed, no communication trenches in those early days. If the reliefs had not moved up in the dark they would never have got to their objectives alive. Nearly all the casualties in this spell in the line took place among men going up to or coming back from the trenches. This trench line in the Rue du Bois was particularly "unhealthy," because it was in a salient and the German enfilade caused more damage than their frontal fire.

The Commanding Officer's orderly, while standing outside Battalion Headquarters, got a shot through his glengarry. "That was a narrow shave," said someone. "Aye, but it's a grand souvenir," he replied. The sniper supposed to have been responsible for this was found and killed by the Battalion Scouts.

Fortunately it was possible to hold the trenches with group sections, as described in the notes just quoted, the picket itself being under cover in the shell-torn houses of the Rue du Bois, thirty to forty yards in rear of the trenches.

It was extraordinary that the men did not suffer in any way from this terrible exposure. Men, rifles, equipment, when they came off duty, were just pillars of walking mud. On being relieved they were sent back to Richebourg St-Vaast, where they were given a very hot bath, a good meal and a stiff hot glass of rum, and were then sent to bed for twelve hours.

One unfortunate, "Gunboat" Smith by name, somehow got left at his post for thirty-six hours. He amused himself by singing hymns and nursery rhymes.

Second Lieutenant L. D. Henderson distinguished himself during this spell of duty in the trenches, and was sent for by the Brigade Commander, who personally complimented him on his gallant conduct.

It is remarkable that more men were not hit during that spell of duty. The German snipers were particularly attentive to anyone moving between the reserve companies and the trench line during the night, and it was impossible to get the men to take any care of themselves. Their one fear seemed to be that someone else might think they were afraid. It was on the first night that the Battalion suffered its first fatal casualty. Private W. Ross, Maryburgh (H Company), was shot while stooping to pick up a shrapnel bullet as a souvenir to send home. He died the next day and was buried in the cemetery at Vieille Chapelle.

Some of the men had crowded into a small room in one of the shell-torn houses in the Rue du Bois. The next morning they found that there were two larger rooms leading out of it. "Kruger" MacDonald had discovered one of these the night before, and there they found him still sleeping in a bed. He had not noticed that in the same room lay the body of a French woman, killed by German shells some days earlier.

Before dawn on 20th January the 4th Seaforths were relieved by the 1st Manchesters and 4th Suffolks and marched to La Couture. A few hours later what had been the Battalion Headquarters and First Aid Post had been reduced to matchwood by the German guns. While resting at La Couture a Staff Officer from the Indian Corps Headquarters came round to see Colonel Mason-MacFarlane. Just before he left he said: "I wish to give you a piece of good news. Your battalion has the name of being the best Territorial Battalion in France. The reason is that its discipline is the best." The discipline of the Battalion was, however, quite unlike that of a Regular unit. It more resembled that of the Highland regiments when first raised in the eighteenth century, and was founded on the fact that most of the men of each company had known each other from boyhood, and all were determined neither to disgrace their district nor to let down their friends.

On Friday, the 22nd, the Sirhind Brigade, consisting of the 1st Battalion Highland Light Infantry, 4th Battalion The Seaforth Highlanders, 1/1st Gurkhas and 1/4th Gurkhas, marched off to Vendin-les-Bethune (eight miles), which was reached at 3 P.M. During one of the halts Major-General Keary, commanding the Lahore Division, came to the head of the Battalion and addressed the leading company, telling them how pleased he was with their work in the line, and ending with a eulogium on the Territorial Force. The 4th Seaforths were billeted in the same billets as on a former occasion and got a very warm welcome from the inhabitants. The Battalion, indeed, got on splendidly at all times when billeted with the inhabitants. It was quite a renewal of the "Ancient Alliance." The diaries—with the one exception of Ecques, where the Battalion was not billeted in the houses—are full of praise of the French. The latter were most hospitable, and there are many references to this. The men were made to feel quite at home, playing with the children and helping "Madame" or "Monsieur" with the daily domestic tasks. It was like the Macleod Fencibles in Ireland; they became veritable members of the family. At 10.45 A.M. on the 23rd the march of twelve miles to Ferfay was resumed *via* Marle-les-Mines and Cauchy. Billets were occupied at 2.45.

On 24th January the Battalion was transferred back to the Dehra Dun Brigade, the following letter being received from the G.O.C. Sirhind Brigade:

24th January 1915.

DEAR MACFARLANE,—I referred your case to our Division Headquarters and they reply that you are again transferred to the Meerut Division. So will you apply to them for orders? You should certainly have at least fourteen days' rest, and leave should be open for your officers, as it is for ours from to-day.

It was a great pleasure having your Battalion with us, and I wish we could have kept you in the Brigade, but your Division won't let you go. I hope to be on leave to-morrow. Good luck to you all. Yours sincerely,

W. G. WALKER.

The rifles were in a terrible state; many had lost their fore-sights, and the barrels of others had burst. Three men of the Ullapool Company, side by side in a trench, had their rifles hit on the night of 19th January. In the first case the trigger was hit and the cartridge in the chamber thereby fired; in the second a hole was punched through the barrel; in the third the wooden hand-guard over the barrel was shot away. In no case was the owner even scratched. These rifles are still preserved at Ullapool.

The Battalion was again temporarily attached to the Sirhind Brigade on the 25th, and was kept for some days in a state of constant readiness to move, first at a half-hour's and later at two hours' notice, owing to heavy German attacks on Givenchy. Five in all were made, but were beaten off each time with heavy loss.

This "rest" period was largely occupied in the training of Battalion telegraphists. On the 30th Major Fraser inspected the left half battalion; his comment on F Company, "I have seen better and I have seen worse, but not to-day," was taken to be high praise!

Lieutenant-General Sir James Willcocks, commanding the Indian Corps, held a conference at his Headquarters on the same day. All battalion commanders and senior ranks were present. He explained the composition of the newly formed First Army, and gave an optimistic account of the war, making everyone feel that things were going well with the British arms.

The 4th Seaforths then received orders to rejoin the Dehra Dun Brigade on the following day. On Sunday, 31st January, the Battalion left Ferfay at 9 A.M., reaching Hinges, where it was billeted for the night, at 1.15. "We were in good form but the weather was bad. The day was foggy, and soon snow fell and continued all day. The roads were soft and slushy, and we felt in anything but good spirits. Just as we were coming to Vendin, where we thought we were to pass the night, we turned off the main road and marched to Hinges—a twelve-mile march. We got the shelter of a cold barn; but any place was welcome if we could stretch ourselves and rest." On 1st February the Battalion left Hinges at 9 A.M., reaching Richebourg St-Vaast at 1 P.M.

"We got to the village we were in before, when we were up here, on Monday afternoon and found it much changed for the worse. The place had been shelled once or twice by the enemy and nearly all its remaining civilians had cleared out."

In the evening Captain Gilbert Fraser, with the machine guns, relieved the 6th Jats in the Rue du Bois. A fatigue party of No. 1 Company carried hurdles and sandbags for a redoubt being built in the Rue du Bois, and Lieutenant Fitzroy, with half a company, garrisoned a redoubt on the east side of the Rue des Berceaux. The rest of the Battalion remained in billets.

On 2nd February No. 3 Company took over a section of a trench from a Gurkha battalion, just south of the Rue du Bois. A private of the Gairloch Company was badly hit in the leg when this line was being taken over. That night Captain James Cameron took 250 men drawn from all companies to work on the reserve trenches. A shell fell in the middle of them, but did not burst. During the night, however, Corporal D. Sutherland was dangerously wounded in the upper jaw and three others were slightly wounded.

A private of the Battalion describes the journey through

the communication trench to the front line: "The guide had disappeared into the communication trench. The sound made the heart sink, but there was nothing for it but to follow; so in we went as bravely as we could. It was no pleasant sensation to feel the cold, icy water splashing up between the legs and then to wade forward through water that smelt like a sewer, along a narrow trench where your feet stuck in the mud, stumbling over branches and other obstacles, bumping and cursing along, gasping, groaning, laughing and joking by turns. After what seemed an interminable time in the communication trench we came into the firing trench, a post known as Wet Picket, and little more than a stream converted into a trench. The only dry place was the firing step. The man I relieved joyfully tumbled into the water I'd just so joyfully come out of, and made off to the end of the trench to join his comrades and get out." He then described the relief: "As you plod forward through the mud, with your heart pumping as if it would break, your chest and your lungs working in gasps, legs burning and feet aching, you feel as if a bullet would be a godsend. But once you get your feet on solid ground and your face turned homewards you seem to tread on air, and look forward with gladsome expectation to your bed on the floor of a draughty barn."

On 3rd February work on the defences continued, and in the evening a shell narrowly missed Battalion Headquarters, where several officers were assembled. From 4th to 8th February the 4th were billeted between Vieille Chapelle and La Couture, but supplied digging parties nearly every day.

Parties going up for digging carried their rifles slung and entrenching tools over their shoulders. They moved through the fields behind the rows of ruined houses, for the "Boches" had the range of the road too accurately to make movement on it safe. The going was, however, very bad; the mud was of the consistency of treacle and deep enough to make it hard at every step to withdraw the feet. It was bad enough for those who had only their entrenching tools to carry; far worse for the fatigue parties of the 1st Battalion (some of whom were passed by those of the 4th), who had to carry up the fascines for revetting the trenches. Wet ditches had to be crossed, and most of the men slipped or fell into these at some time or other. Telephone lines were another trial; they seemed to be everywhere, and the slung rifles continually fouled them as the men stumbled on. Not least of the trouble was the constant whine of the bullets.

The digging was horribly difficult. The mud stuck to the shovels like glue, the men were working in full equipment, and the rain drizzled mercilessly down through the thick darkness. No one could see properly what he was doing, while the treacly mud, when it was finally freed from the shovel, slowly flowed back into the trench wherever it could. When at last the diggers returned to their billets they had to wash the accumulation of mud from their feet by placing them under the pump!

On 8th February the whole Brigade marched to Calonne, about ten miles west of Vieille Chapelle, which was reached at two in the afternoon. The men were well housed here and spent the next ten days in company training, with special demonstrations on entrenchments, varied once a week by a route march. While here, to everyone's regret, Major Brodie went home on sick leave, his place being taken by Captain Gardiner, an Aberdonian.

While at Calonne, Lance-Corporal F. A. Harrop gained a testimonial on vellum from the Royal Humane Society for gallant conduct in saving Private McColl from drowning in the canal on 15th February.

At this time the troops were sent to Richebourg St-Vaast for hot baths. There was a plentiful supply of hot water, and none enjoyed this more than the Gurkhas.

At 9.15 A.M. on 22nd February the 4th Seaforths marched off to join the rest of the Brigade, reaching Vieille Chapelle at noon. The next day the Battalion took over a sector of the Rue du Bois from the 47th Sikhs, the frontage being, roughly, 800 yards from Albert Road to Edward Road. The right half Battalion (Captains Budge, Truslove, J. Cameron and Lieutenant Colin Cameron) went into the firing line, the remainder being in reserve. There were no casualties. The Battalion held the right of the Brigade line, the 2nd Gurkhas being next and the 1st Seaforths on the left. This was a much more satisfactory trench line than the last, and could be held without the horrible physical discomfort that had to be endured there. The line of resistance was some 400 yards from the German trenches and the outpost line, roughly, 300 in front of the line of defence.

Very strict orders had been issued that absolute silence was to be kept in the trench line, so that great was the scandal when, soon after midnight, a rich baritone voice was heard at Battalion Headquarters pouring forth from the direction of the front line the notes of *Annie Laurie*. Heated inquiries down the telephone brought the answer that the singer was in the German and not in the Highland trenches!

The trenches, though fairly dry, were not only not bullet-proof, but were not everywhere deep enough to let the men walk about in safety. Nor had they any parados, which meant that men in this salient could be hit in the back by bullets from the German trenches north of Port Arthur, and in front of Neuve Chapelle. The position was shelled regularly at the same hours two or three times a day, but rifle fire rarely occurred unless anyone showed himself. One day some officers of the Battalion who were in the redoubt on the east side of Albert Road saw the Divisional and Brigade Commanders (Generals Scott [1] and Jacob), with Major Fraser of Leckmelm, enter a house in the Rue du Bois. It was obvious that they had mistaken this house for another which was being used as an artillery observation post. Luckily they discovered their error in time, for within a few minutes the Germans got three direct hits on the house.

On the 27th the 2/2nd Gurkhas handed over a further 250 yards of trenches, which were taken over by No. 3 Company. One of the diarists remarks that they were quite dry, with chairs in them! Just after dusk No. 4 Company relieved No. 2 in the firing line. It was full moon, with a slight haze, and it was very noticeable that visibility was much less than on a dark night with star shells going up. Within 100 yards of the Ullapool (E) half company eighty-six shells fell within twenty-four hours. One struck the ruined house in which it was billeted. The men rushed out and had just got clear when a second shell burst inside it. The Battalion was very lucky during its eight days in this sector, having only three men seriously wounded.

One of the early "casualties" occasioned a ludicrous incident. E Company was in an orchard, well behind the firing line, and the men were throwing apples at one another. One of them accused Sergeant Mackenzie (commonly known as "Doddles") of having hurt him with a stone and began to rub his ankle, when he found that he had been hit by a spent bullet.

On 2nd March the 41st Dogras relieved the 4th Seaforths, who marched back to billets in Vieille Chapelle. It was a relief

[1] General Anderson was at that time on leave.

to all to get a change of clothing and a good night's rest after ten days without once having their clothes off. At Vieille Chapelle was found the first draft of fifty-five men from the Reserve Battalion, under Captain R. de Cardonnell Findlay. Since leaving England on 5th November 1914 no reinforcements had been received, and the strength was now under 700, for, besides killed and wounded, there had been the usual wastage of war. Besides Captain Findlay there arrived at the same time Captain F. Mackinnon and Lieutenant H. A. Summers.

SYNOPSIS OF EVENTS. BATTLE OF NEUVE CHAPELLE

(*10th to 13th March* 1915)

THE attack on Aubers Ridge was to begin by an attack on the village of Neuve Chapelle, which formed a salient in the German line. This was to be followed by the establishment of the British line along the old Smith-Dorrien trench. Finally the First Army was to make a general advance to the Illies-Herlies line. The infantry was to push forward rapidly immediately after an intense artillery bombardment and sweep the Germans out of their positions before they could recover from their surprise. It was indeed the first time that the British attempted an attack on the lines that were afterwards to be the model for almost every operation of any importance. The Germans, though realizing the imminence of an offensive, were in the dark as to its objective and direction, for the greatest secrecy was successfully maintained.

Daybreak on 10th March was cold, damp and misty, but with sunrise the weather improved. The bombardment began at 7.30 A.M., practically obliterating the German trenches and entanglements, except on the left. The batteries that were allotted to this sector had arrived only the previous day. They had been unable to anchor their gun platforms effectively, and hence could not keep an accurate fire, with fatal results to the advance of the 23rd Brigade.

On the right the Garhwal Brigade successfully carried out their attack, reaching the Smith-Dorrien line by 9 A.M. As it was full of water the front troops began to entrench, practically undisturbed, about fifty yards in rear of it. Unfortunately the 1/39 Garhwal Rifles bore too much to the right, and lost heavily in attacking a sector not included in the original plan.

Meanwhile the 25th Brigade had captured Neuve Chapelle and was engaged in entrenching by 10 A.M., but the 23rd Brigade was held up before the undamaged sector of the German line, about 200 yards long. Thus both flanks were held up before more or less intact positions.

The 1st Seaforths from the Dehra Dun Brigade were ordered to support the 1/39 Garhwal Rifles, but for various reasons their attack was delayed till the afternoon.

The advance of the 24th Brigade was also interrupted to clear the German front trench opposite the 23rd Brigade. When the 23rd and 25th Brigades reached their objectives, about 1 P.M., the 24th was ordered to reassemble for a further advance. Thus only the 200 yards sector opposite Port Arthur was still held by the Germans. For various reasons the 24th Brigade, instead of advancing at the time ordered, did not do so until 5.30 P.M., when the light was already beginning to fail, which in turn checked the advance of the 21st Brigade on its left.

At 4 P.M. the Dehra Dun Brigade moved along Edgware Road, and on nearing Neuve Chapelle deployed along the Neuve Chapelle-Port Arthur road. The advance began at 5 P.M. Darkness set in, but a burning cottage near the wood gave the direction. The 2/2nd Gurkhas occupied Les Brulots, and began to dig in at the edge of the wood, but the 1/9th Gurkhas were held up by enfilade fire from the redoubt at Layes Bridge on its left. Consequently, while the Indians were waiting for the advance of the 24th Brigade to bring forward their left flanks, two German battalions reoccupied the Bois du Biez about 6 P.M. The Dehra Dun Brigade, therefore, returned to the west bank of the River Layes.

In the meantime the 1st Seaforth Highlanders, 3rd London Regiment and 1/39 Garhwal Rifles carried the salient left in the German line with heavy losses.

On the 11th March the line consolidated during the night by the Germans was not detected, and was therefore not shelled, so that no advance by the IV Corps was possible. Ambiguous orders also delayed the advance of the Dehra Dun Brigade, which had no indication of what was happening on its left. Indeed the destruction by German shell fire of most of the British telephones resulted in lack of co-ordination, which, together with want of accurate information as to the German position, caused the proposed attacks to be carried out piecemeal.

The Germans counter-attacked along the whole front of the British attack at five on the morning of the 12th March, but were everywhere driven back. Low visibility prevented the British from locating and shelling the German position, although the 7th and Lahore Divisions gained some ground. Lack of ammunition brought the Battle of Neuve Chapelle to a close with a slight but heartening gain for the British arms. In particular it raised the prestige of the British troops among both their enemies and their allies.

MAP 6.

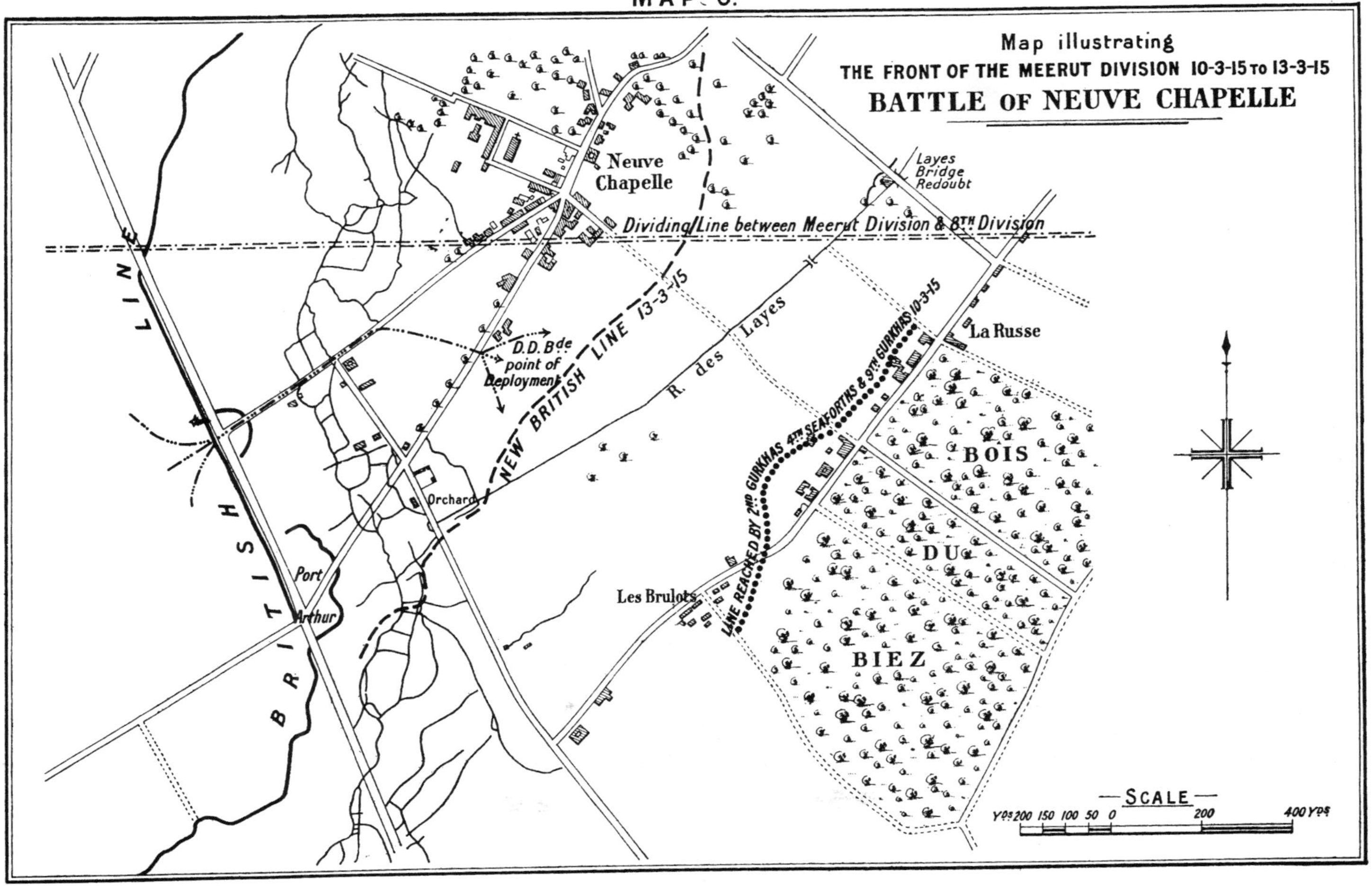

Map illustrating
THE FRONT OF THE MEERUT DIVISION 10-3-15 TO 13-3-15
BATTLE OF NEUVE CHAPELLE

Neuve Chapelle
Layes Bridge Redoubt
Dividing Line between Meerut Division & 8TH Division
La Russe
D.D. Bde. point of Deployment
NEW BRITISH LINE 13-3-15
R. des Layes
LINE REACHED BY 2ND GURKHAS 4TH SEAFORTHS & 9TH GURKHAS 10-3-15
BOIS DU BIEZ
Orchard
Les Brulots
Port Arthur
BRITISH LINE

SCALE
YDS 200 150 100 50 0 200 400 YDS

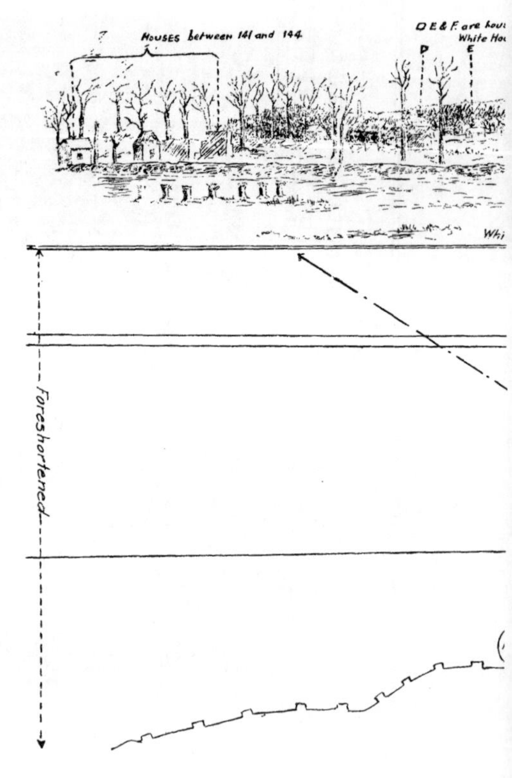
Houses between 141 and 144
D E & F are hou
White Ho
D
E
Foreshortened

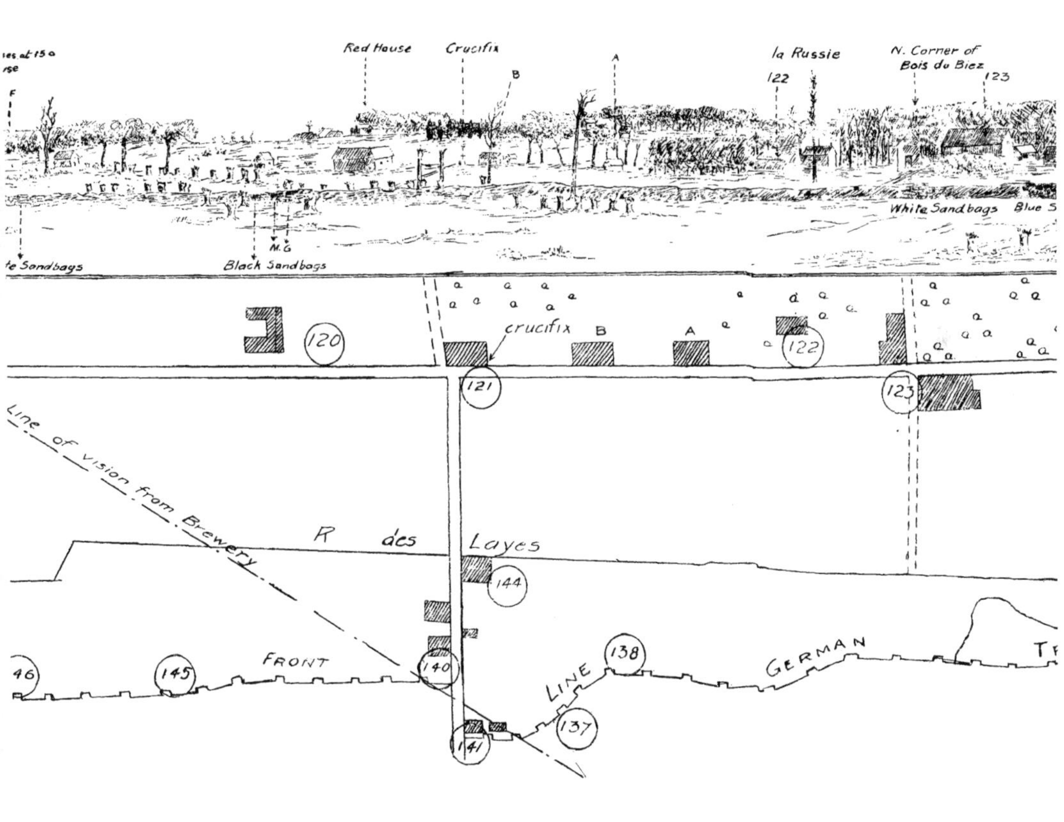

Red House
Crucifix
B
A
la Russie
122
N. Corner of Bois du Biez
123
F
M.G
Black Sandbags
White Sandbags
crucifix
120
121
122
123
R des Layes
144
140
141
145
138
137
FRONT
LINE
GERMAN
Line of vision from Brewery

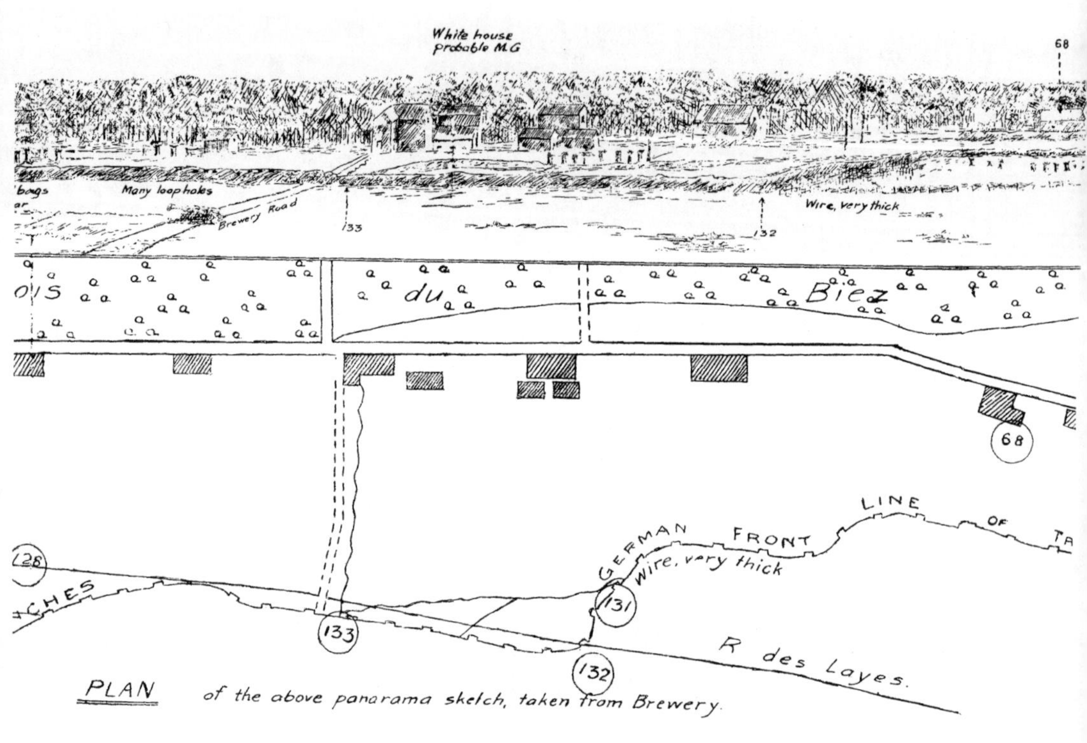

PLAN of the above panorama sketch, taken from Brewery.

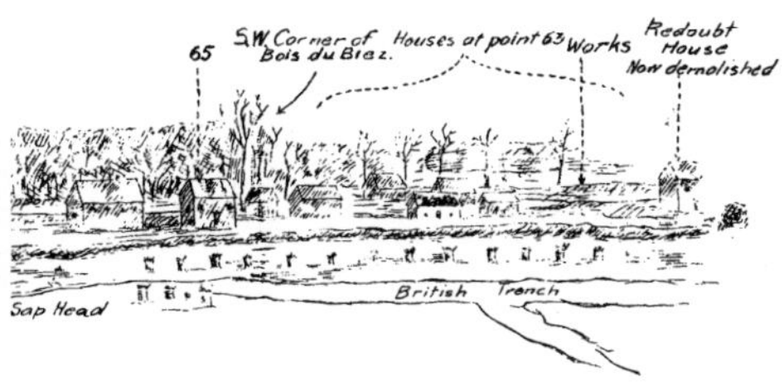
65
S.W. Corner of Bois du Biez.
Houses at point 63
Works
Redoubt House Now demolished
Sap Head
British Trench

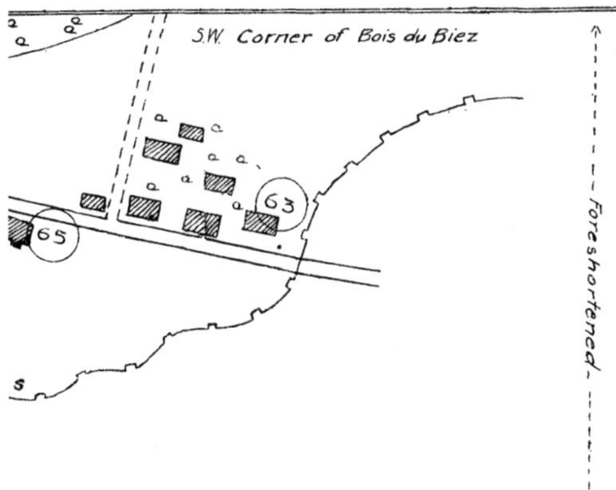
S.W. Corner of Bois du Biez
63
65
Foreshortened

NEUVE CHAPELLE: THE BREWERY

CHAPTER IV

NEUVE CHAPELLE

ON 2nd March 1915 the 4th Seaforths were relieved by the 41st Dogras. "All went like clockwork. The relieving battalion arrived at 7 A.M. and we were all off the ground at 7.40 A.M. Their Colonel told us he had never had a sector of the line handed over to him so carefully before. We were indebted to the Irish Guards for this compliment—we did our best to hand over our line as they had handed theirs over to us. After being relieved we marched back to billets in Vieille Chapelle."

At 3 A.M. on 4th March Lieutenant-Colonel Mason-MacFarlane, the two Majors, the four Company Commanders and the Adjutant walked about three miles to Port Arthur, a redoubt at the east end of the Rue du Bois, close to Neuve Chapelle. They reached the Headquarters of the 2nd Battalion Black Watch, where they had a cup of tea and at dawn were taken all round the British trenches in front of Neuve Chapelle. The German trenches in this sector were from fifty to eighty yards from the British, and an excellent view of them and of the country beyond was got through periscopes. The Germans fired at these whenever they appeared above the parapet, and at that range they ought to have hit them every time! After about two hours' careful inspection the party returned to Vieille Chapelle.

Battalion Headquarters knew by now that a big battle was imminent, but everything was kept secret. On 6th March there was a conference at Brigade Headquarters, at which all arrangements were carefully discussed.

In preparation for the fight enormous numbers of field and heavy guns were brought up. As is well known, the artillery fire, preparatory to the advance on Neuve Chapelle, on 10th March 1915, was the most terrible that had yet been experienced in war. For some days prior to this, and right up to the eve of the battle, guns were arriving and were placed in gun emplacements carefully masked. To allow each artillery commander to get the right range involved a good deal of heavy gun fire, which yet had to be most carefully restricted, lest the Germans should suspect the coming attack.

The last two days had been very full of work, getting everything ready for a move forward. It was certain that no transport would be available, and as each man had to carry food for thirty-six hours, in addition to an extra supply of ammunition, everything else was cut down to a minimum. Sunday, 7th March, found preparations too busily in progress to make a Battalion church parade possible, but each company managed to find time for a company service. The Padre, Mr Macleod, was one of the few who knew what was coming, and none that heard him will ever forget the way in which he spoke.

One of the diaries has an interesting entry referring to the Saturday, which throws some light on the precautions being taken to keep the attack secret: "On guard on bridge crossing up to the firing line. My first experience of real guard. Had to stop all civilians and examine their passes. Also had to stop everything passing after 6 P.M. This was a most interesting day.

"*Sunday*, 7. Just when I was getting home after doing guard for 24 hours, orders had come that all bomb-throwers [1] were to leave their respective companies and join those of the 1st Batt. We heard that serious work was to be done."

In the evening large working parties had to be found for Port Arthur, but fortunately there were no casualties. For the first time the Colonel was able to inspect the new draft, whom he described as a *very* fine body of men.

On Monday, 8th March, orders were received that the attack would take place on the 10th. A conference of battalion

[1] This refers to the trench mortar section.

commanders was held at Brigade Headquarters and Brigadier-General Jacob described in detail the proposed operations, and gave orders that the company commanders were to be informed of the scheme.

On the 10th the guns were to open soon after dawn. The moment they had pulverized the German front line the Garhwal Brigade was to capture it. The Dehra Dun Brigade was then to go straight through the Garhwal Brigade and capture Neuve Chapelle and the Smith-Dorrien line, from which we had been driven in October 1914.

The Indian Corps was to attack on a front of 600 yards, the right flank being Port Arthur redoubt and the left 600 yards north on the La Bassée road. The jumping-off lines were 100 and 200 yards behind Port Arthur, and the troops were to assemble in them under cover of darkness. On the right front of Port Arthur the Germans held a strongly fortified position, which was to be shelled during the attack by a brigade of 6-inch howitzers.

Those who were at Battalion Headquarters on Edward Road on the morning of 10th March will remember seeing the shells from this brigade like coveys of huge birds flying over the high trees at their backs.

For the next forty-eight hours the 4th Seaforths were kept busy, either finding working parties for the assembly trenches (carried out at night) or in preparing for the coming battle. On the 9th superfluous baggage and equipment was stored in an empty hall at La Couture, and each company commander had to inspect his command and report that all was ready for the move. Final orders were received that evening and then followed a last talk over the arrangements at Battalion Headquarters.

At 2 A.M. on 10th March 1915 a good hot meal was served to everybody. At 3 A.M. the Battalion moved off from Vieille Chapelle by La Couture and George Road to Richebourg St-Vaast, and thence to the position of assembly some 600 yards north-east of the remains of the church there. Earthworks had been dug north and south of the road from Richebourg to Edward Road, and the Battalion was safely in its assembly trenches well before dawn.

Dawn broke—a lovely morning—and, except for the occasional report of a gun registering an objective, nothing was to be heard but the larks singing overhead. The men had a ration of biscuits and bully beef, for fires were not allowed. The Garhwal Brigade, which was to carry out the first phase of the attack, was assembled in Port Arthur and in trenches along the Estaires-La Bassée road. The Dehra Dun Brigade, which was to go through the Garhwal Brigade in the event of the latter's success, was assembled in trenches and redoubts behind this line; on the right the 1st Seaforths, supported by the 2/2nd Gurkhas, on the left the 1/9th Gurkhas, supported by the 4th Seaforths, who occupied four redoubts on the road running from the north exit of Richebourg St-Vaast to the Estaires-La Bassée road, Nos. 1 and 2 Companies in front and Nos. 3 and 4 in rear. To the last was allotted the heavy work of carrying the Battalion reserve of ammunition—60,000 rounds—and all the Battalion picks and shovels.

The length of the whole position to be attacked was just over two miles, and against this were massed 480 guns, ranging from 18-pounders to a 15-inch howitzer known as "Mother." She was a source of many rumours. It was alleged that her second shell had destroyed the church at Aubers, and—what still further encouraged the troops—that another had left but two survivors out of a whole German battalion!

All were waiting patiently, wondering what the bombardment would be like, when suddenly a sound burst forth that shook the solid earth and rent the air so that men seemed to sway as before a mighty wind. Small groups of birds swept to and fro like tattered leaves, and where the German trenches lay the ground rose to the skies in writhing columns of flame and earth and smoke. It was 7.30 A.M., and the greatest artillery concentration yet known to history had begun. As suddenly as the bombardment had opened, so suddenly did it stop. At 8.5 A.M. the guns lifted on to Neuve Chapelle itself and the zones behind the German front lines, and the Garhwal Brigade went over the top on a 600 yards' front, the Dehra Dun Brigade moving forward in support.

At 8.30 A.M. came the report that the Garhwal Brigade had carried the German line and that its defenders were in full retreat, while at 9.17 A.M. Neuve Chapelle was in the hands of the 8th Division. On the greater part of the front the guns had done their work, but one section had been missed, which had a decisive effect on the result of the battle. Yet no orders came for the expected advance of the Dehra Dun Brigade.

Meanwhile the trench mortar section had been ordered to

select a position, and one of the men thus describes his experiences: "Our officer left Windy Corner at 8.30 with two men, and I had the good fortune to be one. The bombardment had now slackened considerably. We scurried along the road till we were tired out and then took cover from the shrieking shells overhead. When we were refreshed a little we left this shelter and ran all the way to the communicating trenches. We had cover now, but we had to run still, ducking our heads as a bullet whistled over us. We were quite tired out and breathless when we got in, and the scene before us was one such as we expected. All over the ground were dead bodies. Some lay in the open, some in the trench, and some half buried in the clay. They were mostly Gurkhas, who lay as they fell. . . . It was a gruesome sight, and as we passed on our feeling of awfulness deepened. The Indians were now taking over the first line of German trenches, and the ground over which they trod had been torn by the awful British shells. The place was strewn with lyddite, the dug-outs were broken down, and everything was in confusion. Here and there were mangled remains of German dead, a frozen look of horror on their faces, and in one traverse we saw an officer lying on his back wearing the ribbon of the Iron Cross. Here we could not but wonder at the absence of German dead, but the poor fellows were so scared by the awful bombardment that they surrendered *en masse.* The prisoners we took looked scared out of their wits, and no wonder."

At noon, after three hours of waiting, the Battalion got the order to move forward, not to the attack which everyone had been anxiously expecting, but to assembly trenches which had been occupied in the night by the 1/9th Gurkhas, 700 yards nearer to the jumping-off trenches of the Garhwal Brigade. The Battalion moved by Edward Road and Forester's Lane to Windy Corner, where the left and right half Battalion respectively occupied redoubts to the north and south of the lane. The Commanding Officer went up to Brigade Headquarters and there learnt that the advance of the 1/39th Garhwal Rifles had been held up. He therefore offered to manhandle two guns into the front line so as to smash it with direct fire, but was told that guns were never used in that manner! Finally, the 1st Seaforths were sent to carry the position, which they did at very heavy cost, while their services were lost to their own Brigade both that and the next day.

At 2 P.M. a shell burst over the right half Battalion, killing or wounding seventeen men. Amongst the casualties was Major Robertson (Monteagle), of No. 1 Company, who was mortally wounded. He had only just rejoined from sick leave in the south of France, but had insisted on going into action, and his loss was greatly felt throughout the whole Battalion. He was the first officer casualty in action, and had had the longest service with both the Volunteers and Territorials. Those killed and wounded were nearly all Dingwall men; not a few were men of the first draft, and some of them were University graduates.

The new formation for the attack was as follows: On the right the 2/2nd Gurkhas, supported by the right half of the 4th Seaforths; on the left the 1/9th Gurkhas, supported by the left half. About 4.20 P.M. the advance on the Bois du Biez commenced, the companies at wide intervals gradually working their way to the La Bassée road, and getting a certain amount of cover from low breastworks running parallel to it; for the road was being searched by shrapnel, most of which, fortunately, burst high and short. There were some narrow escapes from short bursts from our own shrapnel: one smashed the pipes of Piper Mackenzie of No. 3 Company, the empty case lodging between Major J. W. Fraser and Captain D. A. MacKenzie.

When the companies turned into the original front trench along the La Bassée-Estaires road progress became very difficult. Not only was it occupied by the Black Watch (of the Bareilly Brigade in divisional reserve), but the Seaforths had to contend with a constant stream of wounded flowing in the other direction, and it was dark before the three leading companies emerged from the trench near Port Arthur. These three companies then worked their way in extended order through and to the right of the village of Neuve Chapelle. Major Cuthbert took on Nos. 1 and 2 Companies, along with Captain J. Cameron. They pushed on to the corner of a little wood leading up to the Bois du Biez, where Major Cuthbert met Major Watt of the 2/2nd Gurkhas, who told him to push on to the support of Major E. P. R. Boileau, commanding that battalion, which was hard pressed. This was done. In crossing the Layes the Seaforths had to plunge in up to about the waist, and found some difficulty in scrambling up the farther bank.

The two companies came up, in extended order, till they reached the Gurkhas, who were lying in line waiting for further orders.

When Major Cuthbert got in touch with Major Boileau he found that orders had just come to hold on where they were, and on no account to go through the wood. By the light of a burning cottage a party went forward. They got right through to the far side of the wood, and in the glare of the fire could make out the enemy retiring. They then returned and reported to Major Boileau that the wood was clear. He in turn reported to Brigade Headquarters, but was told on no account to move.

About 7 P.M. the order came to retire to the old Smith-Dorrien line and dig in, so the whole force retired. After their drenching no one was sorry—even though all felt they were going the wrong way—to get on the move again. The Gurkhas dug in some fifty yards in front of the line, while Major Cuthbert brought back his men and started to dig in on the old line, beside the left half Battalion. The right half Battalion were soaked to the skin in crossing the Layes, and were now so tired that they just scraped small holes, into which they tumbled and fell asleep.

All this time No. 3 Company had remained in support of the 1/9th Gurkhas on the north side of the Layes. No. 4 Company, however, had had great difficulties in the trench, for half was carrying ammunition, two men to a box, and the other half was laden with picks and shovels. It took three hours to struggle through and collect the company at the exit, where Regimental Sergeant-Major Glass was found doing excellent work directing traffic in the darkness. The Leicesters (of the Garhwal Brigade) were now coming out of action by the same route and the utmost congestion and confusion reigned. Eventually No. 4 Company reached the village and got orders from the Commanding Officer to dump the ammunition and dig in behind the Neuve Chapelle-Port Arthur road.

The plight of No. 4 Company is thus described by one of its officers: "Just after passing the third barricade No. 4 lost touch with the remainder. We sat on the road with bullets whistling overhead, and suddenly an H.E. shell landed in a house just on the other side of the road: of course we cleared out at once—so smartly, indeed, that some of the S.A.A. boxes were left lying on the road, but were recovered at once.

"We went up the road till nearly at the Cross Roads, and then entered the trench lately vacated by the British troops—the former front line. This was full of Sikhs and wounded passing up and down, and an awful muddle—not the best thing for one's temper—was the result. If we had only known, there was a fine road just over the parapet which we might have used. Eventually we got out, and at length extricating ourselves from the Indians and Manchesters (of the Jullundur Brigade) succeeded in reaching the village of Neuve Chapelle about 10 P.M. No rest, however, for me, for I was told to take forty men to bring up some bridges. I was almost dead with fatigue, and coming back again I caught myself falling asleep as I walked. However, I got a couple of hours' sleep on a pile of S.A.A. boxes, which served well enough. No. 4 Company was placed in some rough trenches and rifle pits on the west side of the Rue du Bois, the other companies being farther up in support."

The 11th March found the men sleeping as best they might in the little holes they had scraped for themselves. At 6 A.M. orders came for the Brigade to attack the Bois du Biez at 7.30 A.M. in the same formation as had been arranged for the previous afternoon. These orders were explained at a conference of the officers at Battalion Headquarters, during which the Adjutant's batman was hit by a bullet that came through a window in the wall, behind which the conference was being held.

The 2/2nd Gurkhas were on the right, the 1/9th on the left, followed respectively by two companies of the 4th Seaforths in the first support line and two in the second. Owing to an extension of the Brigade left flank Nos. 4 and 2 Companies had to move to the left, under cover of a low breastwork to the east of the road. The attack was preceded by an intense fire on the Bois du Biez, but the enemy had made good use of their respite during the night, and the houses in front of the wood and the sloping ground up to and on its flank appeared to have been heavily reinforced with troops and machine guns. Despite the intense fire the attack made ground, but the company on the left were unable to get in touch with the Division on their flank, and later the Officer Commanding the 1/9th Gurkhas reported to the same effect to Brigade Headquarters.

Very shortly after the Battalion moved off the Commanding Officer, Lieutenant-Colonel Mason-MacFarlane, was hit by a bullet, which went clean through his left thigh bone, fortunately without breaking it. He was carried to a trench and laid under the parapet. Sir John Fowler, the Adjutant, at once reported to Major Cuthbert, who took command, and established his headquarters in a shell hole about two hundred yards east of the village. The Commanding Officer lay there under heavy shell-fire until 1.30 P.M., when a high explosive shell burst overhead, killing two wounded Gurkhas lying beside him and again wounding him in the left thigh. This wound became gangrenous, and but for the fact that he had been a doctor the leg would almost certainly have been amputated at Wimereux. The loss of their Commanding Officer was a great blow to the Battalion, for it was undoubtedly owing to his enthusiasm and real genius for detail (which goes so far to make a successful trainer of men) that the 4th Seaforths had the honour of being amongst the first Territorial battalions to be sent overseas, and to gain and to keep throughout its service its high reputation as one of the best Territorial battalions in the British army.

The attack was not long under way before it became apparent that the Gurkhas were held up. Nothing could live under the intense machine-gun fire that was being poured in from the left flank, where there was no infantry support. An officer who had to work his way along the line under the hail of lead was heard to say: "Now I know what a wretched white hare feels like, madly racing down the line of guns." The assaulting troops had, therefore, to take what cover they could find or make with their entrenching tools. Orders accordingly were issued by Brigade Headquarters to stand fast until the 24th Brigade came into line on the left. From ten till two in the afternoon a very heavy artillery fire was directed over the whole position, and casualties mounted up. It was a trying experience for a battalion engaged in its first general action; for there was nothing to be seen of the enemy—nothing to be done but to set the teeth in the determination to hold on till further orders. With grim humour the War Diary says: "Heavy rifle, machine-gun and artillery fire, mainly directed on the support, encouraged the Battalion to dig in." During this period Captain R. de C. Findlay (Altnamain), who had only just come out from home, was killed by a shell, and Major Cuthbert was wounded in the head, but refused to relinquish the command.

At 2 P.M. a verbal message was received that the attack was to recommence at 2.15 P.M. This was a signal example of the danger of verbal orders, for a rider that the attack was to commence "provided the 8th Division had come up" never reached the 4th Seaforths. The batteries simultaneously opened a very heavy fire on the wood. The noise of this bombardment was different from that of the last; then the guns themselves had been the principal factors, whereas now it was the explosion of the shells. Sometimes five or six high explosive shells would go off together, sending up great columns of greenish smoke. Observation of the ground east of the Layes was extremely difficult owing to the contours, a parapet on the west side completely hiding a dip immediately behind it. Lieutenant John Macmillan (Dingwall) was killed beside Major Cuthbert by a shell, just after selecting a position for his machine guns.

Major Cuthbert decided that to stay in the old Smith-Dorrien line, of which the enemy had the range to a nicety, would only entail needless casualties. He therefore ordered the right half Battalion to rush forward, clear of shell fire, and dig in behind the Gurkhas. The Gurkha trench was, however, too great a temptation to the advancing men, who crowded into it. The left half Battalion, through some misunderstanding that has never been adequately explained, rushed to the support of the 1/9th Gurkhas. As the Gurkhas *had* received the rider to the order concerning the advance of the 8th Division, they had not tried to advance, and the trenches were so badly crowded by the arrival of the Highlanders that the latter had, for the most part, to take what cover they could behind them. Casualties up till now had been heavy: Captain Findlay, Captain Budge (Rarichie) and Lieutenant Macmillan (Dingwall) were killed, and Captain Truslove wounded; about 150 other ranks were killed or wounded. Major Cuthbert discussed the position with the Commanding Officers of the Gurkhas, and it was decided that, should the advance continue, the edge of the wood could be carried in three rushes. This was reported to the Brigade at about 4 P.M., but orders were received to stand fast, owing to the failure of the brigade on the left to come up into line. No. 4 Company was ordered thoroughly to reconnoitre the ground to the front and flanks, and all officers and non-commissioned officers had got a good knowledge of it before darkness set in.

At 6 P.M. orders were received for the Battalion to withdraw and form up in reserve to the west of the Neuve Chapelle road. After dusk parties were sent out to bring in the wounded and collect the dead. Silence reigned over the battle-field, so recently an inferno of thundering guns and shrieking shells; it was as if the very guns were exhausted with the dragging struggle of the day. Figures loomed up in the dim twilight, then vanished in the gloom as they searched in trenches and shell holes — officers seeking their men and men their comrades. Huddled masses approached, gradually taking the shapes of groups carrying still forms on improvised stretchers, or supporting the less seriously wounded over broken ground. The work of the Battalion stretcher-bearers was beyond all praise. Private A. Macleod received the D.C.M. for voluntarily leaving his trench on 11th March and spending a quarter of an hour under heavy shell fire bandaging a seriously wounded Gurkha.

Private A. Thomson (Tong, Lewis) saw a man lying out beyond our front line and went out to bring him in. He proved to be a man of the Black Watch who could not walk by himself. They managed to crawl to a small brook, where Thomson found a plank which just spanned the brook, across which he tried to pass the wounded man. When midway across the plank broke and the man went under. Thomson had hard work to get him to the far side, especially as the enemy had seen him and opened fire on them. He succeeded, however, in getting the man back, and was duly recommended for the V.C. He was wounded next day and was reported to his family as killed. Some weeks later he was found in the Glasgow Infirmary by a gentleman who knew that his family were in mourning for him and had seen in the papers the announcement that he had been awarded the D.C.M. [He was subsequently awarded the Military Cross in October 1918, when serving as an officer in the 5th Seaforths.]

At 2 A.M. on 12th March the Battalion was relieved by the 1st Battalion Highland Light Infantry (of the Sirhind Brigade), and proceeded to its old area in rear of La Couture, which was reached about 5 A.M. Thanks to the foresight of that splendid transport officer, the late Captain P. B. Macintyre, who had succeeded in keeping in touch with the Battalion throughout the whole of the operations, the men had the comfort of finding a hot breakfast in readiness. At 7 A.M. they were again on the march, reaching l'Epinette two hours later. At l'Epinette the Indian Cavalry extended the most kindly hospitality to the Battalion, vivid and grateful memories of which are still warmly cherished by the recipients. Here the Battalion remained till 5 P.M., when it proceeded once more towards the line, for the enemy was delivering a heavy counter-attack. This march in the darkness was a nightmare to the weary troops. The roads were a congested mass of battalions moving up to or down from the trenches, wounded being evacuated, and supplies and ammunition going up. To add to the difficulties always inherent in such a mixture of large and small parties, moving without any common control, the very roads and trenches were, in many cases, new to all, and many of the old ones had been obliterated by shell fire. Richebourg was not entered till 10 P.M. Here the good news reached the Battalion that it was to billet in the disused factory, and by midnight it had settled down to the first night's sleep since the 8th.

The casualties were heavy: four officers killed and four wounded, 37 other ranks killed and 123 wounded; practically a quarter of the number that went into an action in which, for all their valour, the 4th Seaforths never got the satisfaction of coming to grips with the enemy.

It may be of interest to give some of the impressions recorded by men who went through the Battle of Neuve Chapelle. It is noticeable how very simple and matter-of-fact these records are. Nearly all speak of the light-hearted spirit in which the men moved forward to what all knew must be a very serious affair. "We made ourselves as comfortable as possible in these trenches (the assembly position) and passed the time in one game or another, with the same enthusiasm as we might have shown had we been out for enjoyment in far-away Ross-shire."

Another writes: "About 11 A.M. [it was in fact later] we got orders to move forward to occupy a position in front. We hadn't gone far, however, when the results of the morning's work began to show themselves. Wounded were being carried past us by the dozen, the lighter cases making their own way. While still in the trenches, the officers had been informing us of the progress of the bombardment, and we were eager to see for ourselves and to be in the thick of the advance."

Private (later Sergeant) George Ellis wrote of the shell that caused such heavy loss in the Dingwall Company at 2 P.M. on 10th March: "We moved through this trench in single file. Major Robertson was leading; Lieutenant Dewar was behind or alongside of him. I was among the first dozen files; my chum was behind me. How well I remember us joking about the features of the trench, and talking about how fine a place it would be to spend the night in. I rather think B Company was leading. After having gone a distance along this trench we emerged into an open part—built on one side only. The leading files were in the open. I had got in and my chum [the late Edward Watt, B.Sc., son of Mr D. M. Watt, editor of *The Ross-*

shire Journal] had just emerged when a shell burst right overhead. I hear the groan of the wounded yet. About seventeen of us went down. When I recovered I shouted to my chum, asking if he was badly hit, but got no answer. Looking round I got my answer. Stretchers were quickly got, wounds were temporarily bandaged, and all of us hit were out of it for the present."

Another account of 11th March reads: "About 7 A.M. we started for the trenches proper, and then began our worst experience. As soon as we started, the enemy got us with machine guns, and I had not gone 10 yards before the man in front of me went down, and as I stepped, or rather jumped, over him I was vaguely wondering why he was lying there. We had to proceed about 300 yards to take up our position. All the way was along a shoulder-high trench, and, about half way, there was a deep ditch to cross, and about 25 yards of open. We lost two men along this distance, and about 20 yards before I took up my position our Colonel was lying with a bullet through his leg, but not caring a bit, and cheering us with a kindly word as we passed along. We stayed in this place till 1.30 or 2 P.M. and were subjected to an awful rain of shells, bullets from machine guns, lyddite and shrapnel. Many of these burst within 10 yards of me, and all of us had most miraculous escapes. Very often the shells burst on top of the trench and sent down showers of hot earth and iron over us. I do not know how many we lost during this time, but saw personally eight carried away by our own brave stretcher-bearers. At last we were ordered to get over the top of this trench and into a ridge dug in the ground in front. This we did, and after a wait in a crouching position our Major Fraser stood up and ordered the advance. We at once rose, and leaping over the top raced at full pace for the advanced trench 200 yards in front. This run I shall remember for the rest of my life. I reached the trench in safety, and when I regained my breath looked round at the back of me, and the sight was heart-rending. There lay my chums wounded and dead lying about the field. It was awful. Our advance was successful, and we could see the Germans running through the wood in front and away from us for all they were worth. All this time our guns had been showering lyddite into them, and their losses, I afterwards heard, were many times greater than ours. They did most of the damage to our men by their machine guns. We lay in this trench until dusk, when we were relieved, and had the melancholy task of collecting the wounded and dead."

Speaking of the 11th another writer says: "We lay there till 2.15 P.M. When the advance was made our artillery had bombarded the enemy's lines for fifteen minutes, and blew them to bits. Even with the heavy bombardment the Germans managed to get maxims on us. I was lucky enough to get to our first trench before they started, and I lay on my back watching others pushing forward. What a maddening sight it was to see the men fall, some never to rise again. Men who went to help their comrades got shot themselves. Archie Strachan (Maryburgh) was killed going back to the open to help his chum."

Another writer says: "German reinforcements became engaged about 2 P.M., and it was at that stage most of our casualties occurred. We advanced, and suffered from maxim and shrapnel. I managed to get across all right, and got my head behind a roll of barbed wire—luck for me. You see the Gurkhas in front filled the trenches there, and safe cover was limited."

A private in D Company summed up the feelings of the Battalion thus: "Although our losses have been terrible we are not downhearted and never will be. We know that each life given so willingly and fearlessly means a step towards the overthrow of German militarism and oppression, and for the good of humanity in general."

One very notable thing in almost all the letters from the front is the anxiety to allay the fears that might be felt on account of the writers themselves. Nearly all pay a well-deserved tribute to the stretcher-bearers, whose work was magnificently carried out in the face of many dangers. One quotation will suffice. The writer was in F Company and was wounded by a shell about noon on 11th March: "I rolled over and over into a hole occupied by some of Captain Cameron's lads, where one of them dressed my wounds and passed the word along to F Company that I was down. Shortly after I noticed Roderick MacLennan, better known as 'Roddy Alness,' crawling towards me through a perfect hail of machine gun and shrapnel bullets. He came right up, relieved me of my equipment, took out my greatcoat, threw it over me, and placed the water-bottle at hand. Then he crawled to the other boys who were lying around and sang out their names to me. I particularly remember Duncan Jack and Wolfe. Then he called out that he would be back after dark to carry me away and crawled back to his place. Soon after dusk two others came out, Bob Ross and John Calder, who said that Roddy could not get away, and they helped me towards the rear across a trench being dug behind us, and into the village street of Neuve Chapelle, where a temporary dressing station had been, but it was shelled out by the time we reached it. I was laid on some boards in the gutter, and one of them hung around me for longer than I can distinctly recall. Later, up came Roddy, the Laird, Bob Ross, Jock Calder and two others with a stretcher, and I was carried back about a mile or so to a dressing station. You may be sure I have a very warm regard for them all."

At 4.45 P.M. on the 13th the Battalion marched to billets in the neighbourhood of Locon, where it settled down to re-organize and refit. On the 16th it was inspected by the Commander of the Meerut Division, Major-General Anderson. In a very complimentary address he said: "I am not surprised at you officers, non-commissioned officers and men coming out to fight, but what does surprise me is that you are fit in every way to do the work of a Regular battalion."

In his report on the battle Brigadier-General Jacob wrote: "The 4th Seaforths, a Territorial battalion, showed itself to be the equal of any Regular regiment. They worked with a will and with such regularity that it was a pleasure to see this Battalion advance to the attack with a confidence and self-reliance that left very little to be desired."

So ended the Battle of Neuve Chapelle, the Battalion's baptism of blood. They went into it trained up to the highest point that was possible, having passed through their baptism of fire with just so many casualties as had rendered them seasoned to the knowledge of what wounds and death might be, but almost as fresh as when they had landed in France. They came out, having had the punishment that falls to those who have to hold on without the comfort of knowing what effect the effort they make is having on the enemy; they had to put up with hunger, lack of sleep, the weary jostle against a stream of men coming down the trenches against them; cold, soaked through and tired out, they had had all the worst side of battle without once coming to grips with the enemy they sought. Their discipline had stood all tests, they were now fully trained, fully seasoned troops of that strangely detached organism, the British army.

SYNOPSIS OF EVENTS FROM THE BATTLE OF NEUVE CHAPELLE TO THE BATTLE OF AUBERS RIDGE

(*13th March to 27th May* 1915)

WHILE the Allies were concerting plans for a fresh offensive the Germans counter-attacked the Second Army, which had relieved three French divisions and was again covering Ypres as in 1914. Rumours of an impending gas attack passed unheeded or discredited. The capture of Hill 60 on the 17th-18th April and the German efforts towards its recapture were followed on the 22nd by the first gas attack on the French 45th Division, holding the line left of the British, which may be said to have opened the Second Battles of Ypres. The Germans had intended merely to test their new weapon; its success enabled them to make a very serious bid to break the Allied line between the British and Belgians. The battles spread over thirty-three days and nights and ended in mutual exhaustion.

Meanwhile preparations for the Allied offensive continued. The French main objective was to be the crest of the Vimy Ridge, supported by supplementary attacks on Bailleul and Point du Jour to the south, and on the ground north of Souchez, Loos and Hill 70 on the north. The British First Army was again to attack the Aubers Ridge and La Bassée, the main attack being launched by the I Corps and the Indian Corps from the front Festubert-Neuve Chapelle, and a secondary one by the IV Corps towards Fromelles-Aubers. The first objective was to be the line Rue du Marais-Lorgies-Ligny le Grand-la Cliqueterie Farm-Fromelles-Rouge Bancs. Breaches having been forced at points 600 yards apart, the advance would be convergent, and the force thus cut off would be dealt with by units from the inner flanks of the attacking corps. The second phase was to be an advance through Illies and Herlies across the La Bassée-Lille road to the line Bauvin-Don.

The success of the attack on Neuve Chapelle, as well as the shortage of ammunition, led to the employment of a bombardment for forty minutes only, the last ten being intense. The French, however, preferred a deliberate bombardment for four days, with a limited objective for the infantry attacks.

Meanwhile the Germans, taught by the bombardment at Neuve Chapelle, had doubled or trebled the thickness of their parapets, which were now all built with sandbags and large-mesh wire. They were furnished with dug-outs every few yards, and machine-gun emplacements, constructed at intervals of about 20 yards, were sited near the ground-level, so as to get a grazing fire. Their support trenches, 200 to 300 yards in rear, were ready for use as fire trenches, and the communication trenches were screened or blinded by roofing. The British troops had therefore a very much harder task than at

Neuve Chapelle, while the artillery, proportionately to the numbers engaged, was less.

At 5 A.M. the bombardment began. Difficulties at once became apparent, for it was no longer a winter landscape, but one of late spring; the trees were no longer bare, as in the beginning of March, but formed a screen, behind which it was difficult to locate the hostile guns or to observe the effect of our own fire. After half an hour the bombardment became intense, and at 5.40 A.M. lifted 600 yards to the line of La Quinque Rue.

When the infantry went to the assault they were met by a withering fire from machine guns, rifles and guns. The German breastworks and wire were only partially damaged. Wear and tear had told on the British guns, the result being that their fire was short and inaccurate. The 1st Division got as far as the edge of the wire, the Meerut Division only half way across.

A 6.15 A.M. a fresh bombardment was ordered, but the guns could not locate the machine-gun loopholes, and only a hit close to the emplacement could effect disablement. At 7 A.M. a further assault by both divisions failed. At 7.45 A.M. the artillery again bombarded the enemy's position, to which the Germans replied at 8.25 A.M. with a heavy artillery fire on our breastworks and the ground behind, causing many casualties in the second line of the Dehra Dun Brigade and of the Bareilly Brigade which was coming up. The attack of the Meerut Division ceased at 8.27 A.M.

Owing to the congestion in the Indian Corps trenches and to the heavy German fire the renewed attack had to be postponed from 2.40 to 4 P.M. The bombardment had been more successful this time; but, as at Neuve Chapelle, the Germans had had time to re-inforce. In spite of a small success by the 25th Brigade the attack failed all along the line, and by 3 A.M. the British were back in their old trenches.

After some rearrangements of the British front, intended to assist the French to press on with their attack on the Vimy Ridge, a fresh plan of attack was drawn up. The objective was more limited, being the line of La Quinque Rue, to reach which the German line was to be pierced in two places by the 2nd and 7th Divisions. The offensive was to open with a night attack by the 2nd Division, supported by a brigade of the Meerut Division on a front of 2000 yards between Chocolat Menier Corner and Richebourg l'Avoué. At daybreak the 7th Division was to join in immediately north of Festubert. The Meerut Division was to advance on the line of the Port Arthur-La Bassée road. A general bombardment was to assist the consolidation of the position on La Quinque Rue and prepare a further advance on the line Chapelle St-Roch-Violaines-Beau Puits. This was an adaptation to modern conditions of Grant's system of attrition.

A slow bombardment began on 13th May and two more 15-inch howitzers were brought into action. Rain made it difficult to observe the bursts of high explosive shells, and the assault was postponed till the night of the 15th-16th. As the 1/4th Seaforths were not actively engaged in the Battle of Festubert it is unnecessary to describe it in detail. Suffice it to say that by 27th May ground had been gained, German reserves had been drawn in, the French had been well supported and the offensive spirit well maintained; but it was clear that without a much larger supply of ammunition and means for effective close fighting only a partial success could be gained. Meanwhile there was always the danger of a return of German troops from the Russian front, with the consequence of depriving the Allies in the West of the power of taking the initiative.

AUBERS RIDGE

CHAPTER V

AUBERS RIDGE

THE Battle of Neuve Chapelle ended the period of Lieutenant-Colonel Mason-MacFarlane's command of the 1/4th Battalion The Seaforth Highlanders, and it is but fitting that a brief review of his splendid work should here be given. He came in 1913 from the 4th Battalion Berkshire Regiment, to take command of a Battalion which, with excellent material in officers and men, had little to distinguish it from other Territorial units drawn from widely scattered areas, very few of which had as yet realized the possibilities to which a Territorial battalion might attain. By the time war broke out he had already succeeded in paving the way for that rapid progress in war efficiency which resulted in the Battalion being the first unit of the famous 51st Division to go to France.

An enthusiast in all matters military, to which he had devoted his time for ten years, Lieutenant-Colonel Mason-MacFarlane had the advantage of a scientific training in the importance of detail, which enabled him to combine far-reaching ideals with a meticulous attention to those *minutiæ* of administration that are the bedrock of efficiency. Of Highland stock himself, he understood his "laddies," as he always called the men, and it is largely due to this understanding that, when his regular permanent staff were taken to train Lord Kitchener's New Army, their loss was of far less moment than anyone, a few months earlier, would have thought possible. He had the good fortune to command his Battalion in its first general action, and so to see the fruits of his labours in the splendid behaviour of officers and men. Fortunately his great capacity for training soldiers was available till the end of the Great War, and, as Officer Commanding the 3/4th (Reserve) Battalion The Seaforth Highlanders, he was still able to provide his successors in the field with men trained in the same school as the original Battalion. For his valuable services in command of the 1/4th Seaforths Lieutenant-Colonel Mason-MacFarlane was awarded the C.M.G., and for his subsequent services in command of the 3/4th Seaforths the C.B.E. Long may he live to enjoy the honour gained by his thoroughness and enthusiasm!

The week after the Battle of Neuve Chapelle was spent in route-marching and drill. A cross was made by Armourer-Sergeant John Ross (Dingwall) and set up on a small cairn of bricks and grass over the graves of those who had fallen. The Divisional and Corps Commanders inspected the Battalion on 15th and 17th March respectively. In one diary there is a pathetic entry that on the 18th No. 4 Company was disinfected with a new bug-killer that did not kill! The Battalion, like all others, was at this time much plagued by vermin. One lad, who was found to be in a lousy condition, had a tremendous crop of hair, so the Commanding Officer ordered it to be cut short. So thoroughly did the sergeant-major have this done that the lad looked as if he had been shaved!

On Sunday, 21st March, the Battalion paraded for church at 11 A.M., and the rest of the day was spent quietly in or around the billeting area.

On 22nd March the Battalion paraded for a route march, and in the afternoon again paraded to hear a congratulatory message from Seaforth, the Honorary Colonel of the Battalion, as well as a farewell order by Colonel Mason-MacFarlane, read by the Commanding Officer.

COPY OF SEAFORTH'S LETTER TO THE COMMANDING OFFICER

47 BERKELEY SQUARE, W.
19th March.

DEAR SIR,—I cannot find words sufficiently strong to express the great pride and admiration with which I have read of the magnificent bravery displayed by the 4th Seaforths in the recent fighting. I am indeed proud to be associated with such a gallant Regiment, which has so splendidly upheld the name of the Seaforth Highlanders; they are indeed worthy successors of those who have made the name of the Seaforths so well known throughout the army for courage and gallantry. I most deeply deplore the great losses the Regiment has sustained in killed and wounded, and trust the latter are doing well. I can assure you my thoughts are always with you and I follow your fortunes with the greatest interest. My wife joins with me in this letter, and in wishing you all good luck. Yours sincerely,

J. A. Stewart Mackenzie.

The Officer Commanding
4th Seaforth Highlanders.

Copy of Lieutenant-Colonel Mason-MacFarlane's Order

Lieutenant-Colonel D. M. MacFarlane wishes from his heart to tell every Officer, Non-commissioned Officer and Man in his Battalion how intensely proud he is of their magnificent work and splendid bravery during the fighting at Neuve Chapelle.

From what he himself saw before he was wounded, and from what he has heard from Major Cuthbert, he knows that no battalion of the Regular Army could have done better than the 4th Battalion Seaforth Highlanders. One cannot give higher praise than that to any men.

He had always had the most implicit confidence in his Officers, Non-commissioned Officers and Men, and this fight has proved that his belief was more than justified. He regrets extremely that as the result of his wounds caused by a rifle bullet and a piece of high explosive shell, he will be unable to be with the Battalion for some time, but he knows everyone will give Major Cuthbert the same loyal support that has always been accorded to him. He much hopes that he will very soon be with the Regiment again and, in the meantime, he knows that, under Major Cuthbert, all will go well.

The Commanding Officer feels deeply the loss of his brave Officers, Non-commissioned Officers and Men.

The death of each has been to him the loss of a friend.

18th March 1915.

On 23rd March a draft of 128 men arrived from Bedford. One of these, a Cockney, heard for the first time some of the Ross-shire men speaking Gaelic. "My goodness," he exclaimed, "ain't these blokes fairly picked up French!"

At 7 A.M. on 24th March the Brigade moved to Bout de Ville, near Croix Barbée, where the day was spent in an orchard in order to escape observation, moving on at 7 P.M. to billets in the neighbourhood of the Estaires-La Bassée road. The following day some shelling took place in the vicinity of Headquarters, but there were no casualties in the Battalion. Up till 27th March companies were busy in the construction of shelters, burying the dead and collecting equipment about Neuve Chapelle. The next day Captain Ferguson, with Second Lieutenants Macleod, Pender, Hulls and Cartwright, arrived just in time for the trenches, to which the Battalion moved at 8 P.M.

When the 4th relieved the 1st Seaforths in the line on 28th March, Nos. 1 and 2 Companies occupied the firing line, whilst Second Lieutenant L. D. Henderson, with fifty men, was detailed to hold an advanced post, known as the Duck's Bill, No. 3 and the remainder of No. 4 Company being in support. The Duck's Bill was in a very exposed situation, so that work on it could be carried on only under cover of darkness. This was unfortunate, for a great deal was required to make it either tenable or habitable. It had been the scene of very severe fighting on 10th and 11th March, and the dead, both British and German, lay thick around it. In the farm alone there were some six or seven dead Germans together with an old cow, not to mention a multitude of live cats. The atmosphere was almost unbearable, so it was decided to relieve the garrison every two days; while Second Lieutenant Henderson remained in permanent charge to ensure continuity in the work. The nights were, fortunately, frosty, and the breastwork was greatly improved, while hundreds of corpses were interred. Flies were everywhere a terrible scourge to the troops, but here they were in millions. They swarmed round the men's faces and hands, and covered any exposed food in the most disgusting way. The first night was quiet, and, under cover of a screen that lay out in the ditches in front, the trees in the orchard before the breastwork were used as posts for a wire entanglement. Not a shot was fired that night, for each side was too busy working. The detachment materially improved the post as regards strength, comfort and accessibility. Advanced posts are seldom satisfactory, but this one lasted as long as the line stood.

In the afternoon an unfortunate accident occurred. Corporal Moir happened to look into a box of bombs, of which there were two side by side. Noticing that one was smoking he called to those nearest to clear out. This they promptly did, but the bomb exploded, blowing up the box, exploding three other bombs, and slightly wounding two men. After this the bombs were always placed behind the parados.

On 29th March intense rifle and machine-gun fire broke out at about 10.30 P.M., which raked the shallow breastworks held by the Battalion. As it was believed to prelude an attack on the Duck's Bill, work was abandoned and the troops stood to arms. At midnight, however, things became quiet again, and work was continued. On the following morning the trench mortars of the 4th Seaforths were very busy and drew the enemy's artillery fire. The evening was quiet again until about 11.30, when an incendiary rocket fired the thatch of the ruined farm-house in the centre of the Duck's Bill. The fire burned merrily in rear of the breastworks, which made the position of the troops an unenviable one, as it was almost impossible, owing to the intense machine-gun and rifle fire, to show a head above the parapet, lest its silhouette should give the enemy a target. As the men holding the building belonged to the new draft, they were relieved by Sergeant Mackay and a party of seasoned men from F half-Company. A man in No. 1 Company saw this party running up and, thinking they were Germans, shot at them, shouting: "I've got one! I saw him fall!" This was his second error, for no one was hit then. Later on Private Macnab was killed by a sniper. One benefit unwittingly conferred by the Germans was the cremation of the old cow!

When the farm-house in the Duck's Bill took fire the thatched roof burned very quickly, and in a few minutes portions of the house were collapsing. The bomb store for the post—stocked with the old jam-tin bomb, which was never very certain in its behaviour—was immediately under one of the walls, and was a source of grave peril to the whole garrison. Lieutenant Mark Tennant, at great risk to himself, moved the bombs to a place of safety.

The fire had partially burned itself out and the enemy fire was dying down when Major Fraser came dashing through the subsiding flames, after a run partly up a very shallow trench and partly across the open. He remarked to Second Lieutenant Henderson as he arrived: "I came up not knowing what I should find!" What he actually found was the remains of a bottle of vintage port which had that day arrived from home, but which mostly had gone to the revival of the two officers of the post after their strenuous time.

At 9 P.M. on 31st March the Battalion, which had lost three men killed and some twelve wounded, was relieved by three companies of the Connaught Rangers and one company of the 3rd London Regiment. The Battalion rested during the next day, and at 4 P.M. marched *via* Vieille Chapelle and Pont Levis to billets in Croix Marmeuse. These were found to be so inadequate that the transport had to bivouac in their horse lines. The next two days were spent in drill and cleaning up, but on 3rd April No. 4 played a football match against the 1/9th Gurkhas which ended in a draw, three goals all. Church parade was held on the morning of the 4th in an orchard, and on the 6th there was a return match, which was won by the Gurkhas by two goals to one. Maclennan and "Davie" Ross specially distinguished themselves.

Nothing noteworthy happened until 11th April, when the senior officers after church parade went to reconnoitre 400 yards of the line to the right of Brewery Road in front of Neuve Chapelle. In the evening Nos. 1 and 2 Companies relieved companies of the 2nd and 5th Royal Sussex Regiment in the support trenches, and Nos. 3 and 4 relieved the Loyal North Lancashires in the Hills Redoubt. They marched *via* Zelobes, Vieille Chapelle and Pont de Ville to Pont Logy railhead. It was a tiresome march, for the roads were much blocked by traffic. During the 12th the companies were actively engaged in improving the trenches, while the enemy kept up a lively artillery fire, their aeroplanes hovering over our lines in observation.

About this date M. Lorgues, who had been attached to the 1st Garhwal Rifles, joined the 4th Seaforths as their interpreter, a post that he held for a long while. He was an M.A., had held a Fellowship, and was Professor in the Lycée at Marseilles. He was very popular in the Battalion, and gained the Royal Humane Society's Medal.

Life in the trenches at this time was very different from what it had been during the winter. The trenches were now dry enough to allow the men to live in dug-outs, some of which are reported as being "very comfortable." Rations came up ready cooked, the men only having to make their own tea, which, however, had usually to be drunk without milk. The men kept well and fit, and the weather was on the whole good. Everyone was cheerful, even if some of the letters published in *The Ross-shire Journal* betray a longing to see a real hill again.

On 13th April, Private Innes MacIntosh was killed by a bullet which came through a parapet that was badly in need of improvement, and the next day Captain Gilbert Fraser was grazed on the left temple by a bullet. It was a miraculous escape, for the bone was cut through. At one o'clock in the morning of the 16th Lieutenant Fitzroy was killed by a shot through the head. He was a splendid fellow and a fine officer—a great loss to the Battalion. The remainder of the time in the trenches passed quietly enough in improving them and making dug-outs. So many sandbags were used that a shortage occurred, and parties were sent out in rear, with a certain amount of success, to search for any the enemy had left behind. On the 21st a rifle grenade landed among the machine gunners, killing Private Donald Gray (Dingwall) of B Company [his brother was killed later on with the Battalion] and wounding four others, one of whom subsequently died.

The type of man in the ranks in those early days was not to be ruffled by trifles. A sergeant was one day walking along a trench when a trench-mortar bomb landed on the parapet just in front of a sentry, who was blown off the firing step and into the trench on his back by the force of the explosion. The sergeant picked him up, pushed him up on to the firing step, and replaced his cap and rifle—all without a word—while the sentry's only comment on the affair was: "A felt the heat o' yon!"

During the night of the 21st the enemy were exceptionally quiet, but our troops kept up a certain amount of harassing fire in order to interfere with his working parties. The village of Neuve Chapelle was all this time systematically shelled, and a large fire was caused, while the brewery daily changed shape under the effects of high explosive shell.

At 3.15 A.M. on the 22nd the Bareilly Brigade on the right began to harass the enemy, supported by field guns. The enemy became much alarmed, and a perfect blaze of Very lights was kept up over No-man's-land. The following days were uneventful, and rumours of all kinds began to circulate about the fighting round Ypres, not to speak of one, that forty-eight 15-inch howitzers had been concentrated near Neuve Chapelle! On the 26th the Lahore Division moved northwards to take part in the Second Battles of Ypres. A draft of twenty-five sick and wounded returned from the Base hospitals, together with eighty-one new men from Bedford.

On 27th April the Battalion was relieved by the 39th Garhwal Rifles. This fine regiment now consisted of only one battalion. The 4th Seaforths, leaving their machine-gun detachment in the trenches, marched to billets between the cross-roads at Les Huit Maisons and Vieille Chapelle. One of the wounded who had just rejoined says that the men looked fagged out as they marched into billets, for they had been sixteen days in the trenches and had suffered from monotonous diet and lack of regular sleep.

The weather had now greatly improved, so that when orders were received to move the following day, the exchange of billets was carried out in delightful conditions, and the end of April found the Battalion in their comfortable old quarters in Vieille Chapelle. The men thoroughly enjoyed the luxury of being able to wash again, and even to bathe in the ditches and streams, besides having hot baths in the brewery. While the men were disporting themselves, two to each tub of hot water, and amusing themselves by trying to send a surreptitious shower of cold water down some unsuspecting back, their clothes were being systematically baked, to the discomfiture of the unwelcome guests that had sought lodging—not to speak of board—therein.

The last day of the month brought the long-expected and most popular news that Major Cuthbert had been awarded the D.S.O. for his gallantry and splendid leadership, though twice wounded, at the Battle of Neuve Chapelle. He was the first infantry officer of the Territorial Force to receive the D.S.O. At the same time the D.C.M. was conferred on Sergeant J. Maclennan, D Company; Private A. Macleod, E Company; Private W. C. Minchin, C Company; and Private A. Thomson, D Company. The first issue of Balmoral bonnets with khaki covers was made on this day also, much to the improvement of the appearance of the Battalion. In letters written home at this time one comes across requests for condensed milk, dried fruits, soups and any form of tinned meats—except bully beef!

One of the men, who had become anxious to relieve the monotony of trench life, determined to put in for the next job that offered behind the lines. He had not to wait long; for soon it was announced that engineers were wanted for special employment well behind the lines. Our friend at once put in for it—and got it. His disgust can be imagined when it turned out that the engineering work was the making of light bridges which subsequently had to be taken out by the makers and built over the streams and ditches in No-man's-land!

One would have supposed that this would have cured his optimistic views about "cushie jobs." Not a bit. A tailor being wanted in his company, this man applied for the post, for he thought that an "employed man" would have the best of it during a rest period. Unfortunately, as the khaki covers had to be sewn on to the Balmoral bonnets, the new tailor had to spend all his rest period cross-legged among the bonnets, while his unemployed comrades enjoyed themselves. That was the last application he made.

A raw sentry was asked by the Orderly Officer what steps he would take if he saw the enemy coming. "Long ones that way, sir," came the reply, pointing along the communication trench. On one occasion some men were billeted in a loft above a baker's shop. They found a trap door through which they could see the loaves spread out on tables below. A fixed bayonet was found to be just the right length to spear a loaf, but it was long before the baker discovered the fact!

A heavy German bombardment, with which the 1st of May opened, seemed to herald an eventful day. The Battalion stood to arms fully expecting a general attack. But at 9 A.M., no attack having developed, orders were received to "stand easy." In the afternoon the senior officers reconnoitred the sector Orchard-La Bassée road. About 8 P.M. G Company billets took fire. The barn was lost from the beginning, but energetic efforts by the Battalion, assisted by parties from the Gunners (both Field and Marine), the 2nd Black Watch, and 2/2 Gurkhas, saved the main building and some of the out-houses. The Gurkhas particularly distinguished themselves. One officer who redeemed an imprisoned pig had the mortification of seeing the animal rush headlong into the blazing barn. He then removed some fowls from the perch on which they were sitting, with the roof burning over their heads, only to see one of them follow the pig.

Heavy artillery fire was heard to the north in the evening of 2nd May, but otherwise nothing unusual occurred till the 5th, when, much to everyone's delight, Brigadier-General Walter C. Ross of Cromarty, who had commanded its old brigade at Bedford, visited the Battalion. About this time also Major J. W. Fraser of Leckmelm and Captain D. A. Mackenzie left the Battalion to take up Staff appointments at Calais, the first as D.A.Q.M.G., the second as A.M.L.O. Major Fraser was one of the most respected officers in the Battalion. A retired Major of the Cheshire Regiment, and fifty-two years of age, he had offered to join as a subaltern when war broke out, but was at once posted to command E Company, which, having no officers, was mobilized and brought to Dingwall by that other stout-hearted veteran, Colour-Sergeant John Chisholm (Opinan). Major Fraser was a great disciplinarian, and had as much horror of effeminacy as the famous Sir Ewen Cameron, the "Gentle Lochiel" of Montrose's wars. "We were more concerned," says one diarist, "about the Major coming along the trench than about the Germans across the way. Periscopes were used to watch for him, and 'Look out, boys, the Major's coming,' was the quickest message that went along the line." On one occasion he came across a sentry on duty—"What have you in your right hand ?" said the Major. "My rifle, sir." "And what have you in your left hand?" The man was nonplussed, because in his left hand, which he had behind his back, was a biscuit. The long pause was making things awkward, but the Major himself saved the situation by answering his own question: "The lives of all your comrades." Major Fraser was awarded the C.M.G. for his services with the Battalion, and later on was further awarded the O.B.E. for his Staff work.

No. 1 Company and half of No. 2 moved up to a position on the Rue du Bois to the left of the 6th Jats, who were in the orchard. The 6th and 7th May were signalized by heavy artillery fire, and an impending offensive by the British and French began to be talked about. On the 7th the Adjutant explained the mode of attack in which the Battalion was to co-operate, and in the evening Brigadier-General Jacob explained to the officers the plan of operations.

The Dehra Dun Brigade was to lead the attack and carry the German lines till the farther side of the wood was reached and a junction with the IV Corps effected. From right to left in the front line were to be the 2/2nd Gurkhas, 4th Seaforths and 1st Seaforths, with the 6th Jats and 1/9th Gurkhas in support. The Bareilly Brigade was to form the second line, while the Garhwal Brigade was to be in divisional reserve, less two battalions detailed for special duty. Two men were hit this day, one of whom, Lance-Corporal Shaw, died of his wounds.

On 8th May the whole Battalion moved into the line at 11 P.M., Nos. 1, 2 and 3 Companies in the front line, and

No. 4, with reserve ammunition and tools, in support. The night was cold, and, owing to the work in hand and the preparations for the morrow, very little rest could be had.

Shortly before dawn on 9th May the preliminary bombardment of the enemy's position commenced and was vigorously replied to. Shells of all calibres fell in the trenches, and the signal shelter in the front line was blown in, causing many casualties. "It was a brilliant May morning," says one of the men, "with the sun shining and a cloudless blue sky, and I could not help noticing a lark rising out of No-man's-land, singing merrily. Up and up he went, as if he were intent on getting out of the way of the hell that was about to be let loose." Those sitting in the trenches could plainly see the shells flying over.

For reasons already explained in the preceding synopsis the British artillery fire was by no means accurate, a number of shells falling short, and sometimes bursting over our own trenches. The sun soon became obscured by thick clouds of smoke. The First Aid Post was set on fire, several of its personnel being hit, and the wounded men had to be hurriedly removed down a communication trench.

At 5.20 A.M. the bombardment lifted from the German wire to his parapet and at 5.30 A.M. to his support line. No. 1 Company, wearing gas masks, went over the top. The enemy, little disturbed by our artillery, opened a terrific fire from machine guns sited so as to produce grazing fire from every angle, while the infantry stood up to fire, showing themselves waist-high above the parapets. What followed is best told by some of the survivors—here is one narrative[1]: "Of course in the row it was impossible to hear orders shouted from traverse to traverse, so one of our men dashed round. A lyddite shell choked the air with yellow fumes; that was the end of him. Another went round. 'C Company advance: pass it on,' he yelled. C got up, scrambled, with the aid of many hands, from the trenches and flung themselves over the parapet. Immediately an absolute hail of bullets met them, even before they were through our own entanglements, and the hostile shelling was terrific. A short space—'G to advance,' comes the shout. Up we get: machine guns sweep the parapet up and down, backwards and forwards, and many fall back into the trench mortally wounded. Once on the level

[1] Letter from a member of the Battalion, published in *The Morning Post*.

again, down we go flat. The number of dead and wounded lying about is awful, and the shells!

"Inch by inch, foot by foot, yard by yard, we work ourselves forward, through grass in many places even then soaking with blood. No talk or thought of revenge now—everything, anything, for an inch of cover. Thank God! a small ditch—not that, a slight depression, scarcely four inches below the surrounding level, but Cover! Cover! Cover!

"The place is an inferno—a red hell—and oh! those frightful lyddites; blow the place to bits, and rip, and slash, and tear to pieces those puny things lying in the grass—so still.

"Our officer is badly wounded; incapable of doing anything. Our sergeant is somewhere about the middle of a shell—and only two fingers blown off. He gets up and sprints for the parapet, but goes down before he gets there—dead. 'Where are C?' The general opinion is that they are annihilated. The sergeant of the other platoon crawls painfully up. 'There's no one left,' he says tersely. The question about C troubles him too. He crawls up a few yards and somebody screams, but in the din it is impossible to say who it is. Two of us that remain crawl up and drag him by his hands back into the depression. A shell has broken one leg in three pieces above the knee, made two holes through both legs, and torn about five inches of flesh from the other right away—horrible! We do what we can for him—bind up his wounds, put a tight bandage round the top of his leg over the artery to stop the blood, improvise two splints out of a broken rifle and an entrenching tool handle, and pull him into the depression. Farther along, our lance-corporal is lying in a slight cavity. 'Jimmy,' says someone, 'where are we?' No movement. 'I say, Jimmy!' 'Give him a shake, he must be—oh heavens! Look at the ground!' It is saturated with blood. Dead: shot through the head!

"There are some seven dead just in front and five dead in our entanglements just behind. By this time several have their bayonets off and are digging feverishly in the damp ground. Clod after clod, bit by bit. No thought now of dirt or wet; nothing but cover: every inch is of the utmost importance. 'What's going to happen now?' is in everybody's mind. 'It's no use five or six advancing to reinforce some corpses twenty or thirty yards in front. What's to be done?'

"And now, the bravest thing I saw. Suddenly one of the wounded, ten yards or so in front, is seen to be burning and the cartridges in his pouches going off: bang! bang! Without a moment's hesitation the only non-commissioned officer left jumps up, runs to him, takes out his own jack-knife and starts cutting away his jacket and equipment under a deadly rifle fire, and then feels his heart—dead. Fortunately our corporal escaped without injury, but what an escape and what an act!

"Some time in the afternoon word passed from our trenches, shouted from man to man, and where there were no men, brought out by someone crawling on his stomach, that those who could were to retire and get back over our parapet one by one. After digging ourselves in some six inches we occupied our time by bandaging up the wounded and pulling them into places of safety. One by one we crawled painfully up, slung our packs and rifles over, and, with a spring, flung ourselves over the parapet. We were relieved about two hours after by an Indian regiment."

One man who went "over the top" at Aubers Ridge managed to get cover by lying on his back in a very shallow hole. Having made up his mind that he would never escape the bullets that were flying all around him, he got out a pad of notepaper and wrote a farewell letter to his "young lady." Having written it he sealed it and addressed it, and then—went to sleep! He awoke to find men digging a hole through the parapet, so he lent a hand and got back. Before he took cover his glengarry was shot away, and a bullet went through the magazine of his rifle.

Another of the men writes as follows: "Over we tumbled, heart beating six times the normal, and doubled forward. I'd been carrying messages round the traverses, and got back into my trench just in time to see the last man leaping over. I followed, and was one of the last to leave the trenches. One got a dim, hazy vision of the leading platoon doubling forward, and of seeing them simply fade away under the terrific machine-gun and rifle fire which opened on us as soon as we got over. Just in front of our trench was a line of pollard willows running along an extremely shallow depression in the ground. Into this we, seeing the fate of the platoon in front, tumbled hastily, and lay as flat as we could squeeze to the ground. It was only then that we realized the full intensity of the fire poured in on us. As we lay panting, the bullets whizzed overhead, buzzing like a swarm of angry wasps or hitting the trees just about a foot from the ground, or against the sandbags of the parapet with a savage whack, as if angry at not having found a human billet. This went on for what seemed an eternity, but must really have been only a few minutes, when our guns took up the game again and poured their fire on the German trenches. All this took place before six in the morning, and we lay out in the open, a little group of living, surrounded by the huddled bodies of the dead and by the groaning wounded we'd dragged into the shelter of the trees, till one in the afternoon. It was a truly awful experience and one that we don't want repeated."

Another man gives a somewhat different account. He says that half companies of Nos. 1 and 2 went over at 5.30 A.M., but that the other halves did not go till after the second bombardment, which he places at 6.30 to 7 A.M. It is true that after that bombardment the 1st Battalion made another charge, with no better success than before, but Major Cuthbert resolutely refused to allow his left half Battalion to leave the trenches.

"It was really due to Cuthbert's 'unorthodox' ideas," says another who took part in this battle, "that the left half Battalion suffered hardly a casualty; the 1st Seaforths, for instance, sent all their lines over one after the other. They actually reached the enemy's trenches, but they lost terribly, having, I think, less than four hundred men left out of about a thousand."

Failure though it was, the attack had been most gallantly made. It had succeeded in getting about half way across No-man's-land by a series of short rushes, but was held up before the German wire, which had been very imperfectly cut by the guns. The loss, however, had been frightfully heavy; and when that gallant officer, Lieutenant Charles Tennant, headed the final rush, only a handful of men followed him. Their fate was never known, for not a single survivor ever returned. It was an heroic effort. Some of those in the succeeding line thought they could distinguish Lieutenant Tennant's body lying over the wire, but nothing is certain.

A man who was wounded in the advance and had lost a finger tells how he noticed Lance-Corporal Cameron Ross, Privates D. Gair and Pratt sheltering in a shell hole barely large enough to hold them. At great risk they brought him into it, bound up his hand and took off his equipment. Gair then, exposing himself to the bullets, examined the man's chest and found a nasty wound. This they bound up with their own field dressings. Later on the wounded man managed to make a dash for the trench, and succeeded in getting in, after which he lost consciousness. Sergeant Dan Menzies, No. 2 Company, though both his legs were broken, set a splendid example to those in the trenches by coolly smoking cigarettes while he lay out in No-man's-land.

The men were longing for a counter-attack, so that they might have a chance to "get their own back," as one of them puts it. Meanwhile they set about tunnelling through the parapet, so that those in front might have a chance of crawling back to safety.

Almost as soon as it came into action one of the machine guns was knocked out by a shot through the breech casing, while Second Lieutenant Hope's periscope was smashed in his hands. The machine gunners were much hampered by telephone wires, which formed a network, both on the ground and also about six feet above it. The wires were very slack and sagged everywhere, and were cut not only by the German shrapnel but also by the slung rifles of the men.

The Dehra Dun Brigade had suffered too heavily to allow of its being sent to the assault again, and the Bareilly Brigade was ordered to relieve it so as to renew the attack at 2 P.M. The communication trenches were by now in a terrible state; here blocked by shattered parapets, there choked by dead and wounded men; everywhere their direction posts shot away and their very aspect barely recognizable. The Bareilly Brigade was, in consequence, unable to get up in time, and the assault had to be postponed till 4 P.M. The 58th Rifles began to dribble in to relieve the 4th Seaforths about 11 A.M., but the Battalion was not clear of the trenches till 4 o'clock, for it was as hard to get out as to get in.

As soon as it was known that the Battalion was to be relieved, those in the trenches did all they could to get in the men in No-man's-land. A good many were got in through the aforementioned tunnel, but a very large number had to remain till dark. Second Lieutenant Hope and Private Still went out to bring in Private Noble of No. 2 Company. Hope was standing over Noble when a bullet struck his revolver after piercing his left sleeve in three places. It exploded the cartridge in the chamber, the bullet going through his coat pocket. Noble was too badly wounded to be brought in then, so he was bandaged and left in a shell hole with a water-bottle. He eventually died of wounds.

No. 1290, Private H. Macdonald, worked for twenty-four

hours on end bringing in wounded and dying, and once when a poor fellow was buried by an exploding shell Macdonald tore away the earth with his great hands quicker than it could have been done with a spade, until the man was released. Poor Macdonald was killed later on in the war. His skull was fractured in three places, and where most men would have died on the spot he lived on for hours. In the casualty clearing station someone offered him water. He brushed it aside, saying: "No water for me. Bring me beer." A gallant soldier and a splendid man.

The state of the trenches is thus described by a member of No. 4 Company: "In many places the trench was filled in level with the surrounding ground, and to crawl across was a risky business in face of the swarm of bullets flying over. Numbers of dead and wounded were lying in the trench, and many of the wounded were creeping and crawling about in the mud and debris. Stretcher-bearers with their heavy burdens were trying to force their way through and the Gurkhas were going the opposite way, trying to get to the front line. Many of these poor wounded men crawling about unattended and unable to get away from the shambles must have been buried beneath falling parapets."

At the Rue du Bois there was a gap in the trench line where the road ran through, and here the shelling was particularly bad. Indeed the retiring Battalion was shelled the whole way down the trench through the fields, but, although it was only waist-high, conditions were easier than on the other side of the road. Here the 2nd Leicesters were met moving up in diamond formation, as if on parade.

An hour or so before being relieved Sergeant Hugh Ross (Dingwall) sent down one of the machine gunners in advance. This man, Salmon, is described as "a great fellow, but liable to fall behind when loaded with ammunition." Arriving at the reserve trenches, where they were to billet for the night, the sergeant called the roll and found that Salmon was missing. About midnight he heard a noise and shouted the challenge: "Who goes there?" Back came the answer: "It's me, Salmon." "Salmon be damned," said the sergeant; "you ought to be in a tin!"

On first being relieved the Battalion had moved to a redoubt behind the Rue du Bois, in support; but later in the evening it moved to billets near Riez Bailleul. Here, on the morning of 10th May, there was a muster parade. It is said that only five of No. 1 Company answered their names, and that No. 2 was in almost as bad a case. Men, however, had been straggling in all night, and even as the rolls were being called two reported their arrival. Many had been out in that bullet-swept zone from 5.30 A.M. till 10 P.M. Casualties were very heavy. Lieutenants C. G. Tennant, A. T. Railton and Second Lieutenant S. Bastian, with sixty-two other ranks, were killed; Lieutenant Colin M. Cameron, Second Lieutenants J. Watt, R. R. M. MacDonald, I. M. Pender and P. C. Knight, and one hundred and twenty-seven other ranks wounded; and nineteen other ranks missing, all of whom, like Tennant, were certainly killed.

In this battle Sergeant Alick Mackenzie won the D.C.M. for most conspicuous bravery. Although under terrific rifle and machine-gun fire, five times he went over the open and brought in wounded men who were lying in exposed positions.

Thus ended the Battle of the Aubers Ridge, the most terrible ordeal that the Battalion had yet gone through. That the losses were not far heavier is undoubtedly due to Major Cuthbert's courage in acting on his own initiative when an impossible situation arose—a responsibility which few commanding officers would have ventured to take upon themselves. On the 11th the Dehra Dun Brigade marched to Vieille Chapelle, where Second Lieutenant Harris joined with a draft of twenty-seven returned from the Base fit for service again.

One diary has an entry dated 12th May that is not without humour: "Woken up at 1.30 A.M. by the others complaining loudly of cold feet. Henderson shook with laughter for a quarter of an hour before he could stop. I can't think why!"

Brigadier-General Jacob visited the Battalion for a few minutes on the 15th and complimented them on their behaviour in action, but little of interest occurred till the opening of the Battle of Festubert. There was an alarm on the morning of Sunday, 16th May, when the Garhwal Brigade renewed the attack, which, like that on the 9th, was a failure. The Indian Corps continued to attack in conjunction with the 1st Corps till the 22nd; but the Dehra Dun Brigade remained in reserve and was not again actively engaged.

On the 18th the Battalion went into a very poor trench near the Rue des Puits, between Rouge Croix and Croix Barbée. It was a cold, rainy night, and things were not bettered by the noise of a heavy battery firing all night only a short distance in rear. On the 21st the Battalion was once more in Vieille Chapelle.

On the 23rd the 4th Seaforths went up by Queen Mary's Road, the Rue des Berceaux, Windy Corner and Edward Road to a recently captured portion of the German line known as the Glory Hole, No. 4 Company holding the front line, Nos. 1 and 2 in support in the old British line, and No. 3 in reserve in the Rue du Bois. No. 4 Company's part of the line was a listening-post in a sector of the old German trench which was later known as the "Boar's Head." It was extremely unpleasant on account of the numbers of dead lying about. A lot of work was done in the way of strengthening parapets and deepening communications. A few men were wounded by shrapnel on the way up, including Lance-Corporal Allison and Private P. Fraser. The front line was separated from the Germans on the left only by a double barricade, and was quite unsupported on the right. About 4.30 A.M. on the 24th Private C. Sutherland, No. 4 Company, was hit on the head by a bullet and taken down to the First Aid Post. In the evening Lieutenant Daman was shot by a sniper whilst visiting the front line. He was one of the best officers in the Battalion and a very fine fellow. Between 9 and 10 P.M. a piece of shell casing broke the leg of Private Veryard, No. 4 Company.

There were two alarms of gas on the night of 24-25th May. A pillar of black smoke rose to a height of about ten feet above the enemy trenches and then spread over the ground, but the breeze carried it clear of the British line.

On 26th May the Battalion was relieved by the 1st Seaforths and retired to trenches round Windy Corner.

SYNOPSIS OF EVENTS FROM THE BATTLE OF THE AUBERS RIDGE TO THE BATTLE OF LOOS

(*27th May to 13th October* 1915)

BEYOND the normal combats for minor objectives incidental to trench warfare there was no change on the Western front till September 1915.

On the Eastern front the Germans gained success after success, against which the Allies could set only the steady advance up the Euphrates, the occupation of South West Africa, the landing at Suvla, and some slight progress by the Italians in the battles on the Isonzo.

New corps, numbered VI, VII, X, XI and XII, were formed in France, while the arrival of the 2nd Canadian Division completed the Canadian Corps. The VII and X Corps were formed into the Third Army under General Sir C. C. Monro.

The second action at Givenchy was an attempt to support the renewed attack of the Second and Tenth French Armies. The IV Corps carried out the principal attack on 15th June at 6 P.M., after forty-eight hours' slow and twelve hours' heavy bombardment. The ground won could not be held and the troops withdrew. A similar attack on the 16th met with even less success. On 2nd July the Second Army lost the Château of Hooge, a minor affair; while on the 16th the German first line at Bellewaarde was captured. Actions were fought at this point with varying fortune on the 19th, 22nd and 30th, but the British losses were retrieved by an excellently arranged affair on 9th August. The French were similarly occupied.

General Joffre now proposed a general offensive designed to cut the communications of the 300,000 German troops in the Noyon salient and to surround at least a part of their armies. The main attack was to be directed against the more vulnerable flank from the Artois plateau. It was to commence with the capture of the Vimy Ridge and drive eastward across the plain of Douai, while a second attack was to be pressed northward from Champagne along the eastern border of the plain. The final objective was to be the line Mons-Namur. If successful, it was hoped to drive the enemy beyond the Meuse.

The Third Army relieved French troops on a twenty-five-mile front south of Arras, between Chaulmes and Hébuterne.

Meanwhile the Germans were strengthening their defences, and formed a second line on the reverse slopes, defended by wire too thick to be cut by ordinary wire-cutters.

Sir John French did not like this plan; but the collapse of the Italian offensive in June and August, the stalemate in Gallipoli, and the rapid advance of the Germans in Poland made an immediate general offensive in the West imperative, and he agreed under protest.

The attack was to be preceded by four days' deliberate bombardment. The Tenth French and First British Armies were to advance from the twenty-mile front between Arras and the La Bassée Canal, towards the line Tournai - Valenciennes - Le Quesnoy. The eastern attack was to be made on a twenty-two-mile front, with its right on Ville-sur-Tourbe, having as objective the line Sedan-Le Nouvion. Subsidiary attacks were to be made by all other forces and the cavalry was to be ready to follow up a break-through.

The First Army was to attack on 25th September under cover of a smoke screen, preceded by a discharge of gas. The IV Corps was to be on the right, the I Corps in the centre, and the Indian Corps on the left.

In spite of the long bombardment the German casualties were not very serious, and a lot of wire was left uncut. To make things worse, a change of wind interfered seriously with the gas attack. On the right it was effective and terrified the enemy, but on the left it either drifted slowly along No-man's-land or was driven back into the British trenches.

The 47th Division made a very successful advance, reaching all its objectives by 9.30 A.M. The 15th, in spite of serious losses, captured Loos and the western slopes of Hill 70. The 1st suffered from our own gas, and experienced severe losses, but succeeded in gaining ground as far as the Lens-La Bassée road. The 9th captured the Hohenzollern Redoubt, Fosse 8 and the Dump. The 2nd had a disastrous day, and had to withdraw to its original position.

The Meerut Division attacked at 6 A.M. It suffered severely from our own gas, and the Garhwal Brigade was held up in great part by uncut wire. The Bareilly Brigade stormed the German first-line trench, and pressed on into the second-line, but was unable to secure the Moulin du Piètre. Congested trenches prevented the Dehra Dun Brigade from getting up in time to support the attack, with the result that a German counter-attack round the flanks of the Bareilly Brigade compelled it to fall back to its original trenches.

The 8th Division succeeded in straightening out its line; but there were no gains in the second attack on Bellewaarde by the Second Army.

The Second and Fourth French Armies captured the German first position, while the Tenth carried most of the first-line trenches, but failed to carry the Vimy Ridge.

On the 26th the Germans recovered the Quarries and Fosse 8. The raw 21st and 24th Divisions of the XI Corps, which had been in General Reserve, failed in their attacks. Not only were they new troops, but they had had a terribly fatiguing march on the previous day, while the orders they got were confused and misleading. They were relieved by the Guards Division.

On the 28th the French left was extended to Loos. Both on that day and the next, attacks by the Guards Division had little result.

On 3rd October the Germans retook the Hohenzollern Redoubt,

but on the 8th they were repulsed by the French at Loos and Hill 70, and by the Guards at Quarry Trench and Big Willie. Our own attack on Fosse 8 failed.

On 13th October renewed attacks were made by the British. Gas and smoke were successfully launched, but the German wire was but little damaged. The attacks on the new German trench on the Lens-La Bassée road, the Quarries and Fosse 8 were failures, though there were slight gains at Gun Trench and the Hohenzollern Redoubt.

The Battle of Loos was a disappointment, owing chiefly to the failure of the gas attack and the delay on the part of General Headquarters to push up the XI Corps in time to consolidate the gains on our right and centre.

LOOS

CHAPTER VI

LOOS

THERE was little incident during the summer of 1915. The Indian Corps continued to hold the same sectors of the line north and south of Neuve Chapelle, and it was not until late in September that it was involved again in active operations. Units went into the line for four days, came back into reserve for another four, and again returned for four days in the trenches. To be in the line meant a daily routine of sentry duty, water, ration and ammunition fatigues, night patrols and work on the barbed wire. The twenty-four hours were divided into the watches of day and night by "stand to" at the danger periods of dusk and dawn. Being in reserve meant, according to one of the Battalion pessimists, scraping the mud off one's body by day and acting as a pack mule to the Division by night.

To get some idea of what life was like at this time take an extract from the diary of an officer of the Battalion, dated 31st May 1915: "Another nice, warm day, with a little less cloud than yesterday. Fairly quiet in the morning. About 1 A.M. and again about 3 A.M. our guns began a bombardment, why, the Lord only knows. Anyway neither lasted any time, and the enemy's guns actively replied. During the forenoon about a dozen big shells fell into Richebourg St-Vaast from the left front. Two men in the 1st Battalion were hit by shrapnel, one being killed. All, or the great majority, of the enemy's shells above the ordinary field-gun size come evidently from behind the Bois du Biez. Thus they get a somewhat nasty oblique and enfilade fire on our support and front lines.

"About 5 P.M. Quartermaster-Sergeant Cumming (No. 4, Invergordon) was standing near a Gurkha who was playing with the nose of a shell which had the detonator attached. Suddenly the detonator went off; the Gurkha lost two fingers, while Cumming got two or three little punctures in his knee. He did not go to hospital.

"Just after 6 P.M. three shells, about four-inch probably, fell round Windy Corner; the first was just short of the estaminet we occupied originally, the second fell clear of the orchard round our house, and the third fell in the back yard of that house. One or two men got bits of earth, etc., on their bodies, but no one was hurt, though the fright was not a pleasant one.

"Mackinnon and I, who were inside the house, promptly cleared out and went along to the redoubt, where Henderson and Forsyth joined us later on. At 6.55 P.M. another group of 'crumps' came along; these fell short of the Corner.

"We all then walked up to Headquarters *via* Windy Corner, and Forsyth went into the house to get his coat, when another four came on top of us! Duncan was running down at the time, and he had just time to hide round the estaminet. Mackinnon ran for the house, I for a ditch—fortunately dry—and Henderson spread himself over the road.[1]

"The shells burst all round the cross-roads and the narrowest shave was Mackinnon's. Nobody, however, was hurt, and we all promptly cleared out. We had barely reached Headquarters when another three came over. One man in H Company, Ivy Munro, was slightly wounded in the neck, but no other damage was done.

"No. 4 left the redoubt at 9.10 P.M., No. 16 Platoon leading with short intervals, and went along to the next corner at Albert Road, and into some dug-outs in the orchard, where our Headquarters were on 22nd February.

"About 11 P.M., or later, the enemy's guns began a bombardment of our trenches just as the relief was going up. The Connaughts were all but caught in the communication trench. They had, by a miracle, no casualties at all."

[1] All these officers are still alive and well at the time of writing.

Carrying parties had their troubles to contend with. On one occasion, for instance, an officer and sixty men left at 8.45 P.M. with hurdles and other material. First there was some mistake as to their destination, and they lost half-an-hour by going to St-Vaast Post instead of Cour St-Vaast. Headquarters of the 6th Jats was reached at 11.5 P.M., where two guides were allotted to them. They made good progress as far as the communication trench, where Sergeant Robertson was sent down to see that all was correct. The trench was narrow, wire was hanging and lying all about, and the hurdles were hard to carry. The party then turned to the left into the old German line, and after a short distance turned again up a fine new communication trench into the new British front line. It was 11.45 P.M. by now. It was then found that touch had been lost, and it was half an hour ere the rest of the party came up. What had happened was this—when the line broke, the man that led the second lot went on past the entry of the communication trench. The last man of the leading party looked back and shouted "About turn" just as some Indians came round a traverse. The leading man gave the alarm, thinking they were Germans, and the men quite naturally gave back in order to get room to unsling their arms. Then there came an alarm of gas, the author of which was never traced, and the whole party ran back to the next line, where they re-formed. This all meant another half-hour wasted before Sergeant J. J. Sutherland, who had gone down to find them and met them on their way up again, could report all present. Hurdles, sandbags and other material were then piled up, and the party got back at about 1.30 A.M.

The 4th Seaforths remained at Windy Corner supplying working parties until 2nd June, when they relieved the 6th Jats in trenches in front of Albert Road. There had been a few casualties from shell fire. Nos. 1, 2 and 3 Companies were in the firing line and No. 4 in reserve. Visibility was perfect and enemy aeroplanes consequently active; there was a lot of firing, and one shell wounded seven men in No. 3 Company.

About this time Major Cuthbert was promoted Lieutenant-Colonel. One of the men says: "All ranks were pleased that he took up his new rôle with the Battalion. All know that Colonel Cuthbert would do anything for the very least of his men, and all the men would do anything for Colonel Cuthbert."

On 6th June the 4th was relieved by the 1st Battalion,

moving to dug-outs near Cour St-Vaast, whence they supplied working parties till the 8th. They were then relieved by the 3rd London Regiment of the Garhwal Brigade, and moved into billets between Pont Levis and Zélobes. On the 10th, Brigadier-General Jacob spoke to the officers and senior non-commissioned officers, congratulating them on their work, and telling them that for some time to come there would be hard work and plenty of it. On the 11th the Battalion was inspected by the Corps Commander; afterwards F and H Companies had a swimming race in the canal; a man of H Company won, Richford and Bessent of F Company being second and third. On the same day the 1st beat the 4th Battalion at football by four goals to one. This was followed by exhibition rounds of boxing; then came tea, provided by the 1st Battalion for their comrades of the 4th and of the 1/5th, who had by now arrived with the 51st Division; and the day ended with an open-air concert. Till the 16th the time was spent in refitting, providing hot baths for the men, and instruction in the use of grenades.

A senior officer who had fought in other wars, but had little of the lore taught to the young at Woolwich and Sandhurst, was deputed by the Commanding Officer to lecture to the junior officers on the intricacies of topography. Having ascertained the meaning of this unusual word, he at once pounced on his subaltern, who was learned in the subject, and carried him off after lunch to an orchard behind the billet. Here the Commanding Officer found them seated under a tree, and asked what they were doing. Without a moment's hesitation came the reply: "I have a very keen subaltern here who is most interested in topography, so I brought him out here to give him a little extra tuition."

On the evening of 16th June the Battalion relieved the 2nd Black Watch about Chocolat Menier Corner and trenches in front of Dead Cow Post, carrying up their water supply in petrol tins. In this position the enemy line was some distance away; there was, therefore, little rifle or machine-gun fire, but there was sometimes very heavy shelling both of the front-line and communication trenches, fortunately causing very few casualties. These were old German trenches, provided with dug-outs, which were well furnished with chairs and tables, while the walls of some were even papered—a luxury hitherto unknown in British trenches.

On 22nd June the Battalion suffered a severe loss by the

death of Captain and Adjutant Sir John Fowler, who was instantaneously killed by a shell which burst in the Headquarters shelter. He had come to the Battalion before the war, and had seen it grow to its manhood as a fighting unit under his care. He had, from the beginning of the war, unsparingly devoted many hours to making copies of the casualty lists, which were forwarded for publication to Mr Watt, the editor of *The Ross-shire Journal*. By this means the people of Ross and elsewhere were early (and privately) informed of any casualty to their relatives, instead of having to endure the suspense of long silence until the official lists were published. A very short time after his death a General Army Order forbade the continuance of such unofficial lists.

Sir John's death was a heavy loss, not only to the Battalion he loved so well, but to the British army, for he would undoubtedly have risen high in his profession had he lived. He was buried with full military honours at Inverbroom, Ross-shire, on 29th June 1915.

On 23rd June the 1st Seaforths relieved the 4th, who moved back to dug-outs on King's Road. Trench warfare had a demoralizing effect on the troops. The monotony of the trenches, the sameness of the diet, lack of exercise and hours of enforced idleness made them physically soft and mentally slack. "Rest" periods were therefore devoted to strenuous drilling, musketry and route marches, varied by games and bathing parades, the last being the only kind of parade that never evoked any grumbles!

Up till now a good many of the men had succeeded in keeping the longish hair of their civilian days. Henceforth close crops were remorselessly enforced. This led to a good deal of chaff. One man, whose flowing curls had been his chief care, was seen gazing ruefully into his mirror while he vigorously brushed the stubble left by the barber. He was told that if his photograph could be sent home to his relations they would realize to the full the horrors of war!

The men lived very well while in rest billets; for not only was there more variety in the rations, but they were able to obtain excellent food in places like Vieille Chapelle, where the bill of fare in the cafés included salmon, salads and strawberries, while some of the French "madames" had learnt even the secret of making good tea.

The Battalion relieved the 1/9th Gurkhas in "A" sub-section on 28th June. Intermittent shelling took place daily, and on 2nd July the enemy brought a heavy *Minenwerfer* to bear on our advanced post, which had to be temporarily evacuated. Casualties, fortunately, were light, but wet weather made the trenches very uncomfortable. On 3rd July the Battalion was relieved by the 2/2nd Gurkhas and moved back to billets on King's Road. On the 6th a draft of one hundred and fifty men arrived from the 3/4th Battalion, most of whom had already been with the 1/4th.

There were many "characters" in the 4th Seaforths. One exuberant member of the Battalion was promoted Lance-Corporal to enable him to go to a course of instruction for non-commissioned officers. The same day he was heard to say to a sergeant of many years' standing: "Look here, Sergeant, the discipline in this Battalion's rotten. It's up to you and me to put it right."

Then there was No. 1290, Private H. Macdonald of No. 3 Company, whose fine work on 9th May has already been noted. He was admiring the leather braces of one of the London men more fortunately endowed than himself. "Man Mackie," he said, "when I see you lying dead on the battle-field I'm coming to take those gallowses off you." He was never noted for an excessive display of piety, but one Sunday he reprimanded some members of his platoon who were indulging in a music medley. "You may sing psalms or rag-time," said he, "but there's to be no mixing of them."

One day early in July a boxing display was held in an orchard behind some billets, under the supervision of "Wallie" Pack, a London boxer and an incorrigible jester, even in the most solemn and dangerous moments. The first fight was one of six-minute rounds between two youthful members of No. 1 Company. Each was a "character," and their appearance in the ring was greeted by a storm of cheers and laughter. They got as near to the costume of the ring as they could by wearing nothing but their kilt aprons and their boots and socks. The timekeeper sounded his gong—a pick head slung on a string. "Go it, Jerry!" "Give it him, Spack!" the crowd shouted, and go for each other they did. The spectators rocked with laughter as Jerry, a comical Manchester lad, and his opponent, a Cockney with a decided squint, tried between panting and gasping to smile acknowledgment of the vocal efforts of their supporters. In the third round, after a clinch near the ropes, Jerry tumbled into his captain's lap, smothering his riding breeches with blood. At the end of the sixth round the referee solemnly pronounced the result a draw, and insisted that each should make a speech. Jerry stood like a cornered rat, looking as if he would rather have his claret tapped again than do so. "Gentlemen," he began, "in all my fifteen fights I have never met a man before Private Spackman that I have not defeated." The crowd shrieked, and after a bewildered glance round Jerry slipped from "Wallie's" grasp and fled. Spackman began: "Officers and gentlemen of the 4th Seaforths"—the rest was drowned in roars of laughter. He, too, slipped from his second's grasp, hastily arranging his kilt apron.

The next match was between two athletic Highlanders from Tain, who danced and twisted and dodged round the ring. Then Pack, in a costume composed of a grey shirt and bathing drawers tastefully striped in white and blue, called for a volunteer to meet him in a sparring exhibition. The volunteer remarked that he had not had much experience of boxing; but he nobly sacrificed himself for two rounds to the skill of Pack and the entertainment of the company before throwing up the sponge.

It is narrated of "Wallie" Pack that he and a friend each received a new shirt from home. As neither had had a bath for a very long time they determined to do what they could—by heating some water in two pans and standing with a foot in each pan they managed to get tolerably near to cleanliness. They then decided to wash their old shirts. As "Wallie" had had the first "bath," his friend washed his shirt first. After a minute or two at his, "Wallie" said that his shirt had got clean remarkably quickly. It turned out that he had washed the new one!

Jerry Marsh, the hero of the great boxing contest, had a very bad stutter. On one occasion, coming down after taking rations up to the line, he was challenged by a sentry, and being unable to produce any intelligible sound he was within an ace of being shot, for it was supposed that he was a German. After that he always got Spackman to accompany him on such occasions.

Someone who wanted to "get a rise out of" Jerry sent him a packet containing two lance-corporal's stripes, with a covering letter, purporting to come from Lord Kitchener, saying that he had heard of Private Marsh's gallantry, and that he had appointed him to be Lance-Corporal. Jerry duly rose!

The Battalion again relieved the 2/2nd Gurkhas in "A" sub-section at midnight on 7th July, Nos. 2 and 3 Companies in the firing line, No. 4 in support and No. 1 in reserve. The next day was quiet, but at stand-to on the 9th the enemy played on the front line with rifle grenades, and at 6 A.M. sent over three very heavy bombs, one of which fell a few yards behind the trench, making a hole 25 feet in diameter. On the evening of 10th July the Battalion was relieved by the 2nd Yorkshire Regiment, marching by night to La Gorgue, where it arrived at 3.30 A.M. in a very exhausted condition, owing to the lack of opportunity for marching exercise, coupled with want of rest.

La Gorgue was described by someone as a "haven of lazy joy"! Excellent meals were to be had from the inhabitants for one or two francs, and there was always a warm welcome whenever the Seaforths came that way.

When the Battalion was out of the line most of the men spent their time and money in the villages. Some, however, for one reason or another, had no money to spare for this kind of thing. Among them was Private Spackman. Those who were amusing themselves in the villages naturally did not want their rations, which Spackman saved in a sandbag. When they went into the line again rations were not always as plentiful as they might be, in spite of the efforts of the Quartermaster's department. Then would Spackman produce the savings and hand them round. One can only hope that his kindly forethought was appreciated, though it long remained a mystery where he got the rations.

By this time the trench systems were becoming more elaborate and systematic. In early days the front-line trench had been a single line, straight, irregular and occasionally traversed. The lull in the fighting during the summer had left time for improvements, and the units going into the trenches found a fairly complete system, with a front trench, support trench, and numerous communication trenches.

Here is an imaginary description of the city of Trenchville: "Trenches have now grown into little cities with main streets, side streets, devious alley-ways, open spaces, telephone boxes and railways. Over the way live our cousins, but we are not on speaking terms at present. In the city of Trenchville the streets, and even the buildings, have names. Here is 'Pip-Squeak

Promenade,' there is 'Bomb Bay.' That little trench sliding away there is 'Pomme de Terre Alley.' This curve in the line is 'Oui Oui Crescent,' and the rise over there is 'R.I.P. Ridge.' This row of dwellings or dug-outs is known as 'Shrapnel Mansions'; No. 6 is called 'The Bug Walk'; No. 10, 'Hop o' my Thumb House'; No. 15, 'The Angel's Rest'; No. 19, 'The Pig and Whistle.' Over there is a more spacious residence known as 'Hotel de Fleabite.'"

As some of these names suggest, the municipal services were none too highly developed; but, making due allowance for place and circumstance, Trenchville could be quite a nice tenement if the weather was fine; the soldier loved to stretch his imagination and fancy his conditions other than they were. Here is a glimpse of trench life: "Our table consists of a door supported by old casks, our chairs are biscuit boxes, and our tablecloth a copy of *The Daily Mail.* Our dishes are lids of biscuit tins. We feasted on half-hot potatoes and bully beef, while the mess beside us gloated over salmon mayonnaise, gooseberry pudding and cream."

After shells and other inconveniences of warfare, bugs demanded most of the soldier's time, as witness this interesting extract from the same diary: "I had the most successful bug hunt of the campaign to-day. I must have bagged about ten. At home, if I announced the slaughter of ten bugs, I should immediately become a social pariah—here I am a hero. We look upon bug-hunting as a sporting pastime. When there is a lull—and there have been a few lately—you say in an offhand way: 'I think I'll go and bag a few bugs.' You take off your shirt, you arm yourself with a lighted cigarette, and begin patrolling from the collar downwards. When you spot one peacefully taking cover in a seam you place the end of the cigarette gently but firmly upon it, and in a few seconds you will have reason to believe that your bug has ceased to be of any further value as a biting unit."

Many a jest was made about these minor enemies. One man explained that at the first opportunity he was going to salt his shirt well and leave it near a pool. Then when the inhabitants, tortured by thirst, trooped down for a drink, he was going to snatch it away. Another said that he turned his shirt every day, thereby wearing out his guests by long route marches from one side to the other.

Till 14th July the Battalion enjoyed a rest. Companies

were paid, men had baths, clothing was baked and washed, and deficiencies made good. On the evening of the 13th a most enjoyable open-air concert took place. All ranks were delighted to see their old Divisional and Brigade Commanders, Major General Bannatine Allason and Brigadier-General Walter Ross, also Brigadier-General Strickland, Commanding the Jullundur Brigade, and some officers and men of the 1st Battalion. On the 14th a draft of fourteen officers from Fort George, under Major Monro of Allan, reported for duty; and at 8.15 P.M. the Battalion paraded and marched by companies along the La Bassée road to Euston Post, where Nos. 2 and 3 Companies billeted in empty houses, Nos. 1 and 4 proceeding by Hills Redoubt to trenches in front of Neuve Chapelle. The relief was carried out in pitch darkness and torrents of rain, which soaked everyone to the skin. The 15th July was, fortunately, fine, and by hard work the trenches were drained and comfort obtained. The Battalion was now in the Jullundur Brigade, for it had been determined to give the Indian troops a rest during the Mussulman fast of Ramazan. The British units were, therefore, turned over to the Lahore Division and the Indian ones to the Meerut Division, which was sent into rest billets. There were a number of casualties from shell fire during this time. The days were spent, so far as possible, in resting the troops, and the nights in patrolling and cutting the grass in front to prevent the enemy setting fire to it.

Owing to the necessity of extending the front held by the Indian Corps it was found impossible to give the Indian units a full month's rest, and some of them had to be recalled to the Lahore Division. Consequently, at 11 P.M. on 22nd July, Nos. 1 and 4 Companies were relieved by the 47th Sikhs, under very bad weather conditions, and reached Pont du Hem at 2 A.M. On the 29th these companies relieved the other two at Pont Logy, and the following day two officers and fifty men were detached to garrison Curzon Post.

Two notable events occurred during this tour of duty, for on the 21st *The London Gazette* contained the announcement that Regimental Sergeant-Major Glass had been promoted to be Quartermaster, and on the 23rd Sergeant-Major Anderson, an old Scots Guardsman, known to all as "Big Willie," arrived to take over the post of Regimental Sergeant-Major.

Rumour, as usual, was busy. The most persistent at this time was that all who came out in November were soon to be sent home. As one writer pertinently remarks, it would have been easy to have written a book of rumours such as this.

On 31st July the Battalion was relieved by the 1/4th London Regiment. Its billets were once more at La Gorgue, where training, concerts and games were the order of the day. The officers of the 4th beat those of the 1st Battalion at cricket, while the regimental football team beat that of the 8th Gloucesters by 4 goals to 2.

On 6th August Lieutenant W. Gordon, 2nd Battalion Gordon Highlanders, took over the duties of Adjutant.

On the 8th, after the first real rest the Battalion had enjoyed since February, it relieved the 2/2nd Gurkhas in the Duck's Bill section. Four platoons of the 10th Royal Warwickshire Regiment were attached for instruction. At 6.30 A.M. on 10th August the enemy sent over four bombs, one of which failed to burst, and proved on examination to be about 100 lb. in weight. Several of both battalions were wounded, including an officer of the Warwicks. A description of patrol work, written by one of the men, refers to this night. The patrol was under the command of Lance-Corporal Richford, and consisted of Privates Comrie, Smith, Bessent, Tomack Fraser and Ward. "We report to Captain Henderson, who says there is reason to think that the Germans have cut their barbed wire, preparatory to an attack. We start off on our journey of about 200 yards of No-man's-land. It is a slow job, as all must lie flat every time a star shell goes up or machine-gun bullets come too near. At one time we were evidently spotted, as a machine gun started, and as I lay on my stomach, with my head to one side, I could see the top of the grass round me being cut by the bullets! Anyhow, we got across all right and had a good look at the enemy wire, but could find no signs of it being cut. Then commenced the crawl back, after lying outside the enemy barbed wire for about twenty minutes. We accomplished the journey safely; but it is an eerie task, what with sundry frights from rats scampering away from dead bodies, or seeing a form lying on the ground in front of one and not knowing whether it is an enemy or friend, dead or alive. Then, with a kilt on, one's knees suffer from kneeling on stones and tins, and it is not nice to put one's knee into a dead German's face! When we got back the Warwicks looked at us in blank astonishment when we told them we had been over to see the German wire, but we cheered them considerably by telling them that their turn would come ! "

On 12th August the 2/2nd Gurkhas relieved the 4th Seaforths, who moved back to Rugby Road. On the 14th the Battalion took over for the last time from the 6th Jats, who, along with the 41st Dogras, 47th Sikhs and 4th Gurkhas, were withdrawn from the Indian Corps and sent to Egypt. Nos. 2 and 3 Companies, along with four platoons of the 8th North Staffords, held the front line from the right of Min Trench to Winchester Road, including the Birdcage. On the 16th the Battalion took over a further portion of the front line from the 1st Seaforths, occupying this position till the 20th, when it was relieved by the 1st Battalion. Five men were hit on the head during the retirement to Rugby Road. The men had baths at La Gorgue. On 28th August the Battalion beat Brigade Headquarters at cricket by 50 runs. On the following day, after church parade, rumours of an impending gas attack resulted in the 4th Seaforths and 2/2nd Gurkhas being moved up to Pont du Hem as an advanced Divisional Reserve. Here the explosion of a double cylinder bomb killed one man and wounded fourteen in No. 1 Company.

On 4th September a draft of eighty men arrived and a Brigade relief took place, the 4th Seaforths taking over from the 69th Punjabis at Ebenezer Farm. From the 5th to the 8th an immense amount of work was carried out, parties from different regiments working under sappers in the construction of sally-ports and mysterious holes under the fire steps in the old trenches. In addition to these, communication trenches were improved and new ones dug, leading back from the firing line to a position of comparative safety, so that it was possible to pass between front and rear by day as well as by night; emplacements for machine guns, trench mortars and even field guns were made, and dug-outs for the assembly of troops constructed; while artillery officers were constantly in the trenches taking observations.

The troops in reserve were training by day and working by night. " Sometimes armed with picks, shovels and high moral courage we sally forth to dig trenches. Sometimes we carry the sinews of war and the skeletons of dug-outs as far as the front line. But digging has one compensation—it isn't so bad as carrying. If you want to enlarge your vocabulary of expletives, come with a carrying party at night. It is pitch dark.

You can see about as far as the tips of your eyelashes. You are given, say, a huge frame, three feet by four feet, to carry between two of you. The word is passed to 'quick march' —the 'quick' sounds rather unnecessary. You shuffle along over uncertain roads and treacherous fields, exploring as you go. The chap behind you complains because you are going too fast. You growl because he isn't keeping up. 'Step shorter, damn you!' says he. 'Why in the hell can't you . . .' but you've stepped up to the neck into a shell hole. There is a general shuffling and rearranging of limbs, a number of muffled expletives, and on you go again. The other fellow, seeing you are shaken, offers to go in front. By this time the size of the frame feels five feet by seven feet. 'Rhwizz—thwizz—rut-a-tut-a-tut-a-tut-a-rwhizz-thwizz.' The chap in front of you suddenly halts. The frame gives you a jab in the ribs. You both drop down, the frame on top of you. It is a machine gun playing unpleasantly close. You wait until the strafe has ceased, then on again." That the British army was preparing for an offensive was abundantly clear!

Men of a new draft had to fend for themselves; the old hands put as much as they could upon them, and even those who had been out before did not wholly escape. One party leaving Ebenezer Farm had to cross a ditch by means of a crazy foot-bridge full of gaps. One of the last draft was heavily laden with a petrol tin full of water in one hand, his rifle in the other, and a bundle of sandbags slung over his shoulder. He missed his footing in the darkness and his leg slipped into one of the gaps. There he had to remain, while the whole party filed past him, each man using his head as a hand-rail!

At 3.30 P.M. on 10th September a German aeroplane was brought down by the guns at the fifth shot. "It was a lovely, warm afternoon," says one of the diarists, "with brilliant sunshine, and this machine was up a good height, quite 8000 feet, and flying parallel to the trenches. A shell burst exactly in line with it, but some way behind. The second was nearer, and the third nearer still. Then the fourth was almost on the tip of its tail, and the fifth seemed to crash right into it! The machine put its nose down a bit, did a half turn and a sort of a lurch, then put its nose right down vertically and began to spin faster round its own axis. There were several of us watching this tragedy, but all too awed to speak, and each of us must have had at the back of his mind a hope that it would right itself! It was simply appalling! It took such a time to fall—like a wounded bird at first, then—well, it was simply too fascinating, yet utterly repulsive. Down and down it went, spinning all the time, and each wing in turn flashing like a streak of silver, and its black crosses plainly visible. All the time the engine is roaring, pulling the thing down—a sure sign that the pilot is killed or insensible; because if the controls had been severed, accounting for a spin, one would instinctively shut off the engine, which was not done. He fell just inside their own lines, about 100 yards behind. We could see a bit of white behind a hedge and some trees. They waited for the Huns to begin to collect round, and then a battery of field guns put about fifty rounds slap into it in about a couple of minutes. It was a thing to see and to remember. That shooting was marvellous, and I don't expect to see the like again. Five rounds and all was over. Time after time I have seen the sky absolutely speckled with the puffs of shells, and then the machine has got away unharmed."

On 12th September the Garhwal Brigade relieved the Dehra Dun Brigade and the Battalion returned to billets in La Gorgue. In the meanwhile several changes had occurred in the command. Lieutenant-General Sir James Willcocks handed over the Indian Corps to Lieutenant-General Sir Charles Anderson, K.C.B., who was succeeded in the command of the Meerut Division by Major-General C. Jacob, the Dehra Dun Brigade being taken over by Lieutenant-Colonel W. J. Harvey of the 2nd Black Watch.

The men in the trenches read with mixed feelings letters from home describing the Zeppelin raids. One man's brother wrote that the explosion of one of the bombs, about a mile away, was like a million Neuve Chapelles! "A million Neuve Chapelles, indeed!" quoth the indignant recipient; "I'll give him a millionth part of a Neuve Chapelle when I get back, and he won't want another." A girl living near St Pancras said that one Zeppelin came right up Gray's Inn Road. "Well, why in the wide world didn't she run and catch it?" said one of the irrepressibles. There was no sympathy in the trenches for those who squealed before they were hit.

On 18th September the Dehra Dun Brigade relieved the Garhwal and Bareilly Brigades, the 4th Seaforths taking over from the Sunken Road to the left of South Moated Grange Street. No. 2 Company occupied the Duck's Bill. Instructions were issued to keep up a continuous rifle and grenade fire during the night, while the guns kept up a lot of firing. On the 21st they opened at 5.30 A.M. and continued all day, the heavy howitzers making excellent practice. Rumours with regard to further operations materialized with the issue of Brigade Orders of the 22nd. The main offensive was to be carried out by the IV and I Corps, while the Indian Corps was to carry out a local operation, the task being allotted to the Meerut Division, then holding a line from the Estaires-La Bassée road to Winchester Road.

As on 10th March, a break through was to be followed up by an advance to the high ground at La Cliqueterie Ferme and Haut Pommereau, where the direction of the advance was to be changed to south-east, so as to join up with the main offensive in the south.

The attack of the Meerut Division was to be carried out by the Garhwal Brigade on the right and the Bareilly Brigade on the left. The first objective was the line Mauquissart-the Duck's Bill. The Dehra Dun Brigade was to be in reserve, ready to follow up and exploit an initial success of the other two. On the right and left of the Meerut Division the Lahore and 20th Divisions held the line, with orders to cover the attack by concentrated fire, and to form flanks to any advance that might be made.

During the whole of the 22nd our guns continued to bombard the enemy trenches and wire, while heavy firing also was heard far to the south of Givenchy. On this day a party of one hundred men under Lieutenant Morrison was detailed for special duty, and it was soon known that gas and smoke were to aid the attack. The use of the mysterious holes under the fire steps was now apparent; they were to protect the gas cylinders from the enemy fire. On the 23rd, after dark, parties were observed coming out of the communication trenches with large cylinders, which were placed in groups of three or four every twenty or thirty yards by the Royal Engineers. Every care was taken to keep these preparations secret, and the word "gas" was never used in the trenches, the cylinders being spoken of as "Rogers." They were all in position by the following morning, except a few on the left of the line near the Birdcage. This was just as well; for the trench at that point was blown in during the morning by a *Minenwerfer*.

But gas was not to be the only surprise for the enemy. Two field guns and a Hotchkiss gun were placed in emplacements covered with railway metals right in the front line. Needless to say, the infantry had had the pleasing task of carrying these long and heavy rails in the dark up narrow winding communication trenches with indifferent foothold.

On the night of the 24th-25th there was little rest. Packs had to be dumped, rations distributed, extra ammunition and working tools to be issued, and all the hundred-and-one things done that precede an attack. That night the Dehra Dun Brigade returned into support, the 4th Seaforths, with the exception of the gas party, being in some old trenches near Rouge Croix. During the evening the wind was blowing from the south.

At daylight on 25th September there was a slight breeze veering between south-west and south—not very favourable for carrying the gas over the enemy lines. It was a miserable morning, with a slight drizzle.

Zero hour, the time for the attack to start, was 5.50 A.M. Two minutes earlier the mine opposite the Birdcage had been exploded. In a terrific roar, bodies, wire, picks, shovels and rifles flew into the air in a great fountain of earth. Then a red rocket went skywards; it was the signal from Bareilly Brigade Headquarters for the attack to begin. The artillery opened fire and the gas was turned on. Four minutes later the field and Hotchkiss guns in the front line opened, and at 5.55 A.M. a smoke screen was set up; three minutes later the gas was cut off and the infantry attacked under a barrage of artillery and indirect machine-gun fire.

According to instructions, the 4th Seaforth Highlanders in the Dehra Dun Brigade made a forward concentration to the B line, which they reached about 7 A.M.

But the attack was not a success. The Garhwal Brigade failed to reach the enemy front line. A change of wind blew back the gas on the Bareilly Brigade. Lieutenant Morrison's party had twenty men put out of action by this, and the 2nd Black Watch suffered severely. Men came staggering down, looking ghastly, gasping for breath. Nevertheless the Brigade pushed forward and took the enemy line; but though it got into the second line it failed to take the Moulin du Piètre, and its flanks became exposed.

The Seaforths, from their position in the support and

communication trenches, saw the 2nd and 4th Black Watch and the 2/8th Gurkhas going over the top into a thick cloud of smoke and gas. The attack had only just been launched when the rain began to fall in sheets. Shortly after 10 A.M. Lieutenant-Colonel Cuthbert called for company officers and gave orders for a further attack at the point opposite Colvin Trench, where the wire had stopped the Leicesters' assault, and about 11 A.M. the Battalion began to move forward into the front line. But the communication trenches were so crowded with men that movement was almost impossible, and it took three hours for companies to get into position between Colvin Street and South Tilleloy Street.

By this time the enemy guns were getting well into action; the shallow trenches were heavily shelled, and the rain was filling them ankle-deep in water. It was about 11.30 A.M. that the enemy counter-attack began, which by 1.30 P.M. had driven our attack back to our own lines.

While the ground gained was thus being lost the Dehra Dun Brigade was struggling forward, suffering endless delays. A platoon of No. 1 Company found itself held up in a water-logged trench. The men had been leaning dejectedly against the sides in the pouring rain for what seemed an interminable time, when one of the company wits called out: "Where's Sergeant Martin?" "What's the matter?" growled Martin. "Sergeant, I'm fair crippled wi' the rheumatism; I'm goin' sick." Martin pointed out with all the force at a sergeant's command that to go sick in the middle of a battle was irregular and contrary to military discipline. The jester lapsed into silence for the next half hour. Then he went to the sergeant again and said, much to the amusement of the very "fed-up" troops: "Sergeant, I'm feelin' a wee bit better the noo, I'll hang on an' see if we're goin' ower. If we are, I'm goin' sick." And still the attack was being pressed back, and the supports were held up in the congested trenches.

"Wallie" Pack met an Irishman during the Battle of Loos, who was in great excitement, calling out that the Germans were coming in thousands and thousands. "Well," said "Wallie," "that's all right, for I've got thousands and thousands of bullets for them."

Consequent on the failure of the attack the movement of the Dehra Dun Brigade was cancelled. Everything in front was silent, but wounded men and prisoners passed down from time to time. A lad in the Black Watch had his forearm almost blown off. He came down the trenches looking for a dressing station. He came up to one of the Seaforths and asked for the Aid Post. His lips quivered, and he seemed on the point of breaking down when a man beside him whispered: "Stick it, boy, stick it." The words acted like a tonic; he made a great effort, pulled himself together and followed a man to the Aid Post.

Whether the Dehra Dun Brigade could have materially changed the fortunes of the day or not is doubtful. The main cause of the failure was almost certainly the wind, which made the gas attack miscarry, and even recoil on our own lines, and left the smoke screen as a veritable fog of war between the commanders and their units.

About 7 P.M. the Battalion was relieved, and went into reserve trenches on the B line well over the knees in mud and water. It was a miserable night, and the men had left their greatcoats with their packs; but as the Battalion was under one hour's notice to move, the discomfort and cold were of less moment than they might have been.

There they stayed for the next three days, continuously at work to keep the flooded trenches in order. At last, on the evening of 28th September, the Dehra Dun Brigade was relieved by a brigade of the 20th Division, and the Battalion proceeded *via* Pont Logy, Rouge Croix and La Couture to Vieille Chapelle, where it arrived soaked to the skin and coated in mud.

Billets were very welcome again, and the 29th, a cold dreary day, was spent in drying and cleaning up, followed by baths at La Gorgue on the 30th. On 2nd October the Battalion took over a new line in front of Festubert, just north of Givenchy, having two companies in front line and two in support. The weather now was splendid, the communication trenches excellent, and the front-line trenches in very fair condition.

The sector was known as Rothesay Bay. The whole countryside was very flat, so that a good view was obtainable from Givenchy Hill. In rear were the ruins of Givenchy and Festubert, names now for ever linked with the deeds of the British army. Opposite, the enemy trenches curled away like great caterpillars. Puffs of smoke here and there told of the bursting of bomb or shrapnel. Far off, on either side, the life of the countryside seemed to be remote from war.

On the morning of 13th October the First Army again attacked south of the La Bassée canal. A smoke demonstration was carried out for some miles north of the main objective and drew a lot of enemy fire, whereby a dug-out in No. 1 Company's sector was blown in and three officers and one man were wounded. The demonstration was successful in deceiving the Germans as to its object, for they claimed to have repulsed British attacks along the whole front with heavy loss.

On the morning of the 14th the Battalion went into Brigade Reserve in the neighbourhood of Festubert. The village looked like a pile of bricks and wood, with the jagged arch of the old church rising over all. The houses were masses of wreckage—walls, roofs and furniture piled pell-mell on one another. All that was left of the church was that one arch. In the graveyard, monuments were tottering, graves had given up their dead. Above it all stood the undamaged crucifix, one of the many that the war spared in this part of France.

Fatigue parties were called for daily, and at about 5 P.M. on the 19th the Battalion stood to, in readiness to take part in repulsing a German counter-attack to the south. On the 20th the Battalion was relieved and marched to billets at La Couture, but on the next day took over new trenches in front of the Rue du Bois, about 500 yards south of the Estaires-La Bassée road. With the exception of No. 3 Company, garrisoning the keeps, the whole Battalion was in the line, each company finding its own supports. These trenches were mere mud-holes, the water standing three feet deep in parts. Rifle and machine-gun fire swept the ground all night, and the enemy artillery was unpleasantly attentive. Their snipers, too, caused heavy casualties at first, but the Seaforths took effectual measures to keep these pests quiet. The Germans were always shouting over to ask what regiment was opposite them. The reply was a shower of rifle grenades.

This sector was the scene of the attack of 9th May. After more than five months the dead of that battle were still lying out in No-man's-land, and a search party was organized, which identified and buried all that remained of many of our men. The party had gone out under cover of a morning mist, which lifted suddenly and left them exposed to the enemy fire. Everyone got back safely except Sergeant Rogers, who fell wounded seventy yards from our wire. In broad daylight Private H.

Robertson, a stretcher-bearer of No. 2 Company, went out to his assistance. He rolled the sergeant into a shell hole, dressed his wounds, and returned for a blanket and rum, while Private Fraser, who had gone out to help, remained with Rogers. When Robertson returned Fraser went back to the trenches for a stretcher, and after dusk they brought in the sergeant safe. Robertson had done some fine work at this place on 9th May, and for this last act of gallantry he was awarded the D.C.M.

The 4th Seaforths were relieved on the 24th and went into billets between Paradis and Merville. The march was very arduous, for long spells in the trenches had made the men's feet soft and easily blistered. On the 28th the Brigade paraded for inspection by His Majesty the King. After a march of three miles in drenching rain and a long wait it was announced that His Majesty would not arrive. Major-General Jacob then pinned the riband of the Russian Order of St George (4th Class) on the jacket of Lance-Corporal MacRae, No. 1 Company. The men returned greatly disappointed that they had not seen the King, and their disappointment became dismay when it was learned that the cause of his absence was a fall from his horse, which, fortunately, was not followed by serious results. On the 31st a draft of seventeen men came up from the Base. The average strength of the Battalion for the month of October was 640 of all ranks.

When, on 2nd November, the Battalion relieved the 39th Garhwal Rifles in reserve billets at King's Road, near La Couture, rain had fallen continuously for several days, and the mud was approaching the state of the previous winter. On the 4th the 4th Seaforths marched to Vieille Chapelle, and, in the very field in which he had welcomed them to the Dehra Dun Brigade nearly a year before, Major-General Claud Jacob, Commanding the Meerut Division, took leave of the Battalion. After complimenting them on their work in the field, and their appearance that day, he expressed his regret that he was unable to take them to the new theatre of war to which the Indian Corps had been ordered, and bade them farewell.

There were many heavy hearts in the Battalion on the homeward march. They had been through much with the 1st Battalion and their kindness during the year together had been beyond all praise. From all ranks in the 1st Battalion they had received much help and advice, and every soul in the 4th Battalion realized it. Nor was it only with their own regular battalion that the 4th Seaforths had made friends. The Indian battalions had proved themselves staunch comrades on many occasions. The Gurkhas in particular had become great allies of the Ross-shire men, who were very sorry to part from them, and the Gurkhas were sorry too. They liked the Seaforths—" Seaforth teek " was their way of putting it. They left a legacy of many Hindustani words with the Battalion: bread was " rooty," anything good was " teek."

Many stories are told of the Gurkhas. At Neuve Chapelle one was seen to put his head through a hole in a wall. Next moment he reappeared, dragging with him a pair of grey-clad legs. These came through the hole easily—though obviously unwillingly—as far as the junction with the body. This was a tight fit; but Johnny Gurkha, getting a fresh grip, got both feet firmly against the wall and drew through his animated cork.

One very hot August evening Captain P. Macintyre, always the first to do another a good turn, was approaching some very " unhealthy " cross-roads with his wagons about dusk. Here he came upon a wagon in a deep ditch by the roadside. It was in charge of a Gurkha, who was delighted by Captain Macintyre's offer of help. The transport accordingly was halted at this by no means safe spot, while the spare men were set to dragging the wagon out of the ditch. The moment the task was accomplished about half a dozen grinning brown faces appeared over the edge of the wagon, with loud cries of " Teek, Johnnie! " They had been asleep under a tarpaulin and had made no effort to extricate either themselves or the wagon.

One Gurkha, known as *Eebie*, was a particular friend of the 4th Seaforths. While talking to them he would suddenly say, " Me go see Alleman," and be off across No-man's-land. On coming back he would say " Alleman," followed by pantomime —the imitation of a snore, cheek on hand. Sometimes it would be, " Me kill Alleman." This meant that he proposed to carry out a lone-hand raid on their trenches! But the men used to hold him back.

Since Neuve Chapelle great changes had come over the Battalion. It was apparent chiefly to those who, because of wounds or sickness, had been long absent from it. It was less characteristically a Highland battalion, and was becoming more like a Regular unit, filled with men from all parts of the country. Yet in spite of this, in spite of the constant disappearance of well-known faces and the coming of new ones, it kept its old tradition of good comradeship. There was a perfect understanding between all ranks, an absence of restraint in the dealings of officers and men; yet this was never presumed on by the latter, and orders were invariably carried out to the best of the men's ability. Sympathy and the cheery word for all kept the essentials of discipline at the highest pitch of excellence.

Sir Charles Anderson writes: "The 1/4th Seaforths during the whole time they served under me showed that they were worthy of the honour of belonging to the same Regiment as the regular battalion of Seaforths with whom they were brigaded. Higher praise it would be difficult to imagine. Whether in the monotonous and irksome duties of the trenches or in the active fighting on the line, the Battalion always acquitted itself with the greatest credit, and in an incredibly short space of time I came to regard it as an absolutely reliable body of determined fighting soldiers on whom one could bank with confidence in any emergency."

SYNOPSIS OF EVENTS FROM THE BATTLE OF LOOS TO THE MIDDLE OF THE BATTLES OF THE SOMME

(*13th October* 1915 *to 2nd September* 1916)

AFTER the Battle of Loos followed a period of comparative quiet. Winter put an end to the major operations of war; while the assumption by Sir John French of the command of the Home Defence Forces, and his succession in France by Sir Douglas Haig, somewhat modified the plans that were in preparation. The ensuing twelve months were to witness the passing of the initiative in the West from the enemy to the Allies, the decline of the aggressive spirit (though not the fighting capacity) of the French troops, the development by the British of the idea of the war of attrition, and the transfer from the French to the British of the dominant share in events. It is to the student perhaps the most interesting year of the war, for it brought a decisive success very near, and at its end the enemy's *moral* fell to a lower level than it did at any period before the final phase.

On 8th January 1916 the unfortunate expedition to Gallipoli came to an end with an evacuation even more brilliantly carried out than the skilful landings with which it commenced. Henceforth Salonika became the centre of the Allied efforts on the Ægean front.

The French and British were concerting a combined attack on the Germans on a large scale, to coincide with Russian and Italian offensives, when, at the close of February, the Germans flung their armies against Verdun. It was the last bid for an early decision, desperately pushed and almost successful. Some Australian heavy batteries were sent to help the French, and British Divisions were held in readiness to reinforce them, but the French had the glory of repulsing the assailants without calling these latter up. The fighting at Verdun went on right into December, but with the opening of the Battle of the Somme its importance rapidly diminished. The Germans had lost the initiative.

On 29th April British prestige suffered a heavy blow by the surrender of Kut-el-Amara, which was not retrieved until ten months later. The Russian offensive began on 4th May—much earlier than had been expected—and met with gratifying success. On the 31st began the Battle of Jutland, which, under the wise and far-sighted leadership of Admiral Sir John Jellicoe, ended the active career of the German High Seas Fleet. While not so obviously decisive as Trafalgar it assured to Britain the command of the seas, without crippling the Grand Fleet, and thereby risking the loss of the war. On 9th June the Italians began their counter-offensive on the Trentino front, which made good progress.

Long and stubborn fighting round Verdun had exhausted Joffre's reserves and the original plan had to be greatly modified. Instead of thirty-nine French Divisions attacking on a front of thirty miles, only five took part on a front of six miles; while the British, on a front of fifteen and a half miles, attacked with thirteen Divisions in first line and six in close reserve. The plan of battle no longer aimed at mere topographical gains; its object was simply to break through and shatter the German armies. Though to do this it might be necessary to order an attack on this, that, or the other place, the destruction of the enemy units and the enemy *moral* were the essential spirit of the plan.

Fighting commenced on 1st July. On the right, south of the Somme, the French attack took the Germans by surprise; confusion reigned among their commanders, and the French quickly swept forward to Biaches—their ultimate high-water mark in this quarter. North of the river the gains of the XX French Corps, though less striking, were considerable, as were those of the XIII and XV British Corps. Farther north the III Corps also secured valuable results, but the X, though at first very successful, failed to consolidate its gains. Steady fighting went on till, on 8th July, the British attack was held up at Mametz Wood, which was not finally cleared till the 12th.

This was an invaluable delay for the enemy. The attack, none the less, was pushed on, and on the 14th the German second-line system was carried on the whole front of the assault, High Wood being entered by units of the Indian Cavalry Corps. There the attack was stayed by new German field works, and it was not until 15th September that this key position fell to envelopment. This marks the end of the first phase of the Battle of the Somme. The French front now ran roughly north of Soyecourt, through Belloy, Biaches and Hem, to Hardecourt, whence the British prolonged it *via* Longueval and Bazentin to a point midway between La Boisselle and Thiepval.

German counter-attacks took place on 18th and 23rd July, meeting with no ultimate success, and the British settled down to eating their way, bit by bit, for six weeks, into the German positions. The British, having the initiative, were able to allow their troops short periods of complete rest, whereas the Germans had no relaxation from an ever-increasing strain. In consequence, the British *moral* steadily rose, while the German equally steadily fell. This phase ended with the French in possession of Maurepas, their front having been pushed forward for about a mile. The British front had been pushed forward, about a thousand yards to a mile, all along their salient front. They were on the fringe of Guillemont, had captured Pozières, and were able to look over the northern slopes of the ridge towards Martinpuich.

In the meanwhile the Turkish attempt to invade Egypt was effectively checked at Romani, and the Allies had at last begun an advance from Salonika. In Transylvania the Rumanians, who had just entered the war, were driven out by Mackensen, in co-operation with a Bulgarian advance into the Dobrudja. The great Brussilow offensive on the Russian front had now come to an end.

VIMY

CHAPTER VII

THE SOMME

On the night of 4th-5th November 1915 the 4th Seaforths relieved the 1/9th Gurkhas in the line, and from the 6th was attached to the 139th Brigade, 46th Division. Owing to its depleted strength and the condition of the trenches the Battalion was unable to garrison the whole line. Posts were placed at intervals, where a small shelf could be constructed on the side of the trench with a small amount of cover, and in these conditions No. 3 Company took over the firing line, with No. 4 in support in the old British trench. No. 2 Company was in the Rue du Bois and No. 1 in the Rue des Berceaux. Owing to the water it was found impossible to leave companies in the trenches for more than twenty-four hours, when they were relieved and went into reserve, where there was some chance of drying a part of the wet from clothes and boots. The snipers were busy, and claimed to have hit many of the enemy.

At this time Lieutenant Hulls was the only machine gun officer with the Battalion. This was, no doubt, a proud distinction, but it had the one drawback that he was permanently on duty. After a time he felt it was necessary to remonstrate. His representations were most sympathetically received, and he was told that Second Lieutenant Harrop was just about to return from a machine-gun course and that he would be informed when he arrived. Sure enough a message came up almost at once reporting Second Lieutenant Harrop's arrival and asking when Lieutenant Hulls wanted him up. The answer was short and to the point: "At once." He was told that Second Lieutenant Harrop was just starting to report. Hours went by but no sign of the relief, so Lieutenant Hulls sent down an urgent inquiry. The reply was disappointing: "Second Lieutenant Harrop was wounded on his way up to relieve you." He was, in fact, wounded in the arm while going across the open in order to avoid the wet communication trenches.

On the night of 8th November, when the Battalion was relieved, the rain fell in torrents, and three companies were lucky to be in billets at La Couture. No. 1 had to remain as reserve to the relieving battalion, the 3rd Londons.

The Battalion remained at La Couture till the 12th, sending large working parties to the line daily. It then went into Divisional reserve at Calonne-sur-Lys.

On the 16th the Battalion moved in motor-buses to Drouvin, south of the La Bassée Canal, where it was attached to the 46th Brigade of the 15th Division. Accommodation was very limited, and Nos. 3 and 4 Companies had to be contented with canvas tents, which, as the weather now was cold and frosty, were not appreciated.

A draft of one hundred and forty-four other ranks had now arrived, so that when Major-General F. W. N. M'Cracken, C.B., D.S.O., Commanding the 15th Division, inspected the Battalion, on the 17th, it once more paraded in reasonable strength. On the 20th Brigadier-General Torquil Matheson, Commanding the 46th Brigade, himself a Ross-shire man, inspected his new unit. A working party, one hundred and fifty strong, was sent up daily to the trenches.

On 21st November the Battalion moved at 7.30 P.M. through Noeux-les-Mines, Mazingarbe and Vermelles into trenches on the southern face of the famous Hohenzollern Redoubt, where it relieved the 5th Royal Berks. Work had to be carried out continuously, for the trenches were in a very bad condition. There were neither dug-outs nor shelter of any kind from the rain and snow, the only place where a man could snatch a short sleep without lying in water being on the fire step—and that was by no means dry. The terrain was flat and the communication trenches very long, so that rations had to be carried up in sandbags through miles of narrow trench. These conditions made it imperative to relieve the front line every two or three days, the outgoing units finding warmth and comfort in ruined cellars in Vermelles and Sailly Labourse.

The machine gun officer often was alone with his detachment and out of reach of the Officers' Mess, so he shared the morning brew of porridge with his men. On one occasion Sergeant R. Ross was engaged on some rather interesting shooting while the porridge was being shared out. The belt coming to an end he shouted for another, at the same time stretching out his hand for it. It so happened that the officer's batman was handing up a plate of the porridge to his master just as Ross put out his hand. It was a long while before he forgave this.

During bad weather letters home were always full of praise of the kilt, and, curiously, this came from the London men. Its great advantage was that it was easily kept dry on going into the trenches, for it could readily be worn round the neck until the firing step was reached. Even when it got wet the water quickly ran down to the lower edge and dripped off, while the constant swing when in motion helped to dry it. Pity for those who had to spend the time in sodden trousers is often expressed. When, towards the end of the stay in the Neuve Chapelle area, waders were issued, the men adopted the following procedure. A sandbag was cut open along its side, holes were made at the corners of the opposite side, through which the legs were thrust and the whole drawn up, thereby gathering the kilt into a bunch. Another bag was drawn over each leg, which was then thrust into the wader. The appearance is likened to an Elizabethan fashion-plate!

The necessity for carrying rations up to the front line in sandbags while in the vicinity of the Hohenzollern Redoubt made things very onerous. One man of a party going up with the officers' rations had on his back a sandbag in which were some bottles. A shell broke all the bottles, but the man himself got off without a scratch.

Sergeant Hector Mackenzie (Opinan) had to take some men of a new draft up into the trenches, along with the rations for a bomb and gas party. They had to go up through the fields, as the communication trench was full of troops coming down. The shelling was, however, so bad that at last they had to take cover in the trench. On arrival at their destination the sergeant turned to find behind him only Macleod (Coigach) and Mackenzie, the cooks, but never a sign of the draft. "Tug" Wilson was sent down to look for them, and found them sitting in a group about three miles away. A shell had fallen between two of them, and, although no one was hit, they had lost touch and went back to the end of the communication trench.

On 26th November the Battalion went into Brigade reserve at Sailly Labourse, returning to the trenches on the 28th. The following afternoon there was heavy shelling, but no casualties occurred. The Battalion was again relieved on the 30th, going back in its turn to the trenches on 2nd December, which is described as a very quiet day.

This was a most uncomfortable sector. Not only were the trenches in a very bad state, entailing heavy calls for working parties, but there were also many bodies which had to be buried. The retention by the Germans of Fosse 8 and the Dump gave them such observation posts as effectually prevented our placing artillery where it could properly support the troops in this new salient, which was always costly to hold and the scene of constant local actions.

The following incident took place in front of the Hohenzollern Redoubt in December. "Jock Macdonald The Pipes," who had been posted as sentry, began whistling to himself in the pouring rain. This went on for about an hour, till a friend came along and began to talk to him. Only one fragment of the discourse has been preserved. Macdonald was heard to say: "D'ye know, man, I dinna care for these faancy cakes; they are all right for a clairk or a watchmaker, but give me a good bit of oätcake."

On the morning of 6th December the Battalion went on relief to Vermelles, and the following day to Vaudricourt, where it found excellent billets. Here it remained, furnishing fatigues for the front line and cleaning up.

Leave for the men now began, eleven going off daily. The privilege was eagerly sought, the men making light of the interminable waiting at wayside stations and on drizzle-swept quays in the joy of getting home at last. In bad weather the leave-boat was a place of torment, broken limbs and other injuries being by no means rare. Sleep was, moreover, difficult to one wrapped in a cork jacket. The trains were overcrowded and incredibly late. Yet all was endured with the utmost good humour—at any rate on the way home.

Those who were not going on leave amused themselves, when they could, at the expense of those who were. The

Armourer-Sergeant was known as "Fusee." He went on home-leave, and, like the good craftsman that he was, took great pains that his revolver should be spotlessly clean. The arms of men going on leave were always inspected prior to embarkation. When "Fusee's" turn came, he pulled out of his holster, not the immaculate fire-arm that he had put into it, but a very rusty old hammer, which the licensed jester of the Sergeants' Mess had managed to substitute for it. It was a great blow!

On 13th December the Battalion went into Corps reserve at Burbure, where, on the 16th, the Brigade Commander inspected the billets and expressed himself as very satisfied with them.

On the 19th Field-Marshal Sir John French drove through the town, the streets being lined by the troops. This was his farewell visit.

On the 19th Lieutenant-Colonel T. W. Cuthbert, D.S.O., went home on leave. From the time of its arrival in November 1914 he had never left the Battalion for more than a few hours. All ranks naturally expected to see him return in due course. Happenings at home, however, over which he had no control, prevented his coming back to lead again the Battalion that he had led so well.

To rare gifts of leadership, Lieutenant-Colonel Cuthbert added one of the kindest hearts that ever beat. He had a cheery word for everyone, and his indomitable courage and quick decision kept up the spirits and *esprit de corps* of the Battalion in the most difficult situations. He took over the weapon so well forged by Lieutenant-Colonel Mason-MacFarlane, and tempered it till it left his hands fit for any test. There is no better known or more welcome visitor to any gathering of old 4th Battalion men.

Lieutenant-Colonel Cuthbert's departure may be said to mark a very definite period in the life of the Battalion. He was the last of the officers who had come out in a senior rank, and the last who had served with it continuously without any break. He left it, furthermore, at the end of what may almost be called its independent period of existence. Long and closely as it had been associated with the Meerut Division, it was a supernumerary reinforcement, attached partly to make up the numerical deficiencies of the Division, partly to receive its baptisms of fire and blood in the company of seasoned units. There was always the possibility of its being transferred elsewhere. Soon after Lieutenant-Colonel Cuthbert's departure it rejoined its old Highland Division as a unit belonging to and forming an integral part of that Division. It was one of the four normal battalions in its new brigade, in which it was to serve till the end of the war. Finally there was the change in its personnel that has been already referred to, a change that from now on became all the more marked because its commanding officers were always drawn from outside its own commissioned ranks. To the writer of history, moreover, it begins sensibly to lose its strong individuality, in that the diaries and letters which so forcibly impress that individuality on his mind are, for the most part, no longer available. The story has more and more to be drawn from sources that, in great measure, lack the spontaneity and humour of those valuable documents.

Large consignments of good fare were arriving from home, which, coupled with the knowledge that the Battalion probably would be out of the line for Christmas and the New Year, engendered a spirit of real festivity. Time was spent in company-training and lectures, while the baths at Raimbert were allotted to the Battalion. The result was that on Christmas Day the men were in clean shirts and in the very best of form. Voluntary services for all denominations were well attended. On 27th December, Brigadier-General Matheson inspected No. 4 Company in great detail and complimented them on their work.

On New Year's Day, 1916, the Battalion was split up by platoons and sections, each dining in a café, with an officer presiding. One letter says: "Speaking of our own particular 'spread'—I am confident that all others were similar—the regimental cooks prepared a menu worthy alike of themselves and the occasion, and an impromptu programme was also gone through. In the course of the afternoon we were visited by our Chaplain, Captain Macleod (Dame Rumour says that we must shortly write Major Macleod, and whether she speaks truly or not, she at least voices the sentiments of the Battalion), along with the Adjutant, Captain Gordon, who is commanding the Battalion in the absence of Colonel Cuthbert. Captain Gordon expressed the hope that we would all be home ere the year closes. The Chaplain also addressed us, and cheered everyone with his views of the war—religious and otherwise. Perhaps our officers did not fully realize how much pleasure they gave the men in arranging the dinner and being present themselves.

"I wish the folks at home had been present. The happiness and cheerfulness prevailing would have assured them that we are all quite content, and that the *bon camaraderie*, which has ever been a strong point in the Battalion, and which always spells efficiency, is as strong as it was when we marched away from our Depot, the changed personnel of the unit notwithstanding.

"The other day our boys borrowed a *casserole* wherein to cook some delicacy or other, and the lady who had been kind enough to lend it sent her son round the following morning to bring it back. He arrived while the men were washing, and addressed the first he met with '*Maman, casserole*.' The unfortunate private did not understand French, however, and asked if any of the men had promised this kid's mother a bottle of castor oil."

Training continued until 6th January, when the Battalion marched for Lillers to entrain for Amiens. Here it arrived at 9.30 P.M. and marched through the night to Cardonette, where it joined the 154th Brigade of the 51st (Highland) Division, then in the XIII Corps with the Third Army.

Just before the Battalion joined the 51st Division outside Amiens a certain private appeared in orders as Lance-Corporal. That same night he was on leave in Amiens, where he had some small disagreement with the military police, who brought him in next morning. When he appeared at Orderly Room the Regimental Sergeant-Major sent for a pair of stripes and pinned them on the man's arm, to his intense amazement. After he had appeared before the Commanding Officer and duly reverted, he was heard saying to some of his cronies: "Lance-Corporal . . . reverted to permanent grade, an' me never kent A wis a corporal."

The rest at Burbure had done the men a lot of good, and had been much enjoyed because of the kindness of the inhabitants. The time had, moreover, been valuable, for Brigadier-General Matheson was a Guardsman, from whom the 4th Seaforths learned the real value of much that is often contemptuously discarded as "eye-wash."

The 154th Brigade, at this time in process of reconstruction, was composed of the 1/6th Cameronians, 1/4th and 1/5th Black Watch, 1/4th Seaforth and 1/4th Cameron Highlanders.

It was commanded by Brigadier-General C. E. Stewart, C.M.G., lately in command of the 1st Black Watch.

Major-General G. M. Harper, C.B., D.S.O., universally known as "Uncle Harper," commanded the Division, which, from its badge bearing the letters H.D., was of course christened "Harper's Duds."

To avoid confusion it will be best to set forth at once the changes the Brigade went through before taking final shape. On 12th January the 1/6th Cameronians became Divisional troops. On 23rd February the 1/4th Gordon Highlanders joined the Brigade, and two days later both the Black Watch Battalions were transferred to the 118th Brigade. On the 26th the 1/4th Cameron Highlanders were sent to the Base at Etaples for demobilization. The Brigade now consisted only of the 4th Seaforth and 4th Gordon Highlanders, but was completed on 1st March by the 9th Battalion The Royal Scots and the 7th Battalion Argyll and Sutherland Highlanders. Captain C. A. P. Hulls became the Brigade machine gun officer.

On 11th January the Brigadier inspected the Battalion. On the 13th Captain Gordon handed over command to Captain Henderson and went on leave, Second Lieutenant J. Mackie becoming Acting Adjutant.

Very little of note happened during the next few weeks, which were spent in training. Drill in close and extended formations brought the men up to a high pitch of discipline; musketry practice was carried out in all conditions, including shooting in gas helmets; and special training was given in bomb- and grenade-throwing, a Divisional School for officers and non-commissioned officers being formed for the purpose. Reserve signallers also were trained, casualties among signallers being a frequent cause of lack of co-ordination in attacks. Special attention was devoted to Brigade exercises in attack and defence. Training was to some extent interrupted by the chronic call for large working parties; modern warfare, indeed, becomes largely a war between those who wish to train the troops for fighting and those who have got something to build or dig or destroy, so complicated is our modern civilization!

In the Infantry Brigade football matches the Battalion came off rather badly. On 12th January it lost to the 5th Black Watch by 2 goals to 1; on 17th January and 9th

February to the 4th Black Watch, each time by 1 goal to 0; on 19th January to the 4th Camerons, 3 to 1; and on the 29th of that month to the 5th Seaforths, 4 to 1. On the other hand it beat the Brigade Headquarters on 22nd January by 3 to 0; and on 1st February the 8th Devons by 3 to 0. The officers beat the officers of the 4th Camerons by 5 to 1 on 5th February.

On 7th February the Division moved to a new area, the 4th Seaforths being billeted in Neuville-sur-Corbie, close to the Brigade Headquarters at Corbie. Training was continued here. On the 17th the finals of the Brigade boxing tournament, arranged by "Wally" Pack, came off. Corporal A. M. Ross won the final of the 10-stone championship; Lance-Corporal Whitton and Private Pack each won one of the special six-round contests, and Private Smart the four-round contest. Sergeant Mackenzie (Dingwall), the Battalion master tailor, beat Pipe-Major Lamont, 5th Black Watch, in three rounds of Highland dancing.

On the 20th a draft of sixty-six men arrived, and Captain C. G. Hogg returned and took over command. On the 25th Major-General Harper inspected the Battalion but—somewhat characteristically—made no remarks!

On the 28th the well-known "shrapnel helmets," better known as "tin hats," were issued to the Battalion, the khaki Balmoral being retained only for parade dress and for use behind the lines. The officers still retained the glengarry for wear when not on duty with troops outside the shelled area.

On 29th February the 51st Division was transferred to the XVII Corps. A stiff march of about four hours over roads in very bad condition brought the Battalion to Mirvaux, where Lieutenant-Colonel C. H. Campbell, D.S.O., Cameron Highlanders, took over command, in succession to Lieutenant-Colonel Cuthbert, who had been seconded for service at home. March opened with two beautiful days, but on the 3rd the weather broke and the Battalion moved to better billets in Rubempré. On the 6th, after a splendid march over good roads, it arrived at Doullens about 3 P.M. and found excellent billets. Moving on again, the 1/4th Seaforths spent the night of the 8th at Beaudricourt, and that of the 9th at Louez, where it was billeted in a large factory. Considering the close proximity of the front line they were fairly comfortable.

On 10th March, after advanced parties had reconnoitred the line, the Battalion relieved the 138th Regiment in the 23rd French Division. Every kindness and help was extended by their French comrades, and the morning of the 11th saw the Seaforths in the line.

The position held by the 51st Division ran from north of Roclincourt, a fortified village defending the right flank, to Neuville St-Vaast (exclusive). The 154th Infantry Brigade held that part of the line which was astride the Arras-Lille road, the 4th Seaforths being on the right, in touch with the 1st Devons of the 5th Division. The village of Ecurie was about 1200 yards behind the front line and in the 154th Brigade area. It was one of the chief tactical points in the line, and most of the labour of the working parties was spent in strengthening its defences. It is situated on the top of the Ecurie ridge, which gives a good view of the opposing ridge, then held by the enemy, between Thélus and Vimy. A little to the north lay the Labyrinth. The German trenches were from 25 to 200 yards away, and saps led up to within bombing distance of the enemy lines.

When taken over, the first defensive system consisted of three lines: the front line, with saps running forward from it; the support line, about 100 yards behind; and the reserve line, called the *Grand Collecteur*, about 200 yards further in rear. The whole is situated on the forward slope of the hill, running down to the valley between Ecurie and Thélus. The communication trenches back from the support line were from two to three miles long—a matter of necessity owing to the ease of observation from the Vimy Ridge opposite.

The front line was in a very bad condition when taken over. It was very wide, there were no traverses, the parapets were not bullet-proof, and the trenches were very much exposed. Soon after taking over it was decided to turn the support line into the main front line, and to hold the original front-line trench with small garrisoned posts in support of the saps. On the other hand there were features that impressed the troops favourably. The depth and security of the dug-outs were a revelation to men who had spent the whole of the previous year in the corrugated-iron splinter-proofs of Flanders.

There was a certain amount of desultory artillery fire and sniping during the next few days, but casualties were few. The enemy appeared to have been in the habit of moving about rather freely in the open, but once the British snipers got to work this abruptly ceased.

The 14th March opened quietly, and the weather was again splendid. During the morning Lieutenant-Colonel Campbell went up from Headquarters to see the line. He did not return, and later on was found shot through the head at a point where a communication trench crossed the support line. His loss, despite his short time with the Battalion, was very much felt by all. Captain R. S. McClintock, the Adjutant of the 4th Gordons, took over temporary command. Heavy shelling of the reserve trenches on the 15th resulted in some casualties.

On the 16th the Battalion was relieved by the 4th Gordons and went into dug-outs in support, returning to the front line on the 22nd. As the front was a rather long one it was reinforced by the Divisional Cyclists. The next day the enemy attacked a sap on the left of the Brigade front, but after about fifteen minutes' brisk fighting the attack died away and the sap was held. The Battalion grenadiers assisted by firing over one thousand grenades into the enemy trenches. Snow fell on the 24th, on which day a No. 4 Company sniper accounted for two Germans. For the next four days there was a good deal of bombing and shell fire on the front and support lines, but casualties were trifling in proportion to the number of shells that dropped.

On the 28th the Battalion went into billets at Etrun. Cleaning up by day and working parties by night occupied most of the time. On the 31st a draft of forty-four other ranks arrived.

On 3rd April the 4th Seaforths returned into the line, to experience the usual desultory bombing and artillery fire. On the 7th, however, a mine was blown in on the front of the 5th Division, followed by an intense bombardment; but the attack that followed made little headway. On the 8th Lieutenant Mills observed preparations for making a new trench behind the German lines, which was shelled, with good results, at 10 P.M. The artillery on both sides was now becoming much more active and the weather was cold and wet.

On the 9th the Battalion went back to support trenches at Ecurie, where a draft of one hundred and forty joined on the 15th. The same day it went back to the line under the command of Major A. B. A. Stewart of the 1st Battalion, who had been badly wounded at Neuve Chapelle. Continuous rain had made the trenches very wet and uncomfortable, while the artillery and trench-mortar fire had increased in intensity. On the 21st the Battalion proceeded to the comparative comfort of Etrun, though working parties and cleaning up kept the men busy.

The weather now became spring-like. At a Divisional parade at Haute Avesnes Major-General Harper presented medal ribbons to several non-commissioned officers and men, after which a party of four officers and about one hundred and twenty other ranks attended a performance at the Divisional theatre.

The Battalion went back into the line on 27th March, and at about 2 A.M. the following morning a mine was sprung on its left, followed by a heavy-gun and trench-mortar bombardment on saps and trenches, which caused many casualties. No attack of any note, however, developed, and the front and saps were held intact.

A diary entry describes this alarm: "I am lying in a dug-out, reading *The Motor Cycle* and wondering if I shall ever ride again, when there is a terrific explosion. A mine has gone up! The timber supports in the dug-out sway to and fro, my candle goes out, and I am almost buried with dirt that falls from the roof. Almost as soon as I can struggle up and spit the dirt out of my mouth a voice at the top of the dug-out steps shouts: 'All out, with gas masks on!' I pull mine out of its satchel, grab my rifle and run up the steps. I could not smell any gas, but there were clouds of smoke from the mine, which, luckily, being short, had gone up just in front of our front trench, filling a good part of it up, but most of our men were down in the saps. A tremendous strafing was going on from both sides—shells were screaming over and the air was alive with machine guns and rifle bullets, bombs, etc., and star shells of all colours made the scene a very thrilling one. Thinking the Germans were attacking, I jumped on the fire step, but could see only volumes of smoke rolling between the lines, and a big bomb or shell bursting only a few yards in front of me put me on my back at the bottom of the trench. An officer coming along just then picked me up, and finding I was not hurt told me to get down the trench to my right, as it was quieter down there. A German battery, away on the right, and in a direct line with our trench, was enfilading it and giving our fellows a rough time. I could see the flash of those guns, and then along would come four shells all together. Each time I saw that flash I crouched in a corner, and once or twice they came so near, those shells, that bits of them showered around me, and shone brightly phosphorescent, like big glow-worms. I kept working my way down, dodging those shells, and had gone fifty or sixty yards before coming to any of my fellows. How we should have got on if the Germans had attacked I dread to think. We lost a lot of men—some had wonderful escapes. A shell dropped in a trench between two men, and although the explosion set their clothes on fire, only one was slightly wounded. Our casualties would have been much heavier but for the fact that most of the men were out in the saps, too near the enemy front line to be shelled. This awful strafing went on for two hours, and did not subside till day broke. It seems to me that both sides had got the wind up, thinking the other side intended making an attack."

On the 29th two new Lewis guns were issued to the Battalion, making a total on charge of eight.

Exceptional vigilance was called for in this sector, for a great many mines had been sprung in it, and a great many more yet remained, while the British and German saps were often only a few yards apart. The enemy shell fire was, likewise, very heavy at times; but the deep dug-outs that the French had made in the chalky soil in the support and reserve lines made the number of casualties comparatively small. The liaison with the Divisional artillery was exceptionally good in this sector, and the troops holding the front line could count on effective retaliation against trench-mortar fire.

The Battalion scouts and snipers under Lieutenant Mills had been doing very good work, and the enemy front line was under continuous observation from dawn to dusk. Much valuable information was obtained and the enemy snipers were practically silenced.

War affects different men in all kinds of ways. Lieutenant Mills, who was in charge of the scouts, was afflicted by the souvenir mania, as witness this story: "Just as we got settled a big bomb dropped in our trench, a little way off on my left. Going along to see what damage it had done I found that it had made a mess of the (No. 4) Company Sergeant-Major's dug-out; the best one, of course! It was half filled up with dirt, the timbers were all over the place, and the batman, having a nice fire on the brazier and a kettle boiling, was about to make the Sergeant-Major a nice cup of tea, but all went west. About the time I got there Lieutenant Mills arrived on the scene. He is the souvenir fiend. 'Was that bomb dropped here, Sergeant-Major?' 'Yes, sir.' 'And did you get the nose?' asked the Lieutenant. 'Did I get the nose!' replied the Sergeant-Major, with an injured expression. 'I nearly got the bloody lot.' This officer would go crawling about the ground at the back of the trenches, in broad daylight, looking for shell and bomb noses! He would then get a man who happened to have a good fire in a brazier to melt the aluminium off; then finding a man who was due to go on leave, he would load him up with lumps of this stuff, addressed to his wife, to post for him when he arrived in England. He told me that his intention was to have a tea service made of it after the war! I thought he would be lucky if there was any 'after the war' for him. One day he came leaping over the back of the trench, with no hat and his hair standing on end. 'By God, that was a near shave! The devils were not satisfied with turning a machine gun on me, but they shelled me with "whizz-bangs."' "

In spite of the weather the health of the troops was good, and there was a notable absence of trench feet. Considering that the front line and saps were occasionally a foot or more deep in water, which sometimes froze at night, the condition of the Battalion reflected the greatest credit on all concerned. It was maintained only by unremitting care on the part of the junior officers and non-commissioned officers. It even had been found necessary to appoint official "rubbers," whose duty it was to chafe the feet of each sentry when he came off duty, thus restoring the circulation, after which he issued to him a pair of dry socks, of which there was always a plentiful supply.

To mark the opening of May an organized "strafe" of the enemy took place, in which the Battalion bombers and rifle grenadiers played a very active rôle. On thc 3rd, the 4th Seaforths went back into the support lines in warm and sunny weather; but when they came up again on the 9th, cold, rainy conditions had again set in, making the change to the billets at Etrun very welcome.

From 15th to 21st May the Battalion had a delightful rest in splendid sunny weather. On going back to the line the enemy trench-mortar fire caused a lot of annoyance, though his guns were comparatively quiet, and endeavours were made to retaliate with the co-operation of our artillery, even the 8-inch howitzers joining in. From observation, however, it appeared that the mortars must be sited in unusual security, and that they probably were fired from the bottom of the steps of dug-outs.

On the 23rd the Battalion experienced a new misfortune, Lieutenant-Colonel Stewart being instantaneously killed by a trench mortar when making a tour of the line. He had endeared himself to all ranks by his soldierly bearing and sterling qualities, and was, moreover, well known to all from the previous winter as being devoted to the interests of the Regiment. He was succeeded on the 27th by Major J. S. Unthank, who had been in temporary command of the 10th Durham Light Infantry.

After the usual relief the Battalion came back into the line from Ecurie on 3rd June, Nos. 3 and 4 Companies in the firing line. About 7 A.M. a German deserter tried to get over in broad daylight. He crawled for the British line, with a little white flag in his hand; then, when half-way over, sprang up and ran for it, but was shot down by his own side. After dark Lieutenant Mills and Lance-Corporal Bessent went over and found him dead. He was so heavy that two stretcher-bearers had to be fetched to bring him to Headquarters. He proved to be a Lorrainer. It was evident that he had for some time meant to desert, but no documents of value were found on him.

On that day, too, Private Howie, who had a premonition of his own death, was killed by a bomb—the last of four brothers who had come out to France. On the 4th Private Louis Tracy was shot dead through the head. On the 6th there was a change over of companies, and rumours of Lord Kitchener's death began to arrive. On the 8th three men were blown to pieces by a shell and five were wounded, including three Lewis gunners—Still, who was daily expecting a commission, Dean and Comrie Smith. The next day the 4th Gordons came up in relief, and the 4th Seaforths went to Etrun.

On 13th June a grenade company was formed; the men were drawn from all companies and were commanded by Lieutenant Pender.

On the 15th the Battalion returned to their old trenches, and on the 17th—exactly one hundred days since they had arrived in this sector—seventeen men were killed by a bomb while repairing the parapet. As showing how the personnel had changed, one man remarks that one of those killed was the last, save himself, left with the Battalion, out of a group of eight that had come out in 1914; some had got commissions in other units, some had been transferred or invalided, some had been killed.

On 18th June a French aeroplane made a forced landing behind the enemy's lines, and in the evening a Lewis gun was taken down a sap to " liven up " a German working party that could be heard in No-man's-land. There was a very successful interruption, and two Germans came into the sap, shouting " Kamerad." Unfortunately for himself, one threw his arms round the neck of one of our men, on which the latter's " chum," scenting treachery, severely wounded the German.

The 4th Gordons again relieved the Battalion on 21st June. Sergeant Macleod, better known as " Old File," was a veteran of other wars, and was in charge of the Brigade bomb store in the Roclincourt sector. The store was in a shattered house near the reserve line and attracted a good deal of the enemy's attention. On 21st June the store was set on fire and " Old File " escaped from the cellar. Unfortunately discipline proved too strong: he remembered that he had left his equipment, went back for it, and was never seen again. Relays of No. 4, his old company, worked for days on end in the hope of rescuing him; but the house was burned out, the bombs had blown up, and the walls had collapsed, so that it is not to be wondered at that his body was not found. The 4th Seaforths went up in relief of the Gordons on the 28th, in the middle of a demonstration intended to draw the enemy's attention from an attack to be launched elsewhere. The men in the trenches appear unanimously to have voted the demonstration to have been a most successful " draw "! On the 30th the Germans again sprung a large mine. Some of the 2/21st London and the 2nd London Scottish took the places of men of the companies in the firing line. As it was their first spell of duty in the trenches they came in for a good deal of chaff.

One of these London men has described how he went on fatigue with some of the Seaforths. It struck him as peculiar that, whereas every Londoner was laden with large and unwieldy bundles of sandbags, the Seaforths had each a small roll of wire, or something equally compact. On arrival at the front line he found that he had only six of his sandbags, and was duly " crimed " for dropping the others on the way up.

Relief took place on 4th July, and the Battalion went back to Etrun, when its strength was thirty-one officers and seven hundred and forty-six other ranks.

On 10th July the Battalion relieved the Gordons; but its stay in the trenches was short, for on the 13th it was relieved by the 2/23rd London Regiment, and moved to billets at Louez.

Looking back on the four and a half months spent in the Roclincourt sector the principal feature that strikes one is the monotony. The regular sequence of six-day reliefs in the same trenches, always interchanging with the same battalion, with the alternating retirement to Ecurie or Etrun, was a deadly business. Even an officer hardly saw anyone outside his own company, and a man hardly anyone outside his own platoon.

No wonder the idea that men in the trenches required distraction steadily gained ground. First Divisional concert parties were started, then cinemas were added, and finally permission to revive regimental bands was given.

The pipers were collected into a band and went no more into the trenches. Major R. S. Hunt, King's Dragoon Guards, who had come in May as Second-in-Command, took a great interest in the band, and, when on leave, spent much money on kit for them, of which he made a gift to the Battalion, and then the pipers made a gallant show. A regimental canteen and a tailor's shop also were started about this time.

Rats and mice abounded in this sector, in addition to those other "small deer" whose permanence was as that of the poor. The rats appear to have been the black species.

During this period Regimental Quartermaster - Sergeant Wilson went home time - expired, and was succeeded by Company Sergeant - Major Thomas Cumming (Invergordon) of No. 4 Company. He recently had attended a course at one of the schools of instruction held in France; an extract from the official report on his work there speaks for itself: "No. 333, Company Sergeant-Major Cumming, has shown great attention throughout the course. His bearing and appearance have always been in keeping with that of a warrant-officer in such a regiment. He has been very conscientious in all his work in connexion with the course. In every respect he seems a very reliable warrant-officer. He has been a credit to his regiment while at the school."

The usual crop of rumours went the round of the sector. Here is an example of how these things might originate. The Brigade Major and Staff Captain go for a stroll together after dinner. While passing a sentry the Brigade Major, complaining of lumbago, remarks that he hopes that the attack will not last so long as the last one did. The sentry, coming to the present, in saluting the passing officers, makes his hand tell on the magazine of his rifle in the second motion, and the noise thus produced prevents his hearing more than the last part of the Brigade Major's remark. On coming off duty he assures his comrades that there will be a big attack soon, but that it will not last long, and that the war will be over shortly. On being asked for his authority for the statement he explains that he heard one General tell another; for the red band on their caps is evidence enough to him that they were Generals.

There were a large number of time-expired men at this time. It is greatly to their credit that most of them re-engaged after the month's leave to which they were entitled.

Captain Ian Forsyth (Ballintraid) was gazetted to a Majority, much antedated, and Lieutenant Colin Cameron to be Captain about this time.

The following description by an orderly corporal of his duties gives a good idea of the administrative work in a company in the Roclincourt sector: "I really haven't had such a bad time of it. I'm in the usually crowded dug-out in the supports acting as orderly corporal. There's plenty of work going; from eight to about midnight making up the rations into bags for the different platoons; sorting out bread and jam and ham and meat and spuds and cheese and cake and cigarettes and tobacco and matches and candles and butter; all going into the universal sandbags, and all in a manner which would shock you terribly could you see the proceedings; for there's only one pair of hands to do all the actual dividing and no water to spare to wash with after each dose. However, it all goes the same way home, and there are no grumbles. Then from midnight to dawn I sleep, and sleep sound. Then the chaps come for their grub, and after I have satisfied them I get my own breakfast. Then comes, generally, a trip to the Aid Post with a man requiring some medicine or other. Then after dinner comes another short doss, then the round of the trenches for letters to be censored and then tea. Of course this is my own particular programme—the rest of the company do the ordinary trench work; but it shows you I'm pretty busy."

After a night in uncomfortable billets at Louez the 4th Seaforths marched off early on 14th July down the Arras-St-Pol highroad, and after a hot and dusty march of twelve miles reached its billets in Villers Brulin, one of the quiet, secluded, old-world villages of France. Here it settled down comfortably, and was congratulating itself on its lot when, late at night, orders came to march early the next morning to cross-roads at Tincques near by, where it would find lorries for its conveyance.

Not without reluctance the Battalion repacked stores and kit and started in a rush in the dark of the morning. Little did they yet know of the ways of lorries. After a weary wait of several hours they at last arrived, and in got the 4th Seaforths; but not even the officer in charge could tell their eventual destination, for he could not open his orders till he reached a certain spot. Late in the evening he stopped at cross-roads and the Battalion debused. Here it was found that the Brigade had already arrived, and that billets were awaiting the Battalion in Le Souich.

On the 16th the whole Brigade marched in column of route and covered 24 kilometres. It was a hot and tiring march, and the country was hilly. This was the cavalry billeting area behind the Somme battle front, and the Battalion went into Prouville, a village lately occupied by the Indian Cavalry Corps. Here it became part of the XV Corps of the Fourth Army.

After three quiet days there, sudden orders came to entrain at Candas, and on 20th July the Battalion detrained at Méricourt, at this time the rail-head for the Somme battle front. Thence the Brigade marched forward to Méaulte, and there went into bivouac. It was a hot day and the march a tiring one. The road was congested with traffic of all sorts, and all the hustle and confusion inseparable from life behind a battle front reigned supreme.

As the Battalion marched forward the appearance of the country began to change; the fields and crops looked more and more untended, and gradually the trees grew fewer and fewer, the dust became thicker, and the sound of the guns grew louder.

When the Battalion reached its bivouac it found beside it the transport of a battalion of the Durham Light Infantry; and here, shortly after, the Battalion itself marched in—all that was left of it—one officer and about two platoons of men. The roar of the guns went on, the traffic never ceased, and guns, ambulances and wagons jostled on the road.

On the afternoon of 21st July the Division moved up to

MAP 7.

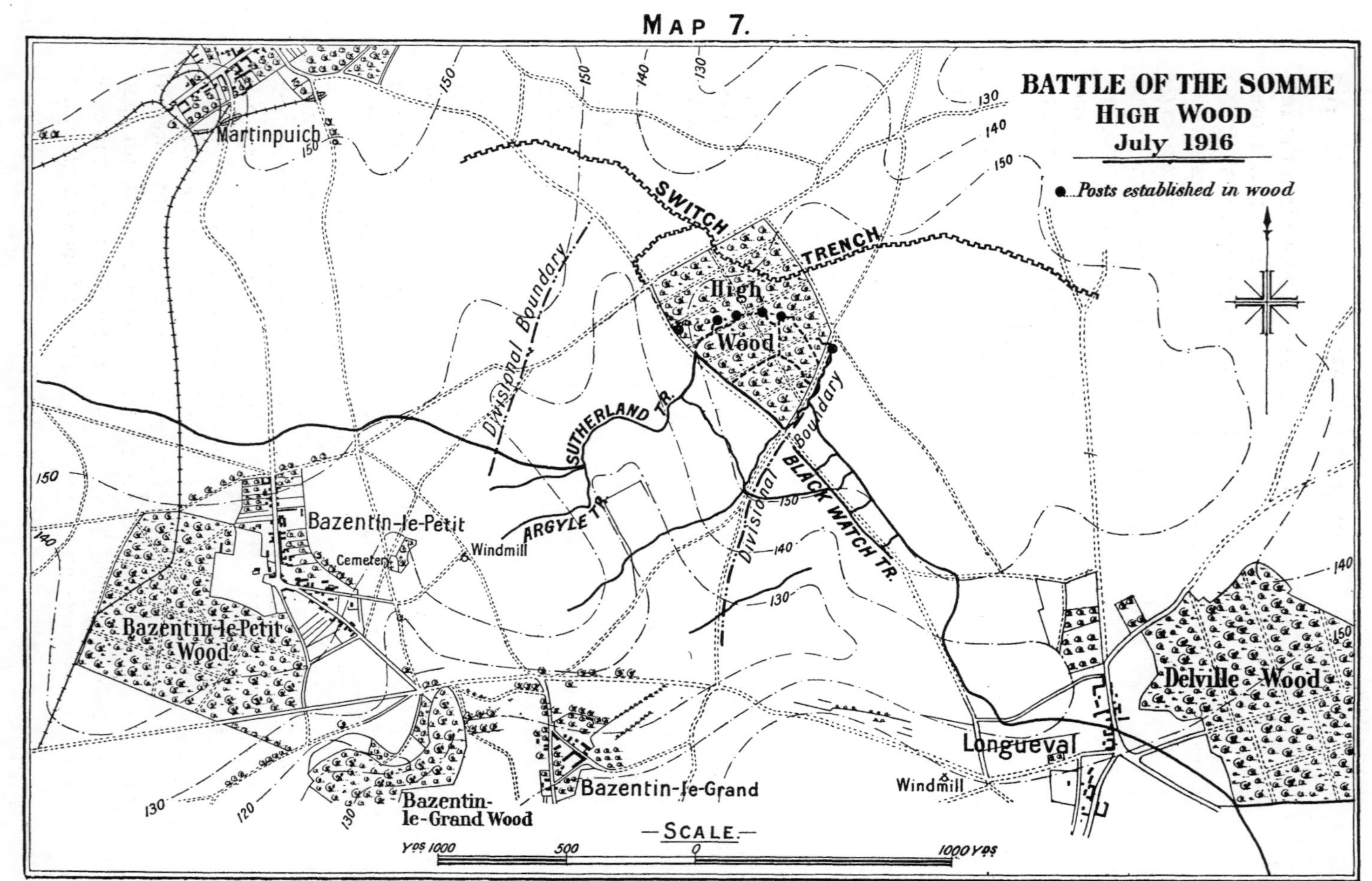

BATTLE OF THE SOMME
HIGH WOOD
July 1916
Posts established in wood
Martinpuich
SWITCH TRENCH
High Wood
Divisional Boundary
SUTHERLAND TR.
ARGYLE TR.
BLACK WATCH TR.
Bazentin-le-Petit
Cemetery
Windmill
Bazentin-le-Petit Wood
Bazentin-le-Grand
Bazentin-le-Grand Wood
Longueval
Windmill
Delville Wood
SCALE
YDS 1000
500
0
1000 YDS

take over its front. The 154th Brigade was to go into the line with the other two brigades in reserve, and all three moved up simultaneously. The 154th Brigade moved across country to Fricourt, where it picked up its guides, and as it marched it could see the other two brigades marching one on each side of the main road. After picking up the guides the route crossed that of one of the other brigades and troubles began, for the 154th had to break the other column at intervals, and, soon after, it entered the stream of traffic going to and returning from Mametz and Mametz Valley and Wood.

The dust was appalling, but in spite of this, and of the gas that was being brought on the wind blowing down the rapidly darkening Mametz Valley, the Battalion got safely through it. As an illustration of the difficulties, the guide of one company lost his bearings and blindly followed a man he saw in front of him for a very long time, until finally the company was found to be marching in a complete circle, with the guide following the last man of the company he was supposed to lead.

The 4th Seaforths were in Brigade reserve and relieved the 9th Highland Light Infantry beyond the Mametz Valley. They had just come down from High Wood (Bois des Foureaux), where they had taken part in one of the numerous attacks on it. They had suffered heavy losses and were very weak.

On the evening of 22nd July, Nos. 1 and 4 Companies were moved up to High Wood in support of the 4th Gordons, and the remaining two companies moved slightly forward. Orders now came for the 4th Gordons and the 9th The Royal Scots to attack in the dark early next morning. The attack was launched accordingly, but met with great resistance, and was unsuccessful. Nos. 1 and 4 Companies were not employed, though they both suffered heavily from the bombardment. By 11.50 P.M. Nos. 2 and 3 Companies had relieved the 4th Gordons; No. 4 remained where it was, with No. 1 in Battalion reserve.

High Wood at this time was still a wood, with trees of considerable size and thick undergrowth of holly, laurel and rhododendron. Both British and Germans were in part occupation of it, so that it was impossible for either side to shell or gas it. Consequently, if the infantry on either side kept quiet, it was a peaceful spot. The ground was littered with dead from the last and several previous attacks, and many wounded were brought in by the Seaforths, some of them having been out for days. Sergeant Macleod of No. 1

Company brought in several from between the lines, until he himself was wounded when going out to fetch another. There was one whom no one could attempt to reach; he lay right under the German parapet outside the wood, away to the right of the Seaforths. Each morning he raised himself and waved his arm, and each morning they looked to see if the Germans had taken him in; but though he lay within two yards of them, they would not lift a finger to help. On the last morning the Seaforths were there he lay motionless.

Such incidents made everyone most bitter against the enemy, for our own men were risking their lives to bring in Germans, and here they deliberately let a man die under their eyes. Indeed at this time the fighting between British and Germans was particularly bitter, probably because the latter had realized that our armies, ever growing in numbers, efficiency and *moral*, were the obstacle that they must break if they would not themselves be broken.

For already the *moral* of the Germans was ebbing. Their troops in High Wood appeared to be quite exhausted, or the position of the Battalion would have been precarious; for on its left was a large and wholly unoccupied gap in the line, so that at night small posts had to be put out to the rear. This gap was closed eventually by the 7th Argyll and Sutherland Highlanders. During the night of the 24th, Nos. 1 and 4 Companies relieved the Norfolks in the front line to the east of High Wood.

Owing to heavy shell fire this relief was not accomplished till the early hours of the 25th; consequently an attack on the north-east corner of the wood, which had been planned for the night 24-25th, had to be postponed. During the day new posts were pushed out in the wood—not, however, without considerable fighting, in which Lieutenant Phillips was killed; but a concrete block-house was occupied and the posts connected up. That night, acting on orders from Corps Headquarters, Lieutenant James A. Ross (Easter Wemyss, Fife), of No. 3 Company, led a storming party against the north-east corner of the wood, under cover of a heavy bombardment. The wood, however, was untouched by shell fire; the Germans were in great strength, and greeted our men, as they charged for the trench, with a heavy shower of hand grenades. Lieutenant Ross alone reached the trench, and was seen by those behind him running along it, firing his revolver till he fell. Sergeant A. Mackenzie and the leading men sheltered under the parapet till the firing ceased, when they crawled back; the remainder got what cover they could in old broken shelters, so that the total casualties were light.

With this abortive effort the activities of the Battalion in High Wood ended, and on 26th July it handed over to the 7th Black Watch. No. 3 Company was delayed on its way out, and became involved in the evening gas shelling at Mametz Wood, suffering some casualties in consequence. The Battalion returned to Méaulte, bringing out of the line a captured machine gun.

During these five days the casualties were:

OFFICERS

Killed: Second Lieutenants Ross and Phillips.
Wounded: Captain R. H. Hay-Will, Second Lieutenants Clark, Mills, Addison (remained at duty), Cowan and Wray.

OTHER RANKS

Killed: 16. *Wounded*: 161. *Missing*: 9.

This proved to be the only appearance of the Battalion in the front line on the Somme until the final phase on the Ancre. It may be mentioned that no further advance was ever made directly in High Wood, which eventually fell to an encircling movement supported by tanks, which here made their first appearance on 15th September.

"During this short tour," says Lieutenant-Colonel Unthank, "a peculiarity of the German soldier struck us all most forcibly, and that was the blind and dazed sort of way he would move about. During our first twenty-four hours in High Wood our snipers were forbidden to shoot, so as to give everyone a chance of finding his feet and the way about the wood. We explored the wood up to the German trench on the far side opposite to us, and from half way along their side of the wood we found a footpath, and, following it, discovered, in the centre of the wood, a concrete block-house occupied by a German post, and all day Germans sauntered up and down this path. The following days, however, the snipers were allowed to shoot, and claimed seventy-seven killed alone; and even if this number is exaggerated they had a lot of shooting all day, mostly in the centre of the wood, and yet the Germans continued to walk openly and blindly across this corner, until it seemed almost a shame to shoot them, it was so easy. One wondered if the awful bombardment they were constantly exposed to had so dazed them that they hardly knew, and were careless of, what they did. Most of us who have watched a German attack have seen the same sort of thing, and many of us have shot man after man on the same spot and yet still another would rise from behind and slowly advance on the same line as the man he had seen fall in front of him, to add to the group. Company Sergeant-Major Mackenzie of No. 3 Company had an experience of this at Roeux the following year. At short range he marked a gap in a bank, behind which Germans were advancing, and so he covered the gap with his rifle. At first he could see only the heads of the men, but before he had finished they were exposed waist-high, and, what is more, they made no effort to get across, but slowly stepped on the dead body in front without even bending, and added one more to the heap.

"Ever since 1914 one had heard similar stories, and, for his own part, the writer had always taken them with a considerable grain of salt, until he had a similar experience himself. The Germans were advancing in attack formation in little groups, one man behind the other, and he dropped the whole of one group on the same spot. The range was about a hundred yards, so missing was out of the question.

"It is hard to believe that any men could be so unintelligent as this, especially the German, and it is difficult to account for. One explanation is that the German soldier had a dope before going into action, but beyond the dope of British high explosives he can have had none in High Wood. Or is it the result of German discipline, depriving him of all mind and making him into an automaton?"

The 154th Brigade rested at Méaulte from 27th to 31st July. The Battalion won the Brigade tug-of-war; its strength was now thirty officers and six hundred and thirty-five other ranks.

On 1st August the 154th relieved the 153rd Brigade in Divisional reserve at Fricourt Wood, providing working parties forward, in one of which Lieutenant E. W. R. Finch was wounded and later died in hospital. Four other ranks were killed, thirteen wounded and one missing. On the 3rd a draft of one hundred men arrived.

On the night of the 6th-7th the Division was relieved, under orders to join the 2nd Anzac Corps in the Second Army.

Captain " Geordie " Levack, R.A.M.C., who had joined the Battalion while it was in the Indian Corps, was transferred to another unit about this time. He came from Tobermory, and the West Coast man — especially if he " had the Gaelic " — always found a soft place in his heart. During his student days at Edinburgh he had been a corporal in the " Dandy Ninth " (9th The Royal Scots), and he liked to " 'shun " and " dress " his sick parades. There was great sorrow in the Battalion when the " Old Doc." was killed later on with another division on the Somme. Captain Levack was succeeded by Captain Healy, imperturbable in temper save when a man came sick, complaining of his boots. Then, in a strong Irish brogue, he would rap out : " Be God, bedad, an' I'm no shoemaker. Away wit' ye ! "

SYNOPSIS OF EVENTS FROM THE MIDDLE TO THE CLOSE OF THE BATTLES OF THE SOMME

(*3rd September to 17th November* 1916)

THE third phase of the Battle of the Somme began on 3rd September and ended on 9th November 1916. Its most intense period began with the French attack on the 12th, followed by the British attack on the 15th. It resulted in the flattening of the German salient between Chilly and Belloy and the attainment by the French north of the Somme of a line running from a point on the river about a mile east of Clery through Bouchavesnes to Morval, which was held by the British. Thence the British line ran by Gueudecourt and Le Sars to Thiepval. Bad weather set in towards the end of September, preventing the rapid delivery of attack after attack on a grand scale, with the result that the enemy had time to make fresh lines of defence in rear. Allied pressure had once more to take the form of local attacks with limited objectives.

The fourth phase, known as the Battle of the Ancre, began on 13th November with the brilliant captures of St-Pierre Divion and Beaumont Hamel. Progress was made here to a depth of over a mile, and lesser gains were made on the British centre and right, while the French got possession of Sailly. On the 17th the Battle of the Somme came to an end.

The battle marks several interesting tactical innovations, two of which must be touched on here. The first was the return to the long-extinct chariot warfare. Just as the chariot had been used to mow a lane through the enemy in combination with the use of missiles, so was the tank to be used: the principle is exactly the same in either case. The second is the advance under cover of a creeping barrage, successive lines pressing on one after another, each in turn consolidating its own gains, while its successors pass through it. The theoretical limit to this kind of thing is the effective range of the guns, but a check may arise from the discovery of a concealed strongpoint such as the Quadrilateral, which, being sited on a reverse slope with a false crest line, was most difficult to locate.

But the outstanding feature of the Somme is that it showed that the hastily raised and trained British troops had now become the dominant factor on the Western front, a position they never lost. From the Commander-in-Chief down was once more exhibited the native capacity for war possessed by the British nations.

THE TRENCHES

CHAPTER VIII

THE ANCRE

On the night of 6th-7th August 1916 the 51st Division was relieved by the 33rd and the Battalion went into bivouac near Dernancourt, where it spent the next two days in bathing and cleaning up. On the 9th it entrained at Méricourt, and, arriving at Longpré-les-St-Coeur, marched to Liercourt, where it remained till the 11th. On that day it entrained at 7 A.M., proceeding *via* Abbeville, Etaples and Calais to Steenbecque, where it arrived at 5.30 P.M. and went into billets at Ebblinghem. It now came under the Anzac Corps.

On 14th August the Battalion entrained at 10.20 A.M. and reached Steenwerck an hour later, going into billets at Armentières, then reckoned a " quiet " area, though the town was subject to occasional shelling, and there was a good deal of trench-mortar fire in the line. This can be extremely unpleasant, and, while it is going on, everyone has to be ready to act on the sentry's warning. Flanders seemed to lend itself particularly to this form of warfare, for there was more of it on the Second Army front than elsewhere, and on most days each side usually discharged a certain number of bombs, either in the morning or the afternoon. After a little practice the sentry could see the shells in the air and judge with fair accuracy where they would fall. He then blew a whistle and warned anyone within range as to how best to take cover. It was annoying, but caused few casualties.

The Seaforths were soon to experience the "quietness" of Armentières, for on the morning of 15th August nine men were wounded during the shelling of the town. That day the Battalion relieved the Wellington Battalion of the 1st New Zealand Brigade. The troops thus relieved were sent straight down to the Somme. The 154th Brigade came under the orders of the 1st New Zealand Division until, on the 18th, the 51st took over the whole sector, on the front Wez Macquart-l'Epinette. The front consisted of a series of small posts.

On the 19th, two men were killed and one was wounded by a bomb. Two days later the 4th Seaforths were relieved by the 4th Gordons and went into the subsidiary line in support. Here they were joined by a draft of one hundred and twenty. The time was, as usual, mainly occupied by working parties; but the men were able to get baths. On the 26th the Battalion was relieved by the 6th Gordon Highlanders and marched to the training camp at Bailleul, where it was joined by a draft of twenty-eight. On the 29th General Plumer inspected the Division and presented some medal ribbons. Sergeant D. Munro, No. 2 Company, was the only recipient in the Battalion.

On 2nd September the Battalion marched to hutments at Romarin, and next day took over from the 11th (Scottish) Battalion, Northumberland Fusiliers, in the Rue du Sac, near Ploegsteert. Three companies were in front and one in support. The line held by the Division at this point extended from the Lys to Le Gheer. This move was made so as to allow the 23rd Division to leave for the Somme before the 19th Division, which was to relieve it, had arrived. The only incident of note was when one of our aeroplanes was hit by a shell and came down behind the German lines. On 8th September the 9th Cheshires relieved the Seaforths, who went back to Armentières.

At Armentières there was the usual round of working parties and cleaning up. On 14th September the Brigade suffered a heavy loss by the death of Brigadier-General C. E. Stewart, who was hit by shell fire near the Headquarters of the 4th Gordons at Houplines.

On the 15th the Battalion relieved the Gordons, Nos. 1, 3 and 4 Companies being in front line and No. 2 in support. There was a great deal of raiding on this front, although the 4th Seaforths did not themselves carry out any raids during this tour.

On the 17th Brigadier-General J. G. H. Hamilton, an officer of the Black Watch, took over command of the Brigade.

On 22nd September the Battalion was relieved by B Battalion, 8th Australian Infantry Brigade, and at 10.30 A.M. marched for Erquinghem, where it went into billets. Two days later Brigadier-General Hamilton made the acquaintance of the officers, and on the 25th the Battalion marched to Estaires, where the Brigade was assembling preparatory to going back to the battle area. The next day General Plumer made a farewell inspection, but it was not till the evening of the 30th that the Battalion entrained at Merville for Candas, where it arrived at 10 P.M. and went into billets.

Lieutenant-Colonel Unthank writes: "We went back for this, our second venture in the Somme Battle, in a very different frame of mind to that in which we had gone before. Our short experience of the Somme in July had given us a glimpse of a modern battle and enlarged our views. The men, whether rightly or wrongly, had come away with the conviction that they had been sent away from this battle in disgrace, and also that they had not been given a fair chance. This put them on their mettle and roused their pride of race, inspiring them with a determination to succeed if given another chance."

The Division took over the line opposite Puisieux on 3rd October, and the 154th Brigade was moved up just behind the front line to help in the preparations. The Seaforths marched nine miles to Sarton on the 3rd, six miles to huts at Bus-les-Artois on the 4th, and to bivouac near Courcelles on the 5th. Here it supplied a working party seven hundred strong for night work on the communication trenches. The two following days were likewise spent in heavy work, for the Royal Engineers were employed in building new trenches, preparing dressing stations, making dumps for rations, water and stores, and laying telephone cables, while strong parties also had to be found to carry up trench-mortar ammunition. On the 8th, bivouac was shifted to Colincamps, where heavy work continued till the 12th, when the 4th Gordons came up in relief and the 4th Seaforths withdrew to billets in Louvencourt. Here a draft of twenty other ranks from the 9th Battalion joined.

Close at hand was a large training area, on which the two other brigades of the Division were practising the attack which they were to carry out, the 154th Brigade being in reserve. As this form of attack was a novel one, the Brigade had much to learn, and after a few days' training practised a brigade attack, the first exercise it had had for a long time in combined training. There were also opportunities for football, and several inter-regimental matches were played; while the Divisional theatre also was within easy reach, so that the Battalion had quite a pleasant time. On the 17th billets were moved four miles to Raincheval, and on the 18th another four miles to Lealvillers, the weather being very bad.

This backward move was due to a hitch in the preparations for the projected attack on Serre, and finally it was decided that the Division should attack at Beaumont Hamel. On 22nd October, accordingly, the Battalion relieved the 6th Gordon Highlanders in reserve, two companies being in Auchonvillers and the remainder in bivouac in the wood behind Mailly Maillet. Frost and snow made bivouacking uncomfortable. Two days later Major Hunt left to take command of the 8th King's Own.

On the 26th the Battalion relieved the 6th Black Watch in the firing line south of Beaumont Hamel, the first three companies being in the front-line trench and No. 4 in support. The 9th The Royal Scots were on the left and the Royal Marines of the 63rd Division on the right. There was great aeroplane activity here and several came down, while artillery and trench mortars were constantly in action, and there was much bombing and several raids.

It was a miserable autumn, cold and wet, sometimes frost and snow and sometimes rain. Hard as the Battalion might work when in the line, the trenches got worse and worse—deeper and deeper in mud and water. Want of revetments helped rain and shell fire to break down the sides and fill the trenches with mud. Several dug-outs collapsed, burying a number of men, some of whom were killed. Fortunately, despite the shell fire, the number of casualties was surprisingly small.

On 30th October the Battalion was relieved by the 7th Black Watch and went back to billets in Lealvillers, where three men were wounded in the town. The next two days were bright. On 4th November Captain Inch, of the 8th Battalion The Royal Scots, joined as Second-in-Command. On the 5th a move was made to huts in Mailly Wood.

On 7th November the Battalion relieved the 4th Gordons in the right sector opposite Beaumont Hamel and found the trenches worse than ever. So bad did the weather become that fears that the intended attack would be impossible were entertained; but, as great preparations had been made and everything was ready, there was great unwillingness that it should be postponed. Failing an improvement in the weather, however, it was clear that the winter must pass before the attack could be made, and opinions oscillated with the movements of the barometer. Orders that had been given were cancelled: no one knew what to expect. The Battalion remained in the trenches longer than had been intended owing to the uncertainty of the weather. So small, at one time, did the chance of making an attack seem to be, that on 11th November the posts in the front line were ordered to be wired. Though quite unpremeditated, this had the good effect of deceiving the Germans, who now thought that all risk of an attack was over.

Next day there was a change for the better. Rain ceased and the forecast was good, so that all seemed more propitious for the effort that had so long been planned. A final decision was reached, and orders issued that the attack would take place on the following morning.

All this time the usual exchange of shells, tear shells and gas took place. The enemy paid particular attention to Essex Trench, Tipperary Communication Trench and Thurles Dump. The Battalion was relieved on the night of the 12th and marched back to Forceville.

At 5.45 A.M. on 13th November the 51st Division attacked Beaumont Hamel. This was part of the great attack by the V Corps, the Divisions being the 63rd, 51st, 2nd, 37th and 3rd supported by the II Corps south of the Ancre. On the right it was successful; Beaucourt fell to the 63rd and Beaumont Hamel to the 51st Division: to the left little progress was made.

Plans for the attack had been most carefully drawn up. For several days our artillery had been methodically shelling the position, with a view to cutting the wire. All ranks were carefully instructed in the disposition of supplies, the recognition of direction signs, the method of aeroplane co-operation, and, most important of all, the systematic advance under the protection of a creeping barrage. The various enemy lines were marked on the map in distinguishing colours, and so came to be known as the Blue, Brown or Green Lines. The attack on the Blue Line was conducted in four lines of men in extended order, termed waves. The duty of the first wave was to keep close up to the artillery barrage as it advanced, usually at a distance of fifty yards, and to clear the first line of trenches, killing or taking prisoner the defenders and dealing with the men in the dug-outs. It then consolidated the position against counter-attacks, and reorganized in readiness for further action.

The second wave passed (or "leap-frogged") over the first, closely following the barrage, and attacking and dealing with the second line in the same way. The third and fourth waves acted in a similar manner, until the whole of the first objective was reached. Further objectives were taken in the same way. It is obvious that the governing factor was the ability of each wave to keep up with the advancing barrage; in this battle the rate of advance was 100 yards in four minutes. While each successive wave was advancing on its particular objective the preceding one was clearing the captured position of the enemy and consolidating against counter-attack. Failure to attain an objective was nearly always caused by inability to keep up with the barrage, whereby the enemy were given time to get their machine guns and rifles into action.

But it is not only from the point of view of the attacker that this method of "leap-frog" has advantages; from the point of view of defence against counter-attacks there is much to be gained by this disposition in depth. The local counter-attack spends its force on the most advanced lines, and, finding an ever-increasing resistance as it penetrates in depth, is finally driven back itself, as by the compression of a spring. The sooner it follows on the attack the more likely is it to be successful, because the attackers have had the less time to consolidate their positions.

The artillery barrage at this time was in three parts. The first consisted of a screen of 18-pr. shrapnel; the second was put up by the 4·5-inch howitzers 100 yards farther forward; the third was the heavy artillery, yet another 100 yards ahead. Special points were engaged by groups of guns told off for the purpose: such as important cross-roads in rear of the enemy position, his artillery positions and strong points from which he might be able to develop enfilade fire on the attacking troops.

The whole system was like a game in which one side, by skilful use of its artillery, sought to keep the defending artillery from concentrating on the advancing infantry, and the defending infantry cowering in its trenches till too late to bring effective rifle and machine-gun fire to bear. It was the triumph of fire over shock tactics—until we revived the old chariot warfare with our tanks!

It was now possible for the infantry to follow the barrage within fifty yards without serious loss. In theory it should be possible for them to stand immediately under the bursting shells, since the shrapnel bullets are thrown forward. In practice, however, shell fire cannot be thus nicely regulated. No two guns are exactly alike; for their accuracy varies with the erosion of the bore with use and from other causes. Shells are not of absolutely equal weight; so that their trajectories vary within certain limits. Fuses, too, differ slightly. The result of all these differences is that there are always a certain number of short bursts, and it was found that fifty yards gave a reasonable degree of security from their effects. So accurate indeed did our artillery become that troops often got well within this distance without serious loss; and it was better to risk a few casualties from short bursts so as to make sure of reaching the enemy trenches before he was ready than to allow him to get his machine guns into action.

Methods of communication had, by now, been greatly improved. On these, perhaps as much as on anything, depends the tactical development of a battle. Headquarters can no longer go forward with the fighting line, but must remain at the spot where all know how to find it, until the unit or formation of which it is the controlling force consolidates and reorganizes. It is, in fact, the nerve-centre on which all but the actual carrying out of an order depends.

Early and reliable information is essential to enable a commander to direct and control his force to the best advantage. The means of communication comprised runners; the telephone, wireless telephony; aeroplanes, pigeons; visual signalling by flags, lamps, shutters, rockets and Very lights. Runners, despite the dangers to which they were exposed, were the most reliable of all. They were men picked for staying power and intelligence, and were distinguished by a red armlet. Many of their deeds of courage and resource were done unnoticed, and unrecorded; but they deserve a high place in the Hall of Fame.

At one time there was an order that runners were to take bicycles wherever they went. When it was discovered that they spent most of the time carrying the bicycles like a kind of collar the order was rescinded.

Mobility being so essential, the pack was discarded when going into action. The remainder of the equipment was worn over the greatcoat, the skirts of which were fastened back, so as to give greater freedom to the legs.

Changes had been made also in the gas mask. The first masks used were handkerchiefs, socks or other closely woven textile fabrics, soaked in water. Later on urine was found to be more efficacious than water. Soon followed specially made masks, chemically prepared, which were held over the nose and mouth. Then followed a kind of helmet fitted with eye-pieces; it was made of flannel and the chemical mixture was kept moist by means of glycerine. The air was breathed in through the flannel and exhaled through a mouthpiece fitted with a one-way valve. It was easy enough to adjust, but was horribly uncomfortable. It induced perspiration, which dimmed the eye-pieces and made observation difficult; while its heat made it unbearable to wounded and exhausted men. It was replaced by the box respirator, which was easy to carry and adjust. The chemicals were contained in a box fitted with valves, which was worn on the breast. It was only when lachrymatory gas was being used that the eyes and face had to be covered.

The men each carried one hundred and seventy rounds of ammunition and two sandbags, and every other man a pick or shovel. In the haversack were carried the "iron ration" and "the unexpended portion of the day's ration."

The attack on Beaumont Hamel began at 5.45 A.M. on 13th November, after a two-days' bombardment. It was most successful, the village and four lines of trenches being carried, and large numbers of prisoners taken. The troops showed great initiative. Where no frontal opposition was made they passed on, ignoring points where it was strong. These points were then out-flanked and their resistance overcome. We had learned much since Neuve Chapelle. The resistance of the Germans in the village and the Y Ravine had, however, caused enough delay to prevent the attacking troops from keeping up with the barrage, so that the advance on Frankfurt Trench was abandoned.

It is said that General Harper first heard of the success of his Division from a wounded Black Watch private. The

MAP 8.

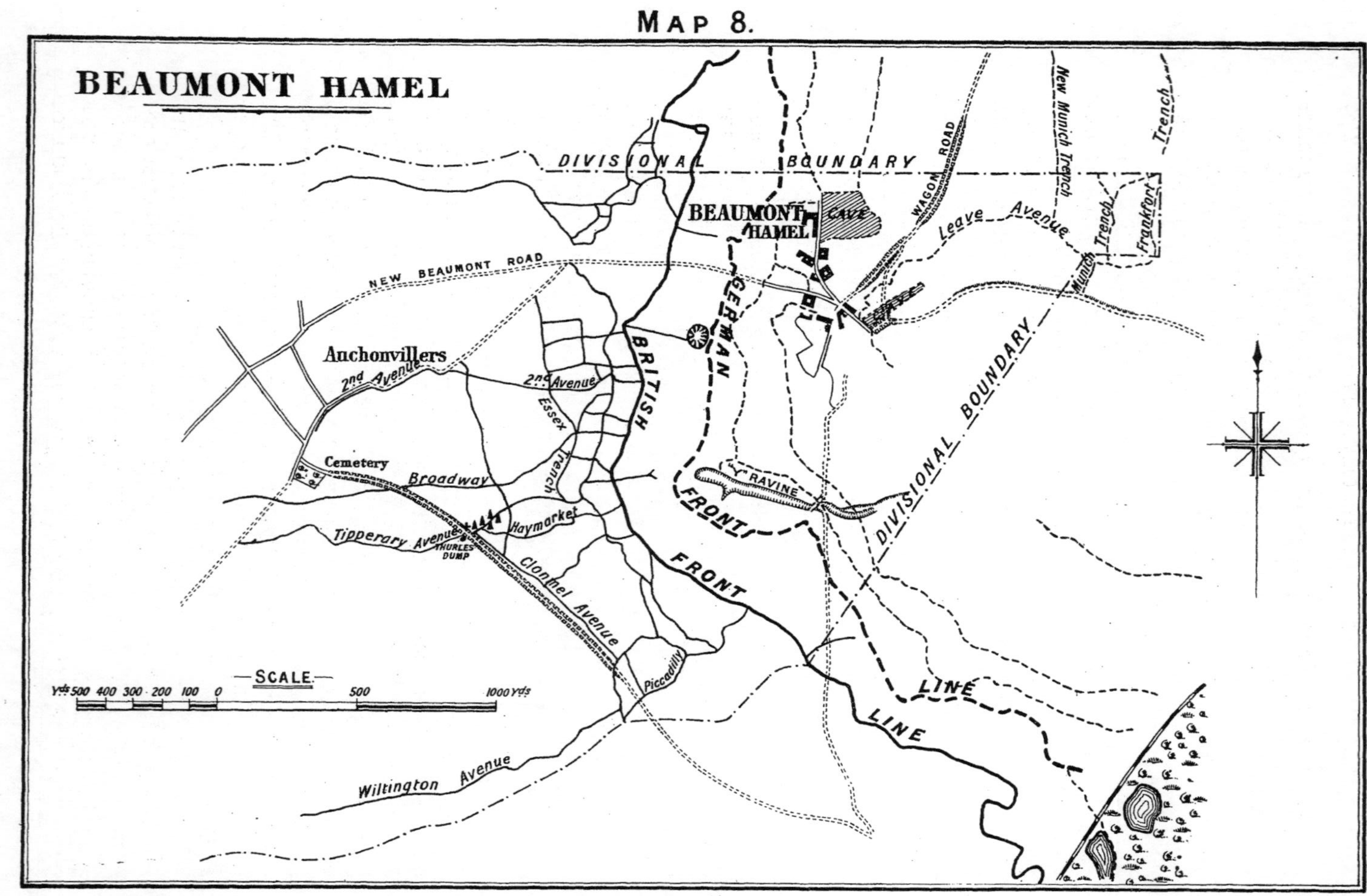

BEAUMONT HAMEL
DIVISIONAL BOUNDARY
BEAUMONT HAMEL
CAVE
WAGON ROAD
New Munich Trench
Trench
Leave Avenue
Munich Trench
Frankfort
NEW BEAUMONT ROAD
GERMAN FRONT LINE
BRITISH FRONT LINE
Anchonvillers
2nd Avenue
2nd Avenue
Essex Trench
Cemetery
Broadway
"Y" RAVINE
DIVISIONAL BOUNDARY
Haymarket
Tipperary Avenue
THURLES DUMP
Clonmel Avenue
Piccadilly
SCALE
Yds 500 400 300 200 100 0 500 1000 Yds
Wiltington Avenue

General was pacing anxiously up and down the road opposite his headquarters when he saw a soldier, covered with dirt, a smile on his face, and a German helmet on his rifle, limping towards him. To his inquiry how things were going he received the laconic, but pertinent, answer: "Well, anyhow, they canna' ca' us 'Harper's Duds' ony mair."

At 8 A.M. on the morning of the attack the 4th Seaforths struck camp at Forceville and moved up into Mailly Wood, where they lay in readiness, but were not called into action that day. On the 14th, the 9th The Royal Scots and the 7th Argyll and Sutherland Highlanders made a further attack and captured Munich Trench, which proved untenable. They therefore withdrew down Leave Avenue and constructed New Munich Trench, 150 yards to the west of Munich Trench, assisted by the divisional pioneer battalion, the 8th The Royal Scots. The 7th Argyll and Sutherland Highlanders made another attack next day, which came to nothing, and in the evening the 4th Seaforths took over the front line from them. The advance to the line was made through a typical November night and was trying in the extreme. The whole countryside was shrouded in deep gloom. Beaumont Hamel was being shelled by the enemy, and as the Battalion came up some 5·9-inch shells fell among it, killing Second Lieutenant Creighton and five men, and wounding Lieutenant Watt and thirteen others, while two were missing. Once past the village, companies had no further difficulties and took over the front without hindrance.

Beaumont Hamel lay in a hollow and was invisible from the former British trenches. So completely had it been destroyed by shell fire that a stranger would have found difficulty in believing that such a place had ever existed. A mound of red brick-dust marked where the church had stood. A fragment of board bearing the letter B was all that was left of the railway station. A cellar was found that had been used as a German canteen, and was still full of stores and a large supply of soda-water, to which the Battalion helped itself freely. The only other fragment of a once thriving village was that part of a factory that contained the bath-house.

Headquarters were established in what had been the German Regimental or Brigade Commander's headquarters. It was partly above and partly below ground, with a fairly good covering of concrete on top. The shelling by German heavies was terrific, particularly on the first day the Battalion was there. Captain Peverell says: "I think I remember Colonel Unthank estimating that during a period of about ten hours they were coming at the rate of about one a minute—mostly 5·9's—in the close neighbourhood of Battalion Headquarters and of the dug-outs in the vicinity, the exact location of which was, of course, known to the Germans. No less intense than the German shelling was the constant clamour from Brigade Headquarters for overdue reports, returns, etc., which it was most difficult to cope with, owing to the telephone lines, both rear and forward, being continually cut by shell fire, and to the almost impossible task of locating the breaks and keeping them repaired. Communication had, to a very large extent, to be maintained by runners, who at times could not get near Headquarters, and, when they did, could not get away from it. As on many other occasions, the Company Battalion and Brigade runners, as well as the signallers, who constantly were out repairing the lines, performed their duties in a way which anyone who realizes the importance, and the dangerous and exacting nature thereof, knows thoroughly how to appreciate."

One of several enormous dug-outs that were found had been a hospital; it was well supplied with beds and stores, while the medical officer congratulated himself on the acquisition of some excellent instruments. Two companies were in New Munich Trench and two in support in the Green Line.

The 16th was spent in consolidating the newly acquired trenches under the continual shelling from 5·9-inch shells. The next day the two companies in the front line were relieved by the 17th Highland Light Infantry, one going to dug-outs in Wagon Road and the other to dug-outs near Battalion Headquarters. During the relief they came under heavy shell fire, which killed Second Lieutenant M. M. Mackenzie and three other ranks and wounded eight other ranks. Two of the killed were runners from Battalion Headquarters, who had been sent up to guide in the companies. Second Lieutenant Kynoch went out into No-man's-land to bring in a wounded Argyll but did not return until 4 P.M. next day. He had lost his way in the darkness in No-man's-land, had several times nearly got into the enemy's lines, and was absolutely exhausted.

There was an unsuccessful attack on the 18th by the 32nd Division, which suffered severely. Beaumont Hamel was shelled, and the Battalion lost eight killed and sixteen wounded.

On 19th November the Battalion was relieved by the 6th Gordons and went back to Mailly Wood. Troops in reserve often get all the dangers of the fighting without the satisfaction of taking any active part. They have to hold the position until shortly before the attack begins. When the enemy replies to the preliminary bombardment they endure the full force of the shelling. While the attack is in progress they are the special object of the enemy heavy artillery, and when it is ended they have to take over the position just as the enemy has located the position of the new front and attempts to prevent its consolidation.

Operations for the year 1916 now came to an end, and left the 51st Division with a reputation second to none, and it was now placed by the enemy as the most dangerous among the British divisions in France.

Beaumont Hamel had been regarded by the enemy as a position of the highest importance. The Upper Silesian Division, which was responsible for its defence, was reckoned as one of the best in the German army. All previous attacks on it had been stubbornly resisted and defeated. Its loss was a serious blow to the German command and to German prestige.

Two incidents at Beaumont Hamel deserve to be recorded.

An Irish soldier belonging to the Battalion had lost his kilt. Sergeant Davidson saw him walking down the road with a peculiar mincing gait, wearing a strange-looking covering on his legs. It turned out that he had converted his cardigan jacket into a pair of trousers by putting a leg through each sleeve!

After the Battalion had gone up to Beaumont Hamel a ration party was going up the Y Ravine. Corporal A. Thomson, D.C.M., the non-commissioned officer in charge, heard a loud bellowing on his right, and went to find out the cause. He found a German lying with both legs broken; his rifle had been recently discharged and his ammunition was exhausted. As he said he had been there three days it was supposed that he was the source of some annoying sniping that had been going on behind our advancing lines. He must have been a gallant fellow.

On the 23rd the Battalion went to Varennes, and the next day marched in very bad weather to Puchevillers. On the 26th it went into huts at Aveluy. There followed a long succession of cold weather. The Battalion supplied large working parties every day, chiefly in unloading engineer stores and improving the trench system. On 2nd December two men were killed and one was wounded. The following day the Battalion moved to the Wolfe Huts, in relief of the 7th Gordons, where it was employed in building up the Courcellette defences. On the 6th it relieved the 4th Gordons in front of Courcellette, where gum boots were issued. It was wet and dark and the men were tired.

The weather was indeed very bad. The trenches were in a very unsatisfactory state and sometimes non-existent. The front line was really a mere line of unconnected posts, between which the telephone was the only possible means of communication in daylight. On the 7th and 8th the weather got worse, making work on the trenches very hard. On the 9th the rain was so heavy that trench work became hopeless, and both sides were busy burying the dead under cover of the Red Cross flag.

That night the Battalion was relieved and went into huts at Ovillers, proceeding on 10th December to Bouzincourt, where it was billeted in barns. The next day was wet. The 12th December was snowy and there were working parties to improve the drainage. The Commanding Officer presented cards to those who had been awarded the Military Medal. Company Sergeant-Major Kenneth Ross was gazetted Second Lieutenant and posted to No. 2 Company.

The weather continued unfavourable for the next four days, during which Second Lieutenants F. Smith and Bessent joined, and a draft of sixty-nine other ranks came up from the Base. On the 19th there was a Battalion concert in the Scots Church Tent, and two days later the Battalion moved, two companies going to the Quarries and two to the Wolfe Huts. The weather continued to be very wet, muddy and windy. Many dead were buried about the Quarries. The two companies in the Wolfe Huts relieved the 4th Gordons in the front line on the 24th, but on the 27th the Battalion withdrew on relief to Ovillers Huts, the men being worn out. On 28th December the 4th Seaforths marched to Bouzincourt. The weather was still bad and there was a great scarcity of fuel, but the Battalion got baths and were able to clean up. On the 30th there was a Commanding Officer's inspection and a Brigade concert. The next day was a holiday and the pipers played in the New Year.

On 1st January 1917 the Battalion went back again to the Wolfe Huts, engaged on the usual round of working parties and suffering from the same horrible weather. On the 4th five men were wounded near the Pozières Dump. That day also the Adjutant, Captain Peverell, left for the Senior Officers' School at Aldershot. On the 5th six men were gassed while working in front of Courcellette, while in the early morning the huts were shelled without result. The next day six more men were gassed.

On 9th January working parties were cancelled because of a three-days' bombardment by heavy artillery. Captain L. D. Henderson returned from a course at the Senior Officers' School.

On the 13th, Headquarters and the "Specialists," under which title were included signallers, machine-gun, Lewis-gun and bombing sections, moved at 2 P.M. and reached Rubempré at 9 P.M., the transport having preceded them on the previous day. On the 14th they went by bus to Berneuil; on the 15th they marched to Millencourt, and on the 16th to Favières. On the 15th the remainder of the Battalion entrained at Acheux, arriving at Abbeville next day, after a cold night in a badly found train. From Abbeville they marched to rejoin Headquarters at Favières.

The period spent in the Courcellette area had been a very wretched one, and trying to the troops in every way. Great care had in particular to be taken to guard against trench feet. For the first time the men wore trousers, which were issued to them as being more suitable for digging, thus allowing the kilts to be kept clean and dry; but it is noteworthy that the percentage of sickness rose very markedly while trousers were in wear. The men did very good work in spite of the difficulties, and earned high praise from the Royal Engineers' officer in charge, especially for a bit of wiring done during the last two days of their tour.

SYNOPSIS OF EVENTS FROM THE CLOSE OF THE BATTLES OF THE SOMME, 1916, TO THE CLOSE OF THE BATTLES OF ARRAS, 1917

(*Approximately from the end of November* 1916 *to the end of May* 1917)

THE British and French Commanders-in-Chief already were agreed that the offensive should begin in February 1917. It was true that it must be long before either Russians or Italians could join in, but it was essential to prevent the Germans from forestalling the Allies, as they did by their attack on Verdun the year before.

The supersession of General Joffre by General Nivelle, the temporary subordination of Sir Douglas Haig to this new Generalissimo, and the removal of General Foch changed all this plan. Nivelle wished the British to take over a large sector of the French front, so that the French army might make a great break-through. It was to be done within from twenty-four to forty-eight hours, and was to be exploited as far at least as Hirson. Very few of those outside his own immediate staff liked Nivelle's plan, and it is not surprising that the British Field-Marshal (as he now was) refused dangerously to weaken his own front in furtherance of a plan of the soundness of which he had the gravest doubts. He did indeed take over a very inconvenient addition to his front as it was; but how entirely the event justified his refusal to take over more was soon to be seen. He therefore kept up a steady pressure with the Fifth Army on the Ancre. For a winter campaign it had wonderful success. By a skilful use of each piece of ground gained to win that which, in turn, would yield similar advantages, Sir Hubert Gough tore away, piece by piece, the enemy's carefully prepared defences. On 11th January and 3rd, 4th, 6th, 13th, 17th and 18th February the tide of victory swept inexorably on, till the enemy, who had long been preparing to fall back, when it suited himself, to the Hindenburg line, found himself compelled to do so when it did not.

For a time he stood on the Le Transloy-Loupart line covering Bapaume, but with the fall of Irles, on 10th March, he found himself forced to fall back on his long-prepared and much-vaunted position.

Nivelle, whose coming offensive, having been discussed in all the political *salons* in Paris, was as well known to the Germans as to the French, called on Haig to take the offensive, so as to hold the German reserves to their ground. While agreeing that the offensive should be at Arras, he deprecated any attempt to take the Vimy Ridge, on which, however, Haig insisted.

On 9th April 1917 the Battle of Arras began on a twelve-mile front, from Henin-sur-Cojeul to Givenchy-en-Gohelle. On the right, south of the Scarpe, were the 12th and 15th Divisions, through which the 37th was to "leap-frog." North of the Scarpe the 9th, supported by the 4th Division, was opposite to Roeux and Greenland Hill. Next on the left came the 34th and then the 51st Division in touch with the Canadian Corps of the First Army.

It is best to trace the events from left to right. The Canadians and 51st Division won all their objectives on Vimy Ridge, while the 9th and 4th Divisions north of the Scarpe bit a great salient into the enemy line about Fampoux. On the south of the river, however, progress was delayed by the obstinate resistance of Monchy-le-Preux, which was not taken till the 11th.

Though the British continued to gain ground up till the 14th, their operations were now directed solely to holding the enemy to his ground during Nivelle's offensive.

On 16th April the French launched the great attack at the Second Battle of the Aisne. This, though marked by great and gratifying success, failed in its object. The great counter-stroke, that was to carry the French arms in a victorious rush to Hirson and beyond, developed into a struggle of the familiar erosive kind.

The French were not prepared to carry the new battle through on these lines, yet Nivelle was loath to break it off. To assist him to continue, Sir Douglas Haig maintained the pressure on the Arras sector on wide fronts but with limited objectives, and on 23rd April the 17th and 51st Divisions attacked respectively south and north of the Scarpe. The objective of the 51st Division was Greenland Hill and the spur running south through Hausa and Delbar Woods, a position not wholly secured till many months later. Yet progress was made, and that with so much success on the south that the Australians actually captured and held a portion of the Hindenburg line.

Nivelle did in fact carry out a further offensive, whereby the French made progress towards getting possession of the long-denied Chemin-des-Dames. His promises, however, had not been fulfilled, and on 15th May he was succeeded by General Pétain, while General Foch was appointed Chief of the General Staff in Paris, with wide powers.

In the meantime operations on all fronts, other than the Russo-Rumanian, were, so far as they went, in favour of the Allies, notably the steady British advance up the Tigris. Two events that were to have far-reaching effects occurred early in the year.

The Russian "Intelligentsia" succeeded in effecting a revolution, and the Tsar abdicated on 15th March. Except for the complete cessation of all action by the Russian army there was no immediately evil effect, and the portent was hailed by too many of our own politicians as a blessing! There were, however, many persons with far more foresight—one only has to read Ludendorff's *Te Deum* for this "crowning mercy" to realize that!

On 6th April the United States of America declared war on Germany. This also was hailed as a great blessing. Had it come a year earlier it might have been a very decisive one.

ARRAS: THE RUINED CATHEDRAL

CHAPTER IX

ARRAS

THE year 1917 has been called the *Annus Mirabilis* of the 4th Battalion The Seaforth Highlanders. It was a year of great battles, in which the Battalion bore a distinguished share in confirming and strengthening that moral ascendancy of the British soldier over his German opponent which, nascent in the days of Mons and Le Cateau, grew slowly during 1915 and became pronounced in 1916.

The Battalion began its stay at Favières with a thorough clean-up. On 20th January, Major Inch, then Acting Commanding Officer, inspected the Battalion. The next day the Commanding Officer returned from leave, and the next the Brigadier inspected the companies. On the 23rd, Major Henderson left to take over Second-in-Command of the 6th Black Watch. The men went for baths and clean underclothing to Ponthoile. On the 31st, Major-General Harper inspected the Battalion in a practice attack from marked-out trenches. This day was the first of the Divisional Sports.

The 30th January and 1st, 2nd and 3rd February were observed by the different companies as occasions for their deferred New Year's dinners at Le Crotoy. On the 30th the officers entertained to dinner the Divisional and Brigade Commanders, with the officers of their staffs and those of the 7th Argyll and Sutherland Highlanders. On the 4th

Map 9.

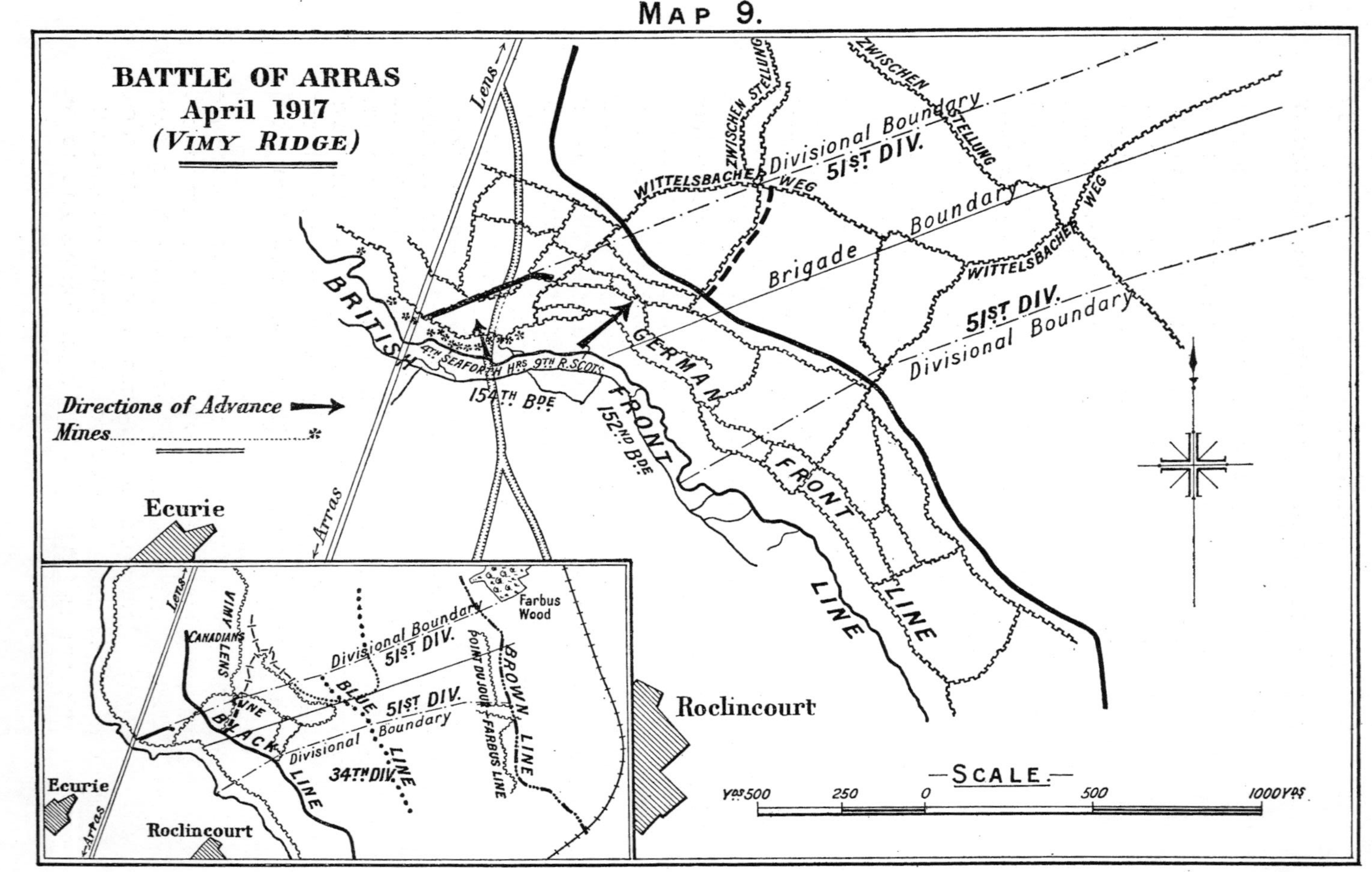
BATTLE OF ARRAS
April 1917
(Vimy Ridge)
Directions of Advance
Mines
Lens
Arras
Ecurie
Roclincourt
BRITISH
GERMAN
FRONT
LINE
FRONT
LINE
4TH SEAFORTH HRS
9TH R. SCOTS
154TH BDE
152ND BDE
WITTELSBACHER WEG
WITTELSBACHER WEG
ZWISCHEN STELLUNG
ZWISCHEN STELLUNG
Divisional Boundary
51ST DIV.
Brigade Boundary
51ST DIV.
Divisional Boundary
SCALE
YDS 500
250
0
500
1000 YDS
Farbus Wood
CANADIANS
VIMY LENS
LINE
BLACK LINE
BLUE LINE
BROWN LINE
POINT DU JOUR
FARBUS LINE
Divisional Boundary
51ST DIV.
51ST DIV.
Divisional Boundary
34TH DIV.
Lens
Arras
Ecurie
Roclincourt

Major Truslove took up the appointment of Staff Captain of the 152nd Brigade.

This rest had been eagerly looked forward to by the Battalion. The winter was exceptionally severe, the hard frost, which had now set in, lasting till April. It was trying enough for civilians living under war conditions, but far worse for soldiers. Not for many years had the cold been so severe. Fuel for the civilian population became extremely scarce; coal hardly could be procured at all, and wood was obtainable only in small quantities with the utmost difficulty; so that even the richest people in Paris suffered from lack of warmth, and some died from this cause.

The farm buildings in which the Battalion was billeted were composed mostly of clay lump. They were inferior in every way to the straw and clay cottages and barns familiar in some parts of England, which are remarkably warm and comfortable. The tenements in which the Seaforths were quartered had not the substantial qualities of these English buildings. They were full of cracks, which it was the custom to patch in the autumn; but during the war no repairs had been made. The walls had become more and more crazy; the cracks had developed into large holes, through which the cold winds found a ready passage. In such billets the Battalion rested. They would have been ideal summer quarters, but gave little alleviation from the severity of winter. The men, however, were so delighted at the prospect of a rest that they showed not the slightest discontent, but were, on the contrary, supremely happy. They might be seen in the early morning coming forth from these wind-swept shelters and breaking the ice on the nearest stream or pond; after which, in a bitter north-easter, with the thermometer below zero, they would strip to the waist and wash as thoroughly and as cheerfully as in the hottest summer. Yet the estuary of the Somme was packed with great blocks of ice, which would have done credit to the Arctic Ocean; although the icicles on the Regimental Sergeant-Major's moustache attracted even more attention from the men.

The hospital, which was under canvas, became an unpopular institution. Colds were very prevalent, and, among others, the Medical Officer, who thus suffered, was persuaded to go there for treatment. Two days sufficed—not, indeed, to cure him, but to bring him out. Another day in hospital, he declared, would have finished him. To lie under canvas and to be roused and get up at 5.30 A.M. would kill any man in such a season!

During this clear frosty weather there was great aeroplane activity. The trains were often pursued by them. One leave-train was watched with great anxiety, because it happened to be known that Captain Macdonald was travelling by it. The train afterwards was hit, and there was one casualty.

The anticipated Divisional Sports never took place. A lecture by the Divisional Commander on the forthcoming attack had warned the Battalion of the imminence of further fighting; but the move came earlier than was expected. On the 5th the 4th Seaforths marched to Forêt l'Abbaye over roads coated with ice, which made the march very arduous, especially for the transport. A draft of eighty-eight other ranks joined at the end of this march. The next day the march was resumed to Fontaine-sur-Maye. Had they not had the good fortune to pass within easy distance of the only colliery then working in France the discomfort of the Battalion would have been greatly increased. Fuel was at the lowest ebb, and when the Quartermaster and Interpreter, who had been sent to the colliery with a lorry, returned with a full load of fuel, all felt that one trouble was, for the moment, surmounted. They had found at the colliery an extraordinary sight. It was crowded with expensive limousine cars, taxis from Paris, farm wagons, and every kind of vehicle, so great was the pressure on the only available source of supply. What fortune their owners may have had in getting coal it is impossible to say.

Marches continued as follows: On the 7th, to Noeux *via* Auxi-le-Chateau; on the 8th, to Nuncq; on the 9th, to Marquay; on the 11th, by the main Arras road to huts at Ecoivres. Here the Battalion spent some days in training and finding working parties. On the 16th German aeroplanes killed two civilians. On the 21st the Battalion marched to tents in Bray Wood, No. 3 Company being in billets in Acq, and next day relieved the 5th Battalion in the front-line trenches at Roclincourt, on the left sector of the XVII Corps, Third Army. The frost had broken and the trenches were everywhere falling in, so that it was necessary to concentrate on clearing and improving them. On the 25th, Second Lieutenants Kynoch, H. F. Smith and Turnbull left for England on transfer to the Machine Gun Corps, and Regimental Sergeant-Major W. Anderson became Regimental Sergeant-Major, Divisional Training Depot. A draft of twenty-nine other ranks arrived. On the 27th the Battalion was relieved by the 9th The Royal Scots and went into billets in Maroeuil.

The Battalion had thus renewed its acquaintance with the front held by it the previous year, and it was fortunate that it was to take part in the impending attack on the Vimy Ridge from ground already so familiar to it. The attack was to be delivered by the 51st Division on the right of the Lille road, the 154th Brigade on the left and the 152nd on the right. On the 154th Brigade front the 9th The Royal Scots were in front line on the right, and the 4th Seaforths on the left, the supports being respectively the 7th Argyll and Sutherland and the 4th Gordons.

Here, for the first time, the Battalion met the Canadians. Their apparent disregard of all the usual precautions struck the Highlanders with amazement. "They strolled about with as little apprehension of danger as if war did not exist," says Lieutenant-Colonel Unthank. "They never made use of communication trenches. Some of them might be seen at almost any time of the day walking in the open right up to the front line. It is true that a few casualties resulted. The Canadians, however, declared that if by chance one of their number was shot, the Germans had good reason to repent of their performance. They never failed, they said, in such an event to cross the line at night and avenge the injury. So effective was their retaliation that the Germans fought very shy of rousing them. The shooting of an exposed Canadian became a rarity."

The time at Maroeuil was spent mainly in providing working parties and training specialists, while on 1st March, Second Lieutenant J. A. Mackenzie and thirty men went to the Divisional Training Depot.

On 11th March the Battalion relieved the 4th Gordons on the Sablière front, Nos. 3 and 4 Companies in front line and Nos. 1 and 2 in support. The trenches were in a bad state, and working parties were detailed for their improvement night and day, while patrols were sent out frequently. On the 13th the enemy artillery and aeroplanes were very active, and raids on the Canadians and the right of the Brigade were unsuccessfully attempted. By the next day the trenches showed an improvement. The supporting companies relieved those in front line, while there was much fire from the German artillery and machine guns. On the 15th Avenue G was blown in, and had to be cleared on the 16th, which was a bright day, remarkable for several air fights. The Battalion was relieved by the 6th Black Watch and proceeded to Ecurie, with one company at Anzin. On the 17th a draft of fifty other ranks arrived. The Battalion was kept hard at work on the construction of assembly trenches, but on the 19th one of these was blown in and much work undone. On the 23rd it was relieved by the 9th The Royal Scots, and went into huts in Maroeuil Wood, sustaining four casualties while leaving Ecurie. It was kept busy cleaning up, having baths at Acq, finding working parties and practising the attack. There was some relaxation, however, for on the 28th the non-commissioned officers beat the officers at football by 3 goals to 2, and on the 30th the Battalion drew with the Divisional Ammunition Column, 2 goals all. This day a draft of twenty other ranks arrived, and on the following day Second Lieutenant Mackenzie and twenty-three other ranks returned from the Divisional Training Depot.

Training for the impending attack began with an explanation of the scheme to all ranks, and a full scale plan of the British and German trenches was marked out on the manœuvre area.

To plan a successful attack on trenches was not so simple as it might appear, for the neglect of some small point which, at first sight, would seem unimportant, might make all the difference between success and failure. It is only necessary to recall how the far-reaching plans of attack in the days about Neuve Chapelle yielded wholly incommensurate results through failure to grasp the importance of apparently trivial detail, to realize the conditions imposed by what was virtually siege warfare.

The problem was to start off the men fit and well in the wake of the artillery barrage, and to do this unnecessary fatigue and casualties had to be avoided on the way up, while the attacking troops had to be put in position as close to the Germans as possible without detection and, above all, clear of the line of their barrage. Finally, just before the time came to attack it was necessary to serve out hot drinks to the men; for these attacks were always made in the early hours of the morning, when men were cold and vitality was at its lowest. In time the troops gained such confidence in the artillery that they knew they could take any system of trenches without a hitch, provided they started correctly.

In many ways the first attack carried out by the Battalion under the conditions now in vogue was the most difficult it ever undertook.

Between the British and German front lines ran the abandoned French system of several lines of trenches, which has been referred to already when dealing with the spring of 1916. These had, to a great extent, fallen in, and had, in addition, been wired by the Division during that period. It was now decided to use them for assembly trenches, and they had, therefore, to be reopened without the Germans finding this out. Every night small parties from each company went up and worked quietly in their positions, laboriously removing the wire and carefully hiding the spoil in shell holes. So well was this done that, in spite of the German command of the British position, they never detected what had been going on. The troops were well rewarded for their trouble, for during all the long wait on the night before the attack there was only one casualty, and that was caused by a German shell falling short. The old British front line, however, was shelled; while away on the right, where these French trenches had been fully dug out and no concealment had been adopted, there was a considerable number of casualties.

Every man in the Battalion was, moreover, taken carefully over the whole route to be followed from where it lay in Maroeuil Wood to his final place in the assembly trench.

Two points gave some cause for anxiety and both had a vital bearing on the events of the day.

The first was that, unlike British trenches, French trenches usually did not run parallel one to another; so that it was impossible to find positions for the second and third waves of the attack directly facing their line of advance. This meant that they would have to change direction after rising to advance—a very difficult thing to do in the dark without any landmarks.

The second was a small knoll behind the German front line near the junction with the Canadians, which was not entrenched, but commanded a good view. The Divisional Artillery would not, however, be able to shell it, for fear of hitting the Canadians, whose advance, echeloned in front of that of the 51st Division, must pass close to it.

On 2nd April the Quartermaster's stores were sent to Maroeuil and the transport to Bray. On the 4th the Battalion returned to Ecurie and Anzin. On the 5th Captain Peverell returned from the Senior Officers' School; but as it was inconvenient at this juncture to hand over to him, Lieutenant Macdonald continued to act as Adjutant till after the battle.

On the 8th, Headquarters, with Nos. 1 and 3 Companies, went up to the front line. There was heavy shelling, and the communication trenches were rather badly damaged. One man was missing from a patrol sent out.

The Battalion was to attack a portion of the German line that curved forward to a salient across the Lille road at a point near which contact had to be made with the Canadians, the right boundary of whose advance ran diagonally across the left of the Battalion front, immediately behind the second German trench; so that, by the time the Battalion reached its final objective, the German third line, its frontage would be reduced by half. The main attack was to be on a front of 600 yards. No. 1 Company (less one platoon), under Captain Hay-Will, was to capture the first German line; No. 2, under Captain C. H. Harris, stationed on the right, and No. 4, under Second Lieutenant MacGregor, stationed on the left, were then to advance in two waves and capture the second and third lines.

The secondary attack was to be made by No. 3 Company and one platoon of No. 1, under Captain "Andy" Fraser. After capturing two German trenches it was to send a platoon to work side by side with the Canadians as they advanced behind the second German trench, until a junction was effected with No. 4 Company on the third German line.

The Battalion moved into position on the night of 8th April. It was dark and snowy, with a cold north-easterly wind. The plans were admirably carried out, and, as stated before, only one man was wounded during the long wait in the assembly trenches. Hot tea was served out at an early hour, and at 5.45 A.M. the attack commenced.

In the main attack No. 1 Company attained complete and immediate success, the front German trench being occupied without opposition and without a casualty. Nos. 2 and 4, which started at the same time as No. 1, bore too much to the right. Second Lieutenant MacGregor made great efforts to change their direction and was wounded in the attempt. A certain amount of confusion, as is sometimes inevitable, now arose, and the capture of the second German trench was by no means certain. The alertness and presence of mind of

Captain Hay-Will saved the situation. He grasped the difficulties with which Nos. 2 and 4 Companies were contending, and knew that not a moment must be lost if the second trench was to be won. He therefore took the responsibility of stopping the consolidation of the first trench, and, leading his company forward, charged and captured the second one, thus carrying out the plan of attack, if not to the letter at least in the spirit.

Meanwhile, on the extreme right of the Battalion front, No. 2 Company had found its way into a communication trench running back from the front German line to the third. It was honeycombed with dug-outs and swarming with men ; but up it Second Lieutenant Kenneth Ross, lately the Company Sergeant-Major, was gallantly fighting his way. His rise to commissioned rank had been rapid, for when it came he was probably the youngest Company Sergeant-Major in the British army. He already had led the first wave of his own company until its aim was achieved, but with this he was not content. At the head of a party composed of men both of his own and No. 4 Company he continued steadily to bomb his way along the trench. When at last he fell, severely wounded in the thigh, the effort which had owed so much to him persisted. The attack reached the German third line, passed along the Zwischen Stellung Trench, and enabled the 4th Seaforths to join hands with the Canadians.

While this bombing fight was proceeding up the communication trench, the advance of the two platoons of No. 4 Company detailed for the capture of the third line was checked. It was impossible for them to move, for the moment the British barrage lifted off the second German trench, enemy machine guns opened fire and swept its parapet and the ground in front. Sergeant John Campbell (Ullapool) realized that these guns must be located and silenced. When he had located them in a position between the German second and third lines he made a bold attempt to put them out of action. Choosing five men from his platoon to accompany him, he proceeded to stalk the guns. To get within bombing distance of machine guns and then to silence them requires as much caution as courage, for a single false step means death.

Campbell's five companions had barely started before they were seen and were at once shot down. Alone, slowly and stealthily, did Campbell crawl on, with every faculty fixed on his set purpose. At length he came within bombing distance of the guns, and, more cautious and vigilant than ever at this, the supreme, moment, he drew a bomb from his pocket with infinite care, withdrew the pin and hurled it. Then, leaping to his feet, he charged with his bayonet, and sprang into the post. He found himself face to face with twelve Germans, resolute to overcome him or to sell their lives as dearly as they could. Single-handed he proved a match for them all. When Company Sergeant-Major Robertson came up at the head of the platoons whom the silencing of the guns had released he found Sergeant Campbell unhurt, with twelve dead Germans lying round him and the guns wrecked.

Lieutenant-Colonel Unthank writes: "I was so struck with the account I had heard of Sergeant Campbell's feat that I went up the next day to look at the ground myself, and made Company Sergeant-Major Robertson describe exactly what occurred from the spot where he witnessed it. It was an even more amazing performance than I had imagined. The ground sloped up gently from the trench from which Sergeant Campbell had started, as far as the strong point occupied by the Germans. There was no cover, except in a few scattered shell holes, and, to make matters worse, the ground was covered with a thick coat of snow. How he managed to stalk the Germans unobserved I do not know, nor do I know whether to admire most his coolness, skill or courage."

Sergeant Campbell was recommended for the V.C. He was awarded the D.C.M. and the French Médaille Militaire.

With the capture of these machine guns, fighting was at an end, for by this time the third-line trench was in the hands of Second Lieutenant Ross's party. All the officers of No. 4 Company had become casualties, and it became the duty of Company Sergeant-Major Robertson to reorganize it. It was now 7.15 A.M., and the Germans could be seen retreating in large numbers up the slope beyond the trench. Heavy shell fire was directed on them, but the limit of the advance was reached.

The German artillery wasted no time in shelling their lost trenches, and no less than thirty casualties were reported in his company by Sergeant-Major Robertson as the result of half-an-hour's shelling. They occurred almost entirely in the German third-line trench. It was fortunate that the shelling had diminished greatly by the time the 4th Gordons moved through to continue the advance.

It will be remembered that in the description of the

Roclincourt sector in the spring of 1916 reference was made to the mining that formed a noteworthy part of the operations. On their return to this area the 4th Seaforths found that the British tunnelling companies had obtained complete mastery over the Germans underground. Beyond listening for signs of countermining they had little to do. No mine of ours was in any real danger. They had been concentrating their energies lately on the construction of large underground chambers designed for the reception of the troops in anticipation of this attack. One of them was spacious enough to house not only No. 3 Company, under Captain "Andy" Fraser, but also a company of the 4th Gordons, for some time before the attack. It lay in No-man's-land, and its exits were within twenty or thirty yards of the German line. Thus during the preliminary bombardment of the German trenches No. 3 Company and the platoon of No. 1 Company remained quietly underground. Shortly before zero the screens that sealed the exits were removed and the men took up their positions in readiness to rush over the top.

On the barrage lifting, the Seaforths immediately seized the two front trenches without opposition and got in touch with the Canadians. This accomplished, Captain Fraser collected his men and got them underground again. It was now the time to send forward a platoon to work with the Canadians as far as the third German line, and link up with the main body of the Battalion.

The platoon found, directly facing them, the small knoll which, as has been said, it was impossible to shell for fear of hitting the Canadians. Over that knoll it now had to advance. Strictly to time, Lieutenant Leslie led forward his men in a perfect double line; but the gloomy anticipations that were connected with this knoll were instantly realized. Without any warning he and his men were greeted with a shower of hand grenades. Hit on the forehead, he fell dead, and a line of men fell behind him. The advance was stopped. Captain Fraser had been anxiously watching it from the exit of his underground chamber, and saw the catastrophe overtake the platoon. He selected a storming party and, covered by the fire of his rifle bombers, charged home at their head. In the fierce hand-to-hand fight that followed the Germans fought to the bitter end, dying where they stood in a rough circle, face to their enemies.

Captain Fraser was now able to lead his men forward to the third German line. So soon as he had secured the position there he finally withdrew with all his men to their quarters underground. There they stayed till the Battalion came out of the line. There was now more space available, for the company of the 4th Gordons that had shared the chamber with them had gone forward to continue the advance.

Immediately the battle was over large parties of stretcher-bearers from the Highland Field Ambulance made every effort to clear the ground of the wounded. The battle had lasted all the morning, but at an early hour of the afternoon every wounded man had been carried to the dressing station. The Highland Field Ambulance, always good, had on this occasion surpassed itself.

The prisoners captured by the Division exceeded its casualties. The share of the Battalion was one hundred and sixty-seven men, six trench mortars and the two machine guns taken by Sergeant Campbell. Its losses were, unfortunately, heavy, consisting of:

OFFICERS

Killed: Second Lieutenants E. V. D. Leslie, H. S. G. Fox, T. B. Waddell, H. E. O. Murray-Dixon, A. I. Davidson.

Wounded: Second Lieutenants D. E. F. MacGregor, K. I. E. Ross, R. I. MacDonald, D. Grant.

OTHER RANKS

Killed: 59. *Wounded*: 151. *Missing*: 7.

The next day, 10th April, Nos. 1 and 3 Companies remained in dug-outs in the old German line, while the other two went forward to support the 4th Gordons. They were relieved in the evening by the 153rd Brigade, and came back to the old German line.

The 11th was spent in collecting salvage, until the 2nd Highland Light Infantry and 17th Royal Fusiliers came up in relief and the Battalion went into huts at Larasset. The next three days were spent in cleaning up, and a draft of thirty-two other ranks arrived.

On the 15th the Battalion went to St-Laurent and relieved a battalion of the 9th Division in reserve. Till the 20th the men were employed in improving dug-outs and mending roads.

MAP 10.

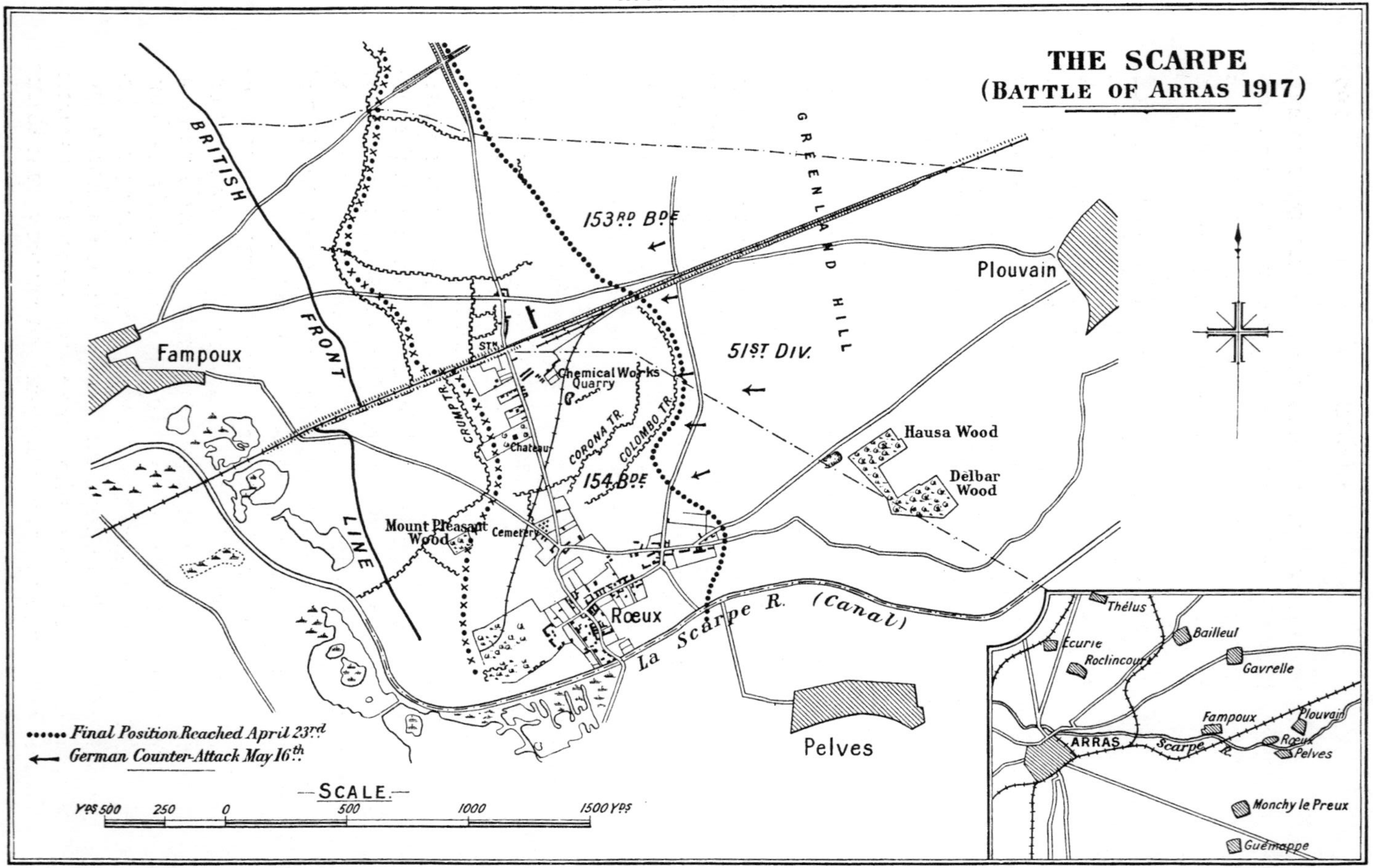

THE SCARPE
(BATTLE OF ARRAS 1917)

•••••• Final Position Reached April 23rd
← German Counter-Attack May 16th

SCALE
YDS 500 250 0 500 1000 1500 YDS

Second Lieutenant Slater was wounded, and a draft one hundred and forty strong arrived. The artillery began active preparation for the impending attack on the 21st, and the next day the Battalion marched by night to its assembly position in Brigade reserve at the cutting near Fampoux.

The attack on Roeux and the Chemical Works was launched at 4.45 A.M. on 23rd April by the 7th Argyll and Sutherland and 4th Gordon Highlanders, supported by the 9th The Royal Scots. A large number of our gunners had been incapacitated by a discharge of gas on the previous evening, and the barrage was, therefore, ineffective. The Germans were but little shaken and stood to their parapet. Fierce hand-to-hand fighting followed, and it was a considerable time before the first trench was finally taken. The casualties on both sides were tremendous. The three battalions engaged had thrown in every available man and had fought themselves to a standstill just short of the Chemical Works and with half the village of Roeux in their hands.

At 8 A.M. Lieutenant-Colonel Unthank received an order to send up two companies in support of the 4th Gordons and to take over the command of the left sector of the Brigade front from Lieutenant-Colonel McClintock of that battalion, who was wounded. The advance began at 8.15 A.M. The adventure looked extremely perilous. In front lay the River Scarpe, with but two ways across it: the first, by a railway bridge on an embankment on the right; the second, a narrow foot-bridge, consisting of a single plank, immediately in front. In either case a very heavy 5·9 barrage had to be faced. The ground, however, was soft and sodden, greatly diminishing the power of the shells, and Lieutenant-Colonel Unthank decided to go by the foot-bridge, as being the shorter route. The result was success beyond expectation; not a single casualty befell the first company that passed over the bridge, while the second had only one—strangely enough from a rifle bullet.

Lieutenant-Colonel Unthank learned from Lieutenant-Colonel McClintock at 8.55 A.M. that, while the right had got on, his left attack had been stopped completely by a machine gun at the intersection of the German front line and the Arras-Douai railway, where about fifty of the enemy were holding out. The bombers of the 4th Gordons had no rifle grenades and were outranged by the Germans, who were using the small egg-bomb. A tank now came up from the right and reported that Roeux was invested on three sides, but that the Germans were still resisting in the centre. It was arranged that the tank should assist in the attack on the strongpoint; but it soon got hopelessly bogged, so Lieutenant-Colonel Unthank determined to proceed without it.

On arrival in the front line the general situation was found to be obscure; but directly in front was the German strongpoint, situated under cover of the railway embankment, which had prevented the advance from reaching the Chemical Works. With this it was decided to deal at once. A party was dispatched to the position under Sergeant Gray, No. 3 Company, and Lance-Corporal Lane. Their attack, which was made from under cover of the railway, met with astonishing success, the position being taken at 11.5 A.M. after a short struggle. Twenty of the enemy were killed and thirty taken prisoners, while not a man of the Seaforths fell. This success enabled No. 3 Company to advance through the Chemical Works and take up a position beyond, with both flanks refused. No. 2 Company could not get level with No. 3, being held up by machine-gun fire from the cemetery. No. 1 was in support and No. 4 in reserve.

Though, for some reason difficult to conjecture, this advance encountered no opposition, a heavy counter-attack from Roeux and Greenland Hill was later on directed against the company. It was broken up by artillery and rifle fire about 5.30 P.M., but was renewed again just before dusk. The "S.O.S." was sent up, and at 8.45 P.M. the artillery responded, but by some mistake the heavy guns shelled the Château and Chemical Works and the position held by Captain "Andy" Fraser's company. This unfortunate mistake added to Captain Fraser's difficulties and caused several casualties, including, later on, himself. Nor was this all. The 153rd Brigade sustained heavy casualties and was forced back on the left of the 154th. Thus left unsupported, with the enemy closing round both his flanks and with no ammunition left, Captain Fraser decided to retire. Immediately before making this decision he was preparing to deliver a bayonet charge. Unhappily he fell wounded before this charge could take place. Still, it may be questioned whether Captain Fraser, with all his courage and resource, could have saved a situation which may fairly be described as desperate. The whole of his left flanking platoon had become casualties, the 153rd Brigade had been forced back, leaving a large and menacing gap, and his force was within measurable distance of being cut off. The Company fell back on the old German front line at 9 P.M.

Curiously enough Battalion Headquarters knew nothing of the German attack until long after it had commenced. Of the three runners dispatched with the news only the third arrived. When he reached Headquarters the Adjutant had just started for an evening tour of the line. No. 4 Company in reserve was being sent to relieve the 4th Gordons and the 9th The Royal Scots. Two platoons had already left and the Commanding Officer was inspecting the other two. These two platoons, therefore, were all the force available, and they were now prevented from moving by a terrific enemy barrage, which was at that moment put down in front of the Battalion Headquarters.

The enemy had by now occupied the Château and a house south of the railway, and established two more machine-gun posts. They bombarded the British position for some hours during the night. After an hour or two of quiet, the bombardment was renewed with intensity at 4.30 on the following morning. The Germans evidently intended to attack. It is a singular coincidence that they made the same mistake as we had made the day before—shelling the Chemical Works, now in occupation of their own men. The Battalion suffered few, if any, casualties from this bombardment, for the German shells—other than those directed on the Chemical Works—fell behind the front line, which, in consequence, had an unimpeded view. Those who looked beyond the Chemical Works towards Greenland Hill at 4.45 A.M. understood the purpose of this bombardment, when they saw large bodies of the enemy advancing from that hill to attack. In spite of their own heavy artillery fire upon the Chemical Works, the waves of the attack passed through it and pressed forward.

Headquarters was fortunate in having just acquired a new telephone instrument called a "power buzzer," by which messages could be sent a short distance without the use of wires. Its name was derived from the loud "buzz" it made. An earth pin was driven into the ground and the signal made. No reply could be obtained by it, so that, having made the signal, the sender had to trust to luck. An "S.O.S." was sent off at 5 A.M. and the result was awaited. The guns at once opened fire, the field guns on the leading waves of the attack and the heavies on the Chemical Works. It was a blast before which the attack was blown away. The survivors fled as best they could to Greenland Hill, from which they had started. Concentrated rifle fire pursued them all the way back, still further thinning their ranks, so that only a remnant could have returned. By 6 A.M. all was quiet. Morning passed into noon and noon into night without further attack. When night came the Brigade was relieved and went far behind Arras for rest and training. The Division was destined once again to hold the same front. Before that happened, however, the 2nd Seaforths, in the 3rd Division, had made a brilliant recapture of the Chemical Works. When the Battalion came into the line again these buildings had disappeared completely—gone was the Château, gone the village and houses; hardly one stone was left upon another. No human habitation remained save one wooden hut by the railway crossing. To this hut is attached a story.

In the attack by the 153rd Brigade on the 23rd an officer of the Gordons, leading his platoon, advanced along the railway behind the barrage. A solitary figure standing by a hut on the railway attracted his attention. The figure did not move. The barrage passed over him and he escaped. He was the gate-keeper of the level-crossing, whom the Germans had forgotten to warn to remove out of harm's way. Here he remained, apparently ignoring every risk. The officer asked him for a drink of coffee. With the courtesy which rarely deserts a Frenchman, even in the most trying circumstances, the old man expressed extreme regret at his inability to oblige. A shell, he explained, had just destroyed his house, and, alas, had spoilt his coffee; but his thanks would be infinite if "Monsieur le Capitaine" would help him to see if his wife were still alive in the cellar.

It chanced in 1920 that Lieutenant-Colonel Unthank passed over the same level-crossing. The wooden hut was still by it, the same old man still standing near. His house had not been rebuilt and his wife was still in the cellar. The hut remained the only human shelter in a district given over to desolation, the old man and his wife the only dwellers in the solitude. There was the same politeness and the same unconscious humour as the old man told his tale and offered his coffee.

It was a sad sight to see the Brigade entrain at Arras, for its losses had been heavy. With the exception of the 4th Seaforths the battalions were mere remnants, and the Seaforths numbered more than the rest of the Brigade put together.

Seaforth casualties were:

OFFICERS

Killed: Second Lieutenant J. Harvey.
Wounded: Captain A. K. Fraser, Lieutenant T. F. Scott and Second Lieutenant A. Macauley.

OTHER RANKS

Killed: 15. *Wounded*: 80. *Missing*: 15.

SYNOPSIS OF EVENTS BETWEEN THE CLOSE OF THE BATTLES OF ARRAS AND THE CLOSE OF THE THIRD BATTLES OF YPRES

(*Approximately from the beginning of June to the middle of November* 1917)

GREAT trouble had broken out in the French army. The agitation of "defeatists" of every complexion, from Anarchists at the one end to Communists at the other, had undermined seriously the discipline of the troops. Nor was this state of affairs improved by the readiness with which French ministers listened to the gossip of *députés* serving with the army, who in too many cases made no scruple of carrying mischievous rumours to political friends already agitated at the length of the casualty lists.

Pétain's first task was to restore the *moral* and discipline of the French army. In these circumstances it fell to Sir Douglas Haig to attack the Germans, and so prevent them from putting too much pressure on the French at a critical time. He had for long planned an offensive in Flanders, designed to clear the Germans out of the submarine bases that were menacing the Channel—a course of action that would have seriously threatened the German flank in Belgium—given fresh bases to the British army, and relieved the Royal Navy from a very heavy responsibility.

Just as, to make sure of successful action at Arras, it was necessary to occupy Vimy Ridge, so, to secure successful action about Ypres, it was necessary to capture the Messines-Wytschaete Ridge. It was brilliantly stormed by the Second Army on 7th June. Nineteen mines were sprung under it; 6000 prisoners were taken and an advance made on a front of nine miles. Further fighting went on till the 14th, adding to the British gains.

About Arras and along the French front there was a good deal of desultory fighting, in which the advantage, for the most part, was with the Allies. The First Army also began to advance towards Lens, a "quiet" area since the Battle of Loos.

On 31st July, after many weeks of careful preparation, began the struggle that gave back to us the positions east of Ypres that were lost in 1914. The main attack was made by the Fifth Army (II, XIX, XVIII and XIV Corps), supported on the right by the Second Army, and on the left by the First French Army, on a front of fifteen miles from La Basse Ville to Steenstraat.

The success of our "leap-frog" attack had led the Germans to hold their front line very lightly, the next more strongly, and so on progressively; with the result that our attacking waves met the enemy in greatest strength when our artillery could give them the least support. To avoid giving the enemy this advantage our attacks were planned with infantry objectives strictly limited to a line well within range of our guns, so that counter-attacks might be efficiently dealt with. While this proved a sure method of advance without heavy casualties, it was slow, and was dependent on favourable weather to enable unrelaxed pressure to be kept up.

The first day's operations were very successful; both on the right and on the left the objectives were in many places exceeded. In the centre, where resistance was greater, there was satisfactory progress on the XIX Corps front, but the II hardly got beyond its first objectives. Still the results were encouraging, for the capture of over 6000 prisoners, in addition to the heavy losses in killed inflicted on the enemy, was at this time of the greatest value. This was to be known as the Battle of Pilckem Ridge.

Unfortunately the month of August 1917 was destined to be the wettest known for many years. Rain stopped further offensive action on a large scale till the 16th, although on the 10th the 18th and 25th Divisions captured Westhoek and got a footing in Glencorse Wood and Inverness Copse. On the 15th the First Army, which had faithfully bided its time, made a conspicuous advance towards Lens. On the 16th came the second attack at Ypres, the Battle of Langemarck, nine British divisions advancing, with the French on their left, on a front of nine miles from the Ypres-Menin Road to Steenstraat.

The right — on the road itself — was severely checked, and the ground prevented the tanks from coming up in support. Ground was indeed gained, but not to the desired extent. The centre and left gained nearly all their objectives, though in some cases strongpoints had to be left to be dealt with later. Unfortunately the exposure of the right flank, consequent on its check, enabled the development of counter-attacks that drove back not only the II but the XIX Corps also, for the state of the ground prevented artillery being brought up near enough to break up the counter-attacks.

The Second Army now took over the front from the Menin Road towards Westhoek, the Australian I and V Corps replacing the II and XIX.

By the end of September the ground was drier and visibility much better. On the 20th began the Battle of the Menin Road Ridge, followed by those of Polygon Wood and Broodseinde (4th October). But for the weather we undoubtedly should have won more ground. As it was, the Germans were driven to "double-banking" their divisions against us for counter-attack, whereby they lost far more than they gained, for our artillery broke them up nearly every time with heavy slaughter.

It is now time to turn elsewhere. The French had almost restored the position at Verdun to what it had been in February 1916. The Russians, after a vigorous oncoming in July under Brusilov, penetrated into Galicia, but were driven back by the Germans in a very disorganized state. The Rumanians gallantly held out till the final defection of Russia compelled them to accept an armistice.

On the Italian front the first noteworthy action was the beginning of the Italian offensive on the Carso on 19th August. The Bainsizza Plateau and 23,000 prisoners were taken on a thirty-mile front. Minor successes followed till 24th October, when the Second Italian Army was routed at Caporetto. The Italians were driven back, first to the Tagliamento and then to the Piave, where the arrival of British and French armies enabled them to stay the pursuit. The loss in prisoners and guns was enormous.

Nothing of interest occurred on the Ægean front. In Palestine a renewed offensive began at the end of October; on 7th November Gaza was taken, and on the 17th, Jaffa.

In Mesopotamia Sir Stanley Maude, after inflicting on the Turks such a series of defeats as prevented them from ever again making any serious threat against us, most unfortunately died of cholera on 18th November.

In East Africa the British were making real progress.

To return to the West. It was obvious that it was now too late to hope to clear the Flemish coast, but, in view of French preparations for a renewed offensive, it was essential to keep as many German troops as possible massed before Ypres. Afterwards the attacks were perforce continued, as being the only means of preventing the Germans heavily reinforcing their Italian front. As in the spring, so in the autumn, the British Commander-in-Chief had to fight battles that, to the ignorant or prejudiced observer, were as pointless as Stonewall Jackson's immortal forlorn hope at Kernstown. A very good reason for the Passchendaele battles is that they well-nigh enabled the Allies to make a great break through the German line at Cambrai in November. It was, moreover, necessary to secure a good defensive line and a good "jumping off" position on this all-important front, gained and held at such a cost. Arm-chair critics forget these remote things: soldiers cannot and do not.

On 22nd October the Allies took the southern end of Houthoulst Forest. The battles of the 26th and 30th gave them a footing in Passchendaele. That of 6th November gave them the village, while that of the 10th rounded the position gained.

Meanwhile, on 23rd October, the French had gained a notable victory on the Aisne, advancing up to two miles on a six-mile front and capturing 8000 prisoners and 70 guns. This went on till the 27th, when it ended in a stalemate on the Oise-Aisne Canal. The French, however, followed this up on 2nd November when the Germans retired from the Chemin-des-Dames on a twelve-and-a-half-mile frontage. The French consolidated the position and pushed on to the Ailette.

YPRES: THE CLOTH HALL

CHAPTER X

THE THIRD BATTLES OF YPRES

On relief by the 11th Suffolks on 24th April 1917 the Battalion went into billets in Arras, entraining next day for Ligny-St-Flochel, whence it marched to billets at Maizières, described as one of the nicest, neatest and cleanest villages yet seen in France.

The long and trying winter was at last over; the weather was fine and warm, and the fruit-trees were in full blossom. On the 29th, Second Lieutenants Robson, J. Davidson, W. N. Collins, W. Surrey Dane, Alec. Brodie, J. N. MacDonald, J. Bain and M. Murray arrived from the Base, and Second Lieutenants D. B. M. Jackson and R. C. Spence-Ross from hospital.

There was a boxing competition and sports on 2nd May. Major-General Harper came over to tea and announced the award of twelve Military Medals for the Battle of Vimy Ridge. The following day Second Lieutenants T. U. Staub, J. T. Jenkins, C. R. Simpson, A. A. Pitcairn, P. H. Ballantyne, H. A. MacIver and J. A. Hermon, with fifty-seven other ranks, arrived; the Commanding Officer went on leave; and there was a concert at which the Divisional Concert Party assisted — quite an eventful day. On the 5th there were Highland Games, at which Lieutenant-Colonel Hon. I. M. Campbell, 2nd Lovat Scouts, presented the prizes. There were plenty of entries and keen competition. The civil population was present in force; and there were cakes and ale free for the men—so everyone was well satisfied. On the 6th the band of the East Lancashires played in the afternoon.

On the 7th there is a doleful entry in the 154th Brigade diary: "G.O.C. 51st Division rode over and saw the 7th Argyll and Sutherland Highlanders and 4th Seaforth Highlanders at training. Not very successful, as the 4th Seaforth Highlanders used ball ammunition and forgot to clear the countryside, with the result that they nearly killed several civilians and their horses who were working in the fields. Naturally the G.O.C. was somewhat annoyed. However it was stopped before any damage was done." There is a scandalized restraint about this account which is wholly delightful, though there is a hint that the apparently blameless Argyll and Sutherland came in for the backwash of the annoyance. This was worse than the hens at Arques!

On the 10th there were sports in the afternoon and a competition with the 7th Argyll and Sutherland; and the next day there was cricket. Thus training and recreation were well blended.

There was a good deal of money about. The men had a few weeks' pay to draw on, and a lucky chance had fallen on some in the attack of the 23rd. In Fampoux an enemy shell blew up a house just as the men were passing it and sent a shower of louis d'ors, the golden hoard of some thrifty Frenchman, among them. This was a great stroke of luck, for the louis, nominally worth twenty-five francs, was now fetching thirty. The relations between our soldiers and the villagers here were even more cordial than usual; and it is probable that the Town-Major had a remarkably small number of claims for lost hens.

On 12th May this pleasant rest came to an end. The Battalion marched *via* Penin and Hermaville to huts near Etrun, and two days later went on to billets in Arras.

Ever since the "race to the sea" Arras had been subject to bombardments, which had caused much damage. The gaunt walls of the great Abbey, in the highest part of the town, rose above its crumbled ruins. All that remained unharmed in the little church of St Gery was the beautifully carved wooden pulpit. In this almost deserted quarter the

Battalion had its billets, Headquarters in the Rue de Jerusalem, and the remainder in the Hospice des Vieillards. Most of the houses were musty and dirty, and the fact that units were billeted in them for only short periods did not tend to make them better.

The South African Scottish were billeted in the next street, so that the Battalion now completed its acquaintance with troops from all the great Dominions of the British Empire.

On 15th May the Commanding Officer returned from leave. That night there was very heavy shelling, and houses just across the street from the Battalion billets were badly dilapidated by shells of large calibre. The shelling was the prelude to a heavy attack on the 152nd Brigade, and by 8 A.M. the enemy were reported to be in the Chemical Works and Roeux. The 154th Brigade was ordered to support the 152nd, the 4th Seaforths being sent up to the Arras-Lens railway embankment north of the Scarpe. At 8.30 they moved off by platoons. "So we left everything, including the breakfast," says one of them.

The situation on the other side of the Scarpe was not clear, and it was uncertain whether the foremost trench of the British line still was held, or whether it was in the hands of the Germans. The latter seemed to be the more probable.

"Things were in a good 'mix-up,' and as no one seemed to know where the Boche was—or in fact where our line really was—we were led to believe that we might meet him in force; so we went prepared for the worst. Luckily he had been too badly mauled, so we were able to get at all our objectives."

At 2 P.M. Lieutenant Dane was sent forward with Nos. 2 and 4 Companies to the cutting south of Fampoux. At 7.30 P.M. he led the companies forward to relieve the 8th Argyll and Sutherland Highlanders. They had been observed by the German artillery, and came under a heavy field-gun barrage; fortunately rain had softened the ground and the shells had little effect. When darkness fell they were in Corona Trench, the support line; and as it was believed that Colombo Trench, the front line, was held by the enemy, Lieutenant Dane prepared to rush it. No. 4 Company advanced silently in open order, and Lieutenant Dane was just about to give the order to charge when he heard a Scots voice coming from the trench. A tragedy was just averted, and he was relieved to find the 8th Argyll and Sutherland still in possession. They said that they had been completely surrounded and attacked all day, but had managed to keep the enemy at bay, the men facing to front and rear alternately.

No. 4 Company held the front and No. 2 the support trench; while No. 1 Company went into a trench west of Roeux, No. 3 into Roeux Wood, and Headquarters into Crump Trench. No further fighting occurred, and the days were spent in consolidating the position, which was commanded by the enemy on Greenland Hill.

"I had," writes Second Lieutenant P. H. Ballantyne (referring to Roeux), "the rather ticklish job given me of establishing posts in a *village that we had not complete possession of before the counter-attack.* I got in all right and found some of our posts still there. I relieved them and spent the night going the rounds or resting in a cellar with four wounded men. The next morning we expected trouble and sniping, but we saw at dusk the Boches clearing out through the small gap that still remained. Then our snipers came up and gradually cleared the village, though they brought a lot of shelling on us, but we were lucky. The houses all round my cellar were blown to dust, but we had no casualties in the two platoons I had under me."

Roeux and the Chemical Works were full of dead and dying. The ground had been the scene of successive attacks and counter-attacks, which have been described as perhaps "the most savage infantry battle that the Division ever took part in." [1]

In the main street of Roeux the German dead lay in hundreds; almost every step was over a dead enemy. In dug-outs and cellars, on the floors and in the beds lay dead Germans, some in a horrible stage of corruption, especially those that had been gassed. The stench in Roeux was vile.

Our troops were busy for the next ten days succouring the enemy wounded who lay out in the open. The stretcher-bearers, cheeriest and bravest of men, risked the enemy fire to bring them in. Some of the wounds were terrible, and gangrene had set in when they had been lying out for several days. These poor fellows were brought into our trenches and given hot tea, spirits, cigarettes, and—when they could take it—food, until they could be carried back to the First Aid Post. Most of

[1] *History of the 51st (Highland) Division*, by Major F. W. Bewsher (Blackwood, Edinburgh and London, 1920).

them were past feeling pain, but they were conscious, and grateful for the treatment they received. With most it was a matter of making easy their last few hours of life.

One poor fellow in particular had been out about ten days with a very bad wound in the thigh, which was appalling to behold, being gangrenous and covered with flies, and giving off a most offensive smell. He had long since finished what rations and water he had had with him, and for drink had, in his misery, resorted to nature to alleviate the thirst that tormented him.

Another was pinned down, the complete lower half of his body, beneath a massive conglomeration of concrete, which defied all attempts at removal. Every effort was made, notwithstanding the close proximity of the enemy, but this circumstance, of course, limited the amount of work that could be done in this direction. He had been in this position for days, and, in addition, was grievously wounded. It was absolutely impossible to do anything for him, except to give him constant doses of morphia till his suffering was at last brought to a merciful end.

The weather was rainy and the trenches very bad, especially Corona Trench, which had been battered out of recognition. When the men started cutting new sides to the trench they cut through the buried German dead.

There was little sleep to be had in Roeux, especially by the officer in charge. At night trenches had to be dug; in the afternoon there was heavy shelling; and in the mornings the name of the visitors was Legion. The Commanding Officer, one or two artillery observers, Brigade and Divisional Intelligence Officers, officers of the battalion detailed to relieve the 4th Seaforths, the Adjutant—each and all seeming to arrive just as the officer visited was dropping off to sleep.

On 18th May, No. 1 Company relieved No. 4 in the front line. The following day an aeroplane was brought down by our Lewis-gun fire; and that night the division on the south of the Scarpe attacked near Monchy le Preux. It was a wonderful sight when our guns opened fire to watch the German line break out into a constellation of golden, red and green lights —until the German counter-barrage came down all along the front. That lasted twenty minutes. The first shell made a direct hit on one of the few remaining houses in Roeux, and after that no one wanted to admire any fireworks!

The troops were in no doubt that German *moral* was shaken. The enemy indeed was in such a state of nervous tension that the imprudence of a burying or fatigue party in letting itself be seen was enough to bring down heavy shell fire all along the front.

The Battalion was relieved on the night of the 20th by the 4th Gordons and went back to Divisional reserve at the railway embankment. There were no casualties among the officers; among other ranks there had been: killed, 2; died of wounds, 1; wounded, 26; missing, 2.

Much variety had been crowded into those few days. There was the excitement of being hurried up to the line, followed by an advance on an obscure position in the dark; the consolidation in mud and rain with constant shelling; the aeroplane activity on either side; the horrors of the dead and wounded. There were many trophies, iron crosses, mark notes, revolvers and field-glasses. In some cellars there was wine, and the Germans had large stores of cigarettes and cigars, which seemed to have been part of the special rations issued on going into action. Our troops got strawberry jam on such occasions, and strawberry jam will always have a special significance for the soldier of 1914-1918. The weather cleared up, and for the next eight days the men were cleaning up and bathing in the canal or the lake of a neighbouring château. On the 25th the Divisional Concert Party gave an entertainment.

On 28th May the Battalion relieved the 7th Argyll and Sutherland in support of the front line; Nos. 2 and 3 Companies in the sunken road west of Roeux, Headquarters and the remaining companies in the railway cutting south of Fampoux. All were kept hard at work improving the trench system.

On the 31st the 5th Cameron Highlanders (9th Division) relieved the Battalion, which went back to billets in Arras.

The Battles of Arras were in some sense a disappointment to the men, who had the soldier's instinctive knowledge of when the enemy was beaten, and who looked in vain for the reserves that should have completed what they had done.

The 51st Division was now a body of shock troops—that is, troops used almost exclusively for attack. While there were obvious disadvantages in belonging to shock troops, there was the great advantage that they did not have the monotony of holding the trenches when there was nothing of interest going on, but went back for rest and training in areas where the presence of the civilian population ensured some of the amenities of peace.

The Battalion entrained at No. 2 station at Arras at 2 P.M. on 1st June, reaching Tinques at 5.30 P.M., whence they marched to billets at Bailleul aux Cornailles. Next day it was joined by Second Lieutenants L. A. Harris, E. St C. Gainer and A. Munro, with one hundred and sixty other ranks. On the 4th it made a two-hours' march to Valhuon, and on the 5th one of five hours *via* Boyaval and Heuchin to Lisbourg. The day was very hot and the men found the unaccustomed hills very tiring. A number fell out, some literally falling unconscious. The cider of Lisbourg was very welcome!

Lisbourg was a fine village and the billets were good. It was here that one of the men threw some onions through a hot-house window. The owner complained volubly and some Company officers went to see what amends could be made. Their soft words appeased Madame, who invited them into the house to partake of coffee and wine. "La fenêtre, monsieur? Ah, c'est la guerre." They accepted the coffee and wine. "Madame est si bonne."

The conversation turned on the village and its amenities. Monsieur's eyes sparkled. He told them all about it, from the best of the estaminet to the worst of the church—and here he waxed eloquent. Monsieur seemed particularly antagonistic to the church. But Madame did not approve of this attitude. She manœuvred behind her guests and, thinking herself unseen by them, shook her fist at her graceless husband.

On 7th June the Battalion left Lisbourg at 8 A.M., at first by route march, but later in buses, and passing through St-Omer reached La Panne, 14 kilometres farther north, at 4 P.M. The billets here were very scattered, the Officers' Mess being about three miles from the parade ground.

France may be divided into three zones, corresponding with the drink of the inhabitants. Wine is drunk in the warm zone of central and southern France, cider in the cooler Brittany and Normandy, and beer in the cold and damp flats of the north, where there is hardly enough slope to carry the waters of the canalized rivers and drainage dykes to the sea.

St-Omer lies on the dividing line between the flats of Flanders and the chalk downs of Artois, which line runs, roughly, from Calais to Arras. La Panne lies within the chalk; and it was on the rolling downs of the Second Army training area that the Battalion now began training and musketry. Special attention was given to musketry practice, but there were also frequent route marches; and the latest methods of attack, especially that of a strong point with rifle grenades—a very necessary matter, as will be seen—were carefully drilled into the troops.

The days at La Panne will always be remembered with pleasure by those who were there, for they had almost all that they could wish. The training ground was excellent, the work interesting; the afternoons were devoted to cricket, bathing and sports. The weather was glorious and enabled the Battalion to make the most of the pleasures that abounded, while the billets were good and the population friendly. Tattoo was the great evening entertainment, to which soldiers and civilians alike turned out. After the buglers had sounded the call the pipes and drums played for half an hour: *Happy we'll be a' thegither*; *The Black Bear*; *The Cock o' the North*—varied by strathspeys and reels. The strut of the pipers, always reminiscent of Stevenson's Alan Breck, and the pomp of the Drum-Major much impressed the French. Leave for two days in Calais also was given to small parties of well-conducted men. This was quite unofficial, but was a much-sought-after privilege.

Drafts, numbering in all one hundred and three other ranks, arrived during this period. One day General Sir Hubert Gough, K.C.B., commanding the Fifth Army, came over to inspect the Battalion at training.

The 4th Seaforths renewed their acquaintance with St-Omer, to which there was a regular service of motor-lorries. Those who missed the last bus had to walk, but as the road was very uneven there were many who preferred this to the jolting lorries.

On 18th June the Battalion held a torchlight tattoo in the grounds attached to its Headquarters, at which the officers and sergeants were "At Home." General Harper and many officers from Divisional and other Headquarters, as well as from neighbouring units, were among the guests. A very warm welcome was given to Major Fraser of Leckmelm, who came over from Calais to see his old comrades. The Divisional band lent its aid; the pipers and others gave exhibitions of dancing. Not even the thunderstorm that came down in the middle of the entertainment could damp the spirits of the guests or check their merriment. The high trees that surrounded the grounds

MAP II.

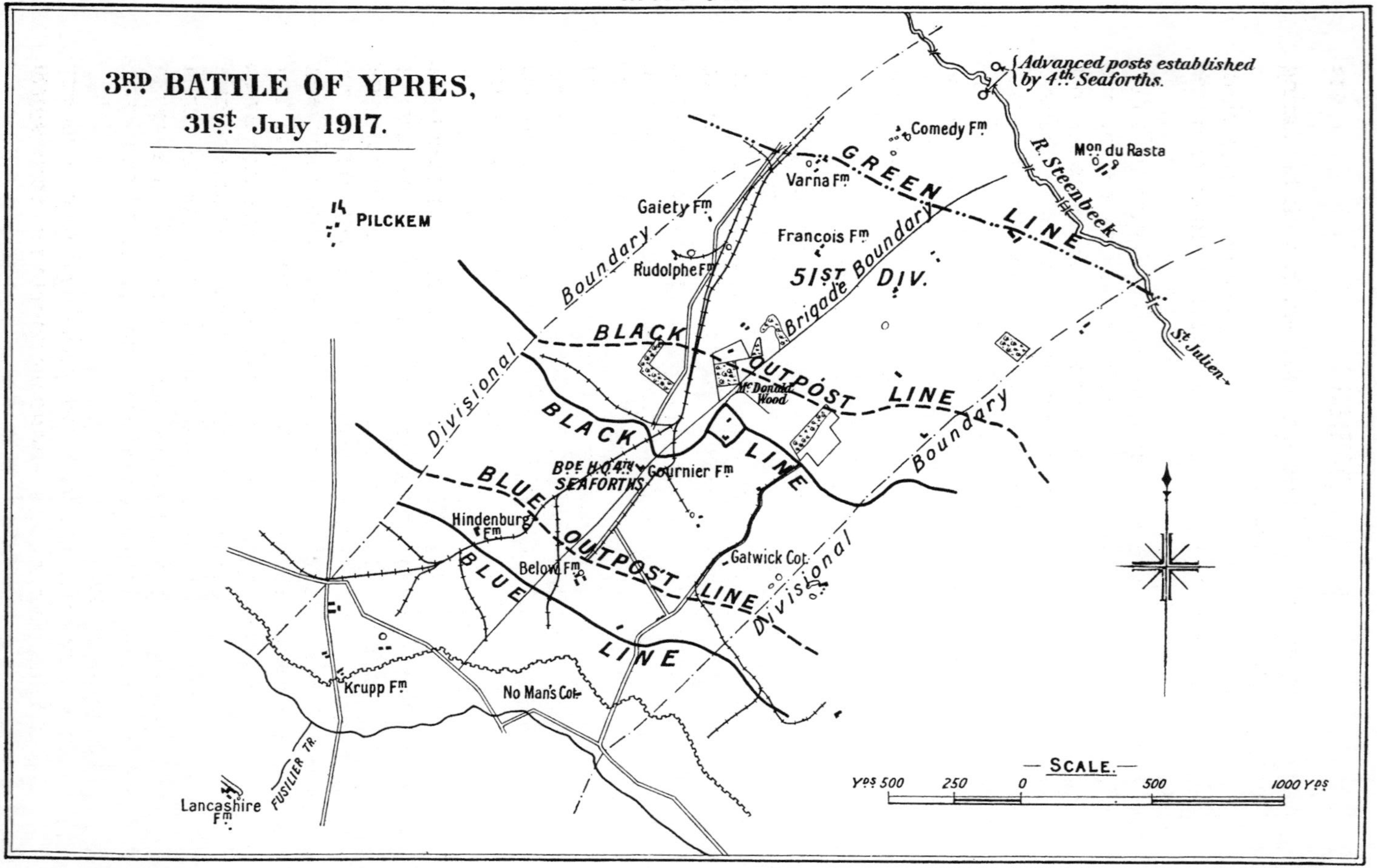
3RD BATTLE OF YPRES,
31st July 1917.
Advanced posts established by 4th Seaforths.
Comedy Fm
Mon du Rasta
R. Steenbeek
St Julien
Varna Fm
GREEN LINE
Gaiety Fm
Francois Fm
Rudolphe Fm
51ST DIV.
Brigade Boundary
Divisional Boundary
PILCKEM
BLACK OUTPOST LINE
McDonald Wood
BLACK LINE
BDE H.Q. 4th SEAFORTHS
Gournier Fm
BLUE OUTPOST LINE
Hindenburg Fm
Below Fm
Gatwick Cot.
BLUE LINE
Krupp Fm
No Man's Cot.
Lancashire Fm
FUSILIER TR.
SCALE.
YDS 500
250
0
500
1000 YDS

were festooned with Chinese lanterns, which, with the flaring torches, lit up the scene.

On the following day there was a Divisional horse show and sports, at which the Battalion was awarded the prize for the best horse or mare.

On 22nd June the Battalion marched *via* Watten to Lederzeele. Despite the continuous rain which had set in, and the sodden roads, the men were now so fit that none fell out on the long march. The Battalion, indeed, was a magnificent sight on the march—the physique was excellent; the march discipline perfect; no troops ever looked better.

Lederzeele was a Flemish-speaking village, and many of the inhabitants "had" very little French. It was an attractive little place. Just opposite the billets was a farm, which was full of live stock, though otherwise deserted. One Friday, which, by the way, was the usual pay day when behind the lines, five hens somehow found their way into the Sergeants' Mess. They were duly served up by the cook, who professed himself wholly in the dark as to how they came there. All looked forward to a succulent meal, when it was discovered that they had not been cleaned before being cooked, and were quite uneatable!

Training went on steadily, but, as at La Panne, amusement was not forgotten. Cricket matches were very popular, for the Battalion at this time numbered many Yorkshiremen. The Divisional Pierrot Troupe, under the guidance of Captain Stanley of Divisional Headquarters, provided most amusing entertainment. One of its performances suggested to the officers the idea of a skit. Captain Stanley and his troupe readily assisted in the preparations. The date had been fixed, when a bolt fell from the blue in the form of orders to move up to the trenches. The promoters were not to be balked; the arrangements were pushed forward, and the performance was given on the night before the Brigade moved. Captain Peverell was the comic lead; Lieutenant L. A. Harris had charge of the beauty chorus; and Lieutenant Cooper—thereafter always "Gladys"—was the leading lady. It was an immense success. The Brigadier and his staff and the officers of the 7th Argyll and Sutherland attended and were highly amused. The topical verses, full of allusive pleasantries that spared no one, had a splendid reception.

It was well that the long rest period ended on a cheerful note, for the Battalion was now going up into the Ypres salient, the mere name of which bore a sinister meaning, and the country round which was thoroughly depressing. As the Battalion marched out on 9th July a solitary old drake was still swimming on the pond at the deserted farm.

Three small drafts, numbering in all fifty-two other ranks, as well as Second Lieutenants F. A. Harrop and G. Robson, had arrived at Lederzeele; so that the Battalion was nearly up to its establishment when it marched out to St-Omer. Here it entrained at 9 A.M. It reached Poperinghe at 2 P.M. and marched to E Camp, three miles away, in the centre of a wood. Officers and men were quartered in huts. It was an " unhealthy " spot, for the Battalion had hardly settled down before an ammunition dump near the camp was blown up by enemy 9-inch high-velocity shells, and some of the men were wounded.

A new officer, who had made his first acquaintance with France on joining the Battalion, was unmercifully quizzed by the Divisional Burials Officer, who was a 4th Seaforth, and had come up on a visit to the Battalion. Just as the new-comer was introduced to him an enemy shell exploded about seventy yards away. With never a smile the Burials Officer surveyed his victim, questioned him about his height and chest measurements, and said that he thought a No. 3 size probably would do. He went on to explain that he had to take the measurements of all new officers and prepare a suitable receptacle " against eventualities." At this point the new-comer's discomfort was relieved by the roar of laughter which those present could no longer repress.

Those who had previously been in Flanders were astonished at the changes which the progress of the war had brought about. New railway lines ran in all directions; enormous dumps were being erected; fresh camps were dotted everywhere. An evil smell pervaded the country—" a very ancient and fish-like smell "—as of damp, dirt and stale humanity. It was a smell that seemed peculiar to Flanders in general and to Ypres in particular.

On 10th July the Battalion relieved the 4th Gordons in the line near Pilckem, Nos. 1 and 4 Companies in front line and Nos. 2 and 3 in support, with Headquarters at Lancashire Farm. The position had remained almost unchanged since 1915. The front line was quiet enough, though Second Lieutenant W. N. Collins was slightly wounded by shrapnel, and of other ranks two were killed and six wounded.

The Gordons had had a bad time there, a number of dug-outs in the bank and a few bridges over the canal having been blown in by heavy shells. A few came over while the Battalion was there, but only one casualty was caused by them, when one burst on the edge of the water, blowing a man right into a dug-out and killing him by concussion.

Here is an interesting description of a night out in the trenches: "The night we were relieved I had a very lively time. I had forty men and we were to work up in the front line under an R.E. officer. First of all the R.E. man turned up late at the rendezvous, thus allowing nineteen other parties, mostly carrying parties, up the line in front of us.

"We were about half way up the trench when the Boche decided to put a barrage on it, just at the time the first of the carrying parties was passing a particularly open and nasty bit of trench. We waited there for some time, but he didn't stop, so we went back to allow the people in front more cover. Then, when he quietened down, we went forward again, to be stopped this time by gas coming from some gas shells of his, so we put on our respirators and waited for things to clear.

"Then we got mixed up in a relief, and altogether things were in a muddle; so, as it was nearly midnight, and there wasn't much time left for working, I got the R.E. officer in charge to say the fatigue was off. Off, accordingly, we went in great glee, for we had to get a good few miles away before dawn.

"We weren't out of the mill even then, for on our way down we had a *pukka* gas alarm, all the hooters and gongs going from the front line onwards, so we put on our respirators again. Fortunately it was either a false alarm or merely gas shells, for we had none of it.

"We finally got out just before dawn, and when we landed at our camp, a good few miles back, we were greeted by a big long-distance shell, which burst just on the borders of the camp —fortunately without doing any damage.

"Notwithstanding our hot last night we didn't have a bad time up there at all. It was nothing like as bad as its reputation has made it, and certainly nothing near so bad as our experience at Roeux.

"The weather was fine and the men enjoyed themselves. One morning I passed one of our corporals standing on a plank in the mud, by the canal bank, fishing, pulling out huge perch from the shallows at the side. He got about half-a-dozen. I went back later and tasted them; they were quite nice, very much like whiting."

The Battalion was relieved on the night of the 12th. Back beyond the Ypres (or Yperlee) Canal the roads were packed with troops and wagons, at which an enemy aeroplane was firing with a machine gun. Fortunately no one in the Battalion was hit. It went back to its former camp, and the next day moved through Proven and Watou to Houtkerque, where it went under canvas in a field near the church. This village is just on the French side of the Belgian march, and the stay was a pleasant one.

A number of the people, especially the girls, spoke English quite well. This was not at once realized, for a certain warrant-officer went into a shop and asked in his best French for what he wanted. After listening most politely to his efforts Madame at last said: " It would be much better that you should speak English, for I would understand better." It turned out that she had lived for some years in England.

The 51st Division was now in the XVIII Corps, commanded by Lieutenant-General Sir Ivor Maxse. Before it went up to the line he had given a lecture to the officers of the Division. He explained that he wished to make the acquaintance of the new comers and to let them make his. He held up the Guards as a model for their imitation, especially in march discipline, and gave them some information about the plans for the coming battle. The effect of the Corps Commander's speech—especially as he had never seen the Division—was to rouse a certain soreness. This was particularly the case as regards march discipline, on which it prided itself.

The Battalion soon had an opportunity to see the model held up to it—two battalions of the Guards marching through its area, one up to the front line and the other back to billets. The immediate effect was an unprecedented demand on the canteen for that useful article, " Soldiers' Friend." Men could be seen polishing every bit of brass in their equipment during their spare time. This was not the end. The Adjutant, who, like all good adjutants, knew what was afoot among the men and was well aware of the general desire to show the Guards how the Seaforth Highlanders could march, suggested somewhat diffidently that the Battalion would like a route march. The Commanding Officer, after some demur, assented to the proposition, insisting, however, that full marching order must be worn, and a distance of not less than ten miles covered. On the day selected, in spite of the sultriness of the weather, the Battalion did a voluntary march of fifteen miles. They were careful to go through all the villages occupied by the Guards Division, and came back without anyone having fallen out, entirely satisfied with their performance. So did the Battalion reply to the Corps Commander's address!

One day the Officers' Concert Party visited the "Balmorals" theatre at Lederzeele to go over some of their items. It was the Commanding Officer's birthday, and on their way back they decided to honour the occasion. At Houtkerque they went to a parlour of the Officers' Restaurant, where they found the Commanding Officer, and thus greeted him:

"Many happy returns of the day, Sir,
We've come back to wish you good-night:
We hope you will kindly observe, Sir,
That none of us are tight.
It's not our fault if your heart don't feel,
For there was no booze in Lederzeele:
If you'll give us a glass we will really try
To drink to your health, for our throats are dry."

This effusion appears to have made Lieutenant-Colonel Unthank's heart feel acutely, for he ordered champagne.

Major M. Jobson, from the 4th K.O.S.B., took over the post of Second-in-Command; Second Lieutenant D. I. G. Clark and a draft of fifty-two other ranks arrived from home; and Captain Harris and the Regimental Sergeant-Major went to the Advanced Divisional Reinforcement Depot as Acting Adjutant and Regimental Sergeant-Major respectively. Company Sergeant-Major Picrce (K.D.G.) relieved Regimental Sergeant-Major Anderson while he was at the Divisional Training School.

The Battalion left Houtkerque on the 21st and marched through Watou and Poperinghe to Windmill Camp, east of the Yser Canal bank. It was here that everyone realized that the expected attack was close at hand—there were issues of strawberry jam! Very hot fighting indeed was expected, for the rations were unusually good; there were butter, jam, vegetables, fresh meat, and even chocolates and good cigarettes. The pill was well sugared!

Captive balloons were up continuously on both sides,

stretching north and south as far as eye could see. One near the Battalion was brought down very hurriedly one day, for long-range guns were using very heavy shrapnel "coal boxes" against it, and the fire was becoming uncomfortably accurate. It was a common sight to see observers jump from their balloons and descend by parachute.

The scheme of the impending attack had been most fully explained. All ranks were pledged to the strictest secrecy; not a man was to open his lips about it to anyone whom he did not know, no matter what his rank. Model trenches were constructed on a very elaborate scale, and the Battalion had been moved up to study them. By model trenches is meant a large-scale map laid out on the ground, with every feature —hills, fences, even single trees (so far as known)—carefully shown. To give some idea of the size of this one it may be mentioned that roads were the width of an ordinary plank, and men walked about the model itself.

In the course of this instruction a young second lieutenant was conducting his platoon round these trenches when he met a General Officer with every outward sign of high rank, and a pleasant and attractive manner. After a few words the General asked the subaltern what part he was taking in the scheme. "Very sorry, sir, I'm afraid I can't tell you. Commanding Officer's orders, and I don't know you." "But you must," came the quick response; "I am your Corps Commander. I command 100,000 men." "Very sorry, sir, I am a Second Lieutenant, and I command 50 men. I don't know you, sir, and my orders are to maintain secrecy."

The impending battle was intended to be the climax of the year, and every preparation had been made for its success. The present objective was Bruges and the sea-coast, including Ostend and Zeebrugge. It was hoped that it would be a shattering blow to the Germans.

The collection of the necessary material and the making of roads had consumed much time, so that it was not until the end of July that all was ready, and the fine weather showed signs of breaking.

Windmill Camp itself was a concentration point for line troops, and therefore received special attention from enemy aeroplanes, particularly at night. There were trenches dug in the camp to give shelter on these occasions, but they were used by very few. It was considered bad form to run and take shelter from aeroplane bombs and machine-gun fire; foolhardy, perhaps, but just the very quality that made it possible for ordinary men to walk open-eyed into a modern battle. There is, furthermore, nothing so infectious as fright or nervousness, and either will break up troops sooner than any mines, bullets or shells. These considerations explain the campaign of frightfulness indulged in by Germany during the war. The German, however, was particularly dense in his appreciation of the *moral* of the British people as a whole, and the British soldier in particular. Not only pride in his country and his regiment, but his own self-respect, combined with his entire detachment from anything out of the ordinary, made him absolutely proof against this kind of attack. Old soldiers, moreover, knew that the odds were in their favour and they were quite willing to gamble on the chance.

On the 24th several men were gassed whilst carrying shells up to the front line. On the 27th there was a bombardment by aeroplanes, followed by another during the night of the 28-29th.

On 30th July the 4th Seaforths moved up into position on the canal bank ready for the opening of the Third Battles of Ypres on the morrow.

The Battalion had a very valuable institution, known as the "hours of silence." Before moving up to take position for an attack, which was always done by night, no work nor duties of any kind were performed. The whole Battalion rested from 2 P.M. till 5 P.M., after which everyone washed and dressed as carefully as if he were going to a ceremonial parade.

The XVIII Corps was operating on the left centre of the Fifth Army, with the 36th Division on the right, then the 51st, the Welsh Division and the Guards. The attack of the 51st Division was made by the 152nd and 153rd Brigades, with the 154th in reserve. The Division had to attack towards the Steenbeck, north-west of Ypres, and establish a defensive line beyond the river, from which a further advance could be made to the Gheluvelt-Langemarck system.

The Germans had the advantage of the ground. The High Command Redoubt in their lines commanded our trenches and battery positions, while screening the whole of their own from direct observation. Our artillery were, therefore, entirely dependent on aerial observation.

The attack was launched at 3.30 A.M. in conjunction with

artillery, trench-mortar and machine-gun barrages. In addition to these normal accompaniments of an attack 206 bombs filled with burning oil and 150 trench-mortar thermite shells were fired on selected positions in the enemy lines.

When the attack began, the *3rd Guard Division* was relieving the *23rd (Reserve) Saxon Division* opposite our front. Strong opposition was met with from a number of concrete emplacements; but these were dealt with systematically, the platoons detailed to capture them advancing from shell hole to shell hole under cover of rifle-grenade fire. The 51st Division alone on the Fifth Army front reached its objectives on 31st July.

Throughout the day the 4th Seaforths remained on the canal bank—a very comfortable place, considering the circumstances. The banks were some thirty to forty feet high, and huts called " elephant shelters," made from arched lengths of corrugated iron, had been built into them. Layers of sandbags, stones, earth and sometimes concrete made these shelters proof against even the biggest shells, though one or two men were killed by 9-inch high-velocity shells falling into the canal. The shelters had doors and windows, and some rose even to the luxury of curtains and flowers! A double duck-board track was the main street of this queer town and was a busy thoroughfare.

When the attack began at 3.30 A.M. the Battalion was standing to in these shelters, ready to move up into the fight at a moment's notice. It was a dull, misty morning, a drizzling rain was falling, and there was just a faint glimmer of dawn in the east. As the attack progressed, various arms of the Service became active—Engineers threw new bridges across the canal; a light railway was built up into No-man's-land with amazing speed; and while the attack was still in progress an engine drawing a load of shells and supplies was puffing away where a few hours before a man dared not show himself.

The Royal Artillery began to advance to new positions. Guns and limbers drawn by six or eight mules charged across the pontoon bridges and dashed up the steep rough road on the other side, the drivers yelling at their beasts and whipping them into a gallop. Overhead flew aeroplanes, while enemy shrapnel burst in clouds of black and greenish smoke.

Here is an eyewitness's account of this day: "We started off from the reserve positions right among the batteries, and at zero we all went to the dug-out door and looked across the canal. Then hell broke loose. The din was awful. As far as the eye could see the air was cleft by innumerable stabbing flashes of light, which followed each other so quickly that the early morning gloom was turned to quite a decent light. And the air above seemed alive and moving. One felt rather than heard the movement of the shells overhead. And as you watched the first simultaneous flashes of the multitude of guns you could picture the sight up in front. Wave after wave of men scrambling over the top to the line, up as close to the shield of bursting shells as they could, and you could feel with them the tense excitement of the moment. They tell me the Boche barrage was pretty heavy, but wild, and I can believe it; for I was up in No-man's-land that was that morning later, and found his brand-new shell holes miles away from anywhere. The pounding of the guns went on for hours and then stopped, after which followed a pregnant calm.

"During the barrage some of our boys were out with improvised fishing lines, fishing for breakfast in the canal!

"Wounded and prisoners began to trickle down, but not many of either, and most of the Boches were acting as stretcher-bearers.

"We expected to be called on any minute, but nothing happened, so we went on top of the bank to see the fun. Then one saw extraordinary scenes. There, where but yesterday there was nothing moving or doing, were batteries in the open, firing away or cleaning their guns; working battalions were clearing tracks and making roads and railways; endless strings of pack mules were coming up with ammunition; and close beside what formerly was the most unhealthy spot in our support line I saw a couple of artillery officers' valises lying dumped beside a tent!"

All the first night and the whole of the second day it rained heavily, making ground that before had been dry and hard into a spongy quagmire, and what had been a wilderness of shell holes and the debris of trenches into an impassable morass. The troops blamed the weather for having prevented a break-through at this time, and the idea, though an exaggerated one, was well founded. As the men put it: "If it hadn't been for the rain we'd have chased 'Jerry' out of Belgium."

Captain Peverell writes: "As had so often been the case before, the conditions during this time were appalling. Almost the whole ground was one series of shell holes filled with water, in which many of the wounded were drowned. Between the shell holes was mud, in which we sank to the knees. What tracks there had been were completely obliterated, and the task of maintaining communication with the various posts, bringing up and distributing rations, water, ammunition and other necessaries, was almost impossible. In this water-logged country there was little in the nature of dug-outs or shelters, and such as existed were death traps; for they had previously been occupied by the enemy, and their exact location was known to his artillery. Quite a large proportion of the casualties were in the neighbourhood of dug-outs. Living under these conditions called for a standard of endurance and fortitude which all ranks displayed, as usual, to the highest degree."

On 1st August the 154th relieved the 153rd Brigade in the Green Line, west of the Steenbeck. Nos. 1 and 2 Companies were in front line, Nos. 3 and 4 in support, while Headquarters were at Gournier Farm.

The trenches were battered and filled in places with the bodies of the enemy. Not a square yard of ground had escaped our artillery fire, and a week's rain had made the whole area a waste of water-holes and mud.

The companies in front line established posts on both sides of the Steenbeck, covering the bridges. The platoon on the west side occupied some German trenches on rising ground; that on the east side dug themselves in, but in a short time water had filled their trenches, and they finally sought cover from the weather in some small corrugated-iron shelters a few yards from the bridge, where they were ready to come into action in a moment.

The river, though only about ten feet wide, was here a serious obstacle, which was important to hold. These posts were isolated from the rest of the Battalion for some thirty-six hours; for it was impossible to move during the day, and they were obliged to remain under artillery fire from both sides until communications were again established. Some dead men of the Black Watch were found beyond the Steenbeck. They must have made a magnificent effort to exploit the successful attack of the first day, but their numbers were insufficient against the concentration of the enemy in the woods and village of Langemarck only a few hundred yards away. Near the Steenbeck, too, were dead and dying horses, the relics of a squadron of King Edward's Horse that had gone up to try to exploit the position under cover of infantry posts. They were stopped by heavy machine-gun fire, and joined the infantry in dismounted action. The officer who established the posts on the Steenbeck has left the following account of his doings:

"The next afternoon [*i.e.* the 1st August], when we moved up, I found myself called on to take over our most advanced positions, which were behind some old concrete German gun-pits just this side of a stream running parallel to our old front line. We had to go down in the early evening, as we had word that the Hun had driven the people on our left in, and so we were to relieve our war-worn people in front, so that if he tried anything, he'd get it hot from fresh troops. As we moved down the slope towards the river we were under observation, and seeing us come, and no doubt 'having the wind up,' he put us under a barrage of heavy howitzers and high-velocity johnnies. It was extremely exciting going along in front of your platoon in single file, winding in and out of shell holes, hearing and seeing the big black beggars bursting all round. Little by little you increased the pace, till by the time you'd reached our half-way house — some other gun-pits — your heart was fit to burst and your knees shaking, what with excitement and the fatigue of pulling your feet from the sticky mud each time. We got up to the pits without a casualty, the Boche shells just following behind all the way; but they caught us up at the gun-pits, and we began to get wounded there. A splinter hit the top of my helmet, tore the cover and dented the steel without piercing it; while the officer I relieved there, an old Ripon acquaintance, got hit by a small piece on the temple, just piercing a vein, so I had to bandage him up and send him off. Then, as soon as things quietened, I moved forward to my objective, and had the same experience—only more so—and this time I had a few casualties, my two corporals and one sergeant being laid out by one unlucky shell. When I reached my destination it was with half a platoon and two unpaid Lance-Jacks as non-commissioned officers. I was then told from Headquarters that my left flank was exposed, and that in addition to holding the front I had to throw out a defensive flank—with less than twenty men!

"When it got dark, the other people cleared off and left me, with about half my original platoon, to hold on. Luckily there was a post of the Division on my left in the same pits, in pretty good strength, so I was all right as regards my flanks.

We had a pretty thick time there for about twenty-four hours, getting shelled very heavily most of the time. The following evening I got orders to re-establish a forward post across a stream in front, from which our people had been driven the day of the attack, and so, after things had settled down a bit—after a terrific strafe from both sides—I went forward and dug in about forty yards in front. The thing was a terrific gamble—a pure gamble with death. If we'd been spotted we'd have been blown to blazes and shelled out of it.

"Luckily I found an old communication trench fitted up with corrugated-iron shelters, the only one of which not blown in was about forty yards from the bridge. So I put my gunners and myself there, and deepened the trench and blocked it and made a cross-piece, so that we could command both sides. I explored the C.T. and found it impassable; anyone coming down must get out and go over the top every few yards.

"Luckily we were in ground that had been shelled fairly heavily, and so our holes weren't conspicuous; and our boys camouflaged their trenches quite nicely, planting thistles and sods all over the fresh turned earth, so that I had great difficulty in spotting them myself when I went round.

"Indeed, when I was coming back from my look at the communication trench, I almost stepped on top of one of my chaps before I saw him. He'd dug down about six feet, leaving a platform at each end of his hole to fire from, had spread his new earth about and stuck it full of thistles and sods, camouflaging it beautifully.

"We lay low during the day and kept good watch during the night, but weren't troubled at all, luckily for us.

"We had two days over there and then went back to our original positions; and getting out was even worse than getting in, for the mud had been stirred up to the consistency of treacle. However, we managed it. I was complimented by the Commanding Officer on what I did, and my company officer has told me he's put my name forward; but I don't for a minute expect to hear anything further about it, for in our Battalion it's very difficult to get anything in that line, and really what I did was just the ordinary and there was nothing exceptional in the doing of it. The doing was simple. It was the gamble element that was awful, and I'm still feeling the strain and the reaction."

While the two leading companies were thus establishing

their posts, the rest of the Battalion occupied the captured concrete emplacements well known as "pill-boxes." They were most formidable affairs, quite unexpected, and caused most of our reverses. They were, for the most part, square boxes, from three to twelve feet in height, with walls of reinforced concrete three to six feet thick, pierced with ports for machine guns. They were cleverly concealed among the debris of ruined farms, so that they did not attract suspicion in aerial photographs. They offered a stout resistance, but were soon captured by men who had been specially trained in the attack of strongpoints. As the doors faced the enemy they had to be sandbagged, but thus treated they made excellent quarters for our men.

Here, too, the 4th Seaforths first met mustard gas. It was a powerful irritant, raising huge blisters on the skin, and causing cuts and abrasions to fester. The kilt was a distinct disadvantage when mustard gas was encountered. The worst feature of it was that it hung about for days where the ground was saturated with it.

Several times was the S.O.S. signal sent up on either flank, being promptly answered with heavy artillery and machine-gun barrages. Thousands of shells and bullets were fired each time and no counter-attack developed.

The artillery was active on both sides during the 2nd and 3rd of August. Headquarters was shelled at intervals and many wounded Germans were brought in. On the 3rd the Battalion suffered a great loss in the death of Captain "Pat" Macintyre (Braelangwell), by then the Brigade Transport Officer, who was mortally wounded by a shell. He was one of the original officers of the Battalion, and his transport was a model of efficiency.

On the 4th, the 4th Gordons relieved the Battalion, which went back to dug-outs on the canal bank, except No. 3 Company, which went to Hindenburg Farm in the old German line.

Casualties for the whole period were:

OFFICER

Wounded: Second Lieutenant M. Murray.

OTHER RANKS

Killed: 20. *Missing*: 1. *Gassed*: 1.
Wounded: 87. *Died of Wounds*: 5.

On the 5th the Battalion went to new dug-outs on the canal bank. On this day an aeroplane bombed the Advanced Transport Camp at Hospital Farm, causing casualties.

On the 6th, on relief by the 8th Duke of Wellington's, the 4th Seaforths went back to huts near their old camp by Poperinghe. Here Company Sergeant-Major J. S. Smith took over the duties of Acting Regimental Sergeant-Major.

On the 8th they moved to St-Jans Ter Biezen, two miles behind Poperinghe; and two days later entrained at Proven at 8 A.M., reaching Watten at 3 P.M., whence they marched to Helvelinghem. Here the Battalion remained for training till the 22nd, Lieutenant Macrae, Second Lieutenants Finlayson and N. Sutherland, and one hundred and fifty-six other ranks, joining during this period.

At Helvelinghem was written the first complaint about the Army Postal Service. It appears that the whole of the newspapers which should have arrived with accounts of the recent battle went astray, so the first numbers received merely recorded that there was nothing special to report. Very annoying for those who wanted to know a little more about the battle than what had happened in their own immediate neighbourhood.

On 23rd August the Battalion was back in St-Jans Ter Biezen, and on the 29th moved to Murat Camp, on the canal bank. On the 31st, Brigadier-General Hamilton went on leave and Lieutenant-Colonel Unthank assumed command of the 154th Brigade. Major Jobson took over command of the Battalion. This night a German aeroplane came over at ten o'clock dropping bombs. It was hit by Lewis guns and fell a mile away.

On 4th September the Battalion went back to Dirty Bucket Camp, near Poperinghe. Everywhere they experienced incessant bombing and shelling. Some of the tents that should have been taken over at Dirty Bucket Camp had been hit the previous night by aeroplane bombs, and blood and flesh were still on the ground. At night the noise reverberated among the trees and disturbed men's sleep.

Here is a sketch of camp life on the Ypres front: "The only excitement we get now is when the Boche 'planes come over and bomb. Then we have thrills—that is if we're not asleep; for it would take a bomb on the hut itself to wake us. We sleep in the hut with a man who suffers from perpetual nightmare. He talks and shouts and screams all night long,

MAP 12.

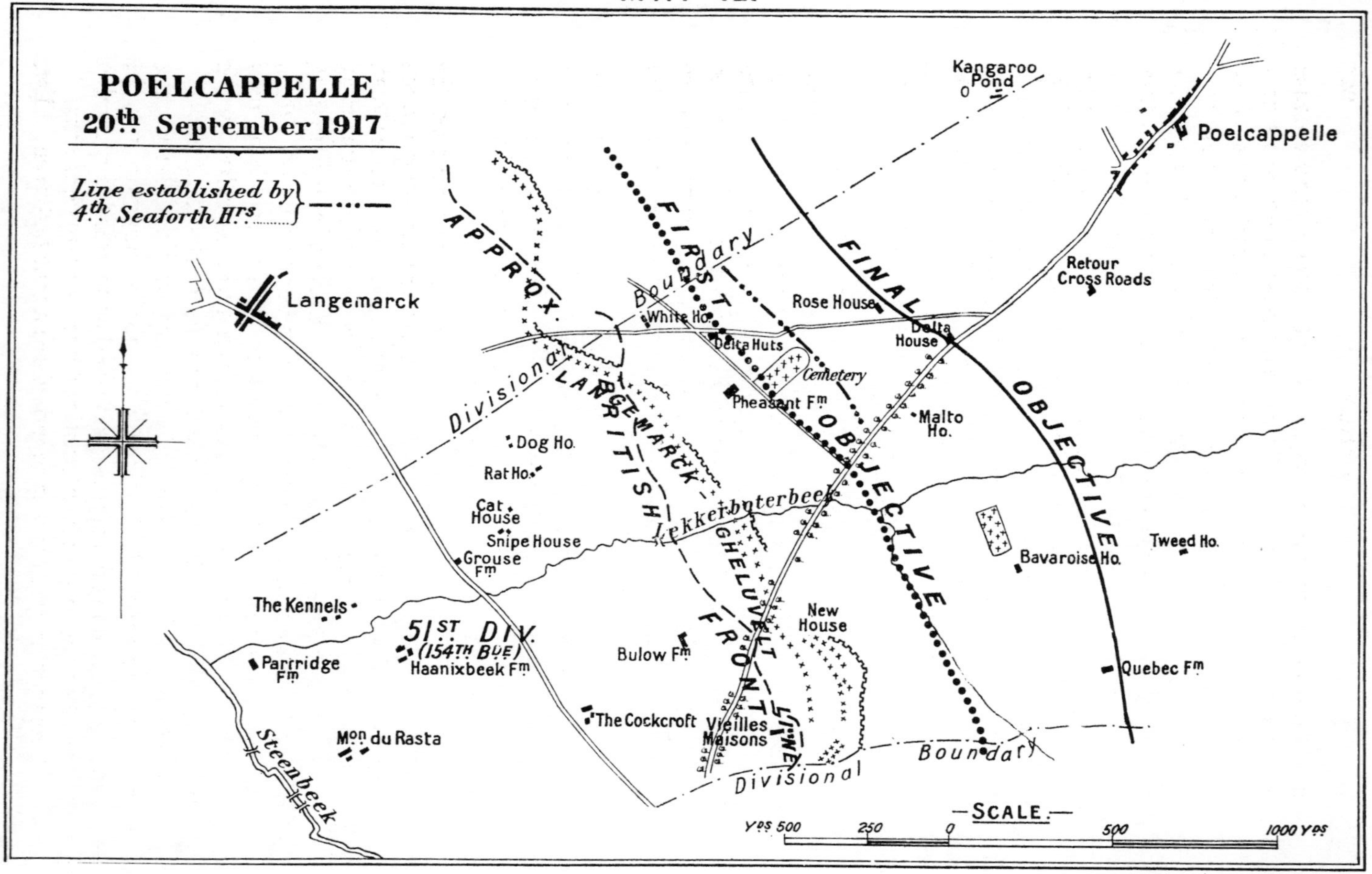

POELCAPPELLE
20th September 1917

Line established by 4th Seaforth Hrs. —··—

Langemarck
Poelcappelle
Kangaroo Pond
Retour Cross Roads
Rose House
Delta House
White Ho.
Delta Huts
Cemetery
Pheasant Fm
Malto Ho.
Dog Ho.
Rat Ho.
Cat House
Snipe House
Grouse Fm
The Kennels
Parrridge Fm
Mon du Rasta
51ST DIV. (154TH BDE)
Haanixbeek Fm
Bulow Fm
The Cockcroft
Vieilles Maisons
New House
Bavaroise Ho.
Tweed Ho.
Quebec Fm
Lekkerboterbeek
Steenbeek
APPROX. LANGEMARCK – GHELUVELT LINE
BRITISH FRONT LINE
FIRST OBJECTIVE
FINAL OBJECTIVE
Divisional Boundary
Divisional Boundary

SCALE
Yds 500 250 0 500 1000 Yds

so we're used to anything now! The old Boche usually comes over every night after dark. First you hear three blasts on a whistle; then every whistle in the camps all round blows. Next the searchlights start and everyone begins chasing round, putting out lights in other people's tents and huts. Now you can hear a drone of engines—perhaps of three or four—and then the 'Archies' begin and Lewis guns by the thousand. And to make more noise, and just stir us up a bit, the old Boche will drop his bombs—generally all at once—and make off for his own lines at top speed. It is the exception for anyone to see him. The searchlights very seldom catch him; but when they do I should think there are from a thousand to ten thousand machine guns, all rapping at once at the ghostly silver 'plane, seemingly standing still in the searchlight's beam, while the air all round is full of the flashes of bursting shrapnel. And, wonderful to say, he generally gets clear. Not always, for we've bagged a good few. One came down near us the other night, and our Lewis gun officer, who had been firing, thought he was the marksman who had done it. So away he chased over the countryside for about two kilometres, clad in pyjamas, trench coat and boots, to see his trophy. Alas, it was only to be told by the captured observer that they had to come down owing to engine trouble!

"Another wonderful thing is where all the bullets and pieces of shell go to. All these thousands of rounds must go somewhere, but so far I've never heard any falling. Yet they must fall somewhere—not that I'm particularly keen on being where they fall, for they must be nasty!"

On 6th September the Battalion moved up and relieved the 6th Seaforths in the front line near Langemarck—1200 yards nearer the Gheluvelt-Langemarck system than on 4th August. The line was held by a series of isolated posts, with headquarters of the companies in German pill-boxes. Little of note occurred, except that Lieutenant Addison was wounded while on patrol. On the 9th the Battalion marched back to the canal bank over three miles of duck-boards, and on the 12th, on relief by the 7th Black Watch, went to Siege Camp, near Elverdinghe.

One day a huge Gotha, escorted by smaller 'planes, flew over, for the enemy had gained a temporary superiority in the air. It dropped some bombs that killed and wounded a number of the Gordons, but only very slightly one or two Seaforths.

One morning a hole was found where a tent had been. Two

men had been killed and some wounded, while one man was thrown several yards clear of the tent. It is alleged that he continued to sleep undisturbed!

Nor were aeroplanes the only troublesome visitors to these camps in Flanders. Here are some impressions of the high-velocity gun: "The H.V. gun is a particularly vicious and nasty creature. It fills you with delight when you see one firing by day, and you hug yourself with glee at the thought of the 'wind up' of some old Boches umpteen miles behind the line. But at night you invariably curse it. It is generally situated—for greater safety for itself—in the middle of some infantry camp. Thus we get all the umpteen thousand shells the Boche sends over searching for the gun, while the beggar lies low beneath his veil of camouflage and grins at us poor mortals. So we catch it during the day, and at night, when we try to sleep off our 'rest day' fatigue, he does his dirty work. We lie strafing and cursing and fuming while the blessed thing poofs off at irregular intervals, partially wrecking the tent each time and making your ears ring. That's how he offends against us in the sending.

"In the receiving it's a bit worse. You hear a distant thud, a screech and a burst at practically one and the same time. However, one gets used to it after a time. It's wonderful how little feeling one has left now. One gets the spirit of the Frenchman more and more with every day that passes—a cold, hard, lack-of-feeling feeling. A shell lands, a bomb bursts, perhaps someone is killed: you shrug your shoulders and perhaps say, if you say anything, *c'est la guerre*. It's the same feeling that takes you through a barrage up the line. What we shall be like after the war, Lord knows. Some will become more sentimental and soppy; others will become the opposite."

Brigadier-General Hamilton had by now returned from leave and the Commanding Officer was back with the Battalion.

On 19th September the 154th Brigade moved to an assembly position west of Langemarck at 8.35 P.M., for it was to carry out the attack on the front allotted to the 51st Division the next day.

To meet the new conditions created by pill-boxes and similar strongpoints the artillery barrage was organized in depth in four zones. The main creeping barrage of 18-pr. shrapnel advanced at the rate of 50 yards in two minutes for the first

200 yards and then increased its pace. The combing barrage of 18-prs. and 4·5-inch howitzers had the special task of dwelling on strongpoints and working up communication trenches. The neutralizing barrage of 6-inch howitzers and 60-prs. worked beyond the combing barrage. The standing barrage of heavy howitzers and 60-prs. concentrated on the back areas where troops might be massed for counter-attack. Thirty-two machine guns opened on suspected strongpoints at zero, lifting as the infantry advanced to the protective S.O.S. barrage lines.

On the right of the Brigade was the 58th Division, on the left the 20th Division of the XIV Corps.

The ground over which the advance must be made rises gradually from the Steenbeck to a slight ridge above Pheasant Farm, which commands Poelcappelle, and covers the valley of the Steenbeck to the south of Langemarck. Though the defences were made up largely of pill-boxes and shell holes, there were still two very well-defined trench lines, Pheasant Trench-New Trench and Kangaroo Trench-Beer Trench.

The Brigade was deployed on a two-battalion front: on the right the 9th The Royal Scots, with the 7th Argyll and Sutherland Highlanders in support, and on the left the 4th Seaforth Highlanders, with the 4th Gordon Highlanders in support. The Battalion boundary was the Lekkerbokkerbeek, a stream some two feet deep and six feet broad. The "leap-frog" attack was still used.

The Battalion attacked on a two-company front: No. 3 on the right, with two platoons of No. 1 in second wave; and No. 4 on the left, with No. 2 in second wave. The remaining platoons of No. 1 Company at Comedy Farm were allotted to the special task of carrying forward ammunition. Battalion Headquarters were at Rat Houses and Brigade Headquarters at Dog Houses.

Major Jobson had marked out the jumping-off positions with tape, which made it comparatively easy to mass the troops very silently well within 100 yards of the enemy front line. Rain fell all night and the men lay in shell holes, where many slept comfortably, waiting for the dawn.

Zero hour was at 5.40 A.M. The rain had ceased and the air was clearing. There was a faint glimmer in the sky. The silence was ominous. Five minutes to go: the order was passed to fix bayonets. One minute: officers and men lay crouched, ready to rush. The seconds passed and the guns began to open, one or two at first, and then swelling into the now familiar roar of the barrages.

No. 4 Company, under Captain Dane, had an easy task on the left, as part of the enemy position had been evacuated, but farther along the enemy stubbornly held out in a strongly built trench with concrete shelters. Sergeant John Campbell, D.C.M., and six men of his platoon pushed on through our own barrage and cleared the trench in front of the right of his Company. Not one of the seven was hit, and this gallant display of initiative saved the Company many casualties. No. 2 Company then went through and attacked Pheasant Farm and the pill-boxes round it. "Captain Jackson," writes Lieutenant-Colonel Unthank, "had trained a small party for this purpose, consisting of himself, his servant, a piper and a Battalion scout, and with these he cleared them all. He himself was wounded slightly by one of our own bombs, but otherwise his party had no casualties. The time was now about 6 A.M., and Second Lieutenant J. Davidson, finding that the Company had taken all its objectives, wheeled his platoon to the right and struck in behind the Germans, who were holding up No. 3 Company."

The Germans had placed well-camouflaged posts in front of their trench, in which men were hidden with light machine guns and bombs. Our barrage did not touch these posts, and immediately No. 3 Company advanced they came under heavy fire from machine guns and hand grenades and were at once involved in fighting. When the barrage lifted, therefore, they were not in a position to charge the trench, so the Germans opened fire and mounted machine guns on the top of blockhouses, placed at intervals along the trench. Lieutenant Mackenzie, the Company Commander, had been killed, and Second Lieutenant Alexander Munro, who was now in command, charged home with the men nearest him, and after fierce fighting the trench was captured. For this Second Lieutenant Munro was awarded the D.S.O. Private H. Macdonald took charge of his platoon when the officer and non-commissioned officers had become casualties, and led it forward to capture the trench and to the final position in advance. He was promoted Sergeant on the spot. Thanks to assistance rendered by Second Lieutenant Davidson, with his platoon of No. 2 Company, the further advance of No. 3 Company was unmolested, and they reached their allotted position.

So far casualties had been remarkably light, being under

one hundred. An artillery officer later in the day counted over two hundred of the enemy dead in 120 yards of trench.

The second phase of the battle was to be carried out by the 4th Gordons on the battalion front. But the Division on the left, except for a few that went forward with No. 4 Company, had been held up by heavy machine-gun fire from Eagle Trench, north-west of Langemarck. The 154th Brigade, therefore, came under heavy enfilade fire from the left, and when the Gordons advanced up to the protecting barrage, from Pheasant Trench, they lost all their officers; wherefore officers of the 4th Seaforths took them on to their objectives. Captain Jackson did brilliant work. After having his wound dressed he returned and took a party of Gordon Highlanders forward and captured an advanced post beyond the objectives of the Division. On his way back he passed a wounded German, to whom he tried to explain that he would send stretcher-bearers to help him. The German threw a grenade, which wounded both the Captain and his servant, Private Seaton. The latter, though mortally hurt, succeeded in throwing a grenade, which killed the German. Jackson dragged himself on until he found two slightly wounded Germans, whom he compelled to carry him. Captain Jackson gained the D.S.O. for his distinguished conduct.

On the right the 9th The Royal Scots and 7th Argyll and Sutherland Highlanders also took all their objectives. But a critical position arose out of the failure of the division on the left to advance, and it became necessary to form a strong left flank over a length of nearly 500 yards, which weakened the Divisional front.

At 9 A.M. it was learned from prisoners that the enemy would counter-attack immediately, and the two platoons of No. 1 Company that were in reserve were sent up to reinforce the right of the Battalion line. The 8th Argyll and Sutherland of the 152nd Infantry Brigade came up and reinforced the left of the line, on the front Delta Huts-Cemetery, suffering heavy casualties on the way.

The first counter-attacks were made by the enemy against the 4th Gordons about 11.45 A.M., and again at 12.30 P.M. They were easily repulsed. But all the morning machine guns had been pushed steadily forward, and the main enemy counter-attack did not develop till 5 P.M. The barrage that accompanied it consisted almost entirely of 5·9-inch shells.

The 4th Gordons having taken up a position in front of the

4th Seaforths, the latter formed a defensive flank. Though the two counter-attacks during the morning were easily repulsed by the 4th Gordons they fell back before a third one at 4.30 P.M., behind the 4th Seaforths' line. Captain "Ray" Macdonald, sent up from Battalion Headquarters to find out the reason for the withdrawal, got together a few men and drove back the enemy into our protective barrage.

Pheasant Farm became the pivot of the Battalion left front, where officers of the 4th Seaforths collected a mixed force of Seaforths, Gordons, and Argyll and Sutherlands, and then counter-attacked and re-established the line in front of the cemetery.

Ammunition had again run short, and every round had to be taken from the dead and wounded. But the enemy was exhausted, and, as night fell, silence settled over the battle-field. The British position was immediately consolidated, the wounded were evacuated and prisoners sent to the rear.

The night passed quietly, and on the 21st all was normal till about 6 P.M., when the enemy were seen massing for a counter-attack. Aeroplanes had reported a forward concentration, and No. 2 Company Headquarters noticed them assembling well in front of the line of our protective barrage. By this time their artillery had opened on the line of Pheasant Trench and communication with the rear was cut off. Fortunately, however, some artillery signallers had come forward to Pheasant Farm and got into direct communication with the Brigade Artillery Signal Station by means of a strong lamp, thus warning the gunners to shorten their range and open fire immediately. The promptness and accuracy with which they carried out these instructions were admirable. The enemy assembly was broken and the counter-attack never materialized. The enemy bombardment was, however, causing heavy casualties; and realizing that, if our own guns stopped, the enemy would stop also, Private David Bannerman volunteered to take a message to Battalion Headquarters. It was a 10 to 1 chance against him; but he won through, and the guns on either side stopped. His brave action saved many lives.

That night the Battalion was relieved by the 5th Seaforths.

The attack of the 154th Infantry Brigade resulted in a gain of about 1000 yards in depth. The high ground commanding Poelcappelle was now in British hands, and the Fifth Army was in a favourable position for an advance on Poelcappelle itself.

The most striking feature about this attack was the prodigious expenditure of ammunition. New supplies continuously had to be sent up on Yukon packs, a dangerous task allotted to the two platoons of No. 1 Company. The pack is a simple affair of two lengths of wood with canvas stretched across, and is carried on the back. A strap round the forehead, like that of a fishwife's creel, takes some of the weight off the neck, and heavy loads can be carried this way.

It had been a notable victory. The magnificent fight of the 154th Infantry Brigade was recognized in a message from the Commander-in-Chief. Sir Hubert Gough also, in a farewell message, quoted below, referred to the battle as one of the proudest records of the Division; and Sir Ivor Maxse congratulated them on their sanguinary defeat of the enemy counter-attacks.

Message from Sir Hubert Gough

"In bidding farewell to the Highland Division the Army Commander wishes to express his great admiration for, and appreciation of, their splendid record during the fighting of the past two months.

"Their fine advance, their gallant defence of ground won against repeated enemy attacks and the severe punishment they inflicted on the enemy during the last battle will ever remain one of their proudest records, and has helped materially to the enemy's final defeat.

"He heartily wishes them all success in the future. *Scotland for ever!*"

It was estimated that more of the enemy were killed than in any previous battle—and that counted for very much at this time.

Considering the results gained the casualties were not really heavy; from the 19th to the 23rd they were:

OFFICERS

Killed: Second Lieutenants T. A. Mackenzie, D. I. G. Clark, G. Robson, T. T. Jenkins.

Wounded: Captain D. B. M. Jackson, Second Lieutenants P. H. Ballantyne, F. A. Harrop, A. Munro.

OTHER RANKS

Killed: 41. *Wounded*: 153. *Missing*: 15.

Brigadier-General J. M. Hamilton, who handed over command of the 154th Infantry Brigade to Brigadier-General K. G. Buchanan at the end of September, records how, during the period of his command, "the 4th Seaforth Highlanders were continually engaged and always maintained the high reputation of their Regiment. At Beaumont Hamel the 154th Brigade was in reserve and had a very trying time prior to the attack, preparing the trenches for the assaulting troops during bitterly cold and wet weather, the 4th Seaforths being continually in the line. The 154th Brigade, though in reserve, was also completely engaged during the attack, and had to hold the captured positions after the assault. In the attack on Vimy Ridge on 9th April 1917 the 4th Seaforths were on the left of the Brigade, and had a particularly difficult task, having to take a triangular set of trenches between the 51st Division and the Canadians, which were not parallel to the general line of advance. The success of this attack caused considerable anxiety to the Higher Command, but was carried out by the 4th Seaforths without a hitch."

SYNOPSIS OF EVENTS FROM THE MIDDLE OF NOVEMBER TO THE END OF DECEMBER 1917

Four outstanding events mark this period: the Battle of Cambrai, the complete occupation of German East Africa (Tanganyika Territory), the armistice at Brest Litovsk, and the surrender of Jerusalem.

Cambrai was something new in our incessant siege warfare. It has been much criticized and much blamed. In fact it came so much nearer success than could have been believed that those charged with its execution were as much surprised as the enemy — and did not recover from their surprise so quickly as he did. The idea was not new—it is, indeed, an old idea in war. Nivelle had tried to put it into execution early this same year. Unfortunately he let his idea be talked about. Cambrai was a well-kept secret. Perhaps it was too well kept. Perhaps a *little* less secrecy might have allowed the machine to work better. Be that as it may, the Germans were completely taken off their guard. Briefly the plan was to take advantage of the concentration of the German troops against the British about Ypres in order to break their front at a weakly held front between the Canal de l'Escaut and the Canal du Nord. It was hoped to break through in from twenty-four to forty-eight hours, to push through three cavalry divisions, supported by infantry, and drive the enemy over the River Sensée. Once in possession of the high ground about Bourlon Wood we were sure of creating a big salient in the enemy lines.

The plan failed. Neither the cavalry divisions nor the III and V Corps, which were to have passed through the gap in the enemy lines and "exploited" his discomfiture, were sufficiently far forward to complete the decision that on 21st November was trembling in the balance, with the weight heavily against the Germans. Bourlon Wood could not be carried. Flesquières was not taken till the morning of the 21st and the high road bridge at Masnières was broken down by a tank. These accidents enabled the Germans to bring up troops from Douai and at least one division recently arrived from the Russian front. By the time the III and V Corps came up the critical moment had passed, and eventually, after heavy and all-too-successful German counter-attacks, the British had to establish a tenable line by withdrawing from most of the ground gained.

The delay in bringing forward the troops for exploitation may have been in great part due to the difficulties of concealing the advance of such large numbers of troops. Yet there is no doubt that we suffered as much from the remarkable success of our surprise attack as did the Germans.

None the less the Battle of Cambrai was a stroke well worth making. In the first place, it showed that, even in what is virtually siege warfare, with all the advantages to be derived from aeroplanes in observation, it is possible to mass sufficient troops against a position to carry it by surprise. The Royal Engineers and the Pioneer Battalion (8th The Royal Scots) of the 51st Division, for instance, were able to make such cover in the woods and ruined villages about Havrincourt as to prevent their presence being observed, and the same applies to the rest of the masses of troops brought up.

Secondly, it proved that artillery working by calibration only and without registration could adequately carry out their task. That the advanced troops were not better supported by artillery at Fontaine-Notre-Dame was not due to such support being impossible, but to weather conditions, as the breaking up of one counter-attack there clearly shows.

Thirdly, the tanks fully justified the time and labour spent on their improvement. Their effective employment during the final advance to victory was due largely to the lessons learnt at Cambrai.

The attack was launched at 6.20 A.M. on 20th November by the 12th, 20th, 6th, 51st, 62nd and 36th Divisions, covered by 324 tanks. Later in the day the 29th Division came up on the right. Both the chief lines of defence were carried and over five thousand prisoners taken.

On the 21st we had penetrated to Fontaine-Notre-Dame, two and a half miles from Cambrai.

On the 22nd Fontaine was lost, but on the 24th the British had gained ground about Banteux, Moeuvres, Quéant and Bullecourt, while Bourlon Wood and village changed hands more than once. Indecisive fighting continued till the 30th, when the Germans penetrated the British line at Gouzeaucourt and La Vacquerie. Both were retaken, but the British found it necessary to withdraw to a better line.

The initiative had passed from the Allies to the Germans. Henceforth the efforts of the former were devoted to preparing for the German offensive that all knew must be imminent.

For with Russia in the hands of the Bolsheviks, who had signed the ignominious armistice at Brest Litovsk, the Germans had decided to concentrate all available troops, with a view to shattering the Allies on the Western front before the American armies could restore the balance of numbers.

MAP 13.

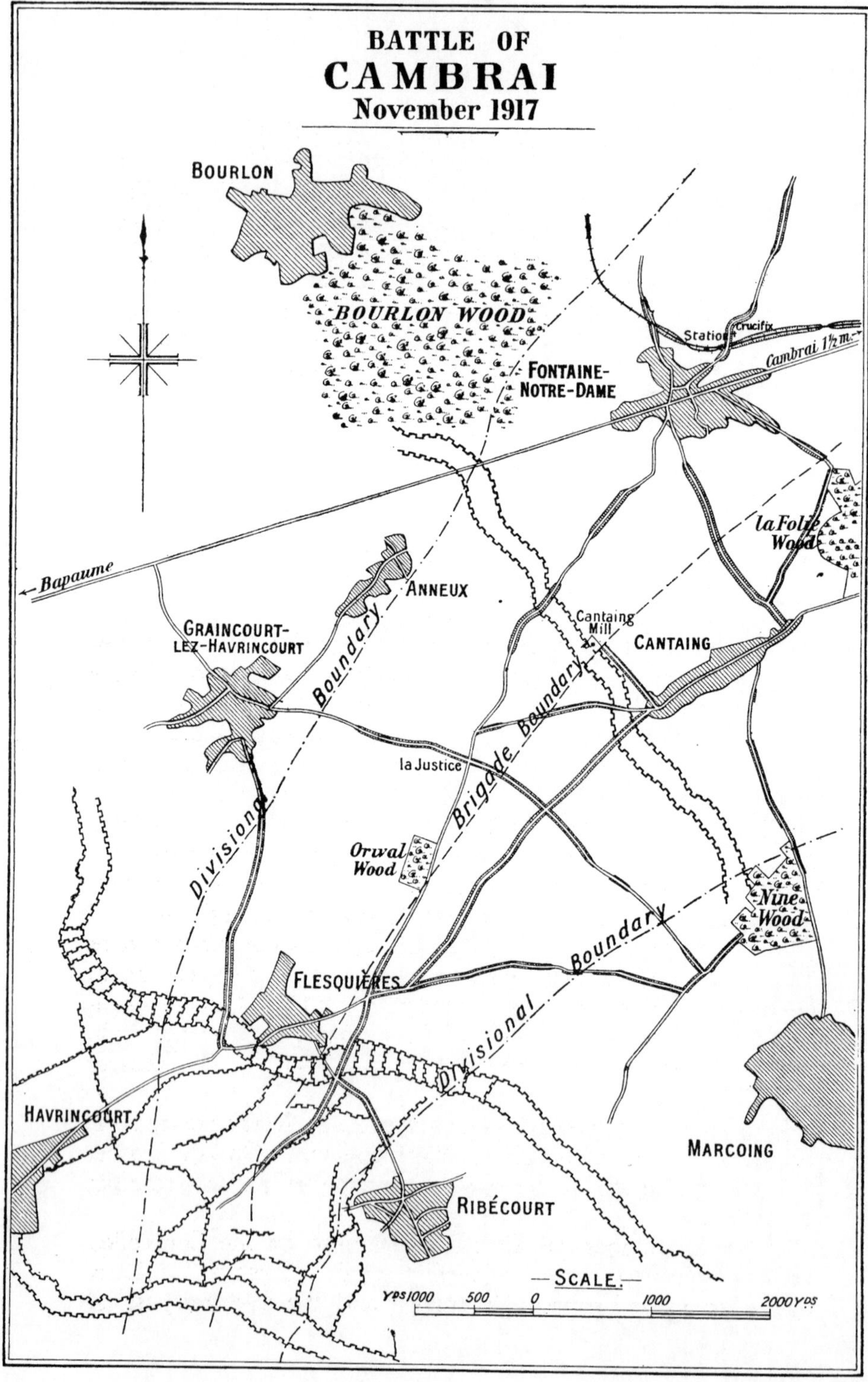
BATTLE OF
CAMBRAI
November 1917
BOURLON
BOURLON WOOD
Station
Crucifix
Cambrai 1½ m.
FONTAINE-
NOTRE-DAME
Bapaume
ANNEUX
la Folie
Wood
Cantaing
Mill
CANTAING
GRAINCOURT-
LEZ-HAVRINCOURT
Divisional Boundary
Brigade Boundary
la Justice
Orival
Wood
Nine
Wood
FLESQUIÈRES
Divisional Boundary
HAVRINCOURT
MARCOING
RIBÉCOURT
SCALE.
YDS 1000
500
0
1000
2000 YDS

FONTAINE-NOTRE-DAME

CHAPTER XI

CAMBRAI

On the night of 21st September 1917 the 4th Seaforths were relieved by the 5th Seaforths and went back to Siege Camp. On the 24th it went into billets at Poperinghe, when Lieutenant-Colonel Unthank went on leave and Major Jobson assumed command. The following day a draft of one hundred and sixty-two other ranks arrived, followed on the 26th by a further one hundred and thirty from the 2/4th Battalion. Two days later the Battalion marched at 9.30 P.M., entrained at 10.30 P.M., and reached Bapaume at 10.30 A.M. on the morning of the 29th. Thence it went to huts at Courcelles-le-Comte for training.

On the march through Bapaume, No. 4 Company's cooker was upset, and the dinners were strewn all over the road. Nothing deterred, the cook—always known as "John"—collected and returned the bulk of it. When remonstrated with, his sole reply was that it was "good enough for the likes of them."

At Courcelles, Second Lieutenants E. A. Mackintosh, L. S. Gander, H. Paterson and E. J. Martin joined. On 4th October the officers drew with the sergeants at football, with a score of 1 goal all.

On 5th October the Battalion embused on the Courcelles-Hamelincourt road and relieved the 5th Yorkshire Regiment in the front line between Guemappe and Vis-en-Artois, astride the Arras-Cambrai road. Nos. 1 and 2 Companies were in front line, No. 4 in support and No. 3 in reserve at Marlière Caves. The 9th The Royal Scots were on the right and the 12th Division on the left. The weather was wet and cold, but the line here had been for long a quiet one.

This state of affairs was not to go on for long. There is a story of a "Jock" who had arrived with the 51st Division in a new area. Meeting a "padre" he, with suitable apologies, asked for a match. The chaplain willingly complied, and when the soldier had lit his cigarette he turned to his benefactor and said: "I've something to tell ye, sir. We've arrived, an' ye're for hell noo."

It was feared that the enemy might fall back on the Drocourt-Quéant line, and that first night the Battalion patrols were out looking for the enemy position. They soon found it, with the result that the suspicions of the Germans were aroused. Enemy aeroplanes came over, flying down the line of the trenches to observe what might be going on. On 7th October a raid by the division on the left brought retaliation from the German side, and Second Lieutenant G. B. Simpson and two other ranks were killed in Southern Avenue by shell fire. On the 9th Nos. 3 and 4 Companies relieved Nos. 1 and 2 in the front line. The enemy shelled Cavalry Trench just after the relief, killing one and wounding four men. On 12th October there was a trench-mortar bombardment of one of the forward posts. It was succeeded by an enemy raid at 4.30 A.M. and, although no prisoners were taken by them, seven men were wounded. Some Germans were killed, and they left one wounded prisoner. The 9th The Royal Scots were less fortunate, for they had several casualties.

On the 13th the Battalion was relieved by the 7th Argyll and Sutherland. The right half Battalion went into shelters near Marlière Caves and the left to Carlisle Huts, near the Arras-Bapaume road.

These Nissen huts were constructed of standardized sections of corrugated iron, with wooden floors, which were put up in large numbers over the wide area desolated by the Germans in their retreat after the Somme offensive.

In spite of the desolation of the countryside it was a pleasant change from Flanders. The nights were clear and starry and the days were bright with the tints and sweet with the scents of a fine autumn. Training was again in full swing and football had displaced cricket. In the League games the 4th Seaforths were beaten by the 7th Black Watch.

On 21st October the Battalion relieved the 7th Argyll and Sutherland in the line, Nos. 1 and 2 Companies in front line, and Nos. 3 and 4 in support and reserve respectively. One man was killed and one wounded by shell fire after the relief, but otherwise everything was very quiet. The 2nd Royal Lancasters came up in relief on the 28th.

The Battalion were taken in buses to Izel-les-Hameaux, the details going by train and the transport by road. This proved to be one of the pleasantest rest billets that the Battalion had occupied.

Several old officers had by now rejoined and new-comers had arrived. These were Captains H. P. T. Gray, A. K. Fraser and G. W. K. Macpherson, Lieutenants Macaulay and MacGregor, and Second Lieutenants Roberts, McMonnies, J. Christie and H. C. Bessent. There was also a draft of fifteen other ranks.

The Battalion trained hard in the mornings and kept mind and body fit in the afternoons with games. There were football leagues and inter-company cross-country runs and boxing. No. 2 Company won the cross-country races. On 12th November the XVII Corps Commander, Lieutenant-General Sir Charles Fergusson, at a Brigade Parade presented medal ribbons for the operations round Ypres. The Brigade held sports on the anniversary of the taking of Beaumont Hamel, which was observed as a holiday. The men had special dinners, and there was an entertainment at the Divisional Theatre.

On 16th November the officers gave what proved to be the final performance of the Officers' Concert Party; for few, alas, of the performers were left when the Battalion next came out to rest. It was a most amusing performance, for the Party was a good one.

That day the transport left at 10 P.M. by road for Boisleux-au-Mont. The following day the Battalion, less its surplus personnel, proceeded to Bapaume by rail and went into tents. On the 18th it moved on again to Railway Camp at Lechelle. Next day the transport was sent to a field between Neuville and Metz-en-Couture, while the Battalion went into cellars in the ruined village of Metz.

For a considerable time there had been a feeling that some big operation was impending. There were vague rumours about tanks, and speculation ran high, but nothing was known, for the secret was well kept. By now, however, it was known that the British army was going to make a surprise attack on the famous Hindenburg Line. Large numbers of tanks (an arm with which the 4th Seaforths had never yet co-operated) were to be employed to plough lanes for the infantry through the enemy's defences. The 51st Division was given the most important task of pushing right through to Cantaing and Fontaine-Notre-Dame, to open a way for the cavalry, who were to exploit the break-through. To the 154th Infantry Brigade was allotted the completion of this task, and the 4th Seaforths were to be in Brigade reserve.

All movements were made at night, with the greatest care that nothing should betray to the Germans that any unusual massing of troops was being made against this part of their line, and by day everything was hidden away in woods and villages.

On 20th November, at 6.20 A.M., the 152nd Brigade on the right and the 153rd on the left opened the assault of the 51st Division, advancing behind the tanks, which crushed the wire and cleared the trenches with small-calibre shell and machine-gun fire. By 9.30 A.M. the whole of the front-line system of enemy trenches was reported captured, so that the 154th Brigade, which had moved out of its billets at Metz-en-Couture, was not called on that day, and returned to its cellars in Metz. The Division had established itself on a line south of Flesquières, where it was held up by uncut wire, and was unable to advance against the second line. The delay before this village was in great part due to the heroism of a German officer, who continued single-handed to serve one of the field guns posted there until he was shot. All honour to him for his gallant stand! But, as was expected, the enemy evacuated Flesquières during the night.

The morning of 21st November was dark, wet and cold. At 4 A.M. the 4th Seaforths took up a position in the old British front-line system. At 6.30 A.M. the 7th Argyll and Sutherland could be seen advancing in front, so Brigadier-General K. G. Buchanan gave instructions for the Battalion to move in support of them.

By 7.15 A.M. the Battalion had passed La Justice, through which ran the front line of the 152nd Infantry Brigade. Beyond thi the advance of the 7th Argyll and Sutherland and of the

4th Gordons on their right was stopped by the heavily wired trench of the Cantaing line and by machine-gun fire from Anneux; because the 62nd Division on the left had failed to advance beyond Graincourt. No. 4 Company therefore was moved up into a gap between the Argyll and Sutherland and Gordons, with No. 2 Company in support to the right of La Justice, while the remaining companies halted on the road behind La Justice.

Captain Gray led his company forward until it was held up by the trench line, and especially by Cantaing Mill, which sheltered two field guns, besides machine guns. Rifle fire also was directed on the Battalion from the village of Cantaing on the right, as well as indirect fire from Anneux, which still was held by the Germans, on the left.

Sergeant A. Ross, No. 1 Company, was sent up with a few men to silence three machine guns that were causing casualties from the direction of Cantaing. These he successfully drove back into the village, putting one out of action; but rifle fire prevented him from crossing the heavy belts of wire round the village.

A squadron of the Queen's Bays had come up and were awaiting developments, but the advance had come to a standstill. Enemy aeroplanes flew low over the ranks lying extended in the open, and poured machine-gun fire on them.

This part of the chalk region of Artois, which resembles the down country in the south of England, had gone out of cultivation. The ground rises slightly for about 200 yards in front of La Justice, and then a long spur runs in the direction of Fontaine, which itself lies on slightly rising ground beyond a shallow valley. The valley marks the line of the main Bapaume-Cambrai road, which at this point crossed the front diagonally. On the left towers Bourlon Wood; on the right, beyond Cantaing, and facing Bourlon Wood, lies La Folie Wood, also in German occupation. The distance to Fontaine-Notre-Dame is 4000 yards over ground exposed to fire from the front and from both flanks.

After Sergeant Ross had returned wounded from driving the Germans machine guns into Cantaing, enfilade fire from that direction ceased. Later in the morning the 62nd Division took Anneux. Meanwhile Captain Gray was hotly engaged with the Germans holding the Cantaing line, and the rifle fire was intense. He himself was wounded at about 1 P.M., while

Lieutenant E. A. Mackintosh was killed and Lieutenant MacGregor wounded.

At about noon tanks appeared, advancing on the right, and, under orders from Corps Headquarters, the Officers Commanding the 4th Seaforths and 7th Argyll and Sutherland, who had established joint headquarters in La Justice Farm, sent up orders for the advance to be resumed, but whether or not they reached the front line before the tanks is doubtful.

No. 1 Company, under Captain "Ray" Macdonald, which was lying in the road close to Battalion Headquarters, was directed to advance with the leftmost of the tanks straight on Fontaine. No. 2 was directed to join in the advance as the tanks passed them.

The tanks soon came under fire from the two field guns in Cantaing Mill, and two were put out of action by direct hits when crossing the sunken road running from La Justice to Cantaing. The rest, however, went on.

No. 1 Company advanced straight up past La Justice in company with the left tank and the attack was launched. Shortly afterwards the first prisoners came in from the Mill, where Nos. 2 and 4 Companies were engaged. The two field guns and the strong body of machine gunners there had been captured, and the advance swept on.

Two platoons of No. 4 Company, however, bore off towards the right in pursuit of some Germans, and became involved in the fighting in Cantaing, where they joined hands with the 4th Gordons, who also were attacking the village. They did not rejoin the Battalion till the following day. The 7th Argyll and Sutherland captured their portion of the Cantaing line and also rounded up Germans from dug-outs in two sunken roads beyond.

Meanwhile Captain Macdonald led forward No. 1 Company with the tanks, which now were advancing on Fontaine under a heavy fire from rifles and machine guns. The village was covered by a line of machine guns, posted along its outer edge.

The tanks advanced straight for the village and then wheeled along it, firing into it and silencing the machine guns. But an advance of 4000 yards under concentrated rifle fire from all sides had sadly depleted No. 1 Company. Captain "Ray" Macdonald himself fell, mortally wounded, forty yards ahead of his company, whilst still three or four hundred yards from the village; but, fired by his splendid example, the gallant remnant pressed on until the village was reached. Here there was no opposition, for the tanks had done their work. Led by the Company Sergeant-Major the company advanced up the main street and formed up at the farther end, facing Cambrai. All the officers and most of the non-commissioned officers were killed or wounded, and of the one hundred and twenty-five men who passed La Justice to the attack only forty were left.

The 7th Argyll and Sutherland, who had reached the north end of the village, had suffered almost equally heavily. They had captured the trench system and fought along the sunken roads and among the dug-outs, and had taken many prisoners. They now pushed through the village.

No. 2 Company and the two remaining platoons of No. 4 Company moved on together after the capture of Cantaing Mill and the trench line to right and left and joined No. 1 on the Cambrai road. All had suffered heavy casualties: 375 men in the ranks had passed La Justice to the attack; now they numbered 120. The total strength of the three companies was less than the nominal strength of one.

Darkness was coming on now, and Captain C. H. Harris, commanding No. 2 Company, as senior officer in Fontaine, was placed in command of the combined force in the village. He at once set about the consolidation of the position. A few prisoners had been taken, but they were all non-combatants, engaged on sanitation or supply services. Except for the machine gunners who had been defending the village, no fighting troops were encountered and the exits of the village were open.

The inhabitants of Fontaine were delighted to see the British troops, for they had not had a happy time under German rule. The proprietor of the café opened up a hidden store of wine in his garden and gave some to the troops. Captain Harris issued it as if it had been a rum ration.

One man wrote thus: "Our reception in the village was a very cordial one. Men, women and children came out of the houses, and recognizing us, they made a great fuss. They called us 'Scotchia,' and many of the men were kissed by the womenfolk. The men were well treated, receiving beer, wine, coffee and various kinds of food. The people could not do enough for us."

The night passed quietly. Rations were sent up by the

Battalion, but no ammunition could be obtained, though urgent demands for it were made on Brigade Headquarters. Unfortunately all the regimental ammunition wagons had been collected into a Brigade Ammunition Column, and through some misunderstanding this, the only means of replenishing supplies, was not available.

About 10 P.M. a German wagon drove down the main road into Fontaine; the captured horses replaced two that had belonged to the Battalion and drew a cooker for the remainder of the war. They were in wretched condition, for the Germans were already short of fodder, but when well fed and cared for they turned out to be a useful pair. This wagon was one of a convoy that came up the road to Fontaine. The escort only discovered that something was wrong when they found across the road four large trees that had been cut down by the retreating Germans. While they were debating what this might portend the 4th Seaforths tried to envelop them right and left. Unfortunately one of the scouts fired too soon, on which the convoy turned about and made for Cambrai. Rapid fire was opened and one wagon taken. The rest disappeared in the darkness; but the last wagon had taken fire and lit up the retreat of the remainder.

When darkness fell the two battalions were disposed, roughly, as follows:

Joint Headquarters . . .	La Justice
3 Companies, 4th Seaforth Highlanders	Fontaine
2 Companies, 7th Argyll and Sutherland Highlanders	
2 Companies, 7th Argyll and Sutherland Highlanders . . .	South-west of Fontaine
1 Company, 4th Seaforth Highlanders	La Justice

This last company was moved under cover of dusk into a position astride the captured Cantaing-Anneux Trench line to guard the exposed left flank.

Late in the evening orders were received from the Division for one of these two battalions to hold Fontaine and for the other to be withdrawn. It was therefore eventually decided that the two companies of the 7th Argyll and Sutherland Highlanders then in Fontaine should be relieved by the company of the 4th Seaforths which had moved from La Justice into the Cantaing-Anneux line; the 4th Seaforths would then be solely responsible for Fontaine and their Headquarters would move there.

"Those who were watching in the front line heard signs of great activity at Cambrai, which was only four kilometres away. Trains arrived in rapid succession, and a great deal of shunting seemed to be going on. These signs were read to mean that a counter-attack was coming and troops being rushed up."

By about 6.15 on the morning of 22nd November No. 3 Company, with Headquarters, were settled in Fontaine. Light was just breaking as they arrived. At the same time a fleet of enemy aeroplanes appeared, and swooped and circled over the village for three hours, like gulls waiting for the nets to be emptied. This delayed the relief and made it more difficult.

No. 3 Company got into position, however, and the greater part of the two Argyll and Sutherland companies got back to the sunken road already mentioned, although it was found impossible to relieve two platoons who were holding an osier-bed almost adjoining the south-west end of the village.

Patrols during the night had failed to get into contact with the enemy, and Lieutenant Campbell, who took out the Battalion scouts on an extended patrol in the morning, had no better success. At about 8 A.M., however, three German deserters came in. They said they belonged to a German division on the march from Douai, which had moved off at 10 P.M. the night before on receipt of sudden orders. They added that the division was just arriving and was preparing to attack.

Even as this disquieting information arrived, a messenger came in from Brigade Headquarters to say that a conference of Brigade Commanders was to be held at 10 A.M. at a neighbouring Brigade Headquarters to discuss further operations. The message continued that the 22nd was to be a day of rest, especially for the Air Force. It was destined to be anything but a day of rest!

The position now was a precarious one. The village of Fontaine was not so large as it looked on the map. Houses lined each side of the long main street, and there were some more up a side street leading to the railway station. The church lay at the eastern end of the village towards Cambrai.

There was, roughly, a parallelogram 3500 yards in perimeter to defend. Unfortunately, lack of men prevented the garrison extending far enough to the north to get a proper field of fire.

It was obvious that no help was forthcoming to meet the enemy attacks, and the remnant of the Battalion was practically isolated. The division on the left not having succeeded in carrying Bourlon Wood, and La Folie Wood being still in the enemy's hands, Fontaine lay "like a nut gripped between two crackers." The ground was broken by quarries and sunken roads, which made much dead ground.

The village was thus defended:

Four machine guns (154th Brigade Company) were posted in a German trench facing Bourlon Wood.

No. 3 Company occupied a quarry north of the village.

No. 1 Company was posted just north of the main road at the eastern end of the village.

No. 2 and the remnant of No. 4 Company held south of the main road facing east, with a flank refused towards La Folie Wood.

A machine gun was posted on the Cambrai road at the western end of the village.

One machine gun was posted south of the village in a position to fire across the main road to Cambrai and to La Folie Wood.

There was a considerable gap between Nos. 1 and 3 Companies, of which the centre was the railway station. Into this the two platoons of No. 4 Company that had joined the 4th Gordons in the attack on Cantaing were sent when they arrived at 9 A.M. They consisted of only one officer, one sergeant and about fifteen men!

Battalion Headquarters in the centre of the village was the only reserve.

At 9.30 A.M. scouts confirmed the information of the German deserters. Half an hour earlier the enemy had begun to shell the end of the village nearest to Cambrai, and now lengthened out and covered the whole village. A party of the inhabitants who had collected in the street were hustled back to the rear, but the majority preferred to hide in their cellars.

The Germans were massing, and the 4th Seaforths sent up an S.O.S., to which, owing to the thick mist, the artillery made no response. One of the artillery liaison officers took a horse and rode back to direct the guns on the area where the scouts had reported that the enemy were moving, and he was just in time to break up the first attack from the north of the village. It was, indeed, a stroke of good luck, for this was the last effective artillery support that the Battalion was to have. Fortunately the enemy artillery fire was equally ineffective, being directed on the village, where only the Aid Post remained. The Adjutant, Captain Peverell, with part of the Headquarter personnel, had gone to the position on the Cambrai road, and the Commanding Officer, with the rest, had taken up a position at the station. Almost immediately afterwards what had been Battalion Headquarters was completely demolished.

The Germans renewed the attack along the whole line, from Bourlon Wood on the left to La Folie Wood on the right, enveloping both flanks. The four machine guns on the left were put out of action as soon as they showed themselves, and the enemy, advancing up a sunken road, penetrated the position. A short fight ensued, but the handful of men there were soon overpowered. The left had gone and the Germans were in the empty village. No. 3 Company were in the quarry, whence a good view could be had. After the artillery broke up the first attack No. 3 had repelled two more before they themselves were driven out, but, by a bayonet charge, recaptured the quarry. Captain "Andy" Fraser could see the Germans advancing into both ends of the village. Accompanied by his Acting Sergeant-Major, he tried to get touch with the troops on his right, and at once met the Commanding Officer, who was looking for him. Neither was in a position to help the other and they parted, never to meet again. The situation was hopeless. Ammunition and bombs were nearly exhausted. At noon Captain Fraser withdrew through the village, under a heavy fire from both flanks, and ordered a further retirement to the sunken road, a few hundred yards in rear, which, as already mentioned, was held by the 7th Argyll and Sutherland Highlanders. Lieutenant Macauley, who was laying a telephone wire, was there, and collected and reorganized the Company. Captain Fraser was seen going back with four or five men to the house where his company headquarters were. The house was surrounded; but not till Captain Fraser fell, mortally wounded, and then, only after bitter fighting, was it captured.

At the east end of the village Captain Peverell had made a desperate stand on the Cambrai road. Here, assisted by Sergeant Robb of the Brigade Machine Gun Company, who formerly had been in the Battalion, he held on till hardly an unwounded man remained. The Germans were fast gaining ground, and when further resistance became a matter only of minutes Captain Peverell ordered those who could to save themselves. He himself was badly wounded in the leg and refused to be moved. None the less he continued the fight until the Germans were on him, thus covering the retirement of the survivors. Captain Peverell gives the following graphic account of what befell him after he had been taken prisoner:

"It was later in the day that a small party of several Germans—I had numerous visitors during the fifteen hours I lay out—debated whether or not to 'give me another.' Opinions seemed equally divided. I hoped that it would not be a bayonet, but something quick. Fortunately some others arrived and gave a casting vote against the proposal. Another one later on amused himself by walking up and down about ten yards away from me for about ten minutes with a stick bomb in his hand. His amusement was at least equalled by my lack thereof. Others helped themselves to my field-glass, etc. One sportsman divided what money I had into two parts, kept one for himself, and gave me back the other; an officer saluted, had a chat, and, quite unsolicited, said he would write to Cox's and tell them I was a prisoner.

"Once the whole thing was over the situation was not without interest, if it had not been for the intense cold and the depressing thought of having to sojourn in durance vile 'for the duration.' It was interesting to watch for once, on the wrong side, the progress of the battle and the relief at night of the enemy troops who had carried out the counter-attack. A particularly distressing thought was the uncertainty as to what had happened to one's friends."

Meanwhile the party from Headquarters were still at the railway station when Lieutenant-Colonel Unthank went to see Captain Fraser. They numbered only some six or seven under Sergeant Grierson, and were occupying some houses near the station. On his return Lieutenant-Colonel Unthank found that the houses had been attacked. The little party had beaten off the enemy, but Sergeant Grierson had been killed. It was evident that the party must either be surrounded or fall back. Step by step it withdrew across the main road where Headquarters had been, then past the church, till finally it emerged on the southern edge of the village. The Commanding Officer had been hitherto conspicuous for his cool indifference to danger, walking about without a helmet, stick in hand, encouraging his men. Now some Germans called on him to surrender, but he shot down two or three and got away. His party were only just in time, for across the open country, stretching from the edge of the village to La Folie Wood, could be seen wave after wave of Germans steadily advancing, the nearest not a hundred yards away. The party hurriedly collected, poured in one minute's rapid fire and doubled for cover. They had to cross the shallow valley and gain the sunken road leading to Cantaing, 200 yards away on the farther slope.

No sooner, however, did they reach the open clear of the village than they came under rifle and machine-gun fire from the Germans on the other side also; for, except at the point where they had come through, the Germans were in complete possession of the village.

The remnant of the Battalion from the right half of the village had fallen back to the sunken road leading to Cantaing, and from there checked any further advance of the enemy. It was 2.30 in the afternoon when the last man from the village reached this road.

Lieutenant A. Macdonnell, R.F.A., who was Artillery Liaison Officer with the Battalion at Cambrai, gives a vivid account of it in three letters:

"What a battle! I've seen and done so much in the last three days that I haven't time to do more than give you an outline now, which I will try and fill up with details later on. All the old 'shock troops' were out on the warpath, and I was liaison to an infantry battalion [the 4th Seaforths] as it went up to attack, and thus I advanced with five different lots.

"The old Division have done, as ever, marvellously. We advanced seven and a half miles in depth into the enemy's lines, took 30 guns and about 2000 prisoners, and finished up on the evening of the 21st with a surprise attack and an impromptu show that took a village no one ever thought we would. Quite apart from that there have been the most astonishing sights—tanks advancing in lines and waves, cavalry galloping across fields with drawn swords and jumping trenches, etc. The last village we captured was intact and without a damaged roof even, and we rescued about sixty civilians. The latter were superb—fell on our necks, rushed off for secret supplies of food for us, and shouted '*Vive l'Angleterre!*' Finally yesterday [22nd] as a climax, the most exciting and hectic day I've ever spent, not even excepting the Somme and Ypres, when the Huns counter-attacked the village from three sides in great strength and drove us out.

"Curiously enough I wasn't a bit afraid, and found myself in command of 50 or 60 Jocks and armed with a rifle. I led a most spectacular rush up the main street, only to find that our right flank was in the air, and then constituted myself O.C. right defence of our village. We held up the Huns for about half an hour, till the centre ran out of ammunition and fell back, whereupon the Huns got up as one man and attacked. We fired off all our ammunition retreating, and eventually ran like blazes! We had a most exciting run across country, and finally tumbled into a sunken road and lined up to hold it. I was then asked to go back for help and had another run across country to the nearest headquarters. After that I found that I had been relieved, but the relieving officer hadn't liked to come up so far, and stayed two miles back overnight!"

He then goes on to a more detailed story:

"On the evening of the 20th the attack started off, preceded by an 'unregistered' barrage, which was wonderfully good, lines of tanks and low-flying aeroplanes firing machine guns. There was a tremendous barrage of smoke shell on the left, with wonderful sparks and phosphorous effects, and it made altogether a splendid sight. About two hours after, Major Thom Davidson appeared on horseback to reconnoitre battery positions, and everyone thought the cavalry was coming, which caused great excitement.

"An hour later the second wave battalion went through, and I went up with their Colonel about two miles forward to a very good dug-out. Then I tried to get into touch with the liaison man on my right, but found he had been killed by a stray shell. I then took on liaison with his battalion as well, and so had to work pretty hard between the two. I got a good sleep that night, and everyone was very hospitable with food and drink.

"The objective for that day was a village on a crest, and

all was going well, with tanks well in front, when two anti-tank guns started to fire from the village [Flesquières], and did wonderful work, knocking out every tank with direct hits. So the village couldn't be got that night, but was almost surrounded, and early on the 21st the Huns retired, and the third battalion [7th Argyll and Sutherland] went through and again I went on.

"This time was extraordinary, as we were over the ridge and could see the whole valley and the attack coming down. Battalion Headquarters was a flag stuck in the middle of a field with a row of officers watching through field-glasses; the infantry was advancing in lines and columns and parties everywhere. Battalions in reserve were streaming up behind, and cavalry patrols were going along the ridges. We had a good deal of machine-gun fire as we went forward, but we fetched up at a farmhouse [La Justice], where we established ourselves.

"Reports came in very soon which made it clear that no more could be done owing to three villages in front, so the Colonel of the infantry and I went forward to see the situation. After going about 500 yards they got machine guns and rifle fire on to us, and we lay in ruts on the road and tried to camouflage ourselves as pancakes for about twenty minutes, and then, being fed up, got up and ran like hares back again—and we were quite glad to be back again! After that we were less ambitious and stayed at Battalion Headquarters at the farm. At about half-past three we happened to glance back and saw rows of tanks advancing, so it was decided to have an impromptu attack, which was a roaring success, and captured all the villages in half an hour, the third being the ultimate objective of the Division—eight miles from the start.

"The next excitement was the arrival of civilians from the village, boys and women, tremendously bucked about it, and we had a long chatter with them. They were wonderfully plucky and cheery, but they almost went off their heads with excitement when, at my suggestion, their kit and baggage was carried to the rear by half a dozen Boche prisoners, of which we had hundreds. It seemed a fitting way of turning the tables on the Huns.

"Further thrills were in store when a Boche ammunition wagon drove peacefully down into the village without seeing our men. They opened fire, killed a driver, set the wagon on fire and captured seven horses, while the blazing wagon went on at full gallop, drawn by the two surviving beasts.

"Next morning another battalion [the remainder of the 4th Seaforths] came up, and on I went again up the village itself [Fontaine-Notre-Dame]. The C.O. of the infantry [Lieutenant-Colonel Unthank] was a splendid man whom I had been with before, and he actually rode forward at the head of the men—another unique sight. We got up about 7 A.M., and I found another gunner officer, with whom I established an R.F.A. Mess! The village was quite intact, and we swanked in arm-chairs and used cups and plates for breakfast.

"The Hun aeroplanes came over and flew round and round the village and fired machine guns at us when we showed our noses. So we didn't show them. At about half-past ten he started shelling the village, and at 11 A.M. reports came in that he was attacking from the left. I enclose a diagram."

[*Note*.—The diagram is not published, but the following references to map 13 will enable the reader to follow the account:

Point A is about the letter C in the words Cambrai 1½ mile.

Point B is at the railway station.

Point C is at the end of the village that points like a finger at La Folie Wood.

Point D is between points A and C.]

"The first attack from the left drove the line across the road at point A, so the Adjutant went up and got back to the north side, whilst the C.O. went off to point B with some more men. The day was so misty that the S.O.S. was put up and not seen, so the other gunner got on to the C.O.'s horse, which we saddled up most feverishly, and galloped off under machine-gun fire back to the batteries—most spectacular. I got a rifle and ammunition and dashed out into the main street, feeling horribly frightened for a moment, for as I reached the street a shell went through the 'R.F.A. Mess.' In the street I found about fifty odd, with no officer, at a loose end. It occurred to me to give some orders, and to my surprise the men obeyed me!

"After that I began to recall O.T.C. days, and started establishing posts in the side streets, and took the rest in a wild dash up the road to A, to help the Adjutant [Captain Peverell], who was in a tight corner. We got there and had a most hectic time in a furious barrage, with the Hun machine guns chipping bricks all round us. The barrage got too bad and was impossible, so we retired in the direction of C. to find another converging attack in the direction of the arrows. [From the S.E.] So we lined the road and held him up for about half an hour, when our ammunition began to give out.

"Our right flank was in the air and I went off to get help and brought another twenty men to prolong our line, but suddenly the centre, D, caved in and the whole Boche line got up and broke into the village.

"We loosed off the remainder of our stuff at them, and then, hotly pursued, we bunked off across the fields with hundreds of shots at us! How we ran for about 1000 yards! but we had not many casualties. We stopped and reorganized in a sunk road, and after posting the men I went to try to secure assistance. I ran like mad over the open, with a machine gun spurting shot round me. I got through and got help. Eventually we were relieved, and I had a huge drink and went to bed. Quite a brisk day's work. I was so pleased that I didn't lose my head at all from the moment that the men did what I told them.

"Altogether it was a wonderful show, but it was an awful pity that we ran out of ammunition. The C.O., on the left, fought to the last gasp, and was surrounded by half a dozen Huns, who told him to surrender. He seized a rifle and went for them club fashion, bald-headed, laid some out and got away. The Adjutant fought to the end, but was wounded in the legs and was taken prisoner. I understand the doctor was also taken, but got away and rejoined another division. It is our first really big attack on the West Front, and I think everyone is feeling quite bucked about it."

A third letter says: "That morning in Fontaine, Peverell and I had a very cheery breakfast together. P. was suffering from rheumatism, but was most lively and cheery trying to interrogate Boche prisoners. He raised a good laugh against himself when he asked one man in German, 'What division are you?' The prisoner replied in English, 'Five days ago.'

"When the situation grew acute he went to readjust the position, and later I joined him there. Later it grew quite untenable with shell fire and so we hopped it. He was roaring with laughter, as though it were the greatest joke in the world. Afterwards we separated and he took the centre position, and I understand he went on fighting until all the ammunition was used up and nearly all the men were out. He was wounded in the legs and very few of his men got away."

As soon as darkness came on, the Battalion moved back to Flesquières on relief by the 7th Black Watch, and on the 23rd went back to its old billets in Metz. While it was marching to Metz the Division again attacked Fontaine, this time employing a whole brigade, which got into the village, but was driven out in two hours. On the 24th the Guards also made an unsuccessful attempt. The men then coined the adage "What the 4th Seaforths can't hold, no one can hold!"

The casualties were very heavy:

OFFICERS

Killed: Captains A. K. Fraser and A. M. Macdonald, Lieutenants E. A. Mackintosh and N. Sutherland, Second Lieutenant S. M. McMonnies.

Wounded: Lieutenant-Colonel J. S. Unthank, Captain H. P. T. Gray, Lieutenant D. E. F. MacGregor, Second Lieutenants N. F. Swan and H. Paterson.

Wounded and Missing: Captain T. H. Peverell.

OTHER RANKS

Killed: 30. *Wounded*: 192. *Missing*: 86.

That the number of the missing was not greater was due to the work of the Medical Officer, Captain Green, and his assistants. Not only did they have an abnormally large number of cases to deal with, but the distances over which the wounded had to be carried were greater than usual, and, what was still more serious, they were under heavy fire all the time. Yet, unaided, they cleared the field on the first day, and on the second worked to the last minute. Fortunately on that day Captain Green had established his Aid Post in Fontaine, where he and his medical staff, helped by Captain Potter, the Roman Catholic chaplain, were dressing wounds and dispatching men to the rear till the enemy were in the village. So successful were they in their exertions that only those whom it was impossible to move were left. Finally when departure was imperative, if Captain Green was to comply with his orders and avoid capture, he reluctantly gave the order to go. Sergeant Robertson of the Aid Post could not, however, endure the idea of abandoning the wounded; with Pioneer-Sergeant "Sandy" Macdonald, Orderly Room Corporal Mott and Corporal Learmonth (R.A.M.C., water duties) he returned to the Aid Post, and, while tending the wounded, all were taken prisoners.

Captain "Ray" Macdonald and some of the fallen were buried in Orival Wood, between La Justice and Flesquières, but the majority could not be buried, and lie in unknown graves. On the anniversary of the battle the following year the Battalion marched to Fontaine and erected a cross at the western end, on which were recorded the names of all who were known to have fallen in the battle. Some of those who were reported missing were not included, because there still was reason to hope that they might yet be found among the returned prisoners of war. Owing to the enormous price demanded for the site, and the high cost of maintaining this monument on the spot, it was decided after the war to bring it to Dingwall, where it now stands, just outside the station. As the original wooden cross had perished, a new one had to be put in its place.

Who shall say which of the acts herein recorded was the finest—Captain "Ray" Macdonald's advance, Captain "Andy" Fraser's defence of the quarry and his fight through the village, Captain Peverell's stand on the Cambrai road, or Colonel Unthank's coolness in an impossible situation? Two of these were killed, one was wounded and taken prisoner, and one, though wounded, brought away his little party at the last moment. Captain Peverell was recommended for the V.C.: as he was wounded and a prisoner of war it was difficult to get him the recognition his gallant action had deserved; but, later, he was awarded the D.S.O. Captain Macdonald, who was the son of the Rector of Dingwall Academy, had been awarded the D.S.O. for his services at Ypres—had he lived he was surely destined for further honours.

It was hoped against hope that Captain Fraser might have survived, and it was not definitely known that he was killed till after the Armistice. His reward is in the memory of his gallant deeds, worthy of the old race and of the father from whom he sprang. Many acts of heroism must be for ever unrecorded. Many a life was lost in the endeavour to bring in wounded comrades; and the Germans of to-day—like their ancestors in the days of Gustavus Adolphus—learned at what a cost the Scots might be driven from their ground.

After a night spent in billets at Metz the Battalion marched on the 24th to the rail-head at Ytres and entrained at 8 P.M. It detrained at Treux and reached its billets at Ribemont at 3 A.M. on 25th November. Here it settled down to a round of recuperation and training.

This was not to last for long. On St Andrew's Day the Germans made their great counter-attack and broke the British line. The Battalion entrained at 8 P.M. at Edge Hill and reached Bapaume at 1 A.M., whence it marched to huts at Rocquigny, which it reached at 5.30 A.M. At 10 A.M. it went on to shelters at Bertincourt.

At 1.30 P.M. on 2nd December the Battalion went into the old British front line, the transport being sent to Lebucquière. On the 3rd it relieved a brigade of the 2nd Division on the extreme left of the battle area, facing Morchies. The position taken over was astride the Hindenburg Line, with the canal on the right. Though the relief was quiet, Captain Green, the Medical Officer, and several others were wounded. Fierce fighting had been going on here since 30th November, and a German attack had been beaten off immediately before the relief.

On the 4th the enemy tried to rush the position between Nos. 3 and 4 Companies at 3.30 P.M. Thanks to Major Jobson, who was commanding the front line, this attack was badly broken up. Battalion Headquarters was in direct communication with an artillery group, and, with Major Jobson acting as observation officer, they were enabled to direct a mass of artillery on to the Germans. The Group Commander had unlimited ammunition and controlled a large number of guns, including heavies, howitzers and field guns. He put down a sudden terrific bombardment and, later, started a rolling barrage, and so thoroughly did he deceive the Germans that they turned their guns on to their own trenches ! After this there was no further trouble; and when, late at night, orders came to withdraw, the movement was carried out without any interference. The 152nd Brigade were holding a position in rear, through which the 154th retired to Frémicourt, where it went into huts.

On 8th December a draft of fifty-two other ranks arrived; next day Lieutenant-Colonel Unthank went on leave.

A private who joined the Battalion at Frémicourt has left an interesting story of his journey from home and his first impressions of the front.

"We left Folkestone," he says, "and crossed the Channel

to Boulogne, whence we motored to the Headquarter Depot at Etaples. After two days there we entrained for Albert, where we saw the church which has been destroyed, and from which is still suspended the Madonna and Child. From Albert we marched to Bouzencourt, where we were billeted for a week.

"At Bouzencourt we had a regular course of training—physical training, bayonet fighting, musketry and squad drill. The weather was frosty, with sunshine through the day, which made conditions very pleasant. For the first time in my life I was under fire, being a marker at the range! And yet it was none too safe. Some erratic shots would persist in hitting the roof of the trench and you had to lie low to be safe.

"One day we marched to Albert for a bath and a change of underwear. There was a room for undressing, and we went in, fifty at a time, and stripped. These fifty figures in the nude with soap and towel marched into a second room. Towels were left at the door and we proceeded into the centre of the room, where twelve spiral columns of lukewarm water flowed from the roof. Everyone started rubbing himself with soap, and when possible trying to get a place under a thin column of water. It was a novel method, not altogether satisfactory, but, I suppose, effective for the purpose. We were next paraded for drying, and then marched upstairs to a room where clean clothing was distributed. I condescended to take a clean towel, but I stuck to my own shirt. Of course the absence of a flannel was discovered, but naturally that was in my pack. However, a quick walk home and a good tea made us all feel fit, and, to a certain extent, clean. The food, generally speaking, was good; and, with a genius of a cook, called Collins, our billet was specially well served.

"We left Albert by train to go to the 4th. We changed at Achiet-le-Grand, and from there re-entrained for Bapaume, which was a journey of only ten minutes. We then marched four kilometres to Frémicourt, where we now lie with the Battalion.

"We had a very warm reception from the boys, among whom I met many old faces. We found the billets very comfortable, and if the floor is hard to lie upon, at least one does get used to it through time. The Battalion had just come down the line and we knew we should have a few days' rest.

"While on rest the work is very easy. Réveillé about 7 or 8 A.M. and breakfast follows immediately. We then parade

R

about 9 A.M. Some do fatigues and others light training, while there are special classes in bombing, Lewis gun, wiring and signalling. The afternoon you have to yourself. The evenings are very long and, with candles difficult to get, one goes to bed about 8 P.M.

"We are out of range here, but Bapaume station gets shelled nightly. On Tuesday, Wednesday and Thursday the Germans attacked incessantly, and it was fearful to a new hand to hear our reply barrage. The ground shook under us and the huts rattled as if there was a terrific storm of wind blowing. We also have visits from Jerry's aeroplanes, and then you have every kind of guns firing from places where you never thought there was a gun. I got a bit of a start when a shell rose exactly six yards from me. I never saw the gun and have not seen it yet.

"This morning at 7 we were wakened by terrific firing, and word was passed round that we must keep to our huts. We knew why almost at once. Jerry was dropping bombs on us and the shrapnel of the anti-aircraft guns was falling thick on the huts. I had a look at it from a window, but returned to bed again quite uninspired and unperturbed. It is practically a daily occurrence and nobody worries.

"To-morrow we go up the line for six days, and we are hoping to get out in time for Christmas, which we are looking forward to spending somewhere near Albert, where it is expected we are to rest for six weeks. That remains to be seen!

"The Pipe Band, under Pipe-Major Mackenzie, is playing just now. It gives us a tune every afternoon, and the men take a great interest in the programme submitted.

"Were it not for the mud, which is six inches deep on the average, the life here would be very tolerable."

The Battle of Cambrai was over, and the usual work of making dug-outs, shelters and the like commenced. The Corps front was held with two divisions in the line and one in reserve. On 16th December the Battalion relieved the 6th Black Watch in the front line. On the 20th one of the patrols ran into an enemy post about 400 yards from the British wire and Second Lieutenant E. J. Martin was wounded by machine-gun fire and died of his wounds.

On the 22nd the Battalion was relieved by two companies of the 5th Gordon Highlanders and two of the 7th Black

Watch. It went back to tents outside Bancourt, where it spent Christmas, with six inches of snow on the ground and enemy aeroplanes bombarding the lines almost every night. On the 27th it moved to Lebucquière, where it spent the New Year in Nissen huts.

SYNOPSIS OF EVENTS FROM THE BEGINNING OF JANUARY TO THE FAILURE OF THE GERMAN OFFENSIVE IN FLANDERS, APRIL 1918

By the beginning of 1918 the course of German strategy was plain to anyone who had eyes to see, ears to hear, and a brain capable of accurate deduction from obvious facts. There was little choice for Ludendorff—either he must shatter the Allied front in France or see his own front shattered. No success in Venezia, in Macedonia, in Palestine or in Mesopotamia could save Germany, unless she could drive a wedge between the British and French before American man-power began to tell. The issue was obvious to Ludendorff. The days of offensives on the Piave were over, for the death-grapple on the decisive theatre was inevitable. Someone must give way on that front. On the others nothing mattered.

Russia was a seething chaos, helpless before the Germans had they chosen to finish her. Turkey, Austria and Bulgaria were crumbling into something almost as hopeless. Yet the Allied Cabinets were still very anxious to knock out these disembodied ghosts, and consequently withheld reinforcements from their commanders on the one decisive front.

The Allied commanders knew, only too well, their danger. Yet at this supreme moment the French and British Governments insisted on the British taking over further frontage in the West, as far as Barisis. This reduced the number of bayonets per yard on the British front below the minimum of safety, while the removal of two out of Haig's five cavalry divisions weakened it yet further.

Hitherto the British troops had been trained almost solely for offensive action; now, when training in defensive tactics was vital, they had to spend invaluable time in constructing new defensive lines and had to suffer a drastic reorganization, whereby each British infantry brigade was reduced from four to three battalions. The whole balance of the organization of our army was destroyed by this blow. Reliefs became a most complicated matter, involving the dislocation of brigades. Rest and training were most seriously interfered with and the effective strength of units grievously reduced; for the smaller the numbers the larger the percentage taken away for administrative purposes.

The British and French commanders set to, to work out plans for mutual support in the impending attack; if they differed in their predictions as to its probable incidence they left no stone unturned to provide for every possibility.

Of the 58 British divisions 40 were in line, 10 in Army and 8 in General reserve. Against this were 40 German divisions in line, 47 in reserve and 30 others available for transfer against the British front. The odds were heavy against us.

Gough had 14 divisions stretched between the Oise and the Somme, which gave him less than one bayonet per yard. The defensive works occupied by these divisions were, moreover, still very far from complete, neither had the Peronne bridge-head been more than commenced.

On 21st March 1918 the biggest battle of the war began in a dense fog. The British lines were held by strongpoints designed to support one another and defend the ground between by the crossed fire of guns and small arms. The fog entirely prevented effective co-operation, with the result that the Germans poured in depth through the uncovered gaps, isolating and masking the points of resistance.

By noon the Germans had pierced the forward zone west of La Fère, had reached Benay, Essigny and Maissemy, and were in our battle zone at Ronssoy. Further to the north they had captured many villages in the Flesquières salient, and had reached St-Leger between Bapaume and Monchy.

On the 22nd the Germans made comparatively little headway against the Third Army; but by night they had penetrated the third line of defence of the Fifth Army, and Sir Hubert Gough, who had thrown in his last reserves, ordered a retirement to the unfinished positions on the Somme.

On the 23rd the Germans had crossed the Somme above Ham, and the Peronne bridge-head had to be abandoned. Here, where the Somme turns westward, Ludendorff endeavoured to drive a wedge between Gough's Fifth and Byng's Third Army, which had now withdrawn from Monchy.

On the 24th the Fifth Army, with some slight help from General Fayolle, was able to delay the German advance on the line of the Somme; but to the north the enemy reached Combles and the Third Army had to abandon Bapaume.

On the 25th the Germans drove the Third Army back on to the Ancre, while the Fifth, forced west of the line Noyon-Nesle, had almost lost touch with the French at Roye and the Third Army on the Ancre.

Early on the 26th the Germans had penetrated the Third Army line and had reached Colincamps, but the arrival of reinforcements from the north enabled this village to be recovered, and their advance here was stayed. The Fifth Army fell back to a line running south from Bray, the Germans still trying to force a wedge between it and the French at Montdidier.

On the 27th the Germans got into Albert, and had actually crossed the Somme behind Gough's left at Chipilly. This forced him to throw back his flank to the line Rosières-Bouzencourt. That day the Germans took Lassigny and Montdidier from the French.

On the 28th Von Bulow made two attempts to take Arras, both of which were beaten off; but to the south of the Somme the Germans forced back the British and French to the line of the Avre.

Steady fighting went on till 4th April, when Von Hutier drove back the Allies to a line running from Mesnil St-Georges, through

Cantigny, Sauvillers and Castel, to Villers Bretonneux and Sailly le Sec. Farther south the French had to fall back behind the Ailette.

The Germans had failed to reach Amiens and to break the Allied front, but they had regained all, and more than all, that they had lost on the Somme since 1916. They claimed 90,000 prisoners and 1300 guns, and they had practically destroyed the Fifth Army, for they had launched against the British above four times the number of divisions that attacked Verdun in 1916.

Foiled in his first object, Ludendorff turned against the Northern front. On 9th April he attacked the Portuguese and the weak divisions withdrawn from the Somme front. By nightfall the Germans were on the Lys at Bac St-Maur and had taken La Couture, but the 55th Division still held Givenchy.

On the 10th the Germans had crossed the Lys and held Estaires, Steenwerck and Ploegsteert.

On the 11th Lestrem and the Messines Ridge were lost.

On the 12th the Germans had crossed the La Bassée Canal and had reached Merville and Merris, but finally were checked at Robecq. By the 16th they had taken Wytschaete, and their advance had reached Meteren, while the British had to withdraw from Passchendaele.

Ludendorff now turned to the Belgian front, where he was repulsed on the 17th; and the attack by his left between Givenchy and Hinges on the 18th fared no better.

On the 25th he attacked on the centre and took Kemmel. Fighting went on till the 29th, but the German offensive was stayed.

Meanwhile 300,000 British troops were sent into France, while the Americans were landing in ever-increasing numbers. Yet, as we shall see, the Germans made one more bid for victory.

One very momentous event had taken place in March. Finding that Pétain was bent on withdrawing towards Paris, Sir Douglas Haig appealed to the Secretary of State and the Chief of the Imperial General Staff. A meeting was arranged at Doullens, under the presidency of M. Clemenceau. It was at first arranged that General Foch should "co-ordinate" the efforts of the Allied armies in front of Amiens, but, at the suggestion of Sir Douglas Haig, the powers given to General Foch were extended to the whole Franco-British front in the West; later the Belgians, Italians and Americans placed their troops under Foch's command.

Map 14.

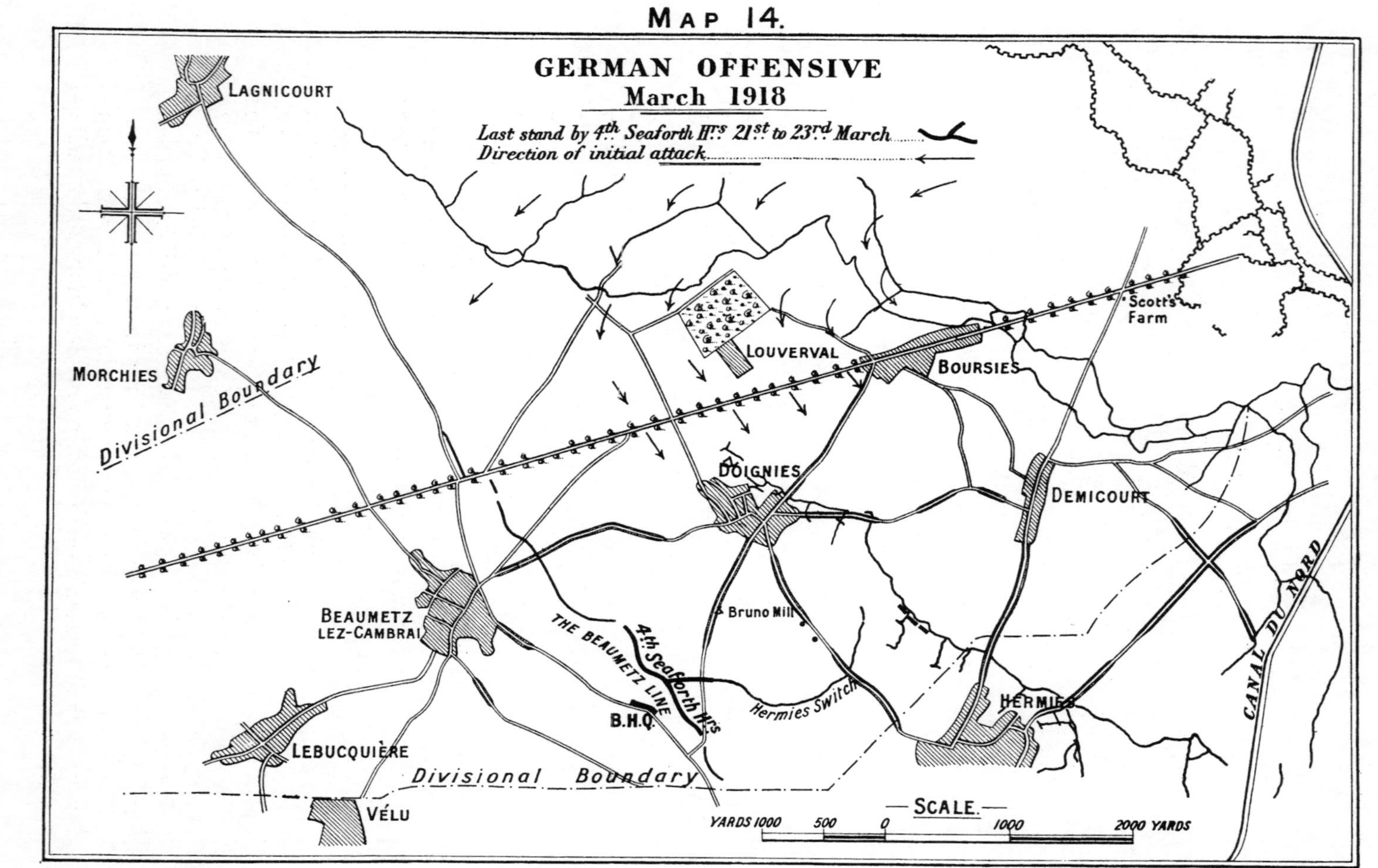

GERMAN OFFENSIVE
March 1918
Last stand by 4th Seaforth Hrs 21st to 23rd March
Direction of initial attack
LAGNICOURT
MORCHIES
Divisional Boundary
LOUVERVAL
BOURSIES
Scott's Farm
DOIGNIES
DEMICOURT
BEAUMETZ
LEZ-CAMBRAI
Bruno Mill
THE BEAUMETZ LINE
4th Seaforth Hrs
B.H.Q.
Hermies Switch
HERMIES
LEBUCQUIÈRE
Divisional Boundary
VÉLU
CANAL DU NORD
SCALE
YARDS 1000
500
0
1000
2000 YARDS

THE GERMAN OFFENSIVE

CHAPTER XII

THE GREAT GERMAN OFFENSIVE, 1918

THE British army was now on the defensive, and, like most other battalions, the 4th Seaforths were very short of their establishment. Unusually large working parties were called for daily; six officers and three hundred other ranks was a quite normal demand. The devastated area was not by any means in a good state of defence; so that, while by day the trenches that did exist were improved, by night new trenches were dug and new wire put in position. When in reserve the troops spent most of their time in preparing the second line between Beaumetz and Morchies. There was little time left for training.

On 11th January 1918 Captain W. Surrey Dane took over the duties of Adjutant, and Captain H. P. T. Gray came back from England.

The next three days were spent in reorganizing the companies prior to going into the line. On the 16th the Battalion relieved the 8th Argyll and Sutherland Highlanders in front of Demicourt, with No. 4 Company at Lebucquière. The trenches were in a bad state and there was mist and heavy rain. On the 18th, enemy working parties were seen in Bourlon Wood. Next day the Battalion was relieved by the 9th Suffolks and went into huts in Middlesex Camp, near Frémicourt.

On the 19th the first three companies moved from Frémicourt by rail to Achiet-le-Grand, going into huts at Courcelles-le-Comte, where they were joined by No. 4, which had come by route march. On the 20th the Battalion marched to rest billets at Bellacourt, the 51st Division being in Corps reserve, while the other two divisions held the line.

On 21st January, Captain P. C. Knight and Second Lieutenants A. G. Williams, W. L. Forsyth and J. S. Ferguson, with forty-eight other ranks, joined the Battalion, which was beginning to recover from the blow it had received at Cambrai. Football and boxing began once more and the Pipe Band gave a concert in the schoolroom at Grosville. Most of the officers turned out at five every morning for a riding class under Captain Gray. Training was very thoroughly organized, and there were courses in bayonet-fighting, rapid wiring, musketry, tactical schemes and gas protection, while every man was taught to load and fire a Lewis gun. Later, when the Brigadier gave prizes for various platoon competitions, the Battalion won those for shooting and march discipline. That for digging was the only one it did not win.

On 2nd February the Division again went back to the front. The 4th Seaforths marched *via* Ransart, Adinfer, Ayette and Ablainzeville to Ritz Camp, at Achiet-le-Grand. On the 6th, the 9th The Royal Scots left the Brigade to join the 61st Division, for the strength of infantry brigades was now reduced from four battalions to three. The distinction marks on the tunics and coats of the Seaforths were therefore altered from two blue stripes to one.

More officers joined about this time — Lieutenant J. K. Calder, Second Lieutenants J. D. Abel and E. T. Hathaway, and a few small drafts. The appearance of the Battalion had changed greatly, for most of the new drafts were undersized men. So much was this the case that, on taking over trenches, it became necessary to build up the fire-steps, whereas in the old days they had to be lowered.

The spirit of the men had, however, recovered, and their smile had returned. A very senior staff officer one day happened to come on a detachment of the Battalion on the march, with pipers playing at their head. He stopped his car to watch them pass, and later remarked to the Commanding Officer that it was the pleasantest and smartest sight that he had seen since he left Aldershot in 1914.

For this recovery much was due to the work of Regimental Sergeant-Major Anderson. Trained in the Scots Guards, and a man of fine appearance, he was always a great example to the non-commissioned officers and men. Associated with him was Sergeant D. D. Davidson (Dingwall) of the Orderly Room, who knew and was known by every man in the Battalion throughout the war. He was the mainstay of many adjutants and only once failed to answer a letter. The Commanding Officer had burned it!

On 13th February the Battalion left Achiet-le-Grand at 8 A.M. and marched through Bapaume to huts at Lebucquière, which it reached at 12.15 P.M., the distance being sixteen kilometres. Here it was in tactical reserve to the 152nd Brigade.

There was now a much greater stir on this front. The rail-heads at Achiet-le-Grand and Bapaume were getting busier every day. More troops were coming and going. Artillery were at work on new gun positions, and the roads were thronged with horses and wagons. The aircraft were particularly active. The front line was often the safest place in the whole of the forward area, for when the moon was high and the sky clear the German aeroplanes swept over villages crowded with troops and showered bombs upon them. The ruins of Lebucquière offered but little shelter to man or beast, and it was no safe place when the moon shone full and the stars were out, for hovering in that empty sky was perhaps a flight of enemy 'planes. A faint, low hum from far beyond the German lines would swell to a roar, and the aeroplanes would come swooping and circling overhead. Having blown out the candles and interrupted a game of bridge there was nothing to do but wait until they had dropped their bombs and moved away; then, if the luck stood, the game was resumed.

Sometimes it happened that an aeroplane was caught in the beam of a searchlight. Then it was a wonderful sight to watch the silvery 'planes gleaming and sparkling; till one would dive and swoop like a pigeon fleeing from a hawk, side-slipping and looping the loop, while round it the shrapnel sparkled as they burst in the sky, and all around the machine guns barked and crackled.

No-man's-land has been called the wonderland of the war. For four years that narrow strip of ground was a more impassable obstacle than any river or mountain range—almost as impassable as the desert itself. From the rugged Jura Mountains to the grey North Sea it ran between its wire boundaries, here swelling to more than a mile in width, there narrowing to a few deadly yards. In parts wild flowers grew and the grass was green; in parts it was covered with shell holes, wire entanglements and the unburied dead of many fights.

At night, patrols from either side silently crept about, trying to gather information. This was eerie work. Tree stumps took the forms of men, and to the beginner it often seemed as if the very stars were the eyes of a stealthy enemy bent on his destruction.

No-man's-land could, however, be a pleasant enough place. Experienced soldiers knew that during a bombardment the safest place was the middle of No-man's-land. And to get out and move about in the open after the confinement to trenches and dug-outs, to be able to look in other directions than skywards, was an inexpressible relief.

During periods of comparative quiet, patrols were sent out as a matter of form to pick up such information as they might happen on and to keep the men in practice for the work. When preparing for the attack, however, the immediate object of patrols was to examine the enemy wire and report on the effect our own artillery fire had had on it, to study the ground for suitable assembly and jumping-off positions, and to capture prisoners. From these latter it was hoped to glean knowledge as to the enemy's preparations and warning of his intentions.

Aeroplane reports, intelligence from secret service sources, and from the interrogation and identification of prisoners, might point to an unusual concentration of troops, and even indicate the intended point of attack. Patrols therefore formed part of a far-flung net for gathering information. It will be remembered that it was because of the unusual precautions taken by the British before the Battle of Cambrai that its initial stages were so very successful. Had the Germans patrolled actively and with daring they might have learned quite enough of what was going on to have saved themselves from surprise.

The conduct of a patrol was left entirely to the officer in charge, whose principal difficulty was to control ten or twelve men, in the most unexpected circumstances, in the dark. One favourite formation was like that of a flight of duck. The officer led, followed by the sergeant. To left and right of the sergeant the men were echeloned to the rear, the last place in each wing being assigned to a junior non-commissioned officer, whose duty was to ensure that the wings conformed to the lead given them. It will at once be seen that this formation gave a free field of fire to the front, and enabled half the patrol to open fire to either flank.

On 20th February the Battalion relieved the 1/6th Gordons in the right sector of the front line of the Division. Nos. 1 and 4 Companies were in front line, No. 2 in support and No. 3 in reserve, with Headquarters in the sunken road near Demicourt. The 7th Argyll and Sutherland Highlanders were on the left and the 17th Division on the right. The line was quiet, for the enemy were from 1500 to 2000 yards away.

On the 21st the Adjutant, Captain Dane, went on leave, and Second Lieutenant G. M. Cooper officiated for him. On the 26th Major Osborne of the Middlesex, at this time Second-in-Command, came back from leave, followed, two days later, by Major Jobson.

On 1st March patrols were sent out from the right and left companies in the line. That on the right encountered an enemy patrol, and, after an exchange of bombs and rifle fire, returned, having lost one man wounded and missing. This was the only casualty during this tour in the line.

The patrol from the left company had been ordered to find out if the enemy were occupying Scott's Farm in the middle of No-man's-land. The officer in command deliberately chose for the patrol men who had come out recently to France, so that they might gain experience of this class of work. The patrol approached to within fifty yards of the house. The officer and sergeant then crept forward alone, leaving instructions with the patrol to rush forward if, after a short interval of time, they heard firing. They searched every nook and cranny of the house without finding any of the enemy, though there were indications that he had been there lately. The two then moved on and explored the enemy outpost lines, but found that he had not occupied them that night. When they reached the wire in front of the enemy's trenches, and found that he was spending a quiet night, it struck them that the patrol had not followed them up. They went back, to find it lying where they had left it, five hundred yards in rear. The men were new to patrolling; but to impress upon them the duties of a patrol the officer in charge took unusual measures. He called them to their feet, ordered them to fall in in two lines, numbered them off, sloped arms, turned to the right and marched towards the British lines at attention. Here he halted them and explained the object of this queer procedure to the wondering and nervous men, after which he dismissed them. It would be interesting to know whether there is any record of another barrack-square parade in No-man's-land.

Aerial photographs had shown that a small overland track leading from the German front line to a forward switch line, which generally was not occupied, had been used. Divisional Headquarters wanted to know if this trench was occupied; for, if it were, it would point to a concentration of troops preparing for an early advance. So soon as darkness had set in a picked patrol crept out through the wire, right up to the enemy line. It was a frosty night, and the grass rustled under foot as the patrol crept stealthily closer. The officer in charge crawled under the enemy wire to peep into the trench, and the patrol was about to follow when, suddenly, a machine gun opened fire. The patrol had been discovered. Sparks flew off the wire entanglements as the bullets struck them. In the trench orders were being shouted, and not five yards separated the patrol from the belching muzzle of the machine gun. That was their salvation. In his excitement the gunner probably forgot that his gun was sighted for a distant objective, or else did not realize how close to him the patrol was. It was a tense moment. Bullets were passing little more than a foot above the ground and lights went up from the trench. Again their close proximity saved the patrol. After a time firing ceased. The ground fell away a little from the trench into No-man's-land. As the patrol began to withdraw, another light went up; the patrol threw themselves on the ground and two machine guns opened. Again no one was hit, but the patrol had quite satisfied themselves that the trench was indeed occupied, and retired as quickly as it could. One or two laughed nervously at the enemy's nervousness, to which another burst of machine-gun fire replied. All got safely into the trenches to the welcome comfort of a tot of rum.

Another night a patrol went out on a general reconnaissance. Lieutenant Williams, who was in charge, walked over some low barbed wire and, without realizing it, entered an enemy trench. He switched on his electric torch, and, walking along, suddenly came across an enemy sentry half asleep. The alarm was given, and Lieutenant Williams made off at top speed, followed by a shower of ineffective rifle shots.

On 4th March, Major Jobson went sick. On the 5th the Battalion was relieved by the 4th Gordons and went into huts at Ambulance Camp, Lebucquière. Here it was in Brigade reserve and supplied many working parties.

The change was not for long, for on the 9th the 4th Seaforths relieved the 4th Gordons in the right sector, while the 7th Argyll and Sutherland relieved them in the left.

The 4th Gordons came up again on the 15th and the 4th Seaforths returned to Lebucquière. On the 16th, Lieutenant-General Harper left the Division to take over command of the IV Corps, being succeeded by Major-General G. T. C. Carter Campbell, C.B., D.S.O. The 17th was a sad day for the Battalion, for Lieutenant-Colonel Unthank, after nearly two years' continuous service in command, left for a period of six months at home. These changes seemed ominous.

Major H. P. D. Osborne, D.S.O., Middlesex Regiment, took over temporary command of the Battalion, only to leave next day to command the King's Own Shropshire Light Infantry in the 6th Division. Captain J. S. Harris joined from the 9th Seaforths and Captain A. M. C. Finch and Lieutenant D. Ross went for a six months' period of duty at home. On 20th March, Major A. C. MacIntyre, M.C., from the 8th Argyll and Sutherland Highlanders, took command of the Battalion.

When the Germans launched their great offensive on 21st March, in the endeavour to separate the French and British armies and to isolate the Fifth Army, the 51st Division on the right centre of the IV Corps was holding about 6000 yards of front astride the Bapaume-Cambrai road. Still further to the right lay the 17th Division, and on the left the 6th.

The forward zone of the Divisional sector comprised a series of spurs and valleys at right angles to the front line. Bourlon Wood commanded the whole position. The defensive zone consisted of three main positions: the front system of trenches, the intermediate line, which was the real battle line, and the Corps line from Beaumetz to Morchies, consisting of a single, almost continuous, trench. It was strongly wired and traversed along the whole of the Corps sector. There were no communication trenches to the rear, but running forward from it were three switch lines up to the intermediate line planned to provide suitable flank defensive positions should the enemy break through on part of the Divisional front. Two battalions of each infantry brigade held the forward zone and intermediate line, the third battalion being in Brigade reserve.

The enemy attack opened at 5 A.M. on 21st March. The

4th Seaforths were lying in reserve at Lebucquière. In a few minutes the whole camp was awake and hurriedly dressing under a bombardment of high-explosive and gas shells. At 5.15 orders were received from Brigade Headquarters to move up and occupy the Beaumetz-Morchies line, and the companies moved up independently under heavy fire, but without any casualties. Long experience of shell fire had taught men to study it and learn the best way through it.

The Battalion took up a position commanding the small valley running south from Doignies and another between Doignies and Hermies. No. 1 Company was on the right, No. 2 in the centre and No. 3 on the left, with No. 4 in support at Battalion Headquarters. No. 1 Company held advanced posts at Bruno Mill and on the Doignies-Hermies road. On the right was the reserve company of the 4th Gordons.

About 7 A.M. the bombardment in front slackened off; but Major A. C. MacIntyre was mortally wounded, and the command of the Battalion devolved on Captain H. P. T. Gray.

The first sign of serious trouble appeared when transport wagons came back at full speed through the Battalion line followed by a number of men of the 152nd Infantry Brigade, which had been holding the left of the Divisional line. The enemy had not made a frontal attack, but had broken through and assaulted the left flank, gaining a spur to the north of the Bapaume-Cambrai road. He had chosen his ground well, for the field of fire in this direction was bad, and after heavy fighting the left flank had to fall back past Doignies.

By the afternoon the enemy had reached the village of Doignies and could be seen assembling in mass on the Beaumetz-Doignies road. No. 3 Company, reinforced by a section of two guns from the Brigade Machine Gun Company, opened fire. The detachment of a field gun out in the front, that had been firing point-blank over open sights at the enemy in Doignies, destroyed their gun before retiring. These gunners had held on to the last and had done excellent work. About 5 P.M. the 8th Gloucesters and 10th Warwicks of the 19th Division came up to counter-attack Doignies, but, through some error, they had to wait until 7.15 P.M. before the tanks (that were to support them) had lined up in the open. This gave the enemy time to prepare for them. His aeroplanes came over, flying not more than 100 feet from the ground; they noted the presence of these battalions and warned the troops in Doignies. When the counter-attack was delivered it met with such fierce opposition that it failed. The tanks and some of the infantry came back at about 8.30 P.M., and the few remaining members of one company of the 8th Gloucesters retired into the trench of No. 3 Company. The 4th Seaforths had the greatest admiration for the cool and determined advance of the Gloucesters.

On the right the Corps had withdrawn from the Flesquières salient, and to conform to the withdrawal of the 17th Division on the right to the Hermies defences the front was reorganized. By 10 P.M. the 5th Seaforth Highlanders and 5th Gordon Highlanders were holding about 1000 yards on the right of the intermediate line and the Hermies Switch. On their left were the 4th Gordon Highlanders and the 4th Seaforth Highlanders, reinforced by one company of the 7th Argyll and Sutherland Highlanders, with another company at Battalion Headquarters. Still further to the left were the 6th Seaforth Highlanders and 8th The Royal Scots between Doignies and Beaumetz, with the 6th and 7th Black Watch and 7th Gordon Highlanders north of Beaumetz.

The morning of 22nd March found the Corps line intact on the whole of the Divisional front. In front of it were the 8th Gloucesters and 10th Warwicks, who had counter-attacked towards Doignies, in a defensive flank position on the Beaumetz-Doignies road. The 4th Seaforths still held their advanced posts towards Doignies.

The enemy opened the bombardment of the British position about 7.15 A.M., but his attack did not develop till 10 A.M. No. 1 Company at Bruno Mill, under Captain Brown, were the first to meet this attack. After a hard fight they were driven in by overwhelming numbers of the enemy, as also were the posts on the Doignies-Hermies road, but not till the officers in charge of both posts had been killed. The attack on the main position was repelled by rifle and machine-gun fire. Two more attacks, at 12.30 and 3 P.M., were similarly driven off, leaving many dead on the wire. During the second attack the artillery support was very good. At night the wire was repaired.

When night fell the Battalion line was intact, but the situation had become precarious. In the first attack the Corps line had been broken north of Bapaume, and the troops on the left flank of the 51st Division again found themselves taken in flank and rear. By evening, therefore, the Corps line had been evacuated on the left as far as the Bapaume road and a defensive flank was formed covering Beaumetz. The situation on the night of the 22nd-23rd was in fact confused. On the right the 7th Argyll and Sutherland and 4th Seaforths were holding a line from near Hermies to near Beaumetz. To the left were the 8th Gloucesters and 10th Warwicks of the 57th Brigade and beyond them mixed units of the 74th, 75th and 153rd Brigades. The 152nd Brigade was re-forming near Bancourt. The 4th Gordons were in reserve to the 154th Brigade.

The morning of 23rd March showed the 4th Seaforths and 7th Argyll and Sutherland alone in the old 51st Division line. The latter were in touch with the 17th Division. The enemy were seen in masses coming over Louverval ridge, and in the Doignes-Boursies valley and Doignes-Beaumetz road. A strong attack was made on the troops on the left as they retired on Beaumetz. The attack on No. 3 Company was held up by rifle and machine-gun fire, for an S.O.S. by pigeon to the artillery remained unanswered. The Beaumetz-Morchies line south-west of Doignes was now evacuated, No. 3 Company holding on till 3 P.M.

During the night the enemy had kept up an intermittent fire from machine guns, especially at those points where the line was pierced by roads leading back from the old front line. This made it difficult to patrol to the front or to communicate with the rear, for the telephone wire had been cut to bits by heavy bombardments. It also made more difficult the grievous task of clearing the trench of the dead.

The enemy had concentrated a large number of troops opposite the Battalion front, and No. 1 Company in the Hermies Switch took two prisoners, who told them what they might expect on the morrow. The Germans had a large number of guns around Doignies, and when they opened at 6 A.M. it was at short range, and the few dug-outs in the front were soon filled with wounded, for under the terrific bombardment casualties mounted rapidly. So soon, however, as the enemy lengthened his range to let his infantry move up, the Seaforths were on the parapet, mowing deep lanes in the advancing lines. The German attack was a good one, for machine-gun posts on the flanks swept the Highlanders' parapet and the infantry came on doggedly. It was a nerve-racking ordeal. Men lay dead and dying in the trench; others were falling every minute. Two of the Gloucesters and some Seaforths were in one bay, making their fire tell with deadly effect on the enemy; first one of the Seaforths fell, next moment one of the Gloucesters was hit through the windpipe. He collapsed, and was choked by his own blood. His comrade stopped for a moment to look at him, but seeing he could not help, quietly took up his rifle and went on with his task. These Gloucesters were gallant men.

Hard fighting went on all that morning, and for a time the German onslaught was checked. Few remained to tell the story of the fight and to record the many acts of bravery and self-sacrifice. Captain J. S. Harris of No. 2 Company had little more than a handful of men left, and they were nearly exhausted; for it was the third day of the battle and they had had little sleep. Thinking to encourage them when the enemy were pressing hard he got up on the parapet and directed their fire, only to fall to an enemy bullet.

By 9 A.M. the Germans had reached Lebucquière, two and a half miles in rear of the position, while the 17th Division on the right withdrew during the morning to conform to movements further south. A sacrifice had been made to save a division, and the victims of the War God were the 4th Seaforth Highlanders and 7th Argyll and Sutherland Highlanders, who were left to hold the Beaumetz-Morchies line alone, and so wrest from the enemy a few more hours' delay. They were found equal to their task.

Nothing was as yet known to the Battalion of the bigger events that were taking place on their flanks and rear, but it was obvious to all that they were almost cut off. The last S.O.S. rocket was sent up, but there were no guns to answer it. The attack continued to develop. The enemy opened fire with his guns again, and the last fight began. Soon ammunition ran short, and the machine gunners were ordered to reserve their fire; the rifle had become the decisive weapon.

The 7th Argyll and Sutherland, after a brilliant resistance to the attack from Hermies, were driven in. At 10.40 A.M. No. 4 Company on the right and No. 2 in the centre withdrew into the sunken road with Battalion Headquarters, to prevent the flank being turned. No. 3 Company on the left commanded the valley leading from Doignies and met the enemy with such deadly fire that they abandoned a frontal attack, and, moving to their right over the ridge, came round the left flank under cover. They got into the trench, and could not be ejected, for there were no more bombs. The fight raged for a time, casualties increased, ammunition was nearly exhausted and the machine guns ceased fire.

The Gloucesters withdrew under orders to link up with the Warwicks, east-north-east of Velu, so as to form a defensive flank. Some of the Seaforths went back with them, but it was too late, and few of them survived. At 3 P.M. the stand of No. 3 Company was over.

An attack had now begun on the last strongpoint of the Battalion in the Headquarters trench, where the Adjutant, Captain Surrey Dane, had collected about a score or so of men. Attacking from the left, the Germans brought up guns to within a few hundred yards, pouring in a terrible fire at point-blank range and reducing the garrison to a mere handful. They kept up a stout resistance although they well knew that there was no hope. They finally were forced to abandon the trench, and only a few got back through the narrow neck of land running towards Velu that was not in enemy hands. In front, in the trench that had been held by No. 3 Company, four men who found themselves surrounded had a few rounds left in the belt of a machine gun, and were taking a last deadly toll of the enemy.

This stand of the 4th Seaforths and 7th Argyll and Sutherland, supported by men of the Brigade Machine Gun Company, is described by Major Bewsher, in the *History of the 51st Division*, thus: "The fighting of these two battalions on this occasion certainly constitutes one of the finest performances of the Division."

The following extracts from "General Remarks on Recent Operations," by Brigadier-General K. G. Buchanan, Commanding 154th Infantry Brigade, are a high tribute to the battalions concerned:

"3. On the 22nd and 23rd March the defence of the Beaumetz-Morchies Line by the 4th Seaforth Highlanders and two companies of the 7th Argyll and Sutherland Highlanders is deserving of the highest praise. On the 22nd the defence was greatly assisted by the batteries of the 293rd (Army) Brigade, R.F.A. These guns fired continuously on the massed enemy, in spite of heavy shelling and the low-flying enemy aeroplanes. Three massed attacks were made during this day and each time they were broken up, though many of the enemy were killed or wounded on the wire in front of the line.

Before dawn on the 23rd March the Artillery had been withdrawn and the 152nd Brigade had withdrawn from Beaumetz, forming a flank North West of the village and joining up with the 10th Warwicks, who were on a line covering the southern exits of Beaumetz. At about 9 A.M. the 152nd Brigade were forced to withdraw by large numbers of the enemy moving on Lebucquière from the North East, and this movement also affected the Warwicks, who withdrew South West. Meanwhile the division on the right had commenced withdrawing from Hermies.

"The 4th Seaforth Highlanders and two companies of the 7th Argyll and Sutherland Highlanders still maintained their position, though completely isolated, and beat off all enemy attempts to advance against 800 yards of the Beaumetz-Morchies Line which they occupied. The Vickers guns on their front did magnificent work. This was made possible by the fact that Major Harcourt, Commanding C Company, 51st Machine Gun Battalion, himself galloped a limber along the positions and supplied the guns with small-arm ammunition.

"At 3 P.M. the line was still held, though the enemy had field guns in action south of Doignies, and was in occupation of Lebucquière and Velu Wood. He also commenced bombing down the Beaumetz-Morchies Line from the North and in several places was in large numbers at very close quarters. It was only then that Captain Gray, Commanding 4th Seaforth Highlanders, gave orders to withdraw South West, clearing to the South of Velu Wood.

"The value of the foregoing defence cannot, I consider, be exaggerated. Apart from inflicting a heavy loss on the enemy, it partly assisted the 152nd Brigade to withdraw, and very greatly assisted the 17th Division on the right in this respect. The defence is also a valuable example of holding out for over five hours with both flanks gone and the enemy having penetrated over 2500 yards directly in rear.

"The 4th Seaforth Highlanders were not engaged East of the Beaumetz-Morchies Line, and they suffered almost all their casualties in the defence of that line (*i.e.* 14 officers and 386 other ranks). I consider, however, that the magnificent stand they made and the results of it fully justifies the depletion in their ranks."

This stand covered the withdrawal of the 153rd Infantry Brigade and of the 17th and 19th Divisions into the Army line and delayed the German advance. The attackers had been ordered to be in Bapaume that day.

Perhaps twenty men, who had come out of the fight, joined the reserve of the Battalion on the Bapaume-Peronne road that night. The 19th Division held the front covering Bapaume.

At 10.30 A.M. on the 24th the Battalion took up a position in shell holes north-east of the reservoir on the Bapaume-Peronne road facing east. The 4th Gordons were on the right near Beaulencourt, with the 7th Argyll and Sutherland in the centre. The Brigade formed a defensive line to support the other two brigades of the Division between Bancourt and Frémicourt.

Early in the afternoon the Army line east of Frémicourt was penetrated and by 3 P.M. the 19th Division was retiring through the Bancourt-Frémicourt line. At 4.30 the 17th Division on the right also fell back, and beyond them there was a general retirement along the whole of the Fifth Army front. The right flank of the 51st Division withdrew about 6 P.M. through the 154th Infantry Brigade, and at dusk it too fell back, fighting rearguard actions, towards Thilloy. On the left the enemy advance from Frémicourt was checked, but the retirement continued. Patrols sent out later encountered no enemy to the west of the Bapaume-Peronne road.

The Division re-formed about Thilloy and received orders to withdraw to the line Butte de Warlencourt-Loupart Wood, as the enemy were advancing from the south-east.

On the morning of 25th March the Division stood as follows: the 7th Argyll and Sutherland Highlanders held the right at the Butte de Warlencourt, then came the 4th Gordon Highlanders, with the 4th Seaforth Highlanders on the left. The 152nd and 153rd Infantry Brigades prolonged the line to the eastern edge of Loupart Wood. The Division had not been able to gain touch with those on either flank and the position had only just been taken when word came that the troops on the right had fallen back on Courcelette and that the Germans were in Delville Wood. The 154th Brigade withdrew, therefore, and formed a defensive flank. The Officer Commanding the 4th Seaforths gave authority to some sappers of the Canadian Overseas Railway Construction Corps to destroy the Miraumont Thilloy railway track.

At 10.30 A.M. reports came in that the troops on the left were falling back and the enemy were seen advancing in large numbers from the east and from the high ground to the south-east, on whom heavy casualties were inflicted. Some of the men began to retire, but were easily rallied and led back into the position. Soon after 1 P.M. the enemy were beginning to envelop the position from the ground north-west of Courcelette, and orders were given to retire by easy stages, while the Argyll and Sutherland threw out a defensive flank to the right.

At 3 P.M. a new position was taken up near Pys. The 152nd Brigade could be seen advancing in extended order against the enemy near Irles, who fell back amazed.

It was now the fifth day of the battle and the 154th Brigade had been in it all the time. They still fought on and fought well, and Brigadier-General K. G. Buchanan rode out in front, mounted on a white horse, and cheered them on. The men recognized his cool courage and responded valiantly. But the flanks were again being threatened and the Division began to withdraw towards Miraumont.

At Colincamps it reorganized and bivouacked to the east of Sailly-au-Bois. At dawn on 26th March an outpost line was thrown out between Sailly-au-Bois and Hebuterne. At 8.30 A.M. another retirement was made to Souastre, where new positions were taken up facing south and south-east. At 3 P.M. an Australian brigade came up, advancing on Hebuterne. They linked up with the 62nd Division on the left and filled up the gap in the IV Corps line.

The 51st Division was now withdrawn from battle. It marched to Pas, where it bivouacked for the night, and on the 27th went *via* Doullens to billets in Barly, near Neuvillette.

The casualties in this very severe fighting were the heaviest the Battalion had as yet experienced:

OFFICERS

Killed: Major A. C. MacIntyre, Captain J. S. Harris, Lieutenant J. K. Calder, Second Lieutenant W. L. Forsyth.

Wounded: Captain H. P. T. Gray, Second Lieutenants L. Gardner, J. W. Macdonald, R. G. Williams.

Wounded and Missing: Captain F. W. Brown, Lieutenant A. MacRae, Second Lieutenant G. M. Cooper.

Missing: Captains P. C. Knight, J. F. Hardesty (U.S.A.M.C.), Second Lieutenant J. Davidson.

Sick: Second Lieutenant J. Christie.

OTHER RANKS

Killed: 29. *Wounded*: 129. *Wounded and Missing*: 21. *Gassed*: 2. *Missing*: 204. *Sick*: 17.

The Battalion had well sustained its reputation; its stubborn resistance against overwhelming odds had gone far to save the 51st and the divisions on its right and left from being surrounded or forced off their line of retreat. It had never failed to stand for as long as it was required in the stress of a gigantic rearguard action. Yet hardly had it been withdrawn from this prolonged and desperate struggle ere it was again called on to hold another front against a similar, though fortunately less powerful, attack.

On 29th March the 4th Seaforths marched to Frévent, where they entrained at 6 P.M. for Lillers. They arrived there about midnight and went into billets at Busnettes. Here began the business of reorganizing and training. On 1st April Lieutenant G. T. Gillies, Second Lieutenants J. P. Anderson, A. Green, A. B. Moncur and J. D. Nixon and seven other ranks reported for duty, and on the 2nd, Major J. O. Hopkinson, D.S.O., M.C., arrived from the 2nd Battalion and assumed command.

On 4th April the Battalion proceeded to Raimbert *via* Allouagne, where the Division became part of the reserve of the First Army. The following day the new Commanding Officer inspected the companies, and Captain H. P. T. Gray rejoined. On the 7th a draft of fifty-six other ranks arrived, but the strength of the Battalion was still far below establishment.

On the 8th the Battalion marched *via* Auchel, Allouagne, Choques and Bethune to Ferme du Roi, just outside Bethune. The 51st Division was now in reserve to the V Corps behind the front held by a Portuguese division, and the 154th Infantry Brigade lay about Gonneheim. The area in which it was to operate when the German offensive began was roughly a triangle, with its base on the Lawe from Locon to Lestrem and Robecq at the apex. The Lawe, a canalized stream joining the La Bassée Canal at Bethune to the Lys Canal at Estaires, was crossed on the Divisional front by several drawbridges. These were defended by a series of entrenched posts on the eastern

MAP 15.

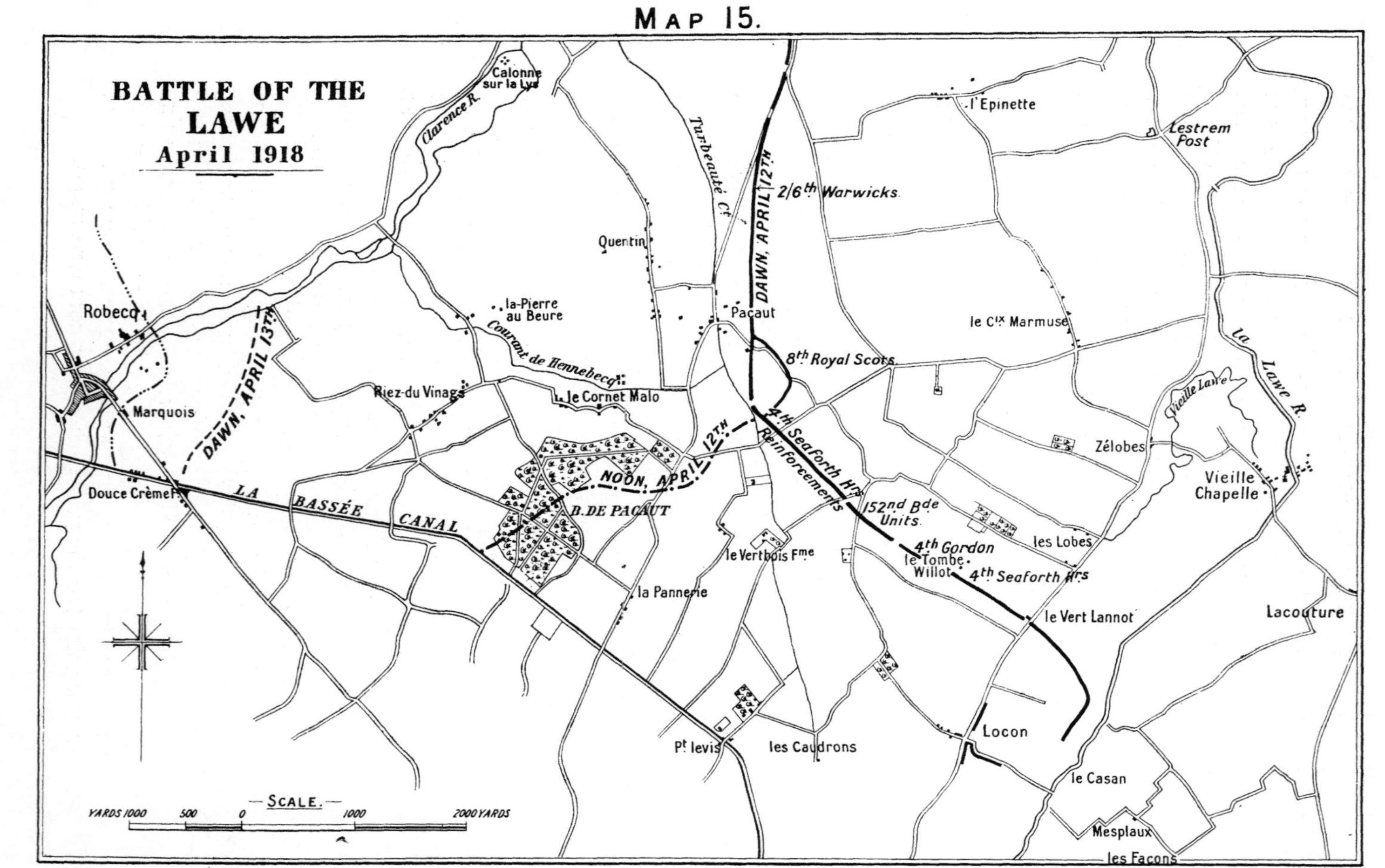
BATTLE OF THE LAWE
April 1918
Calonne sur la Lys
Clarence R.
Turbeauté Ct
l'Epinette
Lestrem Post
2/6th Warwicks
DAWN, APRIL 12TH
Quentin
Robecq
la-Pierre au Beure
Pacaut
le Cix Marmuse
Courant de Hennebecq
8th Royal Scots
la Lawe R.
Vieille Lawe
Riez-du Vinage
le Cornet Malo
Marquois
DAWN, APRIL 13TH
4th Seaforth Hrs
Reinforcements
Zélobes
NOON, APRIL 12TH
Vieille Chapelle
Douce Crème
LA BASSÉE CANAL
B. DE PACAUT
152nd Bde Units
le Vertbois Fme
4th Gordon
les Lobes
le Tombe Willot
4th Seaforth Hrs
la Pannerie
le Vert Lannot
Lacouture
Locon
Pt levis
les Caudrons
le Casan
SCALE.
YARDS 1000 500 0 1000 2000 YARDS
Mesplaux
les Facons

bank and by two others at Lestrem and Zélobes on the western. From the Lawe to Robecq the country was thickly dotted with farms and hamlets, although there were several wide stretches of open ground, over which machine-gun fire was the decisive factor. The ground was low-lying and in places very marshy. When it was learned that the Portuguese front had been pierced the 152nd Infantry Brigade was sent forward to Huit Maisons and La Couture, where the 5th and 6th Seaforths and King Edward's Horse drove back the Germans.

The morning of the 9th broke dull and misty. Heavy gun fire began at 4 A.M. and continued all the forenoon. At 1.15 P.M. the Battalion was ordered to march forward to Le Hamel to report to the 166th Infantry Brigade of the 55th Division in the XI Corps. Here it took up a position east of the Lawe in front of Locon and south of Le Casan, but about 4.30 A.M. it was sent forward to fill a gap west of Le Touret. Battalion Headquarters were at Le Casan, on the right of the 1/4th South Lancashire Regiment.

Le Casan was a comfortable farm, and there were eggs, milk and other luxuries in abundance. The cows, indeed, were suffering from not having been milked. There was no cover, for no trenches had ever been dug in this area, and there was little opportunity even to make rifle pits. It was open, swampy land, where trees and hedges made fewer screens than was usual round about this part of Flanders.

At 9 A.M. on 10th April the enemy attacked the front, trying to dribble forward and to rush up machine guns. Three attempts also were made to work round the flanks, all of which were repulsed. At 1 P.M. the 1/5th King's Own were forced out of Le Touret, and No. 4 Company was ordered up to the Rue du Bois to cover the right flank. No. 1 Company extended its line to occupy the ground evacuated by No. 4.

At 11.30 A.M. renewed attempts to turn the flanks were driven off and a machine gun was taken from the enemy. A further attack at 5.15 P.M. likewise was repulsed.

Advantage was taken of nightfall to adjust the position. For this defence the Brigadier-General Commanding the 166th Infantry Brigade sent the following telegram to Lieutenant-Colonel Hopkinson: "The Brigadier-General Commanding wishes to say that he is very pleased indeed with the fine defence offered by your men yesterday. Please convey to your officers and men the Brigadier's heartiest congratulations."

At dawn, on 11th April, Nos. 4 and 1 Companies occupied a line about five hundred yards west of Le Touret, from the Rue du Bois to the road junction east of Les Facons. Nos. 3 and 2 Companies were in support, the former being about Les Facons. A heavy bombardment began at 8.30 A.M., and about 10 A.M. a determined attack on this front was held up. The troops on the left, however, were forced to retire, and the attack turned against Les Facons. This imperilled the left flank and rear of the front companies, and at noon Headquarters moved to Les Glattignies. The front companies, however, remained in position, brought enfilade fire to bear on their left front, and forced the enemy to retire, with very heavy casualties and the loss of a machine gun, at about 2.45 P.M.

Captain Surrey Dane, the Adjutant, had occasion to go into a farmhouse at Les Glattignies, where he saw a very old couple, sitting one on either side of the fire, looking pitifully sad. When he returned some time after he found that a shell had pitched in the house and had killed them both.

In the cellars at Les Glattignies were a number of cowering Portuguese, who, however, were clinging to their souvenirs! It was here, too, that a German, very drunk and very happy, rode into the 4th Seaforths' lines!

The gap was filled by a company of the 1st Northumberland Fusiliers at about 3 P.M. and the situation up to the Lawe was restored. That night the Battalion was relieved and went into support line between Le Hamel and Les Glattignies, where it remained until the night of the 13th.

Drafts amounting to five hundred and eighteen men in all had arrived meanwhile at the transport lines on the 9th and 10th April. They were there formed into a kind of provisional battalion, under the command of Major Jobson. The companies were commanded in order by Lieutenant W. Weir, Company Sergeant-Major Price, Captain Colin Cameron and Captain A. Campbell.

About 1 A.M. on the 11th, Major Jobson received orders to march at once to Les Choquaux. At 6 A.M. he himself took two of his companies to Le Vert Bois Farm, while the other two were ordered into trenches south-west of Le Vert Lannot, and later went forward to the road south of La Tombe Willot to a position on the right of the 4th Gordon Highlanders.

The Division had fallen back from Vieille Chapelle, and by

4 P.M. the line held by the 4th Seaforth reinforcements and the 4th Gordons had become the front line.

Farther north the enemy was pressing against Merville. The second great attack of the German army extended from the southern defences of Ypres to Givenchy. Messines Ridge, that had cost us so dearly in men and munitions, had fallen. Givenchy and the hill at Kemmel still closed the road to the Channel ports.

Just before dawn on 12th April the left centre of the Divisional line was surprised and broken. The Headquarters of the 152nd and 153rd Infantry Brigades on the outskirts of Riez du Vinage were surrounded and the Brigadier and Staff of the former taken prisoners. The Germans then pushed through to the canal south-west of Pacaut Wood. A flank was formed by a composite force through the wood to the canal; but the position held by the 4th Seaforth reinforcements under Major Jobson was in the air, and the Germans at once attacked it. What happened has never been recorded. It is known that Major Jobson was still holding out with a few men at 4 P.M. and that he died in the enemy's hands some time later. There is no doubt but that he and his party made a gallant stand and one worthy of a more successful issue.

The other party of the draft was relieved at 6 A.M. by a company of the Royal Scots Fusiliers and retired to the canal, whence it went to billets at Busnes. This party had suffered only one casualty.

On the night of the 12th-13th a belt of single-strand wire was erected along the Battalion front. The next day it was relieved by the 1/4th Royal Fusiliers and went to Oblinghem.

The Battalion rejoined the 154th Infantry Brigade from the 55th Division on the afternoon of 14th April at La Miquellerie, where the party of the draft came in from Busnes.

The march back to La Miquellerie was very eerie. The troops were well used to passing through ruined villages, but this march through perfectly untouched towns and villages, all empty and deserted by their inhabitants, was something new and awe-inspiring. To add to the tension on the nerves no one had the slightest idea where the enemy was, and the gun fire that could be heard from every direction might as well be that of German as of British guns.

Casualties were:

OFFICERS

Killed: Major M. Jobson, Captain Colin M. Cameron, Second Lieutenant J. D. Nixon.

Wounded: Second Lieutenants G. L. MacKenzie, R. C. Spence-Ross, B. S. Finlayson.

Missing: Lieutenant W. Weir.

OTHER RANKS

Killed: 15. *Wounded*: 119. *Missing*: 111.

On the 17th the Battalion relieved the 7th Argyll and Sutherland in support to the 61st Division, north-east of Robecq. The last time the Battalion had been in Robecq it was a place of rest; now it was in the front line. Colonel Hopkinson very skilfully selected his Headquarters, which to the last was almost the sole house in the place that was not hit. The safest path to the front line actually ran round the cemetery; it had its drawbacks, however, for there was an almost incredible stench from dead beasts at this spot. The artillery on both sides was very active. On the 21st the Argyll and Sutherland in their turn relieved the 4th Seaforths, who went into reserve at La Brasserie. The War Diary entry for the 22nd is rather quaint, being to the effect that it was a good day and that the enemy shelled No. 4 Company with gas shell!! On the 23rd the Battalion was relieved by a battalion of the Royal Berkshires and went into billets in Busnes. Though there was a lot of shelling by shrapnel during the relief there were no casualties.

On 24th April the Battalion moved *via* Lillers to billets in St-Hilaire, where the Brigade was in reserve to the XI Corps. Here training began again. On the 25th, Major "Jock" Henderson rejoined, and two days later there was a concert in the Y.M.C.A. Hall. On the 29th the Divisional Commander inspected the transport; on 2nd May there were Battalion sports; on the 3rd, Lieutenants T. F. Scott and A. A. Finnigan, Second Lieutenants W. D. Armstrong, F. S. Clark, M. C. Ellis, H. B. Lawson and P. Gray arrived; and on the 4th the transport marched for Divion. The next day the Battalion left St-Hilaire at 7 A.M., entrained at Lillers at 11 A.M., and reached Maroeuil at 3.30 P.M., whence it went into York Huts at Ecoivres.

The 51st Division had been sorely tried by these two attempts by the Germans to end the war, and it now needed rest and time to recuperate its spent force.

SYNOPSIS OF EVENTS FROM THE END OF THE GERMAN OFFENSIVE IN FLANDERS TO THE SIGNING OF THE ARMISTICE

(*May to November* 1918)

LUDENDORFF had made two bids for victory. Had he reached Amiens and cut the Allied line in two, victory was within his grasp. Had he broken the British line in Flanders he might have gained the Channel ports and prolonged the war by a year. His third, and last, bid was purely political, for he struck at Paris—and was lost.

This last German offensive began on 27th May, and was at first brilliantly successful, for by the 31st they held the right bank of the Marne from Dormans to Chateau-Thierry.

There was a lull till 9th June, when a new four-days' offensive against Compiègne met with no little success.

On 15th July the Germans began the Second Battle of the Marne on a front of fifty miles, from about Massiges to Chateau-Thierry. They crossed the Marne, indeed, but Foch counter-attacked on the 18th. French and American troops made a considerable advance towards Chateau-Thierry and Soissons, while, on the 20th, British, French and Italian troops advanced along the valley of the Ardre. The movement continued. Just as when a stream has forced a hole in a dam the breach rapidly widens, till the full head of water is flowing unchecked, so did the Allied offensive spread till it overwhelmed the Germans in a general advance to victory.

First the movement reached the Third French Army opposite Montdidier. Then, on 8th August, the Fourth British and First French Armies began the Battle of Amiens. By the 15th the Germans were falling back from the Ancre, while the British were regaining ground in Flanders. On the 21st the Third and Fourth Armies began the Second Battles of the Somme, 1918, and on the 23rd were attacking on a 33-mile front from Lihons to within five miles of Arras. On the 26th began the Second Battles of Arras, 1918. By 1st September Noyon, Péronne, Bapaume, Bailleul and Kemmel were in Allied hands.

On 2nd September the First Army broke through the Drocourt-Quéant line, and on the 3rd the British were in Lens and Richebourg-St-Vaast.

On 12th September the Americans attacked the St-Mihiel salient, south of Verdun, and on the 15th were within reach of Metz.

On 12th September the British began the Battles of the Hindenburg Line. On the 26th the French and Americans were advancing on a 40-mile front, with their right on the Meuse. On the 27th the Canadians had taken Bourlon Wood and on the 28th the British and Belgians were successfully attacking on a 23-mile front from Ploegsteert to Dixmude. This was the Fourth Battle of Ypres, which carried the advance to the Roulers-Menin Road.

By 3rd October, St-Quentin was in French possession and the British held Le Catelet, Cambrai and Lille. On the 9th the Germans were cleared out of the entire Hindenburg Line. On the 13th there was heavy fighting north of Verdun; the French had taken La Fère and Laon, and the British were having stiff fighting on the Selle. On the 17th the Americans were advancing, while Sissonne, Douai, Lille, Courtrai and Roulers were occupied by the Allies, and Ostend was once more in Belgian hands.

The Battle of the Selle ended on 25th October, when the French were advancing between Rethel and Sissonne.

On 26th October Ludendorff resigned.

On 4th November the Americans reached Stenay, while the First French Army and the Fourth, Third and First British Armies made a deep advance on a 30-mile front.

On the 9th the British had taken Maubeuge, Condé and Tournai, while the French were in Hirson. On 11th November the British captured Mons early in the morning, thus ending the war where they began it. But the front now was one of sixty miles from the right of the Fourth Army east of Avesnes, by the Third, First and Fifth Army fronts, to the left of the Second Army east of Audenarde. Each of these armies was larger than the original British Expeditionary Force.

At 11 A.M. on 11th November 1918 hostilities ceased on all fronts. Only Von Lettow-Vorbeck in East Africa delayed coming in till the 14th. Bulgaria, Turkey and Austria-Hungary had collapsed before this, and Germany was in peril of communist revolution. So ended hostilities, with Marshal Foch's generous tribute to the British armies and their leader as " decisive factors in the final German defeat."

Map 16.

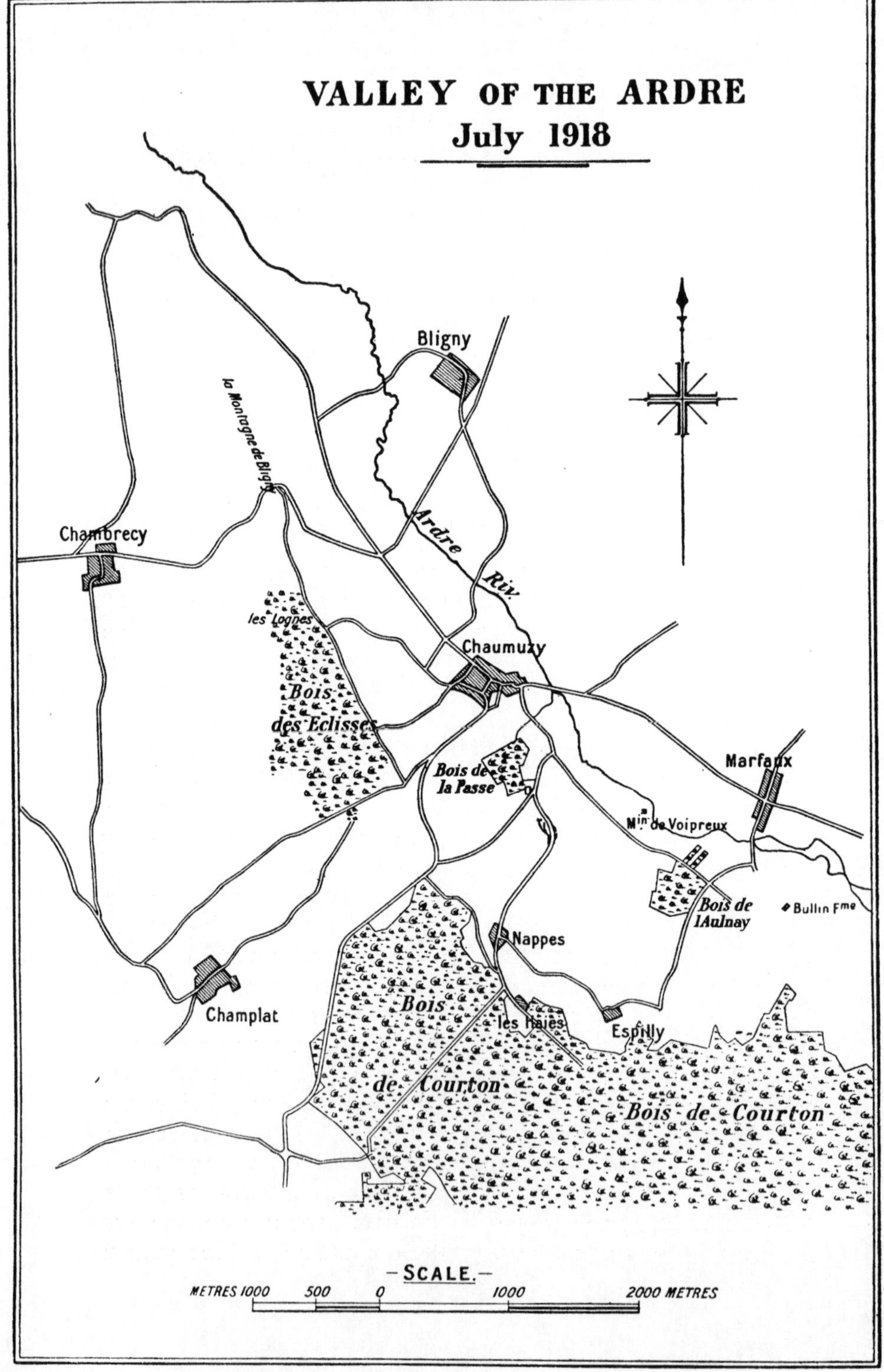
VALLEY OF THE ARDRE
July 1918
Bligny
la Montagne de Bligny
Chambrecy
Ardre Riv.
les Lognes
Chaumuzy
Bois des Eclisses
Bois de la Passe
Marfaux
Min. de Voipreux
Bois de l'Aulnay
Bullin Fme
Nappes
Champlat
Bois de Courton
les Haies
Espilly
Bois de Courton
—SCALE.—
METRES 1000 500 0 1000 2000 METRES

ALBERT

CHAPTER XIII

THE ADVANCE TO VICTORY

THE 51st Division now formed part of the XVII Corps in the familiar country about Roclincourt and Ecurie. Here was the famous Point du Jour on the Vimy Ridge, a redoubt that had been the centre of furious fighting. It was now considered to be a quiet area, and indeed, towards the end of June, very few casualties occurred in the 4th Seaforths.

On 7th May 1918 the Battalion moved from Ecoivres to West Camp at Roclincourt in heavy rain. The following day three platoons relieved posts of the 4th Gordons, and, on the 11th, the 4th Seaforths took over the right front of the Oppy sector from the 7th Black Watch, having the 153rd Brigade on the right and the 7th Argyll and Sutherland Highlanders on the left. On the 21st a German walked across No-man's-land and surrendered. The 154th Brigade went into Divisional reserve on the 23rd, when the 4th Seaforths were relieved by the 6th Seaforths and went back to huts at Ecurie.

While the Battalion was in the Roclincourt sector the British authorities were anxious to obtain some specimens of a new type of German shell which had a projecting nose, designed to ensure that it burst above ground. One of these shells fell by Battalion Headquarters, and was sent to the Brigade by an officer, with a note couched in some such terms as these: "Herewith specimen of shell. To open, smartly tap the projecting portion and the result will be apparent." The Brigade

Major came upon the scene just in time to prevent some of his satellites acting on this ironical jest!

They returned into the line in relief of the 6th Black Watch in the right of the Gavrelle sector on the 29th. Here they had the 15th Division on the right and the 4th Gordons on the left. Nos. 3 and 2 Companies held the right and left of the Battalion front respectively, with No. 4 in reserve and No. 1 in the Post line. The relief was completed in daylight without casualties. On 6th June a patrol reconnoitred Thames Alley as far as the enemy's wire; on the 7th another gained some useful information, while the battalion on the right drove off an enemy raid; on the 8th a third patrol was sent out to raid an enemy post, but as the opportunity was not favourable it returned without casualties. On the 9th a draft of forty-two other ranks arrived, and on the 10th the 5th Seaforths relieved the 4th, which went back to Balmoral Camp at Ecurie. The relief was effected in daylight with no casualties.

A newly posted Sergeant-Major made the acquaintance of a Sergeant-Major of the Royal Engineers who, being more or less a permanency in the sector, had a very fine dug-out. There was a lot of heavy shelling that night, and when the day dawned no Sergeant-Major could be found. There was great consternation and much sympathy for the poor man, who, so it seemed, had been completely obliterated. Entered a Sergeant-Major of the Sappers, crying: "Have you lost a Sergeant-Major?" "Yes, yes, where is he?" "In my dug-out, asleep in my bunk, and I wish you would come and take him away, for I've been on duty all night and want to get to bed!"

On the 11th, Lieutenant F. McCallum, M.C., and Second Lieutenants J. Wood and R. Thomson reported for duty. On the 14th the Corps Commander distributed medal ribbons to the 154th Brigade.

The Battalion again went up into the line by daylight in relief of the 7th Black Watch in the Oppy sector on 16th June. On the 18th, Second Lieutenant P. Gray and five other ranks were killed by a trench-mortar bomb. On the 23rd, on relief by the 5th Seaforths, the 4th went back—again by daylight and without casualties—to Balmoral Camp at Ecurie, in Divisional reserve.

On 4th July the Battalion relieved the 6th Black Watch in the Gavrelle sector, leaving behind No. 2 Platoon and No. 4 Company, which had been practising for a raid that was cancelled later on. On the 7th some excitement was caused by the arrest at the Headquarters of No. 2 Company of a supposed spy. He proved in the end to be an officer of a Labour Company! Abnormal train movement behind the enemy lines was remarked on 10th July. On the 11th the Battalion went to billets in Maroeuil, being relieved by the 54th Battalion of Canadian Infantry.

That a little learning is a dangerous thing needs no great exemplification, yet the following instance is too good to be omitted. In the station hotel at a town behind the lines some young officers attending the Divisional School found a charming barmaid, dressed in a Black Watch tartan blouse. One of them who belonged to that regiment began to tell her that they were both wearing the Black Watch tartan—"Le tartan du Black Watch, vous compris; du Montre Noir, compris, Montre, Montre"—and to emphasize the "watch" he tapped his wrist-watch. Naturally the poor girl was mystified: she knew no English, so "Pardon, monsieur, je vais apporter un dictionnaire," and away she tripped and came back smiling with a small pocket dictionary. The poor French scholar looked very small when one of the Seaforths pulled him out of his difficulties by explaining to the girl that he meant that the design of her blouse was the same as that of the kilts of the famous Scots regiment known as the "Garde Noire," which was the best French he could make out of "Black Watch."

On 12th July the Battalion moved by rail to Monchy-le-Breton, where it was joined by Lieutenant C. M. McEwing and a draft of thirty-eight other ranks. On the 14th it entrained at Bryas for an unknown destination. The whole of the following day was spent in the train, and on the 16th it arrived early in the morning at Nogent, whence it proceeded in a motor convoy to near Chouilly, where it debused at 2 P.M. Here it formed part of the Fifth French Army. For the rest of the day it lay in a wood close by, and at night had orders to billet in Chouilly. The billets, however, proved insufficient, and the Battalion bivouacked under a half-hour's notice to move, while the transport went on by road to Avise. It was bombed during the night and lost eight wounded.

On 17th July the Battalion remained in bivouacs, in readiness to support the 131st French Colonial Division, which counter-attacked the Germans at 11 A.M. There it stayed till 5 P.M. on the 18th, when it moved up to a wood about a mile away.

On the 19th the 4th Seaforths were called out at 6 A.M. to a clearing in the wood north of Champillon, moving by road. In the evening they went into the line: there was heavy shelling, and one man was killed, another wounded, and a third accidentally hurt.

The new battle area was the western edge of the Montagne de Rheims, the great massif that the Germans had tried to seize, so as to turn the southern defences of Rheims and dominate the valley of the Marne. The German advance had been stopped a little to the west of Nanteuil-la-Fosse, and it was here, in the valley of the Ardre, that the 51st and 62nd Divisions were ordered to attack, the latter being on the right.

The northern boundary of the 51st Division was formed by the Ardre, a stream running north to join the Vesle and little more than a ditch at the point where the attack began. Steep, densely wooded hills rose on either side to a height of two to three hundred feet. On the Divisional front the Bois de Courton, spreading south-west for 3000 yards, and north-west (the direction of the attack) for 3500, offered the most formidable obstacle to progress. The hamlets of Espilly, Les Haies and Nappes were strong points of resistance, but the whole valley was full of difficult ground, being cut up by banks, small glens and sunken roads, and dotted with farms and other buildings. The fields were, moreover, full of standing corn, so that there was ideal cover for the enemy's machine guns. Added to this, the Bois de Courton was daily drenched with gas, and the shell fire recalled that on the Somme and at Arras.

Instructions received before the attack began stated that the Germans appeared to be retiring on a wide front, covered by rearguards, and the advance was to be made to a depth of from a mile to a mile and a quarter. The enemy, however, proved to be holding stubbornly to his positions.

The 154th Brigade attacked on the right and the 153rd on the left, each on a one-battalion front. The assembly was delayed by congestion on the routes leading up to it, and the Battalion did not reach its position till 4 A.M. The French guides, who belonged to a battalion that had come into the area only the day before, had very little knowledge of the lie of the land; nor were matters improved by the fact that the maps used were French, supplemented by a few rough sketches issued by Divisional Headquarters.

The attack was launched by the 4th Seaforths at 8 A.M.

They drove in and captured the enemy posts and advanced to the crest of the ridge running south-west from Bullin Farm to the Bois de Courton, where they were checked by heavy machine-gun fire from the Bois de l'Aulnay and Marfaux.

By 9 A.M. No. 1 Company had reached a point 100 yards north-west of Bullin Farm, while No. 2, mistaking Marfaux for Chaumuzy, had gone too far to the right. No. 4 had lost touch with the others and pushed down the forward slope of the crest on which machine-gun fire had first checked it, till it reached the cross-roads 500 yards east of Espilly. Half of No. 3 Company had moved up from support to reinforce No. 4, whose advance had been made with great difficulty, and half went to fill the gaps between Nos. 1 and 4. Touch had been completely lost with the 6th Black Watch in the 153rd Brigade, and the 4th Gordons were sent up into the gap shortly after 9 A.M. They at once became involved in heavy fighting. By noon the Battalion front was slightly withdrawn to the sunken road running south from Marfaux. To the right of Bullin Farm a defensive front was formed facing the river, beyond which the ground in front of the 185th Infantry Brigade was still in the enemy's hands, for the 62nd Division had been given the wrong jumping-off position, and so had to retire on its left.

At 1 P.M. the leading companies of the 7th Argyll and Sutherland Highlanders came up, and by 2 o'clock were heavily engaged alongside the 4th Seaforths. All their efforts to advance during the afternoon were frustrated, for machine guns made it impossible even to crawl through two-foot corn, and later on the positions occupied were consolidated. The line was reorganized with the 7th Argyll and Sutherland on the right and the 4th Gordons on the left. As the Officer Commanding the Gordons had become a casualty, Major L. D. Henderson was sent to take command. In the centre a small party of the 4th Seaforths, who had held on to the crest of the ridge, withdrew for a time, but re-established themselves later.

At 4.30 P.M. the enemy bombarded the position and counter-attacked, but was easily repelled by rifle and Lewis-gun fire. Two hours later there was an intense bombardment round Rectangle Wood, followed by a determined attack from two sides, converging on the top of the hill. The Germans got within a hundred yards of the 7th Argyll and Sutherland Highlanders before being completely caught by the flanking fire of the 4th Seaforths. A section of the former then charged the Germans, on which they turned and ran down the hill.

The Brigade had failed to reach its objectives and the casualties had been heavy, for the enemy, instead of fighting a rearguard action, as had been expected, made a very determined defence. It turned out that he had to do this in order to cover his left flank during the retreat across the Marne.

It was at this battle that the 4th Seaforths gained the only V.C. awarded to them during the war. Sergeant John Meikle (Glasgow), who already had been awarded the Military Medal for gallantry in the Battle of the Menin Ridge Road on 20th September, showed most conspicuous bravery and initiative. No. 2 Company were held up by machine-gun fire, when Sergeant Meikle, advancing for some 150 yards, alone, over open ground, rushed one of the machine-gun nests single-handed, emptying his revolver into the crews of the two guns, and putting the remainder of them out of action with a heavy stick. Then, standing up, he waved the company on.

When, later on in the day, another hostile machine gun checked the progress of the company, Meikle found that most of his platoon had become casualties. Undismayed, he seized the rifle and bayonet of a fallen comrade and again rushed forward against the gun crew. He was killed when almost in the gun position, but his bravery enabled two other men who followed him to put the gun out of action.

The resistance continued on the 21st July and the 152nd Infantry Brigade on the left made very little progress. On the night of the 22nd-23rd it took over the Battalion sector, and at 4 A.M. the 4th Seaforths withdrew into reserve at the wood, 500 yards south-east of Bullin Farm. On the left the 7th Argyll and Sutherland Highlanders and the 4th Gordon Highlanders also advanced, and continued to harass the enemy throughout the 24th. Finally a line was reached running from the southern edge of the Bois d'Aulnay to the western edge of the Bois de Courton.

One day an officer, accompanied by one of the sergeants who was supposed to be an adept at French, saw a French soldier making signs to them and shouting. The officer wanted to know what it was all about. "I think he wants to speak to us," said the sergeant. A moment later a battery of "75's" opened fire close to them. "I think he wants to tell us that there's a battery firing here," said the sergeant.

On the night of 24th-25th July the 4th Seaforth Highlanders relieved the 4th Gordon Highlanders, and on the 25th pushed the line forward another 100 yards in the wood. They were again relieved on the night of the 26th-27th by the 6th Black Watch, and went into billets in the Bois de St-Quentin, being shelled while passing through Nanteuil-la-Fosse. On the afternoon of the 27th the Battalion went up to the Bois de Courton, where they bivouacked.

Meanwhile the 152nd and 153rd Brigades had attacked. By 10 A.M. they had gained their objectives, and it was evident that the Germans were at last retiring. The British troops continued to follow them up, covered by mounted patrols that kept in touch with them. Chaumuzy was occupied at about 2 A.M., and the Bois des Eclisses being reported clear of the enemy, the infantry moved forward during the night and occupied the old French line. All along their front line in the Rheims-Soissons salient the Germans were in retreat.

The morning of the 28th was foggy. The 154th Brigade assembled on the Chaumuzy-Nappes road and took over the divisional line in the evening. The right flank of the Battalion was on the western edge of the Montagne de Bligny on the north-western edge of the Bois des Eclisses. The hill was carried on the 29th by the 185th Brigade on the right. At ten o'clock that night there was a gas bombardment. The 30th opened with haze, but later became bright and warm. The after-effects of the gas bombardment caused some sickness in the Battalion, there being forty-five casualties. At 5.50 A.M., after a fifty-minutes' bombardment, the French attacked on the left. The 31st was very warm, and there was harassing shell fire all day. On being relieved by the 3rd Regiment of French Infantry the Battalion moved back to a wood south of Nanteuil, where it bivouacked for the night. On 1st August it went into bivouac in a wood near Champillon, and on the 3rd entrained at Epernay at 6 A.M. The following day it detrained at Bryas, whence it moved in buses—Headquarters with Nos. 1 and 2 Companies to Villers Brulin, Nos. 3 and 4 with the transport to Bethonsart.

When the Battalion was on the Fère-en-Tardenoise front they had the Italians on their right. These had never seen kilts before, and the sight caused a great sensation. This was one of the rare occasions when the rations failed to come up, and the 4th Seaforths drew them from the Italians, the introduction to spaghetti causing a sensation on our side. The Italian rations are said to have been very good and plentiful.

Writing about this time, an officer of the Battalion says: "We had some Battalion sports yesterday. The day, fortunately, was perfect and the Battalion and villagers greatly interested. There was great excitement and keen competition, especially for the best company. We (No. 3) finished off second, which was a lot better than we expected. We also got the football after replays. There was the divisional band there and the massed Brigade pipes and drummers. So the civilians were pleased too, and they were especially delighted with the dancing competition. The sports lasted the whole day, and we had a very pleasant time. One of our lady-killers routed out a couple of sisters from a Casualty Clearing Station near by, so we had a little element of Blighty femininity there too.

"We were in the mess having an after-dinner smoke when in rushes the old dame, about seventy-five years old, in a great state and lugged us all to the door, where she pointed out about a dozen searchlights which were probing the sky away to the west. They were actually the first she had seen and she thought they must be some diabolical invention of the Hun! Poor old lady, she must have kept very early hours not to have seen any before."

On 8th August, Captain and Quartermaster W. M. Eade of the 2/6th Suffolk, with Second Lieutenants T. E. MacGregor, H. C. Miller, L. H. G. Symington, W. R. Cullen, and seventy-one other ranks joined, followed during the next few days by Lieutenant P. W. Mackenzie and Second Lieutenants W. Boardman and J. A. Hogg.

At 3 P.M. on the 15th the Battalion moved by light railway from Savy to Ecurie, the transport going by road. In the evening it relieved the 7th Cameronians in the front line on the right at the Gavrelle sector. As the strength, including the Medical Officer, was only twenty-two officers and three hundred and sixty-two other ranks for a front of 1000 yards, the usual echelon B could not be left, and the Lewis gun officer, the Regimental Sergeant-Major, and a few details were all that could be spared at the transport lines. A few gas shells fell in the Battalion area, but most behind it.

On 17th August two patrols were sent out; one failed and the other succeeded in locating the enemy. On the 19th two more patrols had exactly the same result. On the 20th night patrols found no sign of the enemy in Thames Alley, but elsewhere got into touch with his posts. The next night a patrol heard the enemy at work, but was prevented from further reconnaissance by machine-gun fire. A number of officers meanwhile had joined the Battalion. These were Captain A. Campbell, Lieutenant C. H. Hodgson, Second Lieutenants Green, H. Paterson, C. J. Boyd, F. J. Conway and D. Kennedy. Also Regimental Sergeant-Major Mason and seventy-one other ranks. A large number of officers and other ranks went away for courses at musketry, Lewis gun, bombing and signalling schools.

The 51st Division now formed part of the XVII Corps on the north bank of the Scarpe. South of the river lay the Canadians. When the Battle of the Scarpe opened the Second Battles of Arras the 51st Division was placed under the command of the Canadian Corps, and it had been arranged that when the Canadians passed Monchy-le-Preux the 51st should carry its line forward in conformity with their advance.

On 25th August, in preparation for the morrow, No. 3 Company moved up from the support trench and took over part of the front line from the battalion on its right. It then advanced some 1000 yards with the attacking units and formed a defensive flank on their left. There was constant sniping, and finally a counter-attack compelled this flank to fall back.

In the early morning of the 26th the advanced position was retaken by No. 3 Company. At 10.30 A.M. the 152nd and 153rd Infantry Brigades advanced, the 6th Black Watch being on the right of the 4th Seaforths. This day No. 2 Company advanced past No. 3 to a depth of 500 yards, thus prolonging the defensive flank, which was stabilized by 1.30 P.M. At 7 P.M., in conjunction with the troops on the right, No. 4 carried the flank beyond No. 2, the movement being completed at 9.40.P.M. In the meanwhile No. 3 Company had reorganized in depth behind Nos. 2 and 4, on the right of the Gavrelle road, while No. 1 prolonged the flank on the left of that road, in advance of the old front line. On their left they were in touch with the 7th Argyll and Sutherland Highlanders, who had "side-stepped" to the right as the 4th Seaforths moved forward. During the day parties of Germans could be seen retreating along the Gavrelle-Fresnes road. By night the two advanced companies sent forward strong patrols through Gavrelle, which established advanced posts in trenches to the east of the village without opposition.

The advanced posts were driven in on the morning of the 27th, but were soon re-established. The line was pushed forward another 500 yards this day, and the Battalion was relieved at night. The two other brigades of the Division had been operating on the familiar battle-ground about Roeux and the Chemical Works, and the 154th Brigade took their place in the attack on Greenland Hill next day. The 4th Seaforths, who were relieved by the 2nd East Lancashires, lay in dug-outs in the Arras-Bailleul railway cutting, just north of the Scarpe.

On 28th August the Battalion was in support of the 4th Gordons and 7th Argyll and Sutherland in the assault on Greenland Hill, but there was little or no resistance. Two companies were with Battalion Headquarters and two further in advance. The attack began at 6.30 A.M. on the 29th and was carried farther by the front line on the 30th, but the 4th Seaforths were not called on to go into action. Ground that a year before had cost so much blood was now taken with trifling casualties. The enemy withdrew to the Rouvroy-Fresnes line, north-east of Plouvain.

Writing from the 51st Division School, an officer of the Battalion describes the appearance of German prisoners: "A huge drove of Boche prisoners came down the road; close on 6000, with 50 officers. They were without exception the most cheerful lot of prisoners I've yet seen, and seemed downright pleased to be prisoners. An old French dame, who has lived on the edge of the war here for four years now, stood and jibed at them: 'Ah, promenade à Paris! Ah, la guerre est fini!' and so on, and they turned and laughed back at her, and occasionally returned her an answer. They were very young, most of them, and a lot of small fellows, but they were clean, and obviously had not done much scrapping. And the escort said there were thousands more in the cages. And now our boys have gone forward for four or five miles easily, taken positions we scrapped mightily for, when I came out here last year, at practically no cost at all. Everyone is mightily hopeful, and that for reasons we can't let you know."

On 1st September the 4th Seaforths relieved the 7th Argyll and Sutherland in the front line on the left of the Greenland Hill sector. The following night they were themselves relieved by the 1/5th York and Lancaster, and went back to Wakefield

Map 17.

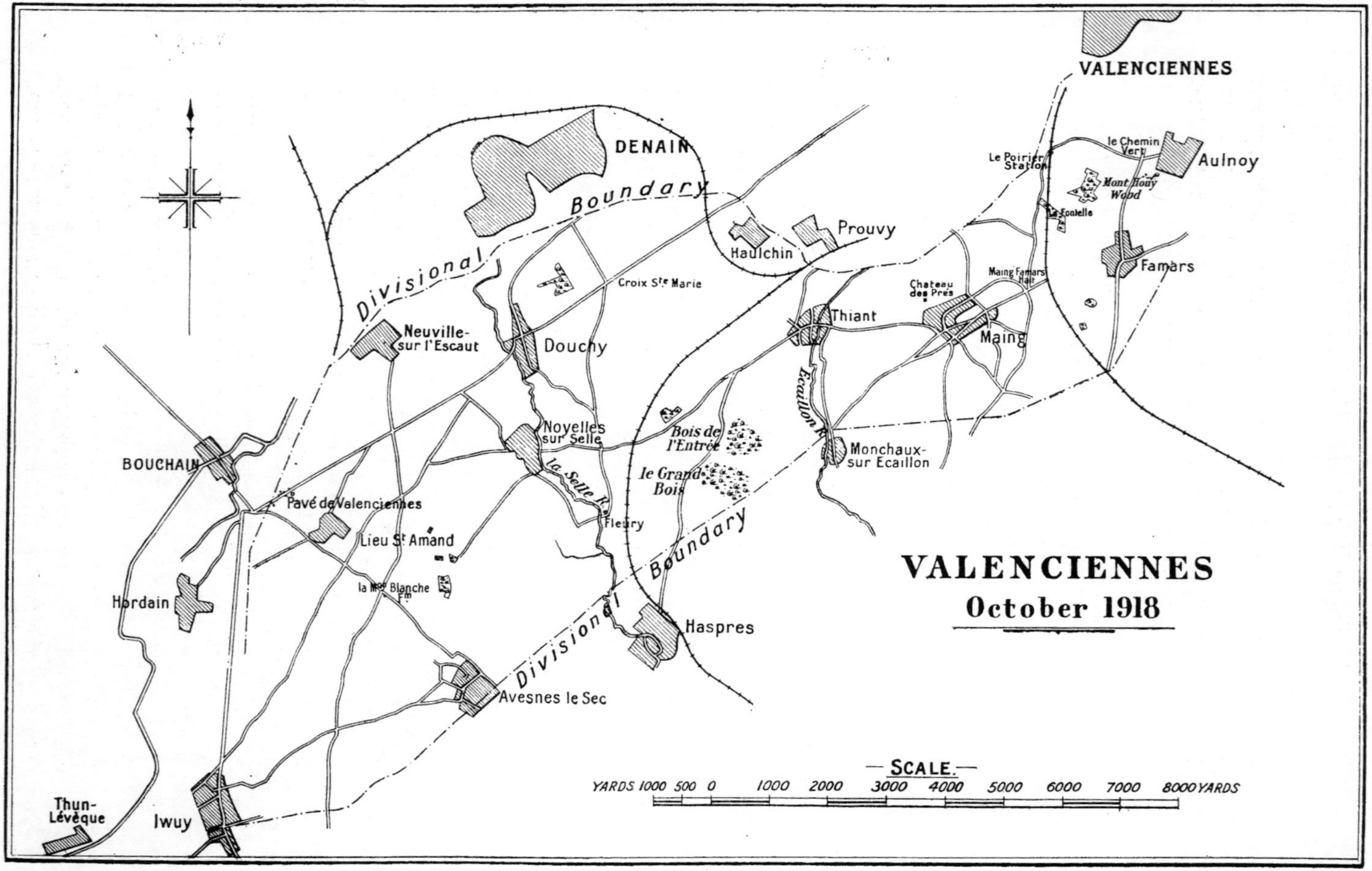
VALENCIENNES
October 1918
VALENCIENNES
DENAIN
Divisional Boundary
Divisional Boundary
le Chemin Vert
Aulnoy
Le Poirier Station
Mont Houy Wood
La Fontelle
Famars
Prouvy
Haulchin
Croix Ste Marie
Maing Famars Halt
Chateau des Prés
Thiant
Maing
Neuville-sur l'Escaut
Douchy
Ecaillon R.
Noyelles sur Selle
Bois de l'Entrée
Monchaux-sur Ecaillon
BOUCHAIN
la Selle R.
le Grand Bois
Pavé de Valenciennes
Fleury
Lieu St Amand
la Mon Blanche Fm
Hordain
Haspres
Avesnes le Sec
SCALE.
YARDS 1000 500 0 1000 2000 3000 4000 5000 6000 7000 8000 YARDS
Thun-Lévêque
Iwuy

Camp, near Roclincourt, where the 154th Brigade was in Divisional reserve. On 4th September a welcome reinforcement of two hundred and ten other ranks came up from the Base. On the 11th the 49th Division relieved the 51st in the line and the Battalion went to Lancaster Camp, Mont St-Eloy, in very bad weather.

The Battalion again went up to Greenland Hill, in relief of the 1/5th York and Lancaster, on the 24th. On the 27th patrols located the enemy, losing two men. The Adjutant, Captain W. Surrey Dane, M.C., went on leave.

The 2nd Rifle Brigade relieved the 4th Seaforths on the night of the 1st-2nd October, and they embused at Athies for Lancaster Camp, where a draft of eighty-one other ranks joined them. On the 7th they again embused, but did not start till 9 P.M. They debused on arrival at Inchy at 4 A.M. on the 8th. Next day, Second Lieutenant Clark and the Battalion scouts reconnoitred the roads to Bourlon for the transport. On the 10th the Battalion moved to Neuville St-Remy, a suburb of Cambrai, where it relieved a battalion of the 3rd Canadian Division.

The Battalion, now under the command of Major L. D. Henderson, moved into the line in front of Iwuy at 10 P.M. on 11th October, relieving the 27th Battalion of Canadian Infantry. Headquarters were in the village. There was much shelling, but the only casualties were in the ration party.

Early the next morning two Germans were found hiding in cellars in the village. The Corps attacked at noon. On the Divisional front the 152nd Brigade advanced on the right and the 154th on the left. Nos. 1, 2 and 3 Companies were in Battalion front line and No. 4 in support. The objective was the village of Avesnes-le-Sec and a line half-way along the road to Lieu-St-Amand, and thence to a point on the railway north-east of Hordain, the jumping-off position being about 1000 yards north-east of Iwuy.

There was little opposition until the crest of the ridge, about 100 yards from the objective, was reached. Here heavy machine-gun fire was encountered, but the companies rushed the objective and consolidated the position. Other units were unable to get through the machine-gun fire on the left in the attempt to carry Lieu-St-Amand. The disposition of the Brigade at night was 4th Seaforths on the right, 7th Argyll and Sutherland on the left. All the divisional objectives were taken.

The casualties were: killed, 5 other ranks; wounded, 61 other ranks.

The line was readjusted, Nos. 3 and 4 Companies being in front line and the other two in support.

The position held by the Division protected the left flank of the British troops on the line of the River Selle and covered Cambrai from the north; for although an enemy counter-attack was improbable, every precaution was taken to strengthen the main line of resistance. The protection of the left flank of the Third Army was, therefore, the principal duty of the Division, the capture of the high ground east of the Selle being of minor importance.

On 13th October the enemy put down a very heavy barrage, his aeroplanes harassed the divisional lines, and he opened intense machine-gun fire. In conjunction with the 49th Division attacks were made on Lieu-St-Amand and Noyelles-sur-Selle; but as instructions were definite that no advance was to be made unless the enemy were retreating, and his machine-gun and artillery fire showed that such was not his intention, the advance was stayed, although No. 3 Company took La Maison Blanche Farm in spite of very heavy fire. The Germans were active all day, shelling the Battalion area with high-velocity and gas shells. Three German machine guns were taken.

On 14th October the enemy got three direct hits on to Battalion Headquarters. Second Lieutenant Clark and the Artillery Liaison Officer were killed and Lieutenant-Colonel Hopkinson was wounded. The Acting Adjutant, Captain A. Campbell, was gassed, and there were several casualties among other ranks. Captain G. W. H. Macpherson assumed command, and Lieutenant D. E. F. MacGregor took over the duties of Adjutant. On relief by the 6th Argyll and Sutherland of the 153rd Brigade the Battalion withdrew to billets in Thun St-Martin, after a most unfortunate day.

On 15th October, the Brigade being in Divisional reserve, Major L. D. Henderson, M.C., again took over command of the Battalion. On the 17th the 154th relieved the 152nd Brigade, the 4th Seaforths taking the place of the 6/7th Gordon Highlanders in Brigade reserve.

Orders were issued for the 51st Division to attack on 20th October, in order to protect the flank of the 4th Division, which was to attack on the right. The enemy, however, having withdrawn from the front of the Canadian Corps on the left, abandoned Bouchain and Lieu-St-Amand on the 19th, and orders were thereon issued to advance to the line Fleury-Noyelles-Douchy.

The Brigade therefore advanced, the 4th Gordon Highlanders on the right, the 7th Argyll and Sutherland Highlanders on the left, and the 4th Seaforth Highlanders in reserve. The troops moved in artillery formation, with patrols out in front. At 11 P.M. on the 19th the 4th Seaforths were marching on Noyelles. After crossing the Selle they formed up about 100 yards from the bank, and at 5.20 A.M. on 20th October moved forward under heavy fire from two machine guns in position about 300 yards to the left of Mont Rouge Farm. No. 1 Company moved to the right and gained dead ground, and the machine guns withdrew to positions behind the railway embankment. Sergeant Morrison of No. 1 Company disabled one of the machine guns with a rifle bullet at 500 yards range and so the company was able to reach the sunken road. Here they filled up a gap between the other two battalions and established a line.

Instructions were received to secure the bridge-heads over the Ecaillon that night. Nos. 2 and 4 Companies, which were in support, sent out patrols beyond the railway and established a line of posts in front of Le Grand Bois and Le Bois de l'Entrée. Heavy machine-gun fire made it impossible to reach the river. In a house entered by one of these patrols there was a fire burning and food still warm.

At 7 A.M. on 21st October the Battalion went forward on the right of the 7th Argyll and Sutherland. Nos. 2 and 4 Companics took up positions beyond the woods, consolidation being assisted by the deep shell holes made by the delaycd-action fuses of our artillery. Lieutenant J. A. Hermon took out a patrol and gained touch with the 4th Division on the right.

At 8 A.M. the leading company of the 7th Argyll and Sutherland Highlanders was in Thiant, and found the enemy holding the village east of the river. The 4th Seaforths, however, came under very hot machine-gun fire from Monchaux and the opposite slopes above the river, and were unable to advance.

The advance of the Canadians had crushed the 153rd Brigade out, and they now covered its front on the left.

Late in the afternoon the front companies moved forward and

scouts were sent out to reconnoitre the river. Corporal Jack of No. 1 Company returned with only one man of his patrol. They had got to within thirty yards of a bridge when a machine gun opened on them. Corporal Jack gallantly tried to bring in his wounded, but was forced to leave them. Another patrol, under Corporal Sutherland, brought back valuable information about the condition of the bridges over the river. They had all been blown up and the enemy was in strength on the other side. Thiant and Monchaux, which had been reported clear, were still in the hands of the enemy. The Battalion therefore withdrew to its position in front of the woods.

Second Lieutenant Murdo Mackenzie, the Transport Officer, who had been Transport Sergeant under Captain Pat Macintyre, continued to carry on the tradition set by him. When the Battalion was facing the Germans on the other side of the Ecaillon he never failed to bring up a ration of hot porridge for breakfast. He also did good work by evacuating women and children from the danger zone in the officers' cart.

It was now decided that the 153rd Brigade should force the passage of the river, with artillery support. Because the villages were crowded with friendly civilians the artillery had been ordered not to fire on them unless it were unavoidable. The 153rd Brigade forced the passage of the Ecaillon on 24th October. The fighting was severe, for the passage had to be made on light bridges or by swimming, and there was a line of wire on the east bank. The 153rd Brigade pushed on and took Maing during the night of the 24th.

On relief the 4th Seaforths went back to Douchy. On the afternoon of 23rd October they moved up to the outskirts of Denain, and were billeted in a mill on the Canal de l'Escaut. Denain was shelled on the 24th.

On 25th October the 154th Brigade was at the tactical disposal of the 152nd, and the 4th Seaforths moved to a position between the railway lines south-west of Haulchin in support of the attacking troops. The 152nd and 153rd Brigades advanced the line, and repulsed heavy counter-attacks between Maing and Famars. On the 26th Famars was taken.

Writing of this part of the country, one of the officers says: "The villages here are quite respectable, houses whole and quite comfortable, and billets quite decent. There are also a good number of civilians just liberated from a four-year domination by the Boche, and as yet they don't quite seem to realize their freedom. They were cowed, timid creatures when we first came here, but are improving now and getting a bit of life. They'd been kept in the cellars while the Boche had the house. He took away all their bedding and all the clothes they had, except what they actually wore and what they had concealed by burying in their gardens and elsewhere. He even took the food with which the American Commission supplied them and gave them his own diluted and artificial stuff. He confined them to their own villages and imprisoned them if they left their boundaries without a pass. The woman in my house has not seen her husband for four years and has so far heard no word of him since July, but she's living in hopes of his turning up one of these fine days.

"They lived in terror of us officers the first few days, but now are quite normal, and are only too keen to talk to us and tell us all their experiences. It's a rare sight to see our boys helping them, wheeling barrows for the refugees, and helping the old people across the rickety bridges constructed over the ruins of those the Boche blew up.

"It's pitiful to see the clamouring crowds of puny, thin, white-faced kiddies, who cluster round the cookers at food times. They've taken properly to porridge, and throng in shoals round the remnants in the porridge dixies.

"Still the time is good and the advance continues, and the folk here are now even spirited enough to jeer at their late oppressors when they pass here as prisoners. The pipes, too, cheer them up, and the band is always sure to get a rare welcome.

"The Battalion did a rare good advance and with really few casualties."

The Battalion moved into the line at 4 A.M. on 27th October, in relief of the 6th Argyll and Sutherland Highlanders, under heavy artillery and machine-gun fire. The position faced Mont Huy Wood, and was occupied by Nos. 1, 2 and 4 Companies in front line and No. 3 in support. Headquarters were at the Château de Pres.

While Headquarters were at the Château, an old woman, who was probably about eighty, though she claimed to be ninety, came in. Whenever gas shells came over she would rub her nose, laughing all the time. All night through she sat drinking tea, with which Headquarters supplied her.

At 5.10 on the morning of 28th October 1918 the 4th Seaforths launched the last attack they were to make. The enemy front was full of machine-gun nests, but they were overcome, and the main objectives reached along a line 100 yards beyond the road from Poirier station to Aulnoy. The right company established a line through Mont Huy Wood; the centre company passed the left of the wood and dealt with the enemy north of Le Chemin Vert; and the left company reached a position 400 yards north of Poirier station after putting the machine guns opposed to it out of action with trench mortars. No. 3 Company from the support passed through No. 1 in Mont Huy Wood to a position between the cross-roads at Le Chemin Vert and No. 2 Company farther north. The front of all companies was very weak, and the advanced positions were flanked by enemy machine-gun posts.

After taking one hundred and eighty prisoners and twenty-one machine guns the Battalion was counter-attacked with great determination and driven back to the southern outskirts of the wood. The 7th Argyll and Sutherland were, therefore, sent up in support, and the two battalions drove off further counter-attacks and consolidated the positions. That night the 6th Argyll and Sutherland relieved the 4th Seaforths, who went back to Maing, whence they proceeded on the 29th to Denain Mill. That day the 51st Division was relieved by the Canadians, and went into billets at Escadoeuvres, a suburb of Cambrai.

Regimental Sergeant-Major Alexander had a party of German prisoners collected at a farmhouse after the last action. They were a miserable lot—cooks, transport, and all kinds of odds and ends. He was trying to drill them in English. One had a piece of black bread which he was wolfing. The Sergeant-Major made him a sign to hurry up and finish it, on which the poor fellow held it out with both hands—a kind of peace-offering!

Valenciennes fell on 6th November. On the 8th the Battalion welcomed back to command Lieutenant-Colonel Unthank, who thus returned in time to share with the Battalion that he had led so long and so well the rejoicings at the declaration of the Armistice at 11 A.M. on 11th November 1918.

The casualties during the fighting on the Selle were:

OFFICERS

Killed: Lieutenant P. H. Ballantyne, Second Lieutenants W. D. Armstrong, F. S. Clark, King's Liverpool Regiment, W. Boardman, D.C.M.

Wounded: Lieutenant-Colonel J. O. Hopkinson, D.S.O., M.C., Lieutenants C. L. Gordon, H. C. Bessent, C. Dickson, W. R. Cullen, Second Lieutenants J. A. Hogg, P. H. M. Mackay.

Missing: Lieutenant J. A. Hermon, Second Lieutenant C. J. Boyd.

OTHER RANKS

Killed: 30. *Wounded*: 192.

DINGWALL: THE FONTAINE-NOTRE-DAME CROSS

CHAPTER XIV

IN THE ARMY OF OCCUPATION

THE signing of the Armistice was followed by a period of clearing up and salvaging—a monotonous anticlimax to the stirring history of the last three months. Every effort was made to relieve the day's work by the encouragement of games, cross-country runs and evening entertainments. The Battalion did well in the Divisional cross-country runs, taking second place on one occasion and fourth on another. At this time, too, the Army Educational Scheme, intended to fit the soldier for civil employment, came into force.

On 11th January 1919 the Battalion moved in buses to Houdeng-Aimeries, in Belgium, where the civil population, on whom they were billeted, could not do enough for them. On the 28th the Prince of Wales visited the place.

Volunteers and men liable for service in the Army of Occupation were mustered on 8th February, and on the 28th the Battalion entrained to join the 62nd Division. It detrained at Meckernich on the 28th and marched to billets in Embken and Ginnick, where it became part of the 187th Brigade. On 6th March it went—partly by route march, partly by train—to Golzheim, where there was a muster parade of men transferred from the 5th and 6th Seaforths to the 4th.

On 17th March the 62nd was renamed the Highland Division.

During April, Colonel Sandilands took over command of the Battalion from Lieutenant-Colonel Unthank, who thus severed his long and honourable connexion with the 4th Seaforth Highlanders.

It fell to Lieutenant-Colonel Unthank's lot to command the Battalion throughout its two most glorious years, and his record is written in the distinguished part played by it at Cambrai and—although he himself had just left it—in the dour stand of the Battalion on the Beaumetz-Morchies line. His wonderful courage and coolness in time of stress, together with his marked ability as a soldier, undoubtedly would have carried him to far higher command than that of a battalion had he studied the art of getting on. A reticent and self-effacing soldier, fearless alike of Germans and "brass hats," he preferred to remain with the Battalion whose interests he had made his own rather than seek self-advancement.

Later on, Lieutenant-Colonel S. Forbes Sharp took over from Colonel Sandilands.

The companies were reorganized at the beginning of May, and on the 12th the Battalion took over a new area at Nideggen, where a ceremonial parade was held in celebration of the King's Birthday.

On 17th June the Battalion moved by rail to Ohligs, to take over perimeter posts in the Lowland Division area, whence they returned to Nideggen on 1st July. Here the signature of peace was celebrated on the 8th, and on the 15th and 16th the Battalion held very successful sports, at which the band of the 3rd King's Own Hussars played.

On the 19th the Battalion, less two companies, went by rail to Lendersdorf, to take over Brigade duties from the 6th Black Watch. No. 1 Company was sent to Herbesthal for duty on train guards, and No. 4 to Bogheim to make a rifle range.

On the 20th the Cadre Party departed with the colours, and on 11th August the Battalion started on its homeward journey *via* Calais and Folkestone, reaching Brocton Camp, in Staffordshire, on the 13th.

The 4th Battalion remained at Brocton, undergoing the process of gradual demobilization, leave being freely granted to enable men to find employment. Finally, on Wednesday, 15th October 1919, all that was left of the Battalion as a unit arrived in Dingwall at 12.35 P.M. This cadre was under the command of Lieutenant-Colonel S. Forbes Sharp, M.C., and comprised the Adjutant, Captain R. M. Bessent, Captain D. E. F. MacGregor, M.C., Lieutenant and Quartermaster Murdoch, Second Lieutenant H. C. Miller and Second Lieutenant M. Mackenzie, M.C.—the last two carrying the colours—together with fifty-two other ranks.

Headed by the pipes and drums, and followed by a large gathering of people, the cadre marched through the High Street to the Municipal Buildings, where they were welcomed by Bailie Crawford, in the name of the Burgh.

After Lieutenant-Colonel Forbes Sharp had returned thanks for the speech of welcome he committed the colours of the Battalion to the temporary care of the town.

The party was thereafter entertained at luncheon by the Burgh at the National Hotel. Bailie Crawford presided, and among those present were Brigadier-General Sir Walter Ross of Cromarty, Seaforth and Mrs Stewart-Mackenzie, Colonels Mason-MacFarlane, Cuthbert and A. F. Mackenzie of Ord. After the usual loyal toasts and speeches the meeting broke up, and the 4th Battalion The Seaforth Highlanders, after five years of war service, was demobilized.

The Rev. J. Macleod, late Chaplain to the Forces, writes: "It is a privilege to 'lay a small stone on the cairn' of men who were true and heroes all. We are proud of them and we want to live up to them and to be worthy of them all. The story which is narrated in this volume can only partially unfold the noble part that they played in the great struggle for right and truth; but it will distinctly establish that the fair fame of the Seaforth Highlanders has received fresh lustre by their exploits. It was in the memorable days of the winter of 1914 that I joined them as their Chaplain, and it was my good fortune to serve with them in the fire zone for over two years. During that time, as I witnessed the cruel and ghastly work, which now appears as a grim nightmare, I was oftentimes moved beyond words to wonder and admiration at the most sublime obedience to duty and service they manifested. They were never embittered by their experiences: on the contrary the sunshine of their mind was invariably in evidence, even when exhausted, dirty, famishing. Their enthusiasm kept them fresh, hopeful, joyful, and even at the darkest they anticipated a good time coming. Under the most trying circumstances they manifested the real heroism and congeniality which safeguarded the best traditions and honour of the British soldier."

Thus ends a magnificent record. A very distinguished man of science once said to the writer that the two most terrible engines of destruction ever made by man were the 51st and the 15th Divisions, both Scottish and both distinguished by the same figures: it is a record that the people of Ross may be proud of, that their Battalion served in both of these divisions, so feared by the enemy and so famous for all time.

And so, as the sagamen would say, "they are out of the story." From the days of that first call to arms on 4th August 1914 to that of handing over their colours to the custody of the County Town on 15th October 1919 they had been through a time of strain such as has probably never before been known in the history of the world. In the retrospect it is hard to say whether those five years were the longest or the shortest in our lives. Yet for most of us, when all is said, despite grief at the loss of many that we loved, despite the strain that for ever separated us from our youth, despite the horrors that we saw and heard of, they were the happiest in our lives.

It is by no means impossible that the nation may again be called to take up arms in defence of things vital to existence. Neither Leagues of Nations nor the most genuine wish for peace can guarantee us against that need. Only the strong man armed can keep his house; and it is the duty of the men of Ross to remember of what blood they are, what proud record they have to sustain, to be ready when the time comes to bear their part as worthily as the men of Neuve Chapelle, of Arras, of Cambrai, of the Beaumetz trenches and the lowlands by the Lawe.

CHAPTER XV

LIST OF HONOURS AND AWARDS

GAINED BY OFFICERS AND OTHER RANKS WHO SERVED IN THE 1/4TH BATTALION THE SEAFORTH HIGHLANDERS

NOTE.—This list is arranged in order of the date of notification of honours and awards in the *London Gazette.* While every effort has been made to ensure accuracy, it is impossible to claim that the list is wholly correct or complete. In many cases, especially in those of honours gained when the recipient was not serving with the 1/4th Battalion, it has been difficult to get the correct dates. Honours gained while serving with other units have, for the most part, been shown separately under the heading "OTHER DATES," whether the actual date happened to be known or not, and whether the recipients originally belonged to the Battalion or not. The rank given is, when possible, that held at the time of notification. Within the dates names of officers and other ranks are arranged alphabetically, under the honour awarded, each within their own list, without regard to rank.

1915

8th April. C.M.G., Mason-MacFarlane, Lieutenant-Colonel D. J.
D.S.O., Cuthbert, Major T. W.

3rd June. D.C.M., 657, Maclennan, Sergeant J.; 1272, Macleod, Lance-Corporal A.; 2110, Minchin, Private W.; 2399, Thomson, Private A.

25th August. ORDER OF ST GEORGE (Russia), 3rd class, 2281, Macrae, Lance-Corporal G. W.

29th November. D.C.M., 2251, Robertson, Sergeant H. J.

1916

14th January. D.C.M., 1652, Mackenzie, Sergeant A.; 2303, Rogers, Lance-Sergeant A.

24th February. CROIX DE GUERRE, 1652, Mackenzie, Sergeant A.
C.M.G., Cuthbert, Lieutenant-Colonel T. W.

3rd June. M.C., Henderson, Captain L. D.
D.C.M., 333, Cumming, Regimental Quartermaster-Sergeant T.

21st September. M.M., 1201, Hendry, Sergeant W.; 3045, Hendry, Private W.; 1015, Munro, Sergeant D.

16th November. M.M., 1461, Mackenzie, Private R.

1917

1st January. M.C., Peverell, Captain T. H.

22nd January. M.M., 2039, File, Private C. E.; 200821, Gardiner, Lance-Corporal G.; 201608, Hancock, Private D.; 201379, Ireland, Private W.; 4038, McPherson, Lance-Corporal W.; 2222, Milton, Private T.; 3798, Moore, Private M. A.

18th June. M.M., 202727, Grubb, Private J.; 3730, Maclennan, Private G.; 1366, Macleod, Corporal W.; 201561, Moir, Lance-Corporal A.; 3851, Rankin, Private R.; 1418, Ross, Sergeant J.; 1664, Sutherland, Lance-Corporal D.

8th July. M.C., MacGregor, Lieutenant D. E. F.

9th July. BAR TO M.M., 200821, Gardiner, Lance-Corporal G.; 2533, Lane, Sergeant C. S.

M.M., 201471, Baker, Private A. W.; 200794, Beattie, Corporal W.; 3160, Brown, Private W.; 3963, Carmichael, Private W.; 3474 Cawtheray, Sergeant G.; 200146, Fraser, Private W.; 261215, Greenwood, Lance-Corporal H.; 201292, Mackenzie, Corporal J.; 1750, Mackenzie, Sergeant M.; 1758, Maclennan, Private A.; 1814, Macpherson, Private K.; 1321, Murdoch, Corporal W.

13th July. MÉDAILLE MILITAIRE (France), 200785, Campbell, Sergeant J.

17th July. M.C., Hay-Will, Captain R. H.; Wells, Second Lieutenant T.

D.C.M., 200785, Campbell, Sergeant J.

M.M., 4551, Seaton, Private H.

18th July. D.C.M., 201290, Gray, Sergeant D.

20th September. PROMOTED SERGEANT ON THE FIELD, 12515, Macdonald, Private H.

26th September. M.C., Addison, Captain D.; Bain, Second Lieutenant J.

6th October. M.M., 200099, Ross, Sergeant J.

18th October. M.M., 4600, Dawson, Sergeant A.; 201446, Hamilton, Private J.; 5108, Mackay, Private A.; 201363, Malone, Private J.; 6175, Parkin, Private J.; 201757, Philben, Private J.; 201307, Stewart, Private P.

19th November. M.C., Brown, Lieutenant F. W.; Fraser, Captain A. K.; Macdonald, Captain A. M. (See 22. 4. 18.)

D.C.M., 202196, Ross, Sergeant A.; 265769, Stewart, Private J.

12th December. BAR TO D.C.M., 200785, Campbell, Sergeant J.; 201290, Gray, Sergeant D.

M.M., 243396, Bannerman, Private D.; 200602, Bolton, Corporal A. J.; 200208, Fraser, Sergeant W.; 202664, Gardner, Sergeant J. G.; 240752, Gunn, Private G.; 10835, Lawton, Private D. J.; 202649, Louttit, Private W.; 1772, Macdonald, Private F.; 241719, McIver, Private C. M.; 13479, Mackenzie, Private D. P.; 201880, Mackenzie, Corporal E.; 1650, Macleod, Corporal R.; 200854, Meikle, Private J.; 203263, Mitchell, Private D.; 201832, Morrison, Private A.; 240065, Murray, Private D. W.; 10865, Ross, Private A. A.; 200439, Ross, Sergeant J.; 757, Smith, Company Quartermaster-Sergeant W.; 200021, Sutherland, Sergeant T.; 6229, Toothill, Sergeant J.; 3790, Veighey, Private A.; 201886, Ward, Private T.

20th December. M.C., Coutts, Lieutenant D. G.

1918

1st January. D.S.O., Unthank, Lieutenant-Colonel J. S.

D.C.M., 1016, Macdonald, Sergeant A.

28th January. M.M., 266030, Main, Lance-Corporal J. A.; 517212, Macdonald, Private C.

4th February. M.C., Campbell, Lieutenant D.

6th February. D.C.M., 43210, Pierce, Acting Regimental Sergeant-Major.

22nd February. BAR TO D.C.M., 2110, Minchin, Lance-Sergeant W.

SECOND BAR TO M.M., 200821, Gardiner, Lance-Corporal G.

BAR TO M.M., 200602, Bolton, Corporal A. J.; 261215, Greenwood, Lance-Corporal H.; 2222, Milton, Private T.

23rd February. M.M., 201795, Donaldson, Lance-Corporal H.; 204310, Forbes, Sergeant A. M.; 202934, Foster, Private T.; 200975, MacCormick, Sergeant W.; 1729, Mackenzie, Private A.; 202205, Mackenzie, Private S.; 200602, Macpherson, Sergeant J.; 200547, Morrison, Lance-Sergeant A.; 6650, Munro, Lance-Corporal C.; 200372, Munro, Corporal W.; 2895, Oldham, Private F.; 201390, Overend, Corporal W.; 201160, Scurrah, Corporal G.; 201425, Telfer, Lance-Corporal A. C.; 200869, Thompson, Lance-Sergeant A. B.; 204146, Wells, Private W. P.

13th March. M.M., 1753, Macdonald, Private D.

22nd March. D.S.O., Jackson, Captain D. B. M.; Munro, Second Lieutenant A.

M.C., Davidson, Second Lieutenant J.

28th March. D.C.M., 200050, McGregor, Company Sergeant-Major S.; 201337, Ross, Lance-Sergeant A.

1st April. LONG SERVICE MEDAL, Glass, Captain and Quartermaster J.

22nd April. D.S.O., Macdonald, Captain A. M. (in substitution of *Gazette* of 19th November 1917).

3rd June. M.C., Macaulay, Lieutenant A.

D.C.M., 201174, Ward, Company Sergeant-Major J. E.

17th June. M.S.M., 1784, Davidson, Sergeant D. D.; 200201, Duff, Sergeant D.; 200381, Keyes, Acting Company Sergeant-Major D.

12th July. CROIX DE GUERRE (Belgium), 200219, Fletcher, Sergeant T.

16th July. M.M., 201135, Smyth, Private D.

26th July. D.S.O., Gray, Captain H. P. T.

M.C., Campbell, Lieutenant A. G.; Davie, Captain W. S.; Mackenzie, Second Lieutenant G. L.; Surrey Dane, Captain W.

M.M., 41513, Priest, Private A.

6th August. M.M., 21055, Simpson, Private G.

22nd August. BAR TO M.M., 202664, Gardner, Sergeant J. G.

28th August. M.C., Finigan, Lieutenant A. A.

D.C.M., 3850, Greenhill, Private C.

3rd September. D.C.M., 1681, Grant, Private A. D.

M.M., 41043, Burton, Private D.

16th September. BAR TO D.S.O., Hopkinson, Lieutenant-Colonel J. O.

M.C., Ferguson, Second Lieutenant J. S.; Harris, Captain C. H.

V.C., 200854, Meikle, Sergeant J.

7th October. M.M., 40112, Barron, Private J.; 201733, Bottomley, Lance-Corporal A.; 201196, Carmichael, Corporal V.; 204347, Coulter, Corporal J.; 21807, Couris, Private J.; 22837, Gellatly, Private P.; 200567, Hearne, Corporal A.; 201417, Ibbetson, Private G.; 200581, McAuley, Corporal J.; 200533, Macdonald, Sergeant G.; 201190, Macdonald, Sergeant J.; 201830, Macdonald, Corporal J.; 200232, Maclennan, Lance-Corporal R.; 200169, Macleod, Corporal J.; 202156, Sheard, Private L.; 241033, Truesdale, Private W.

11th October. CROIX DE GUERRE, Clark, Second Lieutenant F. S.

15th October. BAR TO M.C., Campbell, Captain D.; Coutts, Second Lieutenant D. G.; Dundas, Second Lieutenant G.; Henderson, Major L. D.

30th October. D.C.M., 201286, Gilchrist, Sergeant A.; 200022, Mackenzie, Company Sergeant-Major A.; 200114, Mitchell, Sergeant J.; 242351, Tytler, Sergeant A.

2nd December. M.C., Staub, Second Lieutenant T. V.

11th December. BAR TO M.M., 202649, Louttit, Private W.; 200533, Macdonald, Sergeant A.

M.M., 11466, Bain, Private D. A.; 201431, Bilton, Private S.; 241989, Calder, Private J.; 200643, Coleman, Corporal P.; 201781, Cuthwaite, Private A.; 200219, Fraser, Corporal H. S.; 202655, Hall, Private A. E.; 201751, Kellett, Corporal J.; 201517, Kennedy, Lance-Sergeant C.; 203748, McBain, Private W.; 201938, McMillan, Private N.; 22272, Mitchard, Private S.; 200688, Mitchell, Lance-Corporal E.; 201872, Munro, Corporal J.; 266586, Murdoch, Private N. T.; 240312, Murray, Lance-Sergeant C.; 9298, Newby, Private E.; 202763, Rankin, Private R.; 4650, Shiells, Private J.; 41583, Steele, Private C. B.; 200960, Stewart, Corporal J.; 22273, Swansbury, Private T.; 205742, Walker, Corporal G.

1919

1st January. M.S.M., 333, Cumming, Regimental Quartermaster-Sergeant T.; 200134, Gunn, Sergeant J.

D.C.M., 1552, Macdonald, Company Sergeant-Major M.

18th February. D.C.M., 200786, Mackenzie, Company Sergeant-Major D.

BAR TO M.M., 1552, Macdonald, Company Sergeant-Major M.

22nd February. M.S.M., 200599, Ellis, Sergeant G.; 202813, Greig, Acting Company Quartermaster-Sergeant J.

8th March. BAR TO M.C., Bain, Second Lieutenant J.; MacGregor, Lieutenant D. E. F.

M.C., Brown, Second Lieutenant A. B.; Cullen, Lieutenant W. R.; Hay, Second Lieutenant J. W.

12th March. D.C.M., Adams, Sergeant G. S.

2nd April. M.C., Miller, Second Lieutenant A. M. J.; Willis, Second Lieutenant B. F. W.

5th April. DECORATION MILITAIRE, 202850, Archibald, Sergeant W.

12th May. D.C.M., 202664, Gardner, Sergeant J. G.

14th May. BAR TO M.M., 200097, Ross, Lance-Corporal N.

3rd June. M.S.M., 202788, Green, Sergeant T. W.; 200499, Mandy, Private A.; 9606, Mason, Temporary Regimental Sergeant-Major J.

13th June. M.M., 200159, Forbes, Company Quartermaster-Sergeant J.

23rd July. BAR TO M.M., 3928, Scurrah, Corporal G.

M.M., 238089, Baker, Corporal J.; 235364, Fairbairn, Private D.; 200306, Finlayson, Sergeant H.; 17062, Forbes, Corporal W.; 41060, Harvie, Private J.; 200345, Hendry, Sergeant J.; 203755, Hills, Private W.; 203837, Howie, Corporal H.; 1188, McBain, Private A.; 201917, Macdougall, Acting Sergeant J.; 200060, Mackenzie, Private D.; 200194, Mackenzie, Acting Corporal D.; 20035, Mackenzie, Private J.; 200173, Mackenzie, Sergeant J.; 41671, Mackinnon, Corporal D. N.; 200267, MacLean, Company Sergeant-Major K.; 200140, Macpherson, Private J.; 200105, Martin, Company Quartermaster-Sergeant D.; 265355, Morrison, Private J.; 23855, Paterson, Private W.; 24649, Reid, Private J. S.; 201193, Ritchie, Private T.; 202644, Shiach, Corporal J.; 203084, Strachan, Private R.; 267368, Watson, Corporal C. P.; 25903, Williamson, Private D.; 267069, Wilson, Private J.

20th September. MEDAILLE BARBATIE DI CREDUITA (Rumania), 2nd class, 203478, Hamilton, Corporal A. J. S.; 200101, Macrae, Sergeant R.

7th October. CROIX DE GUERRE (France), Campbell, Captain D.; 203439, Cranston, Private J.; 333, Cumming, Regimental Quartermaster-Sergeant T.; 202749, McBain, Private W.; 22164, McIntosh, Private A.

1920

30th January. D.S.O., Peverell, Captain T. H.

OTHER DATES

C.M.G., Fraser, Major J. W.; Sandilands, Colonel J. W.

C.B.E., Mason-MacFarlane, Lieutenant-Colonel D. J.

O.B.E., Brodie, Captain R., Royal Army Medical Corps; Ferguson, Captain D.; Fraser, Major J. W.; Macleod, Captain J., C.F.

D.S.O., Campbell, Lieutenant-Colonel C. H.; Hopkinson, Lieutenant-Colonel J. O.; Notman, Lieutenant J. P.; Sandilands, Colonel J. W.; Stewart, Lieutenant-Colonel A. B. A.

M.C., Head, Lieutenant V. H.; Hogg, Captain C. G.; Hopkinson, Lieutenant-Colonel J. O.; Hulls, Major C. A. P.; McAllion, Lieutenant F. M.; Mackenzie, Lieutenant M.; Morrison, Second Lieutenant J.

D.C.M., Boardman, Second Lieutenant W.; Fuller, Second Lieutenant W. A.; Vickery, Corporal J. A.

BAR TO M.M., 1391, Munro, Lance-Corporal K. J.

M.M., Mackenzie, Captain and Quartermaster R. W.; Macrae, Second Lieutenant J. D.; 20050, Bain, Sergeant H.; 4388, Dawson, Private S.; 2058, Hendry, Company Quartermaster-Sergeant T.; 4531, Hinchcliffe, Private T.; 4983, Macdougall, Private J.; 1325, Mackenzie, Private D.; 1725, Mackenzie, Private F.; 12632, Malcolm, Private J.; 1391, Munro, Lance-Corporal K. J.; 1523, Munro, Private M.; 201172, Murray, Corporal A.; 624, Ross, Company Quartermaster-Sergeant H. A.

M.S.M., 492, Bain, Company Quartermaster-Sergeant H.; 2168, Urquhart, Company Quartermaster-Sergeant J.

R.H.S. MEDAL, Lorgues, M., Interpreter.

R.H.S. CERTIFICATE, Harrop, Corporal F. A.

PART II

THE STORY OF THE 2/4TH BATTALION THE SEAFORTH HIGHLANDERS

By Lieutenant-Colonel DUNCAN MATHESON, D.L., J.P.

When the 4th Battalion The Seaforth Highlanders went to France in November 1914 the details left behind at Bedford were formed into the 4th (Reserve) Battalion The Seaforth Highlanders, a title soon changed to 2/4th Battalion The Seaforth Highlanders. It was commanded by Captain A. R. Munro. On 3rd December a number of recruits were brought to Bedford from the Depot at Dingwall by Second Lieutenant W. Wilkie, who assumed the duties of Adjutant.

The difficulties the Battalion Staff had to contend with were appalling. The only rifles available had to be used for musketry practice, efficiently conducted by Lieutenant J. G. Russell, and parades had to be carried out without arms. Uniform and equipment were of the scantiest and worst. One man at least was seen wearing a kilt, civilian blue serge jacket and bowler hat; others had civilian trousers with tunic and cloth cap; yet others, kilts and slouch hats. Add to this an extensive billeting area and entire absence of experienced non-commissioned officers, and it is a marvel that the Staff were able to cope at all with the organization of the administrative services, education of officers and non-commissioned officers, and training of the troops. To crown all, a Young Officers' School, 100 strong, was attached to the Battalion for billeting, leave and discipline.

On 19th November Major B. Macleod took over command until the arrival of Colonel J. H. Ewart on 15th December. Both these officers left the Battalion in January 1915, on the 5th of which Lieutenant-Colonel D. Matheson succeeded Colonel Ewart.

Everything was, indeed, lacking, but there was an atmosphere of enthusiasm and determination which made it all seem splendid. Every one did his best to smile at adversities, and the officers, whether experienced or not, were inspired by that fine Highland soldier, Brigadier-General Walter Ross. In Lieutenant Wilkie, with his many years' experience in the Regular army, all ranks had an invaluable guide.

Numbers were still much below establishment, and the idea occurred to Brigadier-General Ross to send a recruiting party to Manchester under Captain A. M. Macintyre. It will be remembered that Prince Charlie did the same in his march to Derby! This "Hielan' Raid," by the pipes and drums, with a selected party of stalwart non-commissioned officers, created a record for the Highland Division by securing 457 recruits in six days. Captain Macintyre created much stir in Parliament and elsewhere, and further action of the kind was forbidden by an Army Council Instruction prohibiting Territorial units from recruiting in areas other than their own.

In 1915 the County Associations were still administering Territorial battalions, and spared no expense. Lieutenant-Colonel Matheson was, therefore, able to obtain from a well-known firm of London outfitters an ample supply of shirts, hold-alls, mess-tins, and the like, and, above all, 500 glengarries at sixpence apiece! True, they all turned green in about six months; still they were uniform, they were glengarries, and the hateful cloth caps, bowlers and slouch hats disappeared for good.

There were amusing incidents in this congeries of semi-civilians. A man was brought before the Commanding Officer and remitted to the guard-room as a deserter, to await escort. When the escort arrived it was found that his Captain had given him leave and he had gone to visit his friends in Manchester! The Commanding Officer was told that he was a very nice man, and that if telegraphed for he would certainly come back. And so he did! Meanwhile the escort expressed themselves as quite agreeable to spend a few days visiting the cinemas in Bedford.

Rather later a non-combatant officer was found fault with in the Orderly Room for slackness. While the Commanding Officer was dressing for dinner this officer entered his room and demanded an apology, giving the name and address of his solicitor!

Three officers were ordered to proceed to France, and as there were no revolvers for them these were ordered by telegram to be sent by the first train from Weedon. No revolvers materialized: the Ordnance Department vowed that they had sent them, the Railway Company were equally positive that they had delivered them, and a long and acrimonious correspondence resulted. When, two months later, the Battalion moved to Fort George, it was found that the Quartermaster's high stool, covered with a blanket, had been made higher by a square box, in which were the revolvers about which he had been writing for two months!

During February Major G. Mackenzie took over the duties of Second-in-Command, in succession to Major Macleod.

On 19th February the first draft left for France under the command of Captain R. de Cardonnell Findlay. Two of its number were marked out for commissions, but refused nomination in order to go to France. One was Private Edward Watt, son of the editor of *The Ross-shire Journal*, who was killed at Neuve Chapelle. Very efficient did they look as they marched off on the command: "Form fours right—to Berlin—quick march!" with the piper leading, and the rear brought up by a lad with a football hanging from his rifle, the gift of his Captain. Alas! not many days later he was killed, the first of the 2/4th Battalion to fall.

The whole Battalion was at this time inoculated. It was, unfortunately, "discovered" that it should have been done a second time. It was not done, with the result that the whole Battalion had to be reinoculated twice at Blair Atholl!

The drafts sent out from Bedford were of fine physique. A curious incident was connected with one of them. About three days before its departure five men presented themselves for enlistment, but only on condition that they were included in the next draft. This was obviously impossible, for their training, musketry course and equipment had to be considered; but it was a pity to lose fine men who claimed to be good shots and to have had experience with the North-West Mounted Police. They were therefore sent to the range that afternoon, where they made good scores, went to London to dispose of their property and settle their affairs—for evidently they were in good circumstances—returned next morning and were enlisted, clothed and equipped. The Brigadier-General, who had already inspected the draft once, noticed nothing, and the new recruits went off to France, where they are said to have acquitted themselves well, whatever may have been their origin and antecedents.

A lad called Greener, probably considerably younger than his officially recorded age, after many failures to get himself included in a draft, slipped down to the station and hid under a seat. The matter was discovered, and the Brigadier-General swore he would try him by court martial. A telegram ordering him to be sent back was sent to Southampton. A man duly returned, but he was not Greener, who got to France. The mystery was never cleared up.

The Gaelic Society of London paid the Battalion a visit in Bedford and gave a most stirring concert. The beauty of the music was a revelation to most of the *Sassenach* present. Soon after, Mr Hugh Patterson, the Secretary of the Society, joined the Battalion. He subsequently rose to commissioned rank and was wounded in France. His recitations and songs always "brought down the house." "*Chuimhnich e air cruadal nan daoine bho'n d'thainig e!*" Another Gaelic stalwart was Norman Macleod, who became an expert bombing instructor. He met with a nasty accident to his hand, for which he had to be operated on in Norwich.

At 1 A.M. on 16th April the Battalion entrained for Fort George. It was a tedious journey; the engine broke down at Beattock, there were endless stops, and it was not till 4 A.M. on the next day that the Battalion detrained at Ardersier. All food had long since been eaten, and everyone was famished. As the 10th Seaforths were in occupation of the Fort, the 2/4th had to put two companies in the horrible casemates, while the Officers' Mess was in a hut half way to Ardersier. After about three weeks the Battalion moved to camp in the Carse of Ardersier in a violent snowstorm, which was not encouraging. It was an uncomfortable camp, as any hole dug was filled with brackish water at high tide, though it was a mile from the sea.

Here the new Brigadier, Colonel J. H. Ewart, arrived, and the Battalion was joined by the 2/6th Seaforths, under Colonel Black, and the 2/4th Camerons, under Colonel Smythe. Here, too, arrived the 3/4th Seaforths, under Major G. M. Cameron, which had been formed recently at Dingwall.

Musketry with "D.P." (*i.e.* suitable for drill purposes only!) rifles was the order of the day at this time, varied by expeditions in search of supposed German spies said to be signalling from the Black Isle—without result. Two German submarines, well known to the Royal Navy as "Fritz" and "Gretchen," were seen off the Fort. It was about this time that H.M.S. *Natal* was blown up in Cromarty Firth.

The Battalion provided the guard of honour of 100 men for the funeral of Captain Sir John Fowler of Braemore. After parading at Inverness station, the guard, with many officers and the Regimental Sergeant-Major, motored over seventy-five miles to Inverbroom for the burial.

On 14th July the Brigade started on the march to Blair Atholl, passing through some of the most delightful scenery in Scotland. The first march was one of fifteen miles to Daviot by Culloden. The rain came down pitilessly, and when the ill-chosen bivouac ground was reached it was found to be ankle-deep in water. In that sparsely inhabited district billets for a brigade are hard to find, and it was midnight before all could be crowded into barns and sheds. The succeeding marches were Carr Bridge, 18 miles; Kingussie, 23; Dalwhinnie, 18; Dalnacardoch, 15; and Blair Atholl, 12.

Lieutenant D. Boyd had succeeded Captain D. Ferguson as Quartermaster. At Blair Atholl he left, and was succeeded by Lieutenant G. P. Simpson.

Here, under the eye of the Divisional Commander, Brigadier-General G. C. I. Stockwell, D.S.O., training became intensive. Few will forget the daily strenuous climb up the sides of Meall Dail-min, and the welcome rest for dinner, usually at Gilbert's Bridge in Glen Tilt. The Battalion was then at the highest pitch it ever reached, and notice was given that that pitch must be maintained, as the Battalion was to proceed to France in three months. Little did they anticipate their fate!

In September the Seaforth and Cameron Brigade marched out on a fortnight's manœuvres against the Gordon Brigade, round about the Braes of Tullymet. Some of the battalions were not wearing the kilt apron, and the conspicuousness of those that did wear it as compared with those that did not was very striking. The tartans were almost invisible among the heather.

A certain Lord of Session, whose home was near by, had driven out to see the fun. In the evening he came across two Seaforth stragglers hardly able to crawl. His heart warming to the tartan, he gave them a lift, and the following conversation took place:

"Well, my lads, what part of Scotland do you come from?"

"From Manchester, sir."

"Oh, indeed" (his heart growing less warm). "How is it you have got so done up?"

"Well, you see, sir, it's this way. We can get on all right on a road, but it's this 'ere 'eather stuff wot kills us."

History does not record whether he turned them out as impostors!

During the marches, when it came to the turn of the company containing the Manchester boys to be next the band, the Commanding Officer used to hear a song to this effect:

"We are the Seaforth 'Ighlanders,
Our 'ome is were the 'eather grows,
We dance the fling on 'eels and toes,
An' we're 'ighly respected werever we goes."

The incessant downpour brought the manœuvres to a close three days before it was intended, and the Battalion plodded through the Pass of Killiecrankie soaked to the skin. Even singing ceased, till, as Blair Atholl was neared, someone struck up *Home, Sweet Home*. This stopped suddenly when the camp came into view—it was all under water, the entrance being knee-deep. The tents were rotten, drainage impossible and the men overcrowded. A hard frost that followed made it difficult to decide whether it was more unpleasant to turn in at night or to turn out in the morning.

On 25th October the Battalion marched to comfortable billets at Pitlochry, where it was most kindly entertained by the inhabitants. They presented the band with a magnificent leopard-skin, while the school children gave a concert in honour of the troops.

The 2/4th Seaforths provided the band and firing party for the funeral of the Brigadier, Colonel Ewart, who had died at Perth. The General Officer Commanding-in-Chief, Scottish Command, and the Divisional Commander were most complimentary about the drill and turn-out of the party, the credit for which was due to the careful preparation of Major Wilkie, who was in command.

Colonel Ewart was succeeded by Brigadier-General Scott-Kerr, who had been severely wounded when in command of the Guards Brigade at Villers Coterets, and about the same time Major-General Bannatine-Allason took over command of the Division, now known as the 64th.

In February 1916 the Battalion entrained for Stirling, where it was quartered in a large disused and half-ruined mill at Cambusbarron. Training was resumed upon the heather-clad hills of Polmaise. Here the Battalion paid its third ceremonial visit to an historic battle-ground. The first had been Culloden, the second Killiecrankie, the third was Bannockburn.

On the appointment of Major Wilkie as Second-in-Command in February, Second Lieutenant G. V. Sibary, Royal Scots Fusiliers, was posted to the Battalion as Adjutant. He was succeeded later on by Captain D. McMonnies.

On 1st March orders were received to entrain for Norwich on the following Saturday, at 1 A.M. Some of the Pitlochry ladies gave a concert in the canteen which lasted from 8 P.M. on Friday till midnight, and was much enjoyed. The march to the station took place in a wild snowstorm, and there were many falls.

Norwich was reached at 2 A.M. on Sunday. There are three stations, but only one was used for the move of the Division, so that there was much confusion. The billets were scattered on the Aylsham road, and even with a guide it was hard to find them in the pitch darkness.

The training-ground was seven or eight miles beyond the billets, and the march there and back, in addition to the hours of training, was a severe tax on the men.

The delay in the expected orders to proceed to France was already beginning toc ause misgivings, when suddenly there arrived a draft of over a hundred "Home Service" men from different regiments—not Highland—and misgiving gave place to certainty. After all the severe work at Blair Atholl, and the official statements made as to its coming transfer to France, it took all the heart out of the Battalion to become a Home Service draft-finding unit. Conscripted men were by this time coming in, many of inferior physique, who gave great trouble to the drill instructors.

A travelling Medical Board visited Norwich, trying to find men who were fit for service. Their methods were both brutal and futile, since it was evident that many men passed as fit for foreign service would break down in a short period. One man who had lost four fingers of the right hand was being passed fit when Lieutenant-Colonel Matheson asked how he was going to pull a trigger. The idea did not seem to have occurred to the Board!

A popular feature in Norwich was the playing of *Retreat* by the massed pipe bands of the 191st Brigade—2/4th Black Watch, 2/4th and 2/6th Seaforths and 2/4th Camerons—in the Cathedral Close, which was a most impressive function.

On 23rd June the Battalion marched fourteen miles to camp in Blickling Park, a delightful old English park, said to be the birthplace of Anne Boleyn. A drawback was that the water supply was a lake, nearly a mile away, from which water for cooking, washing, etc., had to be brought daily in water-carts, and to which animals had to be taken to water.

On 23rd July camp was moved to Kelling Heath, near Holt, a delightful site covered with heather; but the blackish sand in which it grew was not good for the men's clothing. There was excellent bathing about a mile away, and a boat was provided as a safeguard against accidents. The boatman was an elderly fisherman from the Lewis, detailed by the 2/4th Seaforths.

Near the bathing place was a large stranded steamer, which had been torpedoed by the Germans. It probably served as a landmark for Zeppelins, for they all came over it. They could be heard long before they arrived. Lights were immediately put out, with the result that parties going to their appointed rendezvous in pitch darkness had many difficulties, especially in hitching up transport. The Battalion always sent a party with Lewis guns to man a bomb-proof shelter on the cliff near the steamer. The camp was only once bombarded, a cow being killed and a Y.M.C.A. hut blown up; but the raiders could be heard at work farther south.

Twenty-six of the smartest sergeants and twenty-three other non-commissioned officers gave up their stripes to go to France with a very large draft. It was composed of the cream of the Battalion, and was as fine a draft as ever went out. It numbered in all over 1000, of which 340 came from the 2/4th Seaforths. Major Wilkie was the conducting officer.

On 23rd October the Battalion marched to Cromer, perhaps the coldest spot in England during winter, where training went on as before. The billets were very scattered, and lighting restrictions were even more stringent than in Norwich. Nothing was provided for covering the windows, so soldiers' blankets had to be used, and all night long, instead of the watchman's cry of "All's well," as in old days, there was a continuous shout of "Put that light out!"

Great excitement was caused one day by a wreck. A timber steamer was sighted off the lighthouse. Suddenly there was a puff of smoke and she was seen to break in half and drift towards the shore. The Battalion turned out, and all but two of the crew were rescued. Some of the rescuers rushed through the surf with ropes at great risk to themselves. The Battalion was publicly thanked, and Private Stewart Holmes was awarded the medal of the Royal National Life-Boat Institution for conspicuous courage. The life-boat made two ineffectual attempts to reach the ship, but succeeded at the third. Owing to the violence of the storm it was nearly midnight before the last man was got ashore.

A number of the hotels along the coast had been managed by Germans, who were all removed early in the war. As showing the extraordinary rumours that were prevalent on this subject may be quoted the story of the manager of the Golf Links Hotel. It is said that he was arrested by a party of the Welsh Regiment, that he was deported, and that the captain who arrested him, being taken prisoner during the war, entered the prisoners' enclosure in Germany, only to be received by this very manager! The whole tale was a fabrication, for the man was, in fact, interned and not deported.

There was always great trouble about guard-rooms in hotels and private buildings, where rooms are totally unsuited to the purpose. Many non-commissioned officers were "broken" for escapes for which they could not justly be blamed. In camp men under arrest had to be kept in the guard-tent, to the discomfort both of the guard and of themselves. One man was said to have escaped five times. He was caught by another regiment, and his captors, knowing the disastrous results of such escapes to the guard concerned, dealt with him so that "his mother would not know him."

Young lads constantly were arriving at Cromer who had enlisted at the outbreak of war when much under age and who had therefore been sent home. So many were posted to the 2/4th Seaforths that the numbers swelled to nearly 1600, while the establishment of officers and non-commissioned officers remained the same as for a battalion of normal strength (*i.e.* 1026). They were fine young fellows, but resented being posted to a regiment that was not their own, and they gave a lot of trouble. The situation became so difficult that the Brigadier consented to further arrivals being sent on to other battalions.

The Battalion won the silver cup given by Brigadier-General Scott-Kerr, to be competed for by the football teams of the Brigade. On one occasion the champion player of the Battalion —nay, of the Brigade—happened to be in durance vile for some trifling military "crime." After a study of the King's Regulations and a consultation *in camera* it was decided to release him for the match. Victory having been gained, he returned, after a wash and brush-up, to complete the purging of his offence.

Drafts continued to be dispatched, and the Commanding Officer lost several of his best officers and friends. Captain Weston Stewart and Lieutenants R. Hipwell, N. Sutherland and A. A. Mackenzie (known as "Ack Ack") all went out to France never to return.

As there were now a large number of wounded officers with war experience fit for duty at home, they were brought into the Home Service battalions in replacement of the older officers of the Reserve of Officers who had hitherto commanded them. So it fell out that Lieutenant-Colonel Matheson was appointed Quartering Officer for the North of Scotland, with a district extending from Falkirk to Thurso, and Headquarters at Perth. He handed over to Major Wilkie on 17th April 1917.

It is interesting to note that Lieutenant-Colonel Matheson's horse passed from him to Sir Bruce Hamilton, and the last trace that can be found of it is that it carried General (now Field-Marshal) Sir Claud Jacob, then commanding the II Corps, into Brussels.

On 18th April, Lieutenant-Colonel W. B. J. Mitford, Gordon Highlanders, was gazetted to the command of the Battalion, but did not actually take over from Major Wilkie until later.

In May the 2/4th Seaforths moved into Kelling Camp for the second summer in succession, and training was continued, with highly satisfactory results. In June a high compliment was paid to the Battalion, in that it was selected to provide the Royal Guard at Sandringham, being the first Territorial unit to undertake the duty. The training of the guard was entrusted to Major Wilkie, and after its final inspection by Brigadier-General Scott-Kerr the latter said: "When I asked your Second-in-Command to undertake the preparation of this guard I did not think it possible for any unit in this Brigade to turn out as you have done to-day—the smartest and cleanest body of men I have seen since becoming your Brigadier. I have every confidence that you will perform the difficult and exacting duties of a Royal Guard of Honour with credit."

The guard, over eighty strong, was under the command of Captain P. C. Knight. The efficiency and exemplary conduct of its members was so much appreciated, not only by the officers of Queen Alexandra's Household, but also by Her Majesty herself, that the personnel, by special command, was not changed until the final relief of the guard in December 1917.

Early in July an Army Order directed all Territorial officers holding temporary rank to return to their substantive rank and assume seniority as defined by their place on the Battalion roll. This caused some confusion, as officers gazetted in 1915 in some cases became senior to others gazetted in 1914. Captain W. Stewart now assumed the duties of Second-in-Command by reason of seniority, Major Wilkie being appointed Umpire for all tactical exercises of the Brigade. Shortly afterwards this officer, who had been associated with the Battalion from its formation, was appointed Adjutant of the Clackmannanshire Volunteer Battalion, with Headquarters at Alloa.

The very valuable services rendered by Major Wilkie to the 2/4th Seaforths are best expressed in Lieutenant-Colonel Matheson's parting words to him: "I can never thank you enough for all you have done for me and all the help you have given me, all through the happy time we have soldiered together. Always thinking of everything, smoothing over difficulties and taking so much of the burden. Words seem cold, but I assure you that in my heart I have appreciated it very deeply."

The German offensive of March 1918 caused such losses in the army in France that many of the Home Service battalions were drained of their fit men to make good the wastage. Thus it befell that the remnant of the 2/4th Seaforths was absorbed into the 4th Reserve Battalion at Ripon in April 1918.

[So ended the 2/4th Battalion The Seaforth Highlanders. To them fell only the disappointment of having worked for a standard—that of trial by battle—that they were never allowed to attain. Of their Commanding Officer let the following eulogy from one of his most trusted subordinates suffice:

"His departure was an occasion of profound regret to the whole Battalion, for he had brought it from the condition of a crowd of semi-civilians to that of a highly efficient unit. Ever considerate of others, and just in all things, he had endeared himself to all that served under him. He was undoubtedly the best exponent of tactics among the commanding officers of the Division. His appreciation of help rendered to himself and to the Battalion he loved was most marked, and he never missed an opportunity of thanking all ranks for their patience and consideration in trying times."—M. M. H.]

PART III

THE STORY OF THE 3/4TH, LATER THE 4TH RESERVE TRAINING BATTALION THE SEAFORTH HIGHLANDERS

THE 3/4th Battalion The Seaforth Highlanders was, like its predecessor, formed in April 1915 from recruits collected at the depot in Dingwall. Its first Commanding Officer was Colonel C. S. Smyth, D.S.O., who was succeeded by Major G. M. Cameron on 21st May 1915.

On 24th May the 3/4th Seaforths proceeded to Ardersier Camp, where they were stationed until 3rd November, when they moved to Ripon.

At Ripon, Lieutenant-Colonel D. J. Mason-MacFarlane, C.M.G., who had been wounded while leading the 1/4th Seaforths at Neuve Chapelle, was appointed to command the 3/4th Battalion, the appointment dating from 12th February 1916.

On 1st August 1916 the 3/4th, 3/5th and 3/6th Seaforths were amalgamated under Lieutenant-Colonel Mason-MacFarlane's command, being thereafter known as the 4th Reserve Training Battalion The Seaforth Highlanders.

No notable changes thereafter occurred until the German offensive of 1918. In April the details of the 2/4th Seaforths, which had sent all its effective men abroad, were absorbed into the 4th Reserve Training Battalion, which had also sent large drafts to the front. On 24th May the Battalion proceeded to Glencorse, where demobilization began in December, and was completed by 20th June 1919.

Of the methods whereby the 4th Reserve Training Battalion The Seaforth Highlanders was trained, of the standard it attained, of the officers and others concerned in that training, and the attainment of that standard, it is best to let Colonel Mason-MacFarlane speak himself.—M.M.H.

THE TRAINING OF THE 4TH RESERVE TRAINING BATTALION THE SEAFORTH HIGHLANDERS

By COLONEL DAVID MASON-MACFARLANE, C.M.G., C.B.E., T.D., J.P.
Member of His Majesty's Bodyguard for Scotland

IN 1905 many of our leading statesmen, soldiers and sailors began to realize that war with Germany was probable. They knew that although our navy was all-powerful, our army was sadly lacking in numbers and in reserves for a European war. Lord Roberts had failed in his efforts to persuade the nation that universal military training was our only chance of averting a war between Germany and ourselves.

In September 1905 Colonel A. W. A. Pollock, in a powerful letter to the editor of *The Spectator*, after referring to our lack of military strength in the event of a war with Germany, offered to train an experimental company for six months; and guaranteed, at the end of that time, to produce a company of trained soldiers who would, in the event of war, be at once available for *garrison duty*, and thus release every trained soldier for the firing line, and that with a few months' further training the experimental company would themselves be able to take the field against Continental troops.

The following are the qualifications which he said he would guarantee in each of the 100 men after six months' training:

(1) The recruits shall be as good at drill, gymnastics and musketry as any Regular soldier of the same length of service.

(2) On a tactical exercise the recruits shall show themselves tactically more proficient than any company selected from any battalion in the Regular army (with the exception of the Guards) serving in the United Kingdom, provided that the Company chosen to represent the Regular army shall not be selected more than forty-eight hours before the trial takes place.

The cost to train 100 recruits for six months would not exceed £3500.

The result of Colonel Pollock's offer was the formation of *The Spectator's* Experimental Company; no recruit with any previous military training was enlisted.

The training of these 100 men commenced in March 1906, and in September 1906 the Company was disbanded. On the conclusion of the training the Company was inspected by

H.M. King Edward VII.; it was also carefully inspected by the Commander-in-Chief and senior officers in the army.

The reports on the Company were very laudatory, but the inspecting officers did not think that after only six months' training the men would be capable of taking the field against trained Continental troops.

The only definite records of any special training are those of the musketry of *The Spectator* Experimental Company. They are as follows:

Men		103
Marksmen	31	
First-class shots	50	
Second-class shots	13	
Third-class shots	9—103	

The country owes a deep debt to the editor of *The Spectator*, who made the experiment possible. Few of us thought at the time that within ten years from that date Territorial Reserve Training Battalions would be given ten weeks in which to train recruits, who had never seen a rifle, to such a pitch of efficiency as to be able to pit these men against the trained soldiers of the greatest military Power the world has ever seen—and yet such was the case.

To the 4th Reserve Battalion The Seaforth Highlanders recruits during 1916, 1917 and 1918 were coming in at the rate of nearly 100 a week. These men were not only taught drill, gymnastics and musketry, but had an intensive course of musketry, including the Lewis gun, physical training and bayonet-fighting, bombing, anti-gas precautions and signalling, and at the end of their ten weeks' training they were drafted to France, and in the firing line against the most highly trained infantry of the world, all within eleven weeks of their first having seen a rifle. Not only were these men the equals of their opponents, but their superiors.

We will, in this Part, try to do justice to the magnificent body of instructors, to whom all the credit of this result is entirely due. In January 1916 I was passed fit for service at home and was posted to the command of the 3/4 Seaforth Highlanders, stationed at Ripon. Within a few months the 3/4th, 3/5th and 3/6th Seaforth Highlanders were amalgamated, and formed the 4th Reserve Training Battalion The Seaforth

Highlanders, whose function was to train recruits and to form a depot for the officers, non-commissioned officers and men of the 4th, 5th and 6th Seaforths who were convalescent and waiting to be again sent to their fighting units in France. The amalgamation was, as far as possible, carried out by taking one-third of the staff from each of the three Battalions, and thus was formed the Training and Instructional Staff of the 4th Reserve Training Battalion The Seaforth Highlanders. One was thus able to take a very high standard, both in officers and non-commissioned officers, because it meant for each post one had three competent officers available, and in each case one did one's best to choose the most able officer or non-commissioned officer.

One can say, on looking back on the amalgamated Battalion, there was never the least sign of dissatisfaction at the resulting Battalion Staff. No Commanding Officer ever had a more loyal, more willing or more competent staff, and it was entirely as the result of their team-work that the Reserve Battalion was able to send to France such splendid drafts of men. The War Office reported to us, late in 1917, that the type of recruit and his training whom we sent overseas was of a very high standard indeed, and he had not been excelled by any Line regiment.

This standard was kept up only by unceasing attention on the part of every instructor and by most careful selection amongst those instructors. Courses of instruction in all the branches of specialized training were held at the centres of instruction for each special subject—musketry, bombing, physical training, etc.—and after each course the most brilliant instructor was posted to his own specialty in the Reserve Battalion.

Refresher courses, again, were frequently held, and one's best instructors attended for probably a few days' course, to have a fresh, keen edge put on their powers as instructor. It is impossible to write too strongly about the Instructional Battalion Staff—it can have fallen to the lot of very few battalion commanders to have the good fortune to possess non-commissioned officers with so much latent talent. I sent fourteen non-commissioned officers to a school for non-commissioned officers at Edinburgh Castle for a general course of instruction. Of the fourteen non-commissioned officers twelve of them were awarded special certificates and two of them first-class certificates. This explains at once the high standard of training in the Battalion.

There were no two courses more important nor more pregnant with good for the Battalion than the officers' course in drill at the Chelsea Barracks and the course in physical training at Aldershot. Every officer in command of a platoon had been through the former course, and practically every non-commissioned officer, whatever his specialty, had attended the physical training course at Aldershot.

Everyone who knows what these two courses meant to the officers and non-commissioned officers attending them must at once realize what these courses meant to the Battalion.

Certainly 99 per cent. of the efficiency and discipline of the Battalion was directly due to Chelsea and Aldershot, and there is no doubt at all but that the extraordinarily high standard of musketry, which was maintained through these three years of war, was absolutely the result, indirectly, of the physical training standard of the Reserve Training Battalion. For the last two years of the war, 1917 and 1918, the 4th Reserve Training Battalion The Seaforth Highlanders came out first of all the training battalions in Britain in (1) musketry, and (2) physical training and bayonet-fighting.

One always saw every officer and non-commissioned officer at orderly-room on his return from any course of instruction before he joined his unit. One of my captains had returned from an officers' course at Chelsea. I said to him:

"Well, Gunn, what did you think of your course at Chelsea? I expect they have taught you a great deal."

"Well, Colonel, I enjoyed the course very much. I learnt a lot; but it's just like this—all regiments have got their fads, and the Guards' fad is efficiency!"

This spirit permeated through the whole training staff, and each one vied with his fellow-instructor to get the 100 per cent. efficiency at which one always aimed.

The Battalion lines, when we were posted to them at Ripon, were literally a sea of liquid mud. Nobody could walk through the lines without getting mud over the tops of his field-boots. It was a physical impossibility to keep the Battalion lines or barrack huts in any sort of condition except that of a mud swamp. The Battalion strength at the time was over 2000 strong, and in less than ten days, with my Company Commanders and every man in the Battalion working his hardest, the camp was transformed from a soaking ploughed field to a hard parade-ground—all the lines gravelled and drained—and it was possible after the heaviest rain to walk from end to end of the camp without getting a speck of mud on one's boots.

Shortly after this, on making my inspection of the men's living-huts, I was much struck by one part of a hut where one of the Battalion drummer boys slept. He had got his floor section spotlessly white. In recognition of his tidiness he was sent home on a few days' leave. This was the origin of the scheme by which at the end of each month the men whose hut reached the highest standard of cleanliness were granted a few days of privilege leave. In a few weeks what the Reserve Training Battalion had done led to the whole of the divisional camp in Ripon being transformed from wet mud to dry ground.

From January 1916 until the day of the Armistice the work went on all day and every day from dawn till sunset—indeed in the orderly-room very often from dawn till dawn.

The complicated and detailed returns that the War Office called for weekly kept the orderly-room staff at work many nights in the week until the glimmer of daylight made them realize they were burning the candle at both ends. The intensive training went on daily, Sundays excepted, and at the end of the ten weeks every man was granted one week's leave at home before going overseas. On his return he was equipped, and usually left for France within twenty-four or forty-eight hours. The only military offence ever committed by these fine fellows was that occasionally a few of them overstayed their leave. Crime in any other sense was absent, and even the number of cases of recruits who made too merry over their cups was practically *nil*.

One saw each draft before it went on draft leave and carefully explained why it was so important that nobody should overstay his leave—the primary and most important reason being that no man knew whether the others might not also overstay their leave, and if every man did so there would be no draft for that week to go to France, and the draft might be most urgently required in the firing line. In order that the men's discipline should be equal to the strain, and thus ensure their punctual return, one had to hold over their heads certain penalties. Discipline is merely doing something unpleasant because if it is not done one knows something still more unpleasant will follow. On one occasion one of them had overstayed his leave by seventy-two hours and was brought before me at orderly-room. He knew his punishment beforehand, and all I said to him was: "Is it worth it?"

"Yes, sir," he said, with a happy smile, and left the orderly-room.

My Adjutant, the late Captain Colin Cameron, also was smiling, so I said: "What is amusing you, Colin?"

"Well, Colonel, the man got married seventy-two hours before his return!"

My sense of discipline had a temporary lapse, and I cancelled the punishment.

Nothing will show more clearly the hearts and feelings of these good men than the following two incidents. A draft which was going to France the following day had been inspected. One youngster who seemed to me under age, but who stoutly contested the fact, was found on reference to the enlistment sheet to be one year under age. I had reluctantly to take him from the draft. On returning to the orderly-room the Regimental Sergeant-Major asked if I would see the lad, he was so upset, and I did so. He was physically much fitter than several of the recruits older than himself who were going overseas, and he begged to be allowed to go with his own batch of recruits. I told him to telegraph to his father, and if his father and mother did not object I would let him go. Their reply was that he might go. He went to France, was seriously wounded a few weeks later and came back to the Battalion, in which within the next few months he was promoted Sergeant, and did very good work as an instructor. Just about this time, one morning at orderly-room a young soldier was charged with "breaking into the Quartermaster's store, removing a full set of uniform and equipment, rifle ammunition, etc., secreting himself in the ranks of a draft for France and being found under the seat of a railway carriage *en route* for France without a ticket." The young soldier had tears in his eyes while the charge-sheet was read over before him—they quickly disappeared when I told him he was discharged, with a very big good conduct mark on his conduct sheet.

Unless it had been one's good fortune to see those recruits on joining the Battalion and then, too, to bid them "Godspeed" when they left for overseas, I doubt if anyone would have believed the extraordinary change that took place in these men, both physically and in their mental outlook, during that memorable ten weeks.

One must remember that they were extraordinarily well fed and most comfortably housed, not only in their sleeping-quarters but also in their dining huts and recreation huts. They had intensive physical training daily, and in addition all the other instruction which went to transform them from men of peace to soldiers-in-arms.

One recruit especially made a lasting impression on me. When he joined the Battalion he came from Glasgow, where for ten years he had been a clerk in some business house. He looked very thin and ill, and both my Adjutant and myself doubted if he would ever go overseas. We decided, however, to give him his ten weeks' training. At my inspection, ten weeks later, of his batch before going overseas, my Adjutant pointed to him and said: "This is that delicate recruit we thought would fail us!" I hardly recognized him, he looked so fit and well. I asked him if he had enjoyed his training. He replied: "Why did the Government not compel me to undergo this training when I was eighteen years old instead of waiting till I was twenty-eight years of age? I now feel a man! When I came to the Battalion any Glasgow hooligan might have knocked me into the gutter off the pavement and I would have picked myself up and walked on—I should like to see the man to-day who would knock me off the road!"

That gives one in a nutshell the result of the ten weeks' training on these lads.

Every Friday evening for these three long years a draft left Ripon, and after May 1918, Glencorse, for France. The strength of the draft varied, but usually was about fifty men.

The number that passed through the Training Battalion from September 1916, when the three Battalions were amalgamated, until the 20th February 1919, was 12,061. This number includes not only recruits but also the men returned from overseas wounded or invalided home, who on recovery were posted to the Training Battalion for a short course of instruction before again going overseas to the Territorial Battalions in France or the Line Battalion in Mesopotamia.

Those draft evenings seemed to come round every day instead of once a week, but the cheeriness and happiness of the men were really wonderful. Each battalion of the Highland Brigade sent a draft overseas the same day, and the battalion commanders were always on the platform at the station to see their men entrain. On one occasion the Divisional General, an Englishman, had gone down to the station, and took exception to what he thought was an excess of merriment on the part of a draft from a Highland Battalion (not a Seaforth draft). It was dusk, and in the dim light he did not recognize the men's tartan. He reproved them gently for their hilarity, addressing them as "Gordon Highlanders," and referring to the bravery of the Gay Gordons at Dargai. The draft was not a Gordon Highlanders' draft, and as soon as the General had finished his short speech one of the reproved men was heard to say in the dimness: "Wha cares a damn for what the Gordon Highlanders did at Dargai!" That closed the incident, to everyone's satisfaction. When one knows that as a rule 25 per cent. of the drafts going overseas were men who had been wounded two or three times already, one has no words adequate to express one's admiration for them.

If one wished in one word to sum up their dominating quality, that word would be their *Modesty*. I can well remember Sergeant Edwards, V.C., 6th Battalion The Seaforth Highlanders, when he rejoined the Training Battalion at Ripon, after he was wounded and had received his Victoria Cross. As soon as we heard he was rejoining it was arranged that the Battalion, with the pipers and drummers, would form his escort into camp. We failed to find him, and he crept silently and secretly back to his lines, and was only discovered just as he reached the camp.

After more than two years at Ripon, soon after the great German offensive in March 1918, the Reserve Training Battalions were moved with the Highland Brigade to Scotland, and the 4th Reserve Battalion The Seaforth Highlanders to Glencorse. Everyone was glad to get back to Scotland. It meant, however, no slackening of training, and everything, after a few days in which we settled down in our new lines, went on as at Ripon.

One should now refer more in detail to the specialist training of the Battalion, and it seems to me that musketry, certainly from an infantry soldier's point of view, comes first.

The Battalion was more than fortunate in its musketry officer, and it would be impossible for me to speak too highly of the work Lieutenant James B. Connon and his musketry staff did for the Battalion. No commanding officer had a more

Y

competent musketry instructor, nor one who threw himself with more heart and soul into his work. His results were of a very high order, and it was indeed a rare thing to send any recruit to France who was not a first-class shot.

In March 1918 the Inspecting General in Musketry was so struck by the targets in the "mad minute" of a batch of young trained soldiers just going overseas to France that he asked permission to take them to London to the War Office. Unless my memory plays me false, each young soldier had fired off more than the requisite number of rounds in the "mad minute," and every shot was on the target. This exercise was fired on a thirty-yards' range, service ammunition, and painted Boche heads for targets. I have never, not even at the School of Musketry at Hythe—which, in my opinion, is the finest and best instructional school in the British army—seen better musketry instruction than Lieutenant Connon and his officers and non-commissioned officers gave the men in the 4th Reserve Battalion. I am certain that the extremely careful physical training, which each man underwent, had a great deal to do with the high standard of the musketry. They gradually gained so much power in the muscles of their arms and shoulders that they had no difficulty in holding their rifles steady. To assist my memory in writing this chapter I requested my specialists to send me notes on their work. The following account of the Battalion musketry by Lieutenant J. B. Connon is so good that it requires no comment:

"Having been honoured by a request to write a word on the musketry of the Battalion it is with great diffidence that one takes up the pen after a gap of nearly nine years after the greatest known Armistice in this world's history.

"If the war was not won by the rifle fire of the private soldier it certainly was not won without it. In the Reserve Training Battalion the Company officer as such was practically non-existent, and the training of the Battalion was carried on by 'specialists,' and accordingly it was up to every specialist officer and his staff to be imbued with the idea that his department was the one that was to win the war.

"The millions of 'returns' which were compiled by specialist officers and rendered weekly and monthly to the Battalion orderly-room, thence to the Brigade, thence upwards (one wonders were they ever read), must surely by this time have succumbed to the flames—else where are they all stored?

"One is informed that the records of this Training Battalion's musketry stood high among the returns of training battalions, and none are more gratified than those who remain of the musketry staff of the Battalion. Having no records to one's hand as one writes, it is impossible to give comparisons with other units or to go into figures at all.

"It will be recalled that the 3/4th, 3/5th and 3/6th Battalions were united while in camp in Ripon into the 4th Reserve Battalion Seaforth Highlanders. Representatives of the three musketry staffs were taken on the strength of the musketry staff of the new Battalion, and the work carried on. No reader will wish reference to that driest of all publications with which we were at one time supposed to be familiar, known as "*Musketry Regulations*. Part I. 1909. Reprinted with Amendments, 1914. Price Sixpence"—perhaps the greatest amount of unreadable material that was ever offered to the British public at the money. The period of one's existence spent at the *Musketry Regulations* is nearly a nightmare to cast one's memory back to. It was wonderful, however, how this unpalatable food, when served up with the gravy sauce of the lectures of the School of Musketry, concluding with a fortnight at the rifle range, capped by the 'mad minute,' was swallowed by the rank and file of the British army, and to very good purpose.

"If the musketry of the Battalion was a failure, then the blame lay at the door of the Musketry Officer, for in this unit he was given a free hand by the Battalion Headquarters in everything, including selection of his staff. If it was a success it was due to the magnificent body of non-commissioned officers who carried on the great work. It being believed that the instruction of musketry is not of the variety of the soldiers' training, such as drill or physical training, where he must 'jump to it,' but where he must use his brains and imbibe it mentally as a student, the class of instructor selected was not of that type which so often flourished from 1914-1919 by window-dressing or eyewash—in other words, shouting at the pitch of his voice at his squad when he saw anyone in authority coming along, then slacking when the Colonel or Staff Officer had passed by. The type of non-commissioned officer who made the musketry of this Battalion was that with brains, coolness, steadiness, reliability, not afraid to speak when they had to, and who knew what to say—men who backed up those under their charge to the last, and who had their confidence. There were times when three officers and over thirty non-commissioned officers were instructing musketry, and with squads of ten (often twelve) each. There is little wonder that this 'specialist' was regarded as a curse by the Company officers, for during their military training they saw their men only on pay-day.

"The Highland Training Division had the fortune to be under the eye of the well-known major who has been one of the best-known figures on the rifle ranges of Britain for over a quarter of a century, and who in the summer of 1927 was still busy scoring bulls at 1000 yards. To the vast army of 'Green Hats,' to which he belonged, the British army was indebted largely for its efficiency in musketry. These men were all rifle-shots—who knew themselves how to shoot and how to get it out of others.

"But to come back to the Battalion's ability with the rifle; this could hardly help being above the standard of 'passable.' With a Commanding Officer overflowing with energy and enthusiasm for his work, whose target was 'perfection,' and who insisted on getting it, an Adjutant, Captain Colin Cameron, now at rest in Flanders, whose like may tread this earth again, but his better, never (all wondered how so wise a head ever got on so youthful shoulders), non-commissioned officers, instructors who were the cream and brains of the Battalion, the best was got from the rank and file. One may be pardoned for casting one's memory back over ten years for a mental glance at the faces one had the privilege to work alongside of in those now seeming distant times. Where will we ever meet a better type of manhood than Sergeant 'Kenny' M'Rae of the 4th, Sergeant M'Call of the 5th, Sergeants Willie M'Leod and John Christie of the 6th? These and many others ultimately fell where they fought, to rise no more. Of the living the musketry officer in the next war should secure the services of Company Sergeant-Instructor of Musketry John Kellet as his right-hand man. A civilian in 1914 he wore the South African Ribbon, and was ultimately wounded in France in 1918. We cannot pass through Forres without doing ourselves the honour of shaking hands with him and with Sergeant Laurie, now at the head of the British Linen Bank there. The latter will carry the result of his sojourn in Palestine to the grave. With luck we will also meet there our old friend Corporal Singer of the 6th, who often carried the Battalion 'Soccer' team to victory. Can we pass Carr Bridge without looking in to see Sergeant John

Campbell, who was selected by the Adjutant for the secret and mysterious march from Mesopotamia to the Black Sea? He accomplished it, and returned to Glencorse to the Battalion orderly-room and reported to the Commanding Officer that he had done so. Many wondered why the Adjutant selected him—little wonder when, after all, like draws to like. We cannot go through Ross and Sutherland without encountering Sergeants W. Fraser and John Mackay—the former a guardian of the peace and the latter in charge of His Majesty's mails in the northmost Highland county. We would like to mention others, but space forbids. It is good to see that they are as staunch civilians as they were soldiers. Finally, any member of the old Musketry Staff who should fall by the way in Glasgow is sure of a helping hand from their old officer and guardian, Lieutenant Ogilvie, now nearing the top of the tree in the Glasgow Police Force.

"One word in closing. In a service where thirty-six hours' work had to be done in twenty-four, and the same men were wanted by more than one officer at the same time, 'family jars' within a battalion were bound to occur. The driving force from the head of the unit required the work to be accomplished, and an explanation of non-accomplishment was not well received—what else to do, then, but every man to fight for his own hand? Should this meet the eye of anyone who may have 'bumped' against the Musketry Department of the 4th Reserve Battalion Seaforth Highlanders, let it be known that, with the mellowing hand of time, forgiveness is asked and given.

"Good luck to the survivors of the Battalion!"

Company Sergeant-Instructor of Musketry Kellet writes:

"As senior Musketry Non-commissioned Officer of the 4th Reserve Training Battalion The Seaforth Highlanders, it was my privilege to come into contact with many instructors during the three years I was with the Battalion.

"These instructors were, for the most part, young non-commissioned officers with a great enthusiasm for their work, and it says much for their ability and tact that, being called upon at various times to give musketry instruction to returned British Expeditionary Force non-commissioned officers and men, they did so with such success that these men learnt many things they had not known previously, and at the finish of the course returned to their various duties with a deep respect for their instructors.

"The recruits dealt with by these instructors, after one week's instruction, were enabled to go to the range and fire their course, often under the most adverse weather conditions, and did great credit to their teachers. The number of marksmen and first-class shots was always far in excess of the second- and third-class shots.

"These results were due to the fact that the whole Battalion Musketry Staff were as one in their endeavour to do their best for the sake of the regiment, and also to the tact of the senior officers of the Battalion who allowed the 'specialists' to carry on their own work without undue interference.

"I trust it may not be accounted as boasting when I say that finer musketry officers, more loyal instructors and more likeable men could not be found in any other unit of the British army, and I say this because during all the time I was supervising the work of the various musketry parties I cannot recall one instance of any man finishing his musketry course with a grievance against either officer or non-commissioned officer."

Physical training and bayonet-fighting took, without doubt, second place in the training of the Battalion.

We were fortunate in possessing in Colonel Wright, Commandant of the Army School of Physical Training at Aldershot, a friend—who did all in his power for the Battalion.

No officer or non-commissioned officer was ever allowed to act as an instructor until he had passed through the Army School of Physical Training at Aldershot.

Colonel Wright saw the keenness of our Instructional Staff and forwarded it by every possible means.

He was the Inspecting Officer for the whole of the physical training of the troops at home, and for the last two years of the war the 4th Reserve Training Battalion took first place of all the home training battalions in physical training and bayonet-fighting. All I have said about the Musketry Staff Officers and non-commissioned officers applies equally to all the Specialist Instructors of the Battalion, and my physical training officers and non-commissioned officers were no exception. It mattered not whether it were musketry, physical training, gas, bombing or signalling; wherever you took the Inspecting General he saw the same high standard of instruction, and was always full of praise for the work.

One very serious handicap existed during all the three years of intensive training—I was not allowed, and I had no wish, to keep any instructor at home *if* he could be replaced by a disabled officer or non-commissioned officer, and thus released to return to France. This was a real anxiety, because every few weeks I found an officer or non-commissioned officer who had been unfit for service abroad passed fit for France. At once he had to be ready to go overseas and his unfit (physically) understudy had to prepare to fill his shoes. Many a time I have, with a very sad heart, had to part with a brilliant instructor, to be followed by some days of anxiety as to whether or not this understudy would be able to take his place. In nearly every case one found that the mantle of the teacher had fallen on his understudy, and all went well. At the same time one often wondered if it were not bad policy to send an officer or non-commissioned officer to France, already severely wounded, who was a born teacher of men, and who at that time was turning out nearly 100 men a week to reinforce the firing line, while certainly a dozen officers or non-commissioned officers who, from no fault of their own, were not born instructors, and available to fight, were held back as instructors.

In many cases, for the second and third time, my best instructors were sent to France, never to return, and I bitterly resented the War Office attempting to command my Battalion and not allowing *me* to decide in what capacity any officer or non-commissioned officer was doing his best to win the war.

I was, however, almost powerless, and War Office orders had to be obeyed. On one occasion a War Office telegram, ordering my two physical training officers overseas forthwith, was more than I could stand. With my Brigadier's permission I went to the War Office and saw General Sir Francis Davies, and my two officers were returned at once. Had they been taken it meant that, for certainly a few weeks, my drafts for France would have been lowered in efficiency almost 50 per cent., as at that moment I had *no* capable physical training officers available as understudies.

In my opinion the very high standard of the recruits we sent overseas was due entirely to their physical training when the recruits came to the Battalion—without that it would have been impossible to have made soldiers of them. Whatever happened to interfere with the Battalion routine of instruction, nothing was ever allowed to cancel the daily hours of physical training. Musketry, bombing, gas and drill—all might have to be washed out owing to the visit of some Staff Officer, but the physical training never. The result of this was that the physique of the recruit progressed steadily, and at the end of his ten weeks one could only believe the physical improvement because one saw it.

I will allow Lieutenant William Murray, in his own words, to describe the work of Staff Sergeant-Major Matthews and himself—work which, in my opinion, made the 4th Reserve Training Battalion The Seaforth Highlanders what it was.

There was no more cheering sight on the instructional parade ground than a section of young Seaforth Highlanders going over the bayonet assault course. The Battalion owes a debt to the physical training officers, and especially to Staff Sergeant-Major Matthews, that can never be repaid.

Before the war, Matthews was the physical training instructor at Aberdeen University. I have never seen a more capable instructor. During the three years of war while he was with the Battalion he never had one day off duty, and he threw himself, body and soul, into his work. If any one man more than another was responsible for the extraordinarily high standard of efficiency of the Battalion, a standard which evoked the admiration of every Inspecting General, that man was Sergeant-Major Matthews. He literally made the Regiment what it was, and no Commanding Officer could have received more unselfish, loyal and true service from any subordinate than I received from him.

Lieutenant W. Murray's notes on physical training and bayonet-fighting are as follows:

"In the early days of the war both physical training and bayonet-fighting were taught in a very haphazard manner. There was no system, and the spasmodic exercises that went under the name of physical training were worse than useless. The school at Aldershot brought order out of chaos. By the beginning of 1916 a number of non-commissioned officers and one or two officers had undergone a course of training there. Great care was taken in choosing those sent to the school, as it was now realized that the efficiency of the drafts depended largely on the quality of the instructors.

"At this time the Battalion was fortunate in having Sergeant-Major H. Matthews in charge of the physical training and bayonet-fighting. Sergeant-Major Matthews had been for many years lecturer and instructor of physical training in Marischal College, Aberdeen, and knew how to handle men as few instructors did. In a few months a very efficient staff was got together, and by the summer of 1916 the training had progressed by leaps and bounds, receiving the highest praise at the periodical inspections by the Command Staff. The enthusiasm and untiring energy of the Commanding Officer could be seen in every detail of the work, and in no branch of the training more so than in the physical training and bayonet-fighting of the Battalion ; as the physical condition of the man was the groundwork on which everything else rested, the highest standard of efficiency was expected and, as a rule, attained.

"The scheme and methods of training, both in physical training and bayonet-fighting, were in accordance with the scheme of instruction at Aldershot. The new recruits began with a simple table of exercises, and as their physique and efficiency improved they were introduced to table after table in a graded series. A special feature of the training at this time was the mass display, given once a week to encourage the younger recruits and develop *esprit de corps* among the men. It was an inspiring sight to see a whole body of men, who a few weeks previously lacked poise and control, go through exercise after exercise with perfect assurance and grace of movement.

"With regard to method, special stress was laid on the aim of each exercise, as it was found that the men co-operated and entered into the training with greater zest when their intelligence was appealed to. The exercise was then illustrated, detailed, practised and checked. Games formed an important part of the training. These were calculated to develop quickness of response as well as physical fitness. The finest tribute to the tact and skill of the instructors was the testimony of the men themselves. Even those of them who thought they were too old to benefit by any course of exercises, noting the changes in themselves, both with regard to physical well-being and mental outlook, took to the training with enthusiasm.

" Special attention was paid to the training of young non-commissioned officers. Each squad was kept under observation for promising men, and these, on completing their first course, were promoted to a class for specialized training under the Sergeant-Major Instructor. The best of these were sent to Divisional and Command schools and afterwards to Aldershot. Any changes in the scheme and methods of training at the latter school were thus introduced as early as possible in the Battalion training.

"Early in 1916 a special hut was equipped for physical training and bayonet-fighting. Here the physical training staff met daily to discuss possible improvements and to practise any changes or new exercises brought back by non-commissioned officers fresh from Aldershot. The hut was also used for special classes of officers and non-commissioned officers. In the evenings it was open to the men, who took full advantage of the opportunity. About the same time a field was laid out with special erections for practice in jumping, vaulting and climbing. This added greatly to the interest and introduced a healthy rivalry among the men.

"The same general principles were followed both in physical training and in bayonet-fighting. The men were first trained to handle the rifle with ease and, after the preliminary exercises in points and parries, were early introduced to the bayonet-fighting course. This, as in other battalions, consisted of a series of trenches with rows of sacks, placed at varying intervals and in various positions, between them and in them. On these sacks the men practised the points and parries until they were proficient in each singly. They were then put over the course slowly, practising each in turn according to the position of the sack. As the men became expert with the bayonet the speed was gradually increased until the final week of training, when the great majority of the men could carry out each movement of hand and foot and bayonet with admirable precision and confidence. The main aim in this part of the training was to imbue the men with the aggressive spirit, by giving them confidence in the use of their weapons and in their superiority over the enemy.

"'These are fiends,' said a General one day, viewing the wild swing of the kilts as a draft of the 4th Seaforths hurled themselves at the sacks, 'nothing on earth could stop these men.' The grunt of satisfaction that accompanied every point and jab was significant of the spirit in which they were trained.

"During the last two years of the war the 4th Reserve Battalion Seaforth Highlanders had the proud honour of being first in physical training and bayonet-fighting of all the units trained at home."

Staff Sergeant-Major Harry Matthews writes:

"The general training for recruits was ten weeks, included in which was a week given over solely to physical training and bayonet-fighting, other than the usual two hours per day.

Recruits were trained in accordance with army syllabus, greatly augmented by other Swedish exercises and games. The type of recruit: fine strong healthy lads from the north of Scotland, with a very few Englishmen from the Midlands, of whom we made men.

"Great attention was given to the sports side of the Battalion—football, cricket and other outdoor games, including cross-country running.

"I may mention that a swimming-pond was built at Ripon by the Seaforths for their own use, of which they took full advantage.

"There were two competitions in physical training and bayonet-fighting in Ripon open to the Highland Division for squads of twenty drilled by a non-commissioned officer, and on both occasions they were won by Seaforths.

"We never had a man returned as unfit from a draft while passing the test in bayonet-fighting—*i.e.* assault course. The Battalion won the championship football league of both north and south camps while stationed at Ripon."

When one looks back twelve years ago and visualizes the ten weeks' work, one wonders whether or not the men worked twelve or twenty-four hours in the day! The amount of instruction that had to be imparted was almost beyond the hours of work of an ordinary individual.

In those days one had no time to think, one just carried on. I well remember in 1916 receiving a War Office telegram, "Every recruit before going overseas must throw six live bombs." I sent for my bombing officer, Lieutenant Isaac Maciver, and told him we had a draft going overseas that night—could he possibly arrange for the men to throw the live bombs? He replied that he could, and the draft left for France that evening, having complied with the War Office instructions.

No one could have carried out the instructional bombing work in the Battalion better than Lieutenant Maciver. Absolutely fearless, much above the average in brains and full of tact, he was an ideal bombing officer.

Soon after the receipt of the War Office telegram Maciver was instructing a section of recruits in live bombing. One of the young soldiers was very nervous about throwing his bomb—so much so that he absolutely refused to attempt it. Maciver, to show him how safe it was, walked out in front of the line of recruits for about twenty yards, and then ordered his Sergeant-

Instructor of Bombing to draw the pin of a Mills bomb and throw it to him (Maciver). He caught the bomb and threw it on to the target.

Anyone who has any knowledge of a Mills bomb knows what a very brave, daring and risky experiment this was; it gave, however, confidence to the recruit, and he at once threw his bomb.

Personally I was not over-happy at the experiment, as it might easily have resulted in the loss of my talented bombing officer.

On another occasion the bombing class were throwing live bombs—they had to throw them thirty yards on Maciver's word of command and then jump into a traversed trench while the bombs were bursting on the target. The command had been given to throw bombs: all did it, and jumped into the trench, but one of them, instead of throwing his bomb at the target thirty yards away, threw it into the trench and jumped into the trench beside the live bomb! Four seconds was the length of time after drawing the pin before a bomb bursts. Maciver shouted to him to run round the traverse, but the man's brain seemed paralysed, and he stood still. Maciver immediately jumped into the trench and caught him by the collar to drag him away from the danger. As Maciver caught him the bomb burst, killed the man, and Maciver was dangerously wounded, a piece of bomb entering his abdomen, another piece his chest, and another his arm. Had this happened on the field of battle Maciver would have received the Victoria Cross, but at home nothing was given him.

I am thankful to say that although he lay for days between life and death he completely recovered, and although he still has a lump of Mills bomb embedded in the muscles of his back he is as full of life and vigour as ever.

The following detailed account of the Battalion bombing instruction is from the pen of Lieutenant Maciver, and explains very succinctly that invaluable work:

"Bombing training was not taken up seriously by reserve formations in this country until early in 1916. A year and a half of trench warfare had elapsed before the bomb, a weapon so eminently suitable for this type of fighting, had received official recognition as a *sine qua non* of every infantry soldier's training.

"There was no reserve battalion in Great Britain that

responded so quickly as the 4th Reserve Battalion The Seaforth Highlanders to the War Office letter, 'That henceforth every man proceeding overseas will throw live bombs.' On the morning that this instruction was received each reserve battalion in Ripon was sending a draft overseas that night. The Seaforth Highlanders were the only draft that had finished their live bomb training and were the first draft in the British army to proceed thus equipped to France. It must have given our Commanding Officer infinite satisfaction to reply five hours afterwards to this War Office letter: 'Ref. your W.O. Letter No.—— I have the honour to inform you that the draft proceeding overseas to-night from my Battalion have thrown live bombs.'

"From that day not an officer or man was drafted overseas who had not completed a full training in bombing in the 4th Reserve Battalion Seaforth Highlanders.

"In the Battalion our object was to teach men to handle bombs with confidence and to throw them with accuracy. We were never allowed to forget that the bomb was the ferret that drove the enemy into line with the sights of a rifle or proximity to the point of a bayonet.

"In the North Camp at Ripon every officer and man in the Battalion, from the Commanding Officer downwards, was sent to the bombing experts for a full week's training. This consisted of:

"(1) Lectures on explosives—British bombs—principally the Mills No. 5 hand grenade, the No. 3 Hales rifle grenade, and the adaptation of the Mills bomb as a rifle grenade. A general knowledge of enemy bombs and of our Allies' bombs also was given.

"(2) Extensive practice was given in the throwing of dummy bombs on every day of the week's training.

"(3) Lectures were given in trench-fighting with bombs, and squads of eight men and a leader were organized to fight their way along a trench. Practice in this method of fighting was carried out in trenches modelled on our own and enemy trenches.

"The leading bayonet-man in this squad promptly finished off the work of the bomb. A sharpshooter in the squad was detailed off to deal with enemy breaking cover. The whole idea of this class of fighting depended upon a breach being made in the enemy's line.

"Finally, two days' training was given in throwing live

bombs at suitable targets and in firing rifle grenades. Demonstrations also were given in crater-fighting and in demolition work.

" In the specialized form of fighting known as 'The Platoon in the Attack' a section was trained to co-operate with riflemen and Lewis gunners, so that with bombs and rifle grenades enemy machine-gun nests, and other obstacles that would otherwise hold up the attack, would be dealt with.

" It is difficult to give figures, but it is not an over-estimate that 60,000 live bombs were used by the Seaforths alone at Ripon and Glencorse in the training of men. A single life was the casualty list during these three years of training, although twenty padres and one hundred non-commissioned officers and other ranks of the Halifax and Huddersfield National Reserve Defence Battalions were instructed in live-bomb throwing. One officer was wounded, and at the time he was not actually with the Battalion.

" There were no bombing officers who received more encouragement in their difficult and nerve-racking work than ours. Each week a prize of a silver matchbox was given to the bomber who ranked highest for the week's work. We never in the Reserve Battalion experienced the general difficulty in other battalions of obtaining bombing stores, bombing pitches and all the accessaries incidental to the work.

" It was admitted by Major Campbell, who commanded the Bombing School at Troon (and I was then Brigade Bombing Officer to the Highland Reserve Brigade), that this brigade was easily the best trained in Scotland. As Brigade Bombing Officer I can confidently say that the 4th Reserve Battalion Seaforths set the standard of bombing for the Brigade.

" Again it is difficult to give figures, but owing to the careful selection of officers and non-commissioned officers, who were sent to Command Schools to be trained as bombing instructors, our men almost invariably came back with first-class certificates. In the 4th Reserve Battalion Seaforth Highlanders, all our bombing instructors went through a Chelsea course of drill, on the general principle that a man was a soldier first and an instructor afterwards.

" It is gratifying to note that the following inventions were the product of the 4th Reserve Battalion:

" (1) A method of ranging with rifle grenades.

" (2) A method of firing Very lights without the Very pistol.

"(3) An instantaneous fuse lighter for puff bombs to simulate as near as possible the actual live bomb. This lighter, known as the 'Seaforth lighter,' was extensively used in the Northern Command School of Bombing at Otley.

"This short sketch would be incomplete without associating with bombing in the 4th Reserve Battalion Seaforth Highlanders the names of Lieutenant Pat Mackenzie, Lieutenant Herbert Bain and Sergeant Salisbury, and the never-failing encouragement received from the Commanding Officer, Colonel Mason-MacFarlane."

There is no doubt that if the Germans had delayed their first gas attack until they could have carried it out on a frontage of several miles the results for the Allies would have been very grave.

The moment gas was used, our experts set to work to devise a perfect antidote, and the box respirator was this antidote.

If used correctly it never—or humanly speaking never—failed to save the life of its wearer. But here again was more instruction absolutely necessary and essential before any soldier could be trusted to remain alive in the front line. He not only had to know all the various poison gases and their actions, but he had to be an adept in the use of his box respirator as a protection against the different gases; and not only that, but he had to be able to use his rifle, his bayonet, and throw his bombs while wearing the box respirator, and in addition to move at the double over rough ground.

The time for this instruction was very limited, and only an officer of Lieutenant Pat Mackenzie's ability and organization could possibly have taught the recruits this life-saving subject in the time available. His anti-gas instruction and box-respirator drill were of a very high order, and certainly were within measurable distance of the 100 per cent. standard at which we always aimed.

But Lieutenant Pat Mackenzie shall tell his own story:

"In order to teach all men in the Battalion to respect the use of poison gas by the enemy as a powerful and death-dealing weapon, courses of instruction in gas and anti-gas tactics were given at one period of their training.

"Each course extended over a period of two weeks. The first week's work was devoted to lectures and demonstrations on gas production. The effects of the different gases used were demonstrated, and all the men were made familiar with the smell of each different gas. By the end of the first week each man could quickly detect the presence of one or other of the gases, and knew how to act.

"The different types of respirators were described, but in particular every man was made familiar with the construction and function of the box respirator. He was taught to have implicit faith in his respirator. During both weeks of training gas drill was practised daily, and all the men became expert in manipulating the respirator. Tests were repeatedly made in donning gas helmets against time. Before finishing the course each man went through a chamber densely filled with either chlorine or mustard gas, and on emerging from it, after having been in it for about ten minutes, he felt fully confident in the powers of his respirator and lost all fear of gas. After completing the gas course each man had to acquire experience in bayonet-fighting, musketry and bombing with his respirator on. On suddenly getting up against gas in the battle areas of France the training in 'holding his breath and donning his respirator' stood every man in very good stead."

We have now gone over every special subject of training which applied to all ranks in the Battalion.

One subject—signalling—was confined almost entirely to the Signal Section. Lieutenant Alister Macpherson-Grant was in charge of the signalling, and right well did he carry out his instructions. What he had forgotten about signalling was more than most signallers ever know, and when he went to France in 1918 his departure was a very serious loss to the Battalion.

In addition to all specialized training, section and platoon and company training went on daily, followed by instruction in attack and defence and outdoor schemes for young officers. Major Manson, my Second-in-Command, and Major Robertson took charge, in the main, of these subjects.

I must place on record the devoted service of Major Manson, Major Robertson, Major Ramsay, my Quartermaster, Captain Gair, my Regimental Sergeant-Major Fraser, my Orderly-Room Sergeant, George Ellis, and my Adjutant, Captain Colin Cameron. The loyal support and the extent of the work of these officers and non-commissioned officers no one but myself can ever know or realize. During the three years' most arduous and unceasing strain in the life of the amalgamated Battalion, the Headquarters and Training Staff of which was composed of the officers and non-commissioned officers of three battalions, there was never a suspicion of a rift in the lute of harmony, and the real friendship and good feeling which permeated the Battalion was a thing to conjure with.

One object was uppermost in everyone's thoughts: to turn the young Highlanders committed to our charge into the best soldiers possible, to give them such training and such knowledge in the game of war that when the moment came, and they were face to face with the foe, each one was full of confidence begotten of the knowledge that his handling of his rifle, bayonet and bombs could not be equalled.

I much regret that the limits of this chapter make it impossible for me to attempt to do justice to the officers and non-commissioned officers of the Battalion, whose magnificent work produced the results so well known to us all. To each and all of them I can only say that no men ever did their duty more thoroughly and conscientiously. They will forgive me if I thank from my heart our padre, the Rev. Doctor Gillies, for all his goodness to every man in the Battalion—he was beloved by all.

I have left to the last my brilliant young Adjutant, Captain Colin Cameron. He was dangerously wounded—shot in both lungs in 1915—and after leaving hospital joined the Battalion. At the first opportunity I appointed him my Adjutant. I nearly failed in my effort, but was strongly supported by my Divisional General, Sir Cecil Bingham. No one ever for a moment regretted my choice. It would have been quite impossible for any commanding officer to have had a more loyal or more brilliant young officer for his Adjutant. He was universally respected by everyone in the Battalion.

He was passed fit for service early in 1918 and was ordered overseas during the German offensive in March 1918. He went to France in command of one of the finest drafts of young soldiers—about 150—ever sent overseas, and was killed by a shell, leading his men to the attack a few hours after he landed in France.

His death was a great personal sorrow. I had rarely met his equal.

No one is more conscious than I am of the imperfections of this Part. It has been written at the pressing request of the Committee which is publishing the 4th Battalion The Seaforth

Highlanders' war history. Every statement, not only my own but those of my brother officers, is from memory, almost ten years after the Battalion was demobilized.

Looking back from this date on the work of the Battalion one simply marvels that human flesh and blood carried on as they did. Those officers and non-commissioned officers who were not passed fit for overseas never relaxed for one day from the hour they were posted to the unit until the Armistice.

The memory of the three and a half years during which I had the very great honour and privilege to command the 4th Reserve Training Battalion The Seaforth Highlanders is a memory which, for me, time can never dim.

[Although the foregoing account of the training of the 4th Reserve Battalion tells its own tale, this Part would be incomplete without the following tribute to the Commanding Officer from one who worked in close association with him :

"Throughout the whole existence of the Battalion the dominant presence of the Commanding Officer brought success. With the thoroughness for which he was widely known he brought every department to a state of the highest efficiency.

"His worth was recognized by higher authorities as well as by every officer and man who served under him, for, in addition to being selected to command the amalgamated battalions of the Seaforth territorial units under the name of the 4th Reserve Battalion, he was awarded the C.B.E."—M.M.H.]

AFTERWORD

As the last Brigade Commander under whom the 4th Battalion The Seaforth Highlanders served in the War, I have been given the distinction of adding a few words to this volume.

When I took over Command of the 154th Infantry Brigade in September 1917 the 4th Seaforth Highlanders was a veteran battalion, with already a magnificent record.

Those last fifteen months saw the Battalion engaged in a succession of some of the severest fighting of the long struggle —at Cambrai—in the German March offensive—on the Lys—in Champagne—and in the final advance. Not many battalions have been put to such a test, but because of the unbounded cheerfulness of spirit and the determination to win displayed by all ranks, under all conditions, the Battalion stood the test and finished the War with a record difficult to equal.

I am proud to be a Seaforth. The story of the 4th Battalion alone gives us all due cause to be so.

K. G. BUCHANAN, *Colonel.*

1st September 1927.

INDEX

This Index is not intended to be exhaustive, but merely to provide a general guide to the references of those persons and places which the general reader may wish to look for.

PERSONS

(*Chapter XV has not been indexed, since its arrangement permits of easy reference.*)

PLACES

(The numbers in brackets immediately following the names show the maps on which the names appear. The index is thus a gazetteer of the maps.)